AF559745

SOCIAL
IN
AGEING

SOCIAL IN AGEING

Dr. Afroze Eqbal

RANDOM PUBLICATIONS
NEW DELHI - 110 002 (INDIA)

Social in Ageing

ISBN 978-93-51117-30-8

© Reserved

All Rights Reserved. No Part of this book may be reproduced in any manner without written permission.

Published in 2015 in India by

Reprint 2019

RANDOM PUBLICATIONS

4376-A/4B, Gali Murari Lal, Ansari Road

New Delhi-110 002

Phone: +9111-43580356, 23289044

E-mail: randomexports@gmail.com; sales@randompublications.com; info@randompublications.com

Type Setting by: Friends Media, Delhi-110089

Printed at : Mehra Printers, Delhi-110092

Preface

Ageing is both a biological and sociological process wherein human beings experience and accomplish stages of biological and social maturation. Aging may be seen as a relatively objective biological process whereby one becomes older and experiences varied biological developments. Aging may also be seen as a subjective series of social processes whereby people interpret, negotiate, and make sense of biological development in relation to existing conceptualizations of what it means to be a certain age. While aging, itself, is a bio-social process, the ways people and cultures interpret ages (e.g., "old," "young," "mid-life") and the ways these interpretations are distinguished by varied biological age markers vary dramatically. In Western societies, where youth is highly valued, people are considered "old" at much younger ages than in Eastern societies where age is often seen to beget wisdom. This emphasis on youth translates into considerable expenditures on makeup, cosmetics, and surgeries to hide signs of aging, particularly among women, but also among men. Ironically, among adolescents, just the opposite approach is taken, as adolescents often try to appear "older", though obviously not too much older. The labels of "old" and "young" also vary by life expectancy. In societies where lifespans are relatively short or in areas within a given society where violence and / or other means of "early" death are common, one could be considered "old" or "middle-aged" by her mid-twenties, whereas in countries and social settings with longer lifespans and lower levels of "early" death, mid-twenties is still considered young-adulthood.

The activities that are expected of one at different ages is also socially constructed and relative to culture. For instance, retirement only became a "universal" American ideal in the post-World War I era, as the growth of Social Security and private pensions dramatically expanded the safety net available to aging workers who were leaving the labour market. Likewise, the idea of childhood being an age of innocence when children should be kept from adult worries and spend their time pursuing education and recreating is only widely held in highly developed countries and is a relatively recent invention, following the industrial revolution and the introduction of child-labour laws. Ageism is prejudice on the grounds of age. While it can be targeted toward individuals of any age, two groups that are often targeted are the young and the elderly. While most people are aware of the mistreatment of the elderly, few people seem to realize that young people are often subjected to discrimination because of their age. Discrimination against young people is primarily in the area of behavioural restrictions, often by parents, but also in public places like malls and stores. Some stores have gone so far as to limit the hours young people can be in their stores. Population ageing is the increase in the number and proportion of older people in society. Ageing has a significant impact on society. Young people tend to commit most crimes, they are more likely to push for political and social change, to develop and adopt new technologies and to need education, the latter of which tend to lose political significance for people in the ageing process. Older people have different requirements from society and government as opposed to young people and frequently differing values as well, such as for property and pension rights. While the elderly have seen substantial improvements in their economic situation in recent decades, those improvements have not equally affected men and women. Women, whether working or not, are more likely to fall below the federal poverty line than are men. Globally, most countries are seeing the average life expectancy of their populations increase. While aging is often associated with declining health, current research suggests there are some things people can do to remain healthy longer into old age. For instance, maintaining a positive attitude has been shown to be correlated with better health among the elderly. Older individuals with more positive attitudes and emotions engage in less risky behaviour and have lower levels of stress, both of which are correlated with better health.

This student friendly textbook provides both a thorough explanation of the issues, as well as current research and controversies, exploring health care, socioeconomic trends, and the life course.

I thank all members of my team who have helped in the preparation of the book. My special thanks go to "Random Publications" who have published the book.

— Dr. Afroze Eqbal

Contents

Chapter 1

Ageing

Ageing

Ageing (British English) or ageing (American English) is the process of becoming older. It represents the accumulation of changes in a person over time. Ageing in humans refers to a multidimensional process of physical, psychological, and social change. Some dimensions of ageing grow and expand over time, while others decline. Reaction time, for example, may slow with age, while knowledge of world events and wisdom may expand. Research shows that even late in life, potential exists for physical, mental, and social growth and development. Ageing is an important part of all human societies reflecting the biological changes that occur, but also reflecting cultural and societal conventions. Ageing is among the largest known risk factors for most human diseases. Roughly 100,000 people worldwide die each day of age-related causes.

Age is measured chronologically, and a person's birthday is often an important event. However the term "ageing" is somewhat ambiguous. Distinctions may be made between "universal ageing" (age changes that all people share) and "probabilistic ageing" (age changes that may happen to some, but not all people as they grow older including diseases such as type two diabetes). Chronological ageing may also be distinguished from "social ageing" (cultural age-expectations of how people should act as they grow older) and "biological ageing" (an organism's physical state as it ages). There is also a distinction between "proximal ageing" (age-based effects that come about because of factors in the recent past) and "distal ageing" (age-based differences that can be traced back to a cause early in person's life, such as childhood poliomyelitis). Chronological age does not correlate perfectly with functional age, i.e. two people may be of the same age, but differ in their mental and physical capacities. Each nation, government and non-government organisation has different ways of classifying age.

Population ageing is the increase in the number and proportion of older people in society. Population ageing has three possible causes: migration, longer life expectancy (decreased death rate) and decreased birth rate. Ageing has a significant impact on society. Young people tend to commit most crimes, they are more likely to push for political and social change, to develop and adopt new technologies and to need education, the latter of which tend to lose political significance for people in the ageing process. Older people have different requirements from society and government as opposed to young people and frequently differing values as well, such as for property and pension rights. Older people are also far more likely to vote and in many countries the young are forbidden from voting. Thus, the aged have comparatively more, or at least different, political influence.

Recent scientific successes in rejuvenation and extending a lifespan of model animals (mice 2.5 times, yeast and nematodes 10 times) and discovery of variety of species (including humans of advanced ages) having negligible senescence give hope to achieve negligible senescence (cancel ageing) for younger humans, reverse ageing or at least significantly delay it.

However, human ageing may differ in significant respects from the ageing of worms and even mice. Recent progress in deciphering the ageing of human cells aged in culture as first described by Leonard Hayflick led to the demonstration that human cells age largely because of a genetic "clock" in the DNA region known as the telomere. By isolating the telomerase gene, scientists then at Geron demonstrated that telomerase was an immortalizing enzyme likely necessary for the immortality of germ-line cells, but absent in most cells in the body. This observation led to the mainstreaming of the concept of regenerative medicine, in which human embryonic stem cells may potentially be used to repair aged tissues with young cells, and induced pluripotent stem (iPS) cell technology capable of making cells of various kinds that are potentially useful in repairing tissues for the treatment of age-related degenerative diseases.

Some aspects of bacterial senescence may lend support to contemporary theories of ageing, including the free radical, antagonistic pleiotropy, and disposable soma theories. Ageing is the major cause of mortality in the developed world.

Senescence

Senescence (from Latin: *senescere*, meaning "to grow old", from *senex*) or biological ageing (also spelled biological ageing) is the gradual deterioration of function characteristic of most complex lifeforms, arguably found in all biological kingdoms, that on the level of the organism increases mortality after maturation. The word "senescence" can refer either to cellular senescence or to senescence of the whole organism. It is commonly believed that cellular senescence underlies organismal senescence. The science of biological ageing is biogerontology.

Senescence is not the inevitable fate of all organisms. Organisms of some taxonomic groups (*taxa*), including some animals, even experience chronological decrease in mortality, for all or part of their life cycle. On the other extreme are accelerated ageing diseases, rare in humans. There is also the extremely rare and poorly understood "Syndrome X", whereby a person remains physically and mentally an infant or child throughout one's life.

Even if environmental factors do not cause ageing, they may affect it; in such a way, for example, overexposure to ultraviolet radiation accelerates skin ageing. Different parts of the body may age at different rates. Two organisms of the same species can also age at different rates, so that biological ageing and chronological ageing are quite distinct concepts.

Albeit indirectly, senescence is by far the leading cause of death (other than in the trivially accurate sense that cerebral hypoxia, *i.e.*, lack of oxygen to the brain, is the immediate cause of all human death). Of the roughly 150,000 people who die each day across the globe, about two thirds—100,000 per day—die of age-related causes; in industrialized nations, moreover, the proportion is much higher, reaching 90%.

There are a number of hypotheses as to why senescence occurs; for example, some posit it is programmed by gene expression changes, others that it is the cumulative damage caused by biological processes. Whether senescence as a biological process itself can be slowed down, halted or even reversed, is a subject of current scientific speculation and research.

Cellular Senescence

Cellular senescence is the phenomenon by which normal diploid cells cease to divide. In cell culture, fibroblasts can reach a maximum of 50 cell divisions before becoming senescent. This phenomenon is known as "replicative senescence", or the Hayflick limit in honour of Dr. Leonard Hayflick, co-author with Paul Moorhead, of the first paper describing it in 1961. Replicative senescence is the result of telomere shortening that ultimately triggers a DNA damage response. Cells can also be induced to senesce via DNA damage in response to elevated reactive oxygen species (ROS), activation of oncogenes and cell-cell fusion, independent of telomere length.

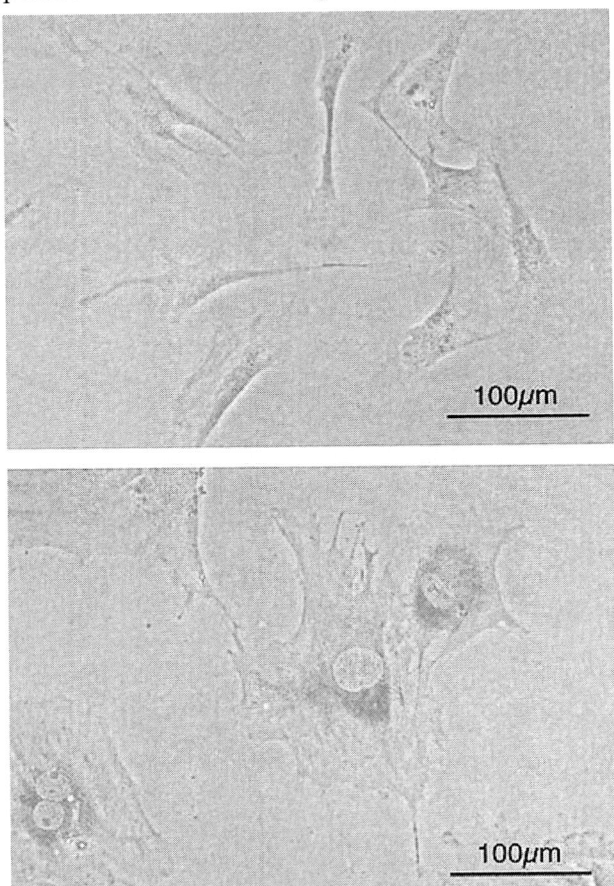

Figure: *Cellular Senescence— (upper) Primary mouse embryonic fibroblast cells (MEFs) before senescence. Spindle-shaped. (lower) MEFs became senescent after passages. Cells grow larger, flatten shape and expressed senescence-associated â-galactosidase (SABG, blue areas), a marker of cellular senescence.*

As such, cellular senescence represents a change in "cell state" rather than a cell becoming "aged" as the name confusingly suggests. Although senescent cells can no longer replicate, they remain metabolically active and commonly adopt a phenotype including flattened cell morphology, promiscuous gene expression, a pro-inflammatory secretory response and positive senescence-associated â-galactosidase staining. Senescent cells are known to play important physiological functions in tumour suppression, wound healing and possibly embryonic/placental development and paradoxically play a pathological role in age-related diseases. The elimination of senescent cells using a transgenic mouse model led to greater resistance against ageing-associated diseases, suggesting that cellular senescence is a major driving force of ageing and its associated diseases.

Ageing of the Whole Organism

Organismal senescence is the ageing of whole organisms. In general, ageing is characterized by the declining ability to respond to stress, increased homeostatic imbalance, and increased risk of ageing-associated diseases. Death is the ultimate consequence of ageing, though "old age" is not a scientifically recognised cause of death because there is always a specific proximal cause, such as cancer, heart disease, or liver failure. Ageing of whole organisms is therefore a complex process that can be defined as "a progressive deterioration of physiological function, an intrinsic age-related process of loss of viability and increase in vulnerability".

Differences in maximum life span among species correspond to different "rates of ageing". For example, inherited differences in the rate of ageing make a mouse elderly at 3 years and a human elderly at 80 years. These genetic differences affect a variety of physiological processes, including the efficiency of DNA repair, antioxidant enzymes, and rates of free radical production.

Senescence of the organism gives rise to the Gompertz–Makeham law of mortality, which says that mortality rate accelerates rapidly with age.

Some animals, such as some reptiles and fish, age slowly (negligible senescence) and exhibit very long lifespans. Some even exhibit "negative senescence", in which mortality falls with age, in disagreement with the Gompertz–Makeham "law".

Whether replicative senescence (Hayflick limit) plays a causative role in organismal ageing is at present an active area of investigation.

The oft-quoted evolutionary theorist George Williams wrote, "It is remarkable that after a seemingly miraculous feat of morphogenesis, a complex metazoan should be unable to perform the much simpler task of merely maintaining what is already formed."

Theories of Ageing

The exact etiology of senescence is still largely unclear and yet to be discovered. The process of senescence is complex, and may derive from a variety of different mechanisms and exist for a variety of different reasons. However, senescence is not universal, and scientific evidence suggests that cellular senescence evolved in certain species because it prevents the onset of cancer. In a few simple species, such as those in the genus *Hydra*, senescence is negligible and cannot be detected.

All such species have no "post-mitotic" cells; they reduce the effect of damaging free radicals by cell division and dilution. Another related mechanism is that of the biologically immortal planarian flatworms, which have "apparently limitless [telomere] regenerative capacity fuelled by a population of highly proliferative adult stem cells." These organisms are biologically immortal but not immortal in the traditional sense as they are nonetheless susceptible to trauma and infectious and non-infectious disease. Moreover, average lifespans can vary greatly within and between species. This suggests that both genetic and environmental factors contribute to ageing.

In general, theories that explain senescence have been divided between the programmed and stochastic theories of ageing. Programmed theories imply that ageing is regulated by biological clocks operating throughout the lifespan. This regulation would depend on changes in gene expression that affect the systems responsible for maintenance, repair, and defence responses. The reproductive-cell cycle theory suggests that ageing is caused by changes in hormonal signalling over the lifespan. Stochastic theories blame environmental impacts on living organisms that induce cumulative damage at various levels as the cause of ageing, examples of which ranging from damage to DNA, damage to tissues and cells by oxygen radicals (widely known as free radicals countered by the even more well-known antioxidants), and cross-linking.

However, ageing is seen as a progressive failure of homeodynamics (homeostasis) involving genes for the maintenance and repair, stochastic events leading to molecular damage and molecular heterogeneity, and chance events determining the probability of death. Since complex and interacting systems of maintenance and repair comprise the homeodynamic (old term: homeostasis) space of a biological system, ageing is considered to be a progressive shrinkage of homeodynamic space mainly due to increased molecular heterogeneity.

Evolution of Ageing

Enquiry into the evolution of ageing aims to explain why almost all living things weaken and die with age. There is not yet agreement in the scientific community on a single answer. The evolutionary origin of senescence remains a fundamental unsolved problem in biology.

Historically, ageing was first likened to "wear and tear": living bodies get weaker just as with use a knife's edge becomes dulled or with exposure to air and moisture iron objects rust. But this idea was discredited in the 19th century when the second law of thermodynamics was formalized. Entropy (disorder) must increase inevitably *within a closed system*, but living beings are not closed systems. It is a defining feature of life that it takes in free energy from the environment and unloads its entropy as waste. Living systems can even build themselves up from seed, and routinely repair themselves. There is no thermodynamic necessity for senescence. In addition, generic damage or "wear and tear" theories could not explain why biologically similar organisms (e.g. mammals) exhibited such dramatically different life spans. Furthermore, this initial theory failed to explain why most organisms maintain themselves so efficiently until adulthood and then, after reproductive maturity, begin to succumb to age-related damage.

History

August Weismann was responsible for interpreting and formalizing the mechanisms of Darwinian evolution in a modern theoretical framework. In 1889, he theorized that ageing was part of life's program because the old need to remove themselves from the theatre to make room for the next generation, sustaining the turnover that is necessary for evolution. This theory again has much intuitive appeal, but it suffers from having a teleological or goal-driven explanation. In other words, a *purpose* for ageing has been identified, but not a *mechanism* by which that purpose could be achieved. Ageing may have this advantage for the long-term health of the community; but that doesn't explain how individuals would acquire the genes that make them get old and die, or why individuals that had ageing genes would be more successful than other individuals lacking such genes. (In fact, there is every reason to think that the opposite is true: ageing *decreases* individual fitness.) Weismann disavowed his own theory before his life was over.

Theories suggesting that deterioration and death due to ageing are a purposeful result of an organism's evolved design (such as Weismann's "programmed death" theory) are referred to as theories of programmed ageing or adaptive ageing. The idea that the ageing characteristic was selected (an adaptation) because of its deleterious effect was largely discounted for much of the 20th century, but is now experiencing a resurgence because of new empirical evidence as well as new thinking regarding the process of evolution.

Mutation Accumulation

The first modern, successful theory of mammal ageing was formulated by Peter Medawar in 1952. It formed from discussions in the previous decade with J. B. S. Haldane and the selection shadow concept. Their idea was that ageing was a matter of neglect. Nature is a highly competitive place, and almost all animals in nature die before they attain old age. Therefore, there is not much reason why the body should remain fit for the long haul - not much selection pressure for traits that would maintain viability past the time when most animals would be dead anyway, killed by predators or disease or by accident.

Medawar's theory is referred to as *Mutation Accumulation*. The mechanism of action involves random, detrimental mutations of a kind that happen to show their effect only late in life. Unlike most detrimental mutations, these would not be efficiently weeded out by natural selection. Hence they would 'accumulate' and, perhaps, cause all the decline and damage that we associate with ageing.

Modern genetics science has disclosed a possible problem with the mutation accumulation concept in that it is now known that genes are typically expressed in specific tissues at specific times. Expression is controlled by some genetic "program" that activates different genes at different times in the normal growth, development, and day-to-day life of the organism. Defects in genes cause problems (genetic diseases) when they are not properly expressed when required. A problem late in life suggests that the genetic program called for expression of a gene only in late life and the mutational defect prevented proper expression. This implies existence of a program that called for different gene expression at that point in life. Why, given Medawar's concept, would there exist genes only needed in late life or a program that called for different expression only in late life? The *maintenance mechanism* theory avoids this problem.

Medawar's concept suggested that the evolution process was affected by the age at which an organism was capable of reproducing. Characteristics that adversely affected an organism prior to that age would severely limit the organism's ability to propagate its characteristics and thus would be highly "selected against" by natural selection. Characteristics that caused the same adverse effects that only appeared well after that age would have relatively little effect on the organism's ability to propagate and therefore might be allowed by natural selection. This concept fit well with the observed multiplicity of mammal life spans (and differing ages of sexual maturity) and is important to all of the subsequent theories of ageing discussed below.

Medawar did not suggest that there were fundamental limitations on life span. Organisms exhibiting negligible senescence suggest that ageing is not a fundamental limitation, at least not in the scale of mammal life span.

Antagonistic Pleiotropy

Medawar's theory was further developed by George C. Williams in 1957, who noted that senescence may be causing many deaths, even if animals are not 'dying of old age.' In the earliest stages of senescence, an animal may lose a bit of its speed, and then predators will seize it first, while younger animals flee successfully. Or its immune system may decline, and it becomes the first to die of a new infection. Nature is such a competitive place, said Williams, (turning Medawar's argument back at him), that even a little bit of senescence can be fatal; hence natural selection does indeed care; ageing isn't cost-free.

Williams's objection has turned out to be valid: Modern studies of demography in natural environments demonstrate that senescence does indeed make a substantial contribution to the death rate in nature. These observations cast doubt on Medawar's theory. Another problem with Medawar's theory became apparent in the late 1990s, when genomic analysis became widely available. It turns out that the genes that cause ageing are not random mutations; rather, these genes form tight-knit families that have been around as long as eukaryotic life. Baker's yeast, worms, fruit flies, and mice all share some of the same ageing genes.

Williams (1957) proposed his own theory, called *antagonistic pleiotropy*. Pleiotropy means one gene that has two or more effects on the phenotype. In antagonistic pleiotropy, one of these effects is beneficial and another is detrimental. In essence this refers to genes that offer benefits early in life, but exact a cost later on. If evolution is a race to have the most offspring the fastest, then enhanced early fertility could be selected even if it came with a price tag that included decline and death later on. Because ageing was a side effect of necessary functions, Williams considered any alteration of the ageing process to be "impossible."

Antagonistic pleiotropy is a prevailing theory today, but this is largely by default, and not because the theory has been well verified.

In fact, experimental biologists have looked for the genes that cause ageing, and since about 1990 the technology has been available to find them efficiently. Of the many ageing genes that have been reported, some seem to enhance fertility early in life, or to carry other benefits. But there are other ageing genes for which no such corresponding benefit has been identified. This is not what Williams predicted. This may be thought of as partial validation of the theory, but logically it cuts to the core premise: that genetic trade-offs are the root cause of ageing.

Another difficulty with antagonistic pleiotropy and other theories that suppose that ageing is an adverse side effect of some beneficial function is that the linkage between adverse and beneficial effects would need to be *rigid* in the sense that the evolution process would not be able to evolve a way to accomplish the benefit without incurring the adverse effect even over a very long time span. Such a rigid relationship has not been experimentally demonstrated and, in general, evolution is obviously able to independently and individually adjust myriad organism characteristics.

In breeding experiments, Michael R. Rose selected fruit flies for long life span. Based on antagonistic pleiotropy, Rose expected that this would surely reduce their fertility. His team found that they were able to breed flies that lived more than twice as long as the flies they started with, but to their surprise, the long-lived, inbred flies actually laid more eggs than the short-lived flies. This was another setback for pleiotropy theory, though Rose maintains it may be an experimental artifact.

Disposable Soma Theory

A third mainstream theory of ageing, the *Disposable soma* theory, proposed in 1977 by Thomas Kirkwood, presumes that the body must budget the amount of energy available to it. The body uses food energy for metabolism, for reproduction, and for repair and maintenance. With a finite supply of food, the body must compromise, and do none of these things quite as well as it would like. It is the compromise in allocating energy to the repair function that causes the body gradually to deteriorate with age. A caveat to the disposable soma theory suggests that time, rather than energy, is a limiting resource that may be critical to an organism. The concept is that each organism must reproduce in an optimal period in order to ensure the greatest chance of success for the offspring. This optimal period is dictated by the ecological niche of the organism but in essence, it limits the time that any given organism can devote to growth and development prior to bearing offspring. Thus, developmental rate and gestational rate are subject to evolutionary pressure. The need to accelerate gestation limits the time allocated to damage repair at the cellular level, resulting in an accumulation of damage and a decreased lifespan relative to organisms with longer gestation. This concept stems from a comparative analysis of genomic stability in mammalian cells.

The term *disposable soma* came from the analogy with disposable products—why spend money making something durable, if it will only be used for a limited amount of time?

The disposable soma theory has great appeal because its basis is so sensible and intuitive, but there are arguments against it. The theory clearly predicts that a shortage of food should make the compromise more severe all around; but in many experiments, ongoing since 1930, it has been demonstrated that animals live longer when fed substantially less than controls. This is the caloric restriction (CR) effect, and it cannot be easily reconciled with the Disposable Soma theory. Though by decreasing energy expenditure the damage generated (by free radicals for instance) is expected to be reduced and the total energy budget might indeed be reduced, but the investment in repair function might still be relatively the same. But dietary restriction has not been shown to increase lifetime reproductive success (fitness), because when food availability is lower reproductive output is also lower. So CR does thus not completely dismiss disposable theory.

Experimentally, some animals lose fertility when their life spans are extended by CR and some suffer no appreciable loss. Males, for example, typically remain fertile when underfed, while females do not. And, even females present an enigma because their fertility decline is not tightly coupled to their longevity gain. For example, in female mice that are restricted to 60% of a free-feeding diet, reproduction is shut down altogether. But female life span continues to increase linearly right up to the threshold of starvation - around 30% of free-feeding levels.

A difficulty with the disposable soma theory is that the energy required for maintenance and repair would appear to be relatively minor when compared to the energy required for gestation (repair should take less energy than producing an entire new organism). Yet gestating animals seem able to perform the maintenance while post-reproductive animals do not. A similar difficulty is that male animals seem to have similar life spans as females despite the apparently higher energy requirement for gestation and other reproductive activities.

With respect to such limitations Kriete proposed consideration of systems-level properties like robustness (evolution) to characterize ageing as a robustness tradeoff. According to this concept living systems evolve into a state of highly optimized tolerance promoting traits beneficial for survival and fitness at the cost of fragilities driving the ageing phenotype. The view is compatible with aspects of the antagonistic pleiotropy and the disposable soma theory, but offers additional mechanisms rooted in complex systems theory.

Other Problems with the Classical Ageing Theories

A raised criticism for all three mainstream theories based on classical evolutionary process concepts is the potential existence of 'deliberate' metabolic mechanisms that work to promote death.

One is *apoptosis*, or programmed cell death. Apoptosis is responsible for killing infected cells, cancerous cells and cells that are simply in the wrong place during development. There are clear benefits to apoptosis, so the existence of apoptosis isn't a problem for evolutionary theory. The problem is that apoptosis seems to ramp up late in life and kill healthy cells, causing weakness and degeneration. And, paradoxically, apoptosis has been observed as a kind of 'altruistic suicide' in colonies of yeast under stress. This seems to be a direct hint that senescence arose because it conferred a direct evolutionary advantage, rather than some kind of side effect of genes that have other evolutionary advantages (pleiotropy).

A second 'deliberate' mechanism is called *replicative senescence* or cellular senescence. Metaphorically, a cell may be said to 'count' (with its *telomeres*) the number of times that it has divided, and after a set number of replications, it languishes and dies. It has been proposed that this mechanism evolved to suppress cancer. Many invertebrates experience replicative senescence, though they never die of cancer. Even one-celled organisms count replications, and will die if they don't replenish their telomeres with conjugation (sex).

More strictly, of course, cells cannot 'count' the number of times they have divided. Telomeres are not a counting mechanism, though they may be used to indicate the number of times a particular chromosome has been replicated. Cellular processes for genetic material replication occurs in both directions along DNA, 5' to 3' and on the other strand, 3' to 5'. As the 3' to 5' end is impossible for DNA polymerase to grab at the 1 base pair mark, a handful of basepairs (10-15) are cut off each replication. Over time, this cutting short of the DNA results in no telomeres, and the cell is unable to replicate that chromosome without cutting into genes.

The dilemma is that classical evolutionary theory says that what is maintained in a lineage is that which ensures the viability of an organism and its offspring. Ageing can only cut off an individual's capacity to reproduce. So, according to classical theory, ageing could *only* evolve as a side effect, or epiphenomenon of selection. The disposable soma theory and antagonistic pleiotropy theory are examples in which a compensating individual benefit, compatible with classical evolution theory is proposed. Nevertheless, there is accumulated evidence that ageing looks like an adaptation in its own right, selected for its own sake.

Semelparous organisms and others that die suddenly following reproduction (e.g. salmon, octopus, marsupial mouse (Brown Antechinus), etc.) also represent instances of organisms who incorporate a life span limiting feature. Sudden death is more obviously an instance of programmed death or a purposeful adaptation than gradual ageing. Biological elements clearly associated with evolved mechanisms such as hormone signalling have been identified in the death mechanisms of organisms such as the octopus.

Impact of New Evolution Concepts on Ageing Theories

At the time most of the non-programmed ageing theories were developed there was very little scientific disagreement with classical theories (i.e. Neo-Darwinism or modern evolutionary synthesis) regarding the process of evolution. However, in addition to suicidal behaviour of semelparous species (not handled by the classical ageing theories) other apparently individually adverse organism characteristics such as altruism and sexual reproduction were observed. In response to these *other* conflicts, adjustments to classical theory were proposed:

- Various group selection theories (beginning in 1962) propose that benefit to a group could offset the individually adverse nature of a characteristic such as altruism. The same principle could be applied to characteristics that limited life span and theories proposing group benefits for limited life spans appeared.
- Evolvability theories (beginning in 1995) suggest that a characteristic that increased an organism's ability to evolve could also offset an individual disadvantage and thus be evolved and retained. Multiple evolvability benefits of a limited life span were subsequently proposed in addition to those originally proposed by Weismann.

Ageing Theories Based on Group Selection

Group selection is often criticized to be too slow to happen in real biology. However, Jiang-Nan Yang recently showed with an individual-based model that the evolution of altruistic ageing occurs under fairly general conditions by kin/group selection. Group selection can be based on population viscosity (limited offspring dispersal, first proposed by Hamilton (1964) for kin selection) that is widely present in natural populations. This population structure builds a continuum between individual selection, kin selection, kin group selection and group selection without a clear boundary for each level. Although early theoretical models by D.S. Wilson et al. (1992) and Taylor (1992) showed that pure population viscosity cannot lead to cooperation/altruism because of the exact cancelling out of the benefit of kin cooperation and the cost of kin competition, this exact cancelling out also suggests that any additional benefit of local cooperation would be sufficient for the evolution of cooperation. Mitteldorf and D.S. Wilson (2000) later showed that if the population is allowed to fluctuate, then local populations can temporarily store the benefit of local cooperation and promote the evolution of altruism. By assuming individual differences in adaptations, Yang (2013) further showed that the benefit of local altruism can be stored in the form of offspring quality and thus promote the evolution of altruistic ageing even if the population does not fluctuate, this is because local competition among the young will result in an increased average local inherited fitness of survived progenies after the elimination of the less adapted by natural selection, since the young do not have strong age-associated abilities and have to depend more on inherited abilities to compete. In Yang (2013)'s model, altruistic ageing is stabilized by higher-level selection instead of just kin selection.

Mitteldorf proposed a group benefit of a limited life span involving regulation of population dynamics. Populations in nature are subject to boom and bust cycles. Often overpopulation can be punished by famine or by epidemic. Either one could wipe out an entire population. Senescence is a means by which a species can 'take control' of its own death rate, and level out the boom-bust cycles. This story may be more plausible than the Weismann hypothesis as a mechanistic explanation, because it addresses the question of how group selection can be rapid enough to compete with individual selection.

Libertini also Suggests Benefits for Adaptive Ageing

Inversely, within a *Negative Senescence Theory* R.D. Lee (similarly J.W. Vaupel) considered positive group effects performing a selection force directed to survival beyond the age of fertility. Often also postreproductive individuals make intergenerational transfers: bottlenose dolphins and pilot whales guard their grandchildren; there is cooperative breeding in some mammals, many insects and about

200 species of birds; sex differences in the survival of anthropoid primates tend to correlate with the care to offspring; or an Efe infant is often attended by more than 10 people. Lee developed a formal theory integrating selection due to transfers (at all ages) with selection due to fertility.

Ageing Theories Based on Evolvability

Goldsmith proposed that in addition to increasing the generation rate and thereby evolution rate a limited life span improves the evolution process by limiting the ability of older individuals to dominate the gene pool. Further, the evolution of characteristics such as intelligence and immunity may specially require a limited life span because otherwise acquired characteristics such as experience or exposure to pathogens would tend to override the selection of the beneficial inheritable characteristic. An older and more experienced but less intelligent animal would have a fitness advantage over a younger more intelligent animal except for the effects of ageing.

Skulachev has suggested that programmed ageing assists the evolution process by providing a gradually increasing challenge or obstacle to survival and reproduction and therefore enhancing the selection of beneficial characteristics. In this sense ageing would act in a manner similar to that of mating rituals that take the form of contests or trials that must be overcome in order to mate (another individually adverse observation). This suggests an advantage of gradual ageing over sudden death as a means of life span regulation.

Weissmann's 1889 ageing theory was essentially an evolvability theory. Ageing or otherwise purposely limited life span helps evolution by freeing resources for younger, and therefore presumably better adapted individuals.

Yang (2013)'s model is also based on mechanisms of evolvability. Ageing accelerates the accumulation of novel adaptive genes in local populations. However, Yang changed the terminology of "evolvability" into "genetic creativity" throughout his paper to facilitate the understanding of how ageing can have a shorter-term benefit than the word "evolvability" would imply.

Ageing Mechanism Concepts

If organisms purposely limit their life spans via ageing or semelparous behaviour, the associated evolved mechanisms could be very complex just as mechanisms that provide for mentation, vision, digestion, or other biological function are typically very complex. Such a mechanism could involve hormones, signalling, sensing of external conditions, and other complex functions typical of evolved mechanisms. Such complex mechanisms could explain all of the observations of ageing and semelparous behaviours as described below.

It is typical for a given biological function to be controlled by a single mechanism that is capable of sensing the germane conditions and then executing the necessary function. The mechanism signals all the systems and tissues that need to respond to that function by means of organism-wide signals (hormones). If ageing is indeed a biological function we would expect all or most manifestations of ageing to be similarly controlled by a common mechanism. Various observations (listed below) indeed suggest the existence of a common control mechanism.

It is also typical for biological functions to be modulated by or synchronized to external events or conditions. The circadian rhythm and synchronization of mating behaviour to planetary cues are examples. In the case of ageing seen as a biological function, the caloric restriction effect may well be an example of the ageing function being modulated in order to optimize organism life span in response to external conditions. Temporary extension of life span under famine conditions would aid in group survival because extending life span combined with less frequent reproduction would reduce the resources required to maintain a given population.

Theories to the effect that ageing results by default (mutation accumulation) or is an adverse side effect of some other function are logically much more limited and suffer when compared to empirical evidence of complex mechanisms. The choice of ageing theory therefore is logically essentially determined by one's position regarding evolutionary processes and some theorists reject programmed ageing based entirely on evolutionary process considerations.

Maintenance Theories of Ageing

It is generally accepted that deteriorative processes (wear, other molecular damage) exist and that living organisms have mechanisms to counter deterioration. Wounds heal; dead cells are replaced; claws regrow.

A non-programmed theory of mammal ageing that fits with classical evolution theory and Medawar's concept is that different mammal species possess different capabilities for maintenance and repair. Longer lived species possess many mechanisms for offsetting damage due to causes such as oxidation, telomere shortening, and other deteriorative processes that are each more effective than those of shorter lived species. Shorter lived species, having earlier ages of sexual maturity, had less need for longevity and thus did not evolve or retain the more effective repair mechanisms. Damage therefore accumulates more rapidly resulting in earlier manifestations and shorter life span. Since there are a wide variety of ageing manifestations that appear to have very different causes, it is likely that there are many different maintenance and repair functions.

A corresponding programmed maintenance theory based on evolvability suggests that the repair mechanisms are in turn controlled by a common control mechanism capable of sensing conditions such as caloric restriction and also capable of producing the specific life span needed by the particular species. In this view the differences between short and long lived species are in the control mechanisms as opposed to each individual maintenance mechanism.

Summary of Empirical Evidence Favouring Programmed Ageing

- Existence of complex programmed death mechanisms exist in semelparous species (e.g. octopus) including hormone signalling, nervous system involvement, etc. If a limited life span is generally useful as predicted by the programmed ageing theories, it would be unusual for an octopus to possess a more complex mechanism for accomplishing that function than a mammal.
- Discovery of "ageing genes" with no other apparent function.
- Caloric restriction effect: *reduction* of available resources *increases* life span. This behaviour has a plausible group benefit in enhancing the survival of a group under famine conditions and also suggests common control.
- Progeria and Werner syndrome are both single-gene genetic diseases that cause acceleration of many or most symptoms of ageing. The fact that a single gene malfunction can cause similar effects on many different manifestations of ageing suggests a common mechanism.
- Although mammal life spans vary over an approximately 100:1 range, manifestations of ageing (cancer, arthritis, weakness, sensory deficit, etc.) are similar in different species. This suggests that the deterioration mechanisms and corresponding maintenance mechanisms operate over a short period (less than the life span of a short-lived mammal). All the mammals therefore need all the maintenance mechanisms. This suggests that the difference between mammals is in a common control mechanism.

- Life span varies greatly among otherwise very similar species (e.g. different varieties of salmon 3:1, different fish 600:1) suggesting that relatively few genes control life span and that relatively minor changes to genotype could cause major differences in life span—suggests common control mechanism.

Problems with Programmed Ageing Theories

Contrary to the theory of programmed death by ageing, individuals from a single species usually live much longer in a protected (laboratory, domestic, civilized environment) than in their wild (natural) environment, reaching ages that would be otherwise practically impossible. Also, in majority of species there doesn't exist any critical age after which death rates change dramatically as intended by the programmed death by ageing theory, but the age-dependence of death rates is very smooth and monotonic. However, as mentioned above, V.P. Skulachev explained that a process of gradual ageing has the advantage of facilitating selection for useful traits by allowing old individuals with a useful trait to live longer. It is also easy to imagine that animals with gradual ageing will live longer in a protected environment.

The death rates at extreme old ages start to slow down, which is the opposite of what would be expected if death by ageing was programmed. From an individual-selection point of view, having genes that would not result in a programmed death by ageing would displace genes that cause programmed death by ageing as individuals would produce more offspring in their longer lifespan and they could increase the survival of their offspring by providing longer parental support.

Biogerontology Considerations

Theories of ageing affect efforts to understand and find treatments for age-related conditions:

- Those who believe in the idea that ageing is an unavoidable side effect of some necessary function (antagonistic pleiotropy or disposable soma theories) logically tend to believe that attempts to delay ageing would result in unacceptable side effects to the necessary functions. Altering ageing is therefore "impossible" and study of ageing mechanisms is of only academic interest.
- Those believing in default theories of multiple maintenance mechanisms tend to believe that ways might be found to enhance the operation of some of those mechanisms. Perhaps they can be assisted by anti-oxidants or other agents.

- Those who believe in programmed ageing suppose that ways might be found to interfere with the operation of the part of the ageing mechanism that appears to be common to multiple symptoms, essentially "slowing down the clock" and delaying multiple manifestations. Such effect might be obtained by fooling a sense function. One such effort is an attempt to find a "mimetic" that would "mime" the anti-ageing effect of calorie restriction without having to actually radically restrict diet.

Gene Regulation

A number of genetic components of ageing have been identified using model organisms, ranging from the simple budding yeast *Saccharomyces cerevisiae* to worms such as *Caenorhabditis elegans* and fruit flies (*Drosophila melanogaster*). Study of these organisms has revealed the presence of at least two conserved ageing pathways.

One of these pathways involves the gene *Sir2*, a NAD+-dependent histone deacetylase. In yeast, Sir2 is required for genomic silencing at three loci: The yeast mating loci, the telomeres and the ribosomal DNA (rDNA). In some species of yeast, replicative ageing may be partially caused by homologous recombination between rDNA repeats; excision of rDNA repeats results in the formation of extrachromosomal rDNA circles (ERCs). These ERCs replicate and preferentially segregate to the mother cell during cell division, and are believed to result in cellular senescence by titrating away (competing for) essential nuclear factors. ERCs have not been observed in other species (nor even all strains of the same yeast species) of yeast (which also display replicative senescence), and ERCs are not believed to contribute to ageing in higher organisms such as humans (they have not been shown to accumulate in mammals in a similar manner to yeast). Extrachromosomal circular DNA (eccDNA) has been found in worms, flies, and humans. The origin and role of eccDNA in ageing, if any, is unknown.

Despite the lack of a connection between circular DNA and ageing in higher organisms, extra copies of Sir2 are capable of extending the lifespan of both worms and flies (though, in flies, this finding has not been replicated by other investigators, and the activator of Sir2 resveratrol does not reproducibly increase lifespan in either species). Whether the Sir2 homologues in higher organisms have any role in lifespan is unclear, but the human SIRT1 protein has been demonstrated to deacetylate p53, Ku70, and the forkhead family of transcription factors. SIRT1 can also regulate acetylates such as CBP/p300, and has been shown to deacetylate specific histone residues.

RAS1 and RAS2 also affect ageing in yeast and have a human homologue. RAS2 overexpression has been shown to extend lifespan in yeast.

Other genes regulate ageing in yeast by increasing the resistance to oxidative stress. Superoxide dismutase, a protein that protects against the effects of mitochondrial free radicals, can extend yeast lifespan in stationary phase when overexpressed.

In higher organisms, ageing is likely to be regulated in part through the insulin/IGF-1 pathway. Mutations that affect insulin-like signalling in worms, flies, and the growth hormone/IGF1 axis in mice are associated with extended lifespan. In yeast, Sir2 activity is regulated by the nicotinamidase PNC1. PNC1 is transcriptionally upregulated under stressful conditions such as caloric restriction, heat shock, and osmotic shock. By converting nicotinamide to niacin, nicotinamide is removed, inhibiting the activity of Sir2. A nicotinamidase found in humans, known as PBEF, may serve a similar function, and a secreted form of PBEF known as visfatin may help to regulate serum insulin levels. It is not known, however, whether these mechanisms also exist in humans, since there are obvious differences in biology between humans and model organisms.

Sir2 activity has been shown to increase under calorie restriction. Due to the lack of available glucose in the cells, more NAD+ is available and can activate Sir2. Resveratrol, a stilbenoid found in the skin of red grapes, was reported to extend the lifespan of yeast, worms, and flies (the lifespan extension in flies and worms have proved to be irreproducible by independent investigators). It has been shown to activate Sir2 and therefore mimics the effects of calorie restriction, if one accepts that caloric restriction is indeed dependent on Sir2.

Gene expression is imperfectly controlled, and it is possible that random fluctuations in the expression levels of many genes contribute to the ageing process as suggested by a study of such genes in yeast. Individual cells, which are genetically identical, nonetheless can have substantially different responses to outside stimuli, and markedly different lifespans, indicating the epigenetic factors play an important role in gene expression and ageing as well as genetic factors.

According to the GenAge database of ageing-related genes there are over 700 genes associated with ageing in model organisms: 555 in the soil roundworm (*Caenorhabditis elegans*), 87 in the bakers' yeast (*Saccharomyces cerevisiae*), 75 in the fruit fly (*Drosophila melanogaster*) and 68 in the mouse (*Mus musculus*).

Chapter 2

Genetics of Ageing

Genetics of ageing is generally concerned with life extension associated with genetic alterations, rather than with accelerated ageing diseases leading to reduction in lifespan.

The first mutation found to increase longevity in an animal was the *age-1* gene in *Caenorhabditis elegans*. Michael Klass discovered that lifespan of *C. elegans* could be altered by mutations, but Klass believed that the effect was due to reduced food consumption (calorie restriction). Thomas Johnson later showed that life extension of up to 65% was due to the mutation itself rather than due to calorie restriction, and he named the gene *age-1* in the expectation that other genes that control ageing would be found. The *age-1* gene encodes the catalytic subunit of class-I phosphatidylinositol 3-kinase (PI3K).

A decade after Johnson's discovery *daf-2*, one of the two genes that are essential for dauer larva formation, was shown by Cynthia Kenyon to double *C. elegans* lifespan. Kenyon showed that the *daf-2* mutants, which would form dauers above 25 °C (298 K; 77 °F) would bypass the dauer state below 20 °C (293 K; 68 °F) with a doubling of lifespan. Prior to Kenyon's study it was commonly believed that lifespan could only be increased at the cost of a loss of reproductive capacity, but Kenyon's nematodes maintained youthful reproductive capacity as well as extended youth in general. Subsequent genetic modification (PI3K-null mutation) to *C. elegans* was shown to extend maximum life span tenfold. According to the GenAge database of ageing-related genes, there are over 800 genes extending lifespan in model organisms: 454 in the soil roundworm (*Caenorhabditis elegans*), 236 in the bakers' yeast (*Saccharomyces cerevisiae*), 79 in the fruit fly (*Drosophila melanogaster*) and 68 in the mouse (*Mus musculus*).

Genetic modifications in other species have not achieved as great a lifespan extension as have been seen for *C. elegans*. *Drosophila melanogaster* lifespan has been doubled. Genetic mutations in mice can increase maximum lifespan to 1.5 times normal, and up to 1.7 times normal when combined with calorie restriction.

Cellular Senescence

As noted above, senescence is not universal. It was once thought that senescence did not occur in single-celled organisms that reproduce through the process of cellular mitosis. Recent investigation has unveiled a more complex picture. Single cells do accumulate age-related damage. On mitosis the debris is not evenly divided between the new cells. Instead it passes to one of the cells leaving the other cell pristine. With successive generations the cell population becomes a mosaic of cells with half ageless and the rest with varying degrees of senescence.

Moreover, cellular senescence is not observed in several organisms, including perennial plants, sponges, corals, and lobsters. In those species where cellular senescence is observed, cells eventually become post-mitotic when they can no longer replicate themselves through the process of cellular mitosis; i.e., cells experience *replicative senescence*. How and why some cells become post-mitotic in some species has been the subject of much research and speculation, but (as noted above) it is sometimes suggested that cellular senescence evolved as a way to prevent the onset and spread of cancer. Somatic cells that have divided many times will have accumulated DNA mutations and would therefore be in danger of becoming cancerous if cell division continued.

Lately, the role of telomeres in cellular senescence has aroused general interest, especially with a view to the possible genetically adverse effects of cloning. The successive shortening of the chromosomal telomeres with each cell cycle is also believed to limit the number of divisions of the cell, thus contributing to ageing. There have, on the other hand, also been reports that cloning could alter the shortening of telomeres. Some cells do not age and are, therefore, described as being "biologically immortal". It is theorized by some that when it is discovered exactly what allows these cells, whether it be the result of telomere lengthening or not, to divide without limit that it will be possible to genetically alter other cells to have the same capability. It is further theorized that it will eventually be possible to genetically engineer all cells in the human body to have this capability by employing gene therapy and, therefore, stop or reverse ageing, effectively making the entire organism potentially immortal.

The length of the telomere strand has senescent effects; telomere shortening activates extensive alterations in alternative RNA splicing that produce senescent toxins such as progerin, which degrades the tissue and makes it more prone to failure. Cancer cells are usually immortal. In about 85% of tumors, this evasion of cellular senescence is the result of up-activation of their telomerase genes. This simple observation suggests that reactivation of telomerase in healthy individuals could greatly increase their cancer risk.

A research team led by Jan M. van Deursen at the Mayo Clinic in Rochester, Minn., purged all the senescent cells in mice by giving them a drug that forces the cells to self-destruct. The mice's tissues showed a major improvement in the usual burden of age-related disorders. They did not develop cataracts, avoided the usual wasting of muscle with age, and could exercise much longer on a mouse treadmill. They retained the fat layers in the skin that usually thin out with age and, in people, cause wrinkling.

Chemical Damage

Figure: *Elderly Klamath woman photographed by Edward S. Curtis in 1924*

One of the earliest ageing theories was the *Rate of Living Hypothesis* described by Raymond Pearl in 1928 (based on earlier work by Max Rubner), which states that fast basal metabolic rate corresponds to short maximum life span.

While there may be some validity to the idea that for various types of specific damage detailed below that are by-products of metabolism, all other things being equal, a fast metabolism may reduce lifespan, in general this theory does not adequately explain the differences in lifespan either within, or between, species. Calorically restricted animals process as much, or more, calories per gram of body mass, as their *ad libitum* fed counterparts, yet exhibit substantially longer lifespans. Similarly, metabolic rate is a poor predictor of lifespan for birds, bats and other species that, it is presumed, have reduced mortality from predation, and therefore have evolved long lifespans even in the presence of very high metabolic rates. In a 2007 analysis it was shown that, when modern statistical methods for correcting for the effects of body size and phylogeny are employed, metabolic rate does not correlate with longevity in mammals or birds.

With respect to specific types of chemical damage caused by metabolism, it is suggested that damage to long-lived biopolymers, such as structural proteins or DNA, caused by ubiquitous chemical agents in the body such as oxygen and sugars, are in part responsible for ageing. The damage can include breakage of biopolymer chains, cross-linking of biopolymers, or chemical attachment of unnatural substituents (haptens) to biopolymers.

Under normal aerobic conditions, approximately 4% of the oxygen metabolized by mitochondria is converted to superoxide ion, which can subsequently be converted to hydrogen peroxide, hydroxyl radical and eventually other reactive species including other peroxides and singlet oxygen, which can, in turn, generate free radicals capable of damaging structural proteins and DNA. Certain metal ions found in the body, such as copper and iron, may participate in the process. (In Wilson's disease, a hereditary defect that causes the body to retain copper, some of the symptoms resemble accelerated senescence.) These processes termed oxidative stress are linked to the potential benefits of dietary polyphenol antioxidants, for example in coffee, red wine and tea.

Sugars such as glucose and fructose can react with certain amino acids such as lysine and arginine and certain DNA bases such as guanine to produce sugar adducts, in a process called *glycation*. These adducts can further rearrange to form reactive species, which can then cross-link the structural proteins or DNA to similar biopolymers or other biomolecules such as non-structural proteins. People with diabetes, who have elevated blood sugar, develop senescence-associated disorders much earlier than the general population, but can delay such disorders by rigorous control of their blood sugar levels. There is evidence that sugar damage is linked to oxidant damage in a process termed *glycoxidation*.

Free radicals can damage proteins, lipids or DNA. Glycation mainly damages proteins. Damaged proteins and lipids accumulate in lysosomes as lipofuscin. Chemical damage to structural proteins can lead to loss of function; for example, damage to collagen of blood vessel walls can lead to vessel-wall stiffness and, thus, hypertension, and vessel wall thickening and reactive tissue formation (atherosclerosis); similar processes in the kidney can lead to renal failure. Damage to enzymes reduces cellular functionality. Lipid peroxidation of the inner mitochondrial membrane reduces the electric potential and the ability to generate energy. It is probably no accident that nearly all of the so-called "accelerated ageing diseases" are due to defective DNA repair enzymes.

It is believed that the impact of alcohol on ageing can be partly explained by alcohol's activation of the HPA axis, which stimulates glucocorticoid secretion, long-term exposure to which produces symptoms of ageing.

DNA Damage Theory of Ageing

The DNA damage theory of ageing proposes that ageing is a consequence of unrepaired accumulation of naturally occurring DNA damages. Damage in this context is a DNA alteration that has an abnormal structure. Although both mitochondrial and nuclear DNA damage can contribute to ageing, nuclear DNA is the main subject of this analysis. Nuclear DNA damage can contribute to ageing either indirectly (by increasing apoptosis or cellular senescence) or directly (by increasing cell dysfunction).

In humans and other mammals, DNA damage occurs frequently and DNA repair processes have evolved to compensate. In estimates made for mice, on average approximately 1,500 to 7,000 DNA lesions occur per hour in each mouse cell, or about 36,000 to 160,000 per cell per day (Vilenchik & Knudson 2000). In any cell some DNA damage may remain despite the action of repair processes. The accumulation of unrepaired DNA damage is more prevalent in certain types of cells, particularly in non-replicating or slowly replicating cells, such as cells in the brain, skeletal and cardiac muscle.

DNA Damage and Mutation

To understand the DNA damage theory of ageing it is important to distinguish between DNA damage and mutation, the two major types of errors that occur in DNA. Damages and mutation are fundamentally different. DNA damages are physical abnormalities in the DNA, such as single and double strand breaks, 8-hydroxydeoxyguanosine residues and polycyclic aromatic hydrocarbon adducts. DNA damages can be recognised by enzymes, and thus they can be correctly repaired if redundant information, such as the undamaged sequence in the complementary DNA strand or in a homologous chromosome, is available for copying. If a cell retains DNA damage, transcription of a gene can be prevented and thus translation into a protein will also be blocked. Replication may also be blocked and/or the cell may die. Descriptions of decrements in function, characteristic of ageing, associated with accumulation of DNA damages, are given later in this article.

In contrast to DNA damage, a mutation is a change in the base sequence of the DNA. A mutation cannot be recognised by enzymes once the base change is present in both DNA strands, and thus a mutation cannot be repaired. At the cellular level, mutations can cause alterations in protein function and regulation. Mutations are replicated when the cell replicates. In a population of cells, mutant cells will increase or decrease in frequency according to the effects of the mutation on the ability of the cell to survive and reproduce. Although distinctly different from each other, DNA damages and mutations are related because DNA damages often cause errors of DNA synthesis during replication or repair and these errors are a major source of mutation.

Given these properties of DNA damage and mutation, it can be seen that DNA damages are a special problem in non-dividing or slowly dividing cells, where unrepaired damages will tend to accumulate over time. On the other hand, in rapidly dividing cells, unrepaired DNA damages that do not kill the cell by blocking replication will tend to cause replication errors and thus mutation. The great majority of mutations that are not neutral in their effect are deleterious to a cell's survival. Thus, in a population of cells comprising a tissue with replicating cells, mutant cells will tend to be lost. However, infrequent mutations that provide a survival advantage will tend to clonally expand at the expense of neighbouring cells in the tissue. This advantage to the cell is disadvantageous to the whole organism, because such mutant cells can give rise to cancer. Thus DNA damages in frequently dividing cells, because they give rise to mutations, are a prominent cause of cancer. In contrast, DNA damages in infrequently dividing cells are likely a prominent cause of ageing.

The first person to suggest that DNA damage, as distinct from mutation, is the primary cause of ageing was Alexander (1967). By the early 1980s there was significant experimental support for this idea in the literature (Gensler & Bernstein, 1981). By the early 1990s experimental support for this idea was substantial, and furthermore it had become increasingly evident that oxidative DNA damage, in particular, is a major cause of ageing (Bernstein & Bernstein, 1991; Ames & Gold, 1991; Holmes et al., 1992; Rao & Loeb, 1992; Ames et al., 1993).

In a series of articles from 1970 to 1977, PV Narasimha Acharya, Phd. (1924–1993) theorized and scientifically proved that cells undergo "irreparable DNA damage," whereby DNA crosslinks occur when both normal cellular repair processes fail and cellular apoptosis does not occur. Specifically, PVN Acharya noted that double-strand breaks and a "cross-linkage joining both strands at the same point is irreparable because neither strand can then serve as a template for repair. The cell will die in the next mitosis or in some rare instances, mutate." (PVN Acharya; PVN Acharya & Bjorksten et al.) Acharya's research also showed how irreparable DNA damage is caused by environmental pollutants, low dose ionizing radiation and food additives, particularly nitrites and nitrates and such damage to the DNA is a causal factor for pre-mature ageing and cancer.

Age-associated Accumulation of DNA Damage and Decline in Gene Expression

In tissues composed of non- or infrequently replicating cells, DNA damage can accumulate with age and lead either to loss of cells, or, in surviving cells, loss of gene expression. Accumulated DNA damage is usually measured directly. Numerous studies of this type have indicated that oxidative damage to DNA is particularly important. The loss of expression of specific genes can be detected at both the mRNA level and protein level.

Brain

The adult brain is composed in large part of terminally differentiated non-dividing neurons. Many of the conspicuous features of ageing reflect a decline in neuronal function. Accumulation of DNA damage with age in the mammalian brain has been reported during the period 1971 to the present in at least 29 studies. A review (/book published) of the role of DNA damage in ageing, including a comprehensive summary of the studies showing DNA damage accumulation with age in brain, muscle, liver and kidney, was presented by Bernstein et al. (2008). Here, we mention only some recent studies involving rodents plus one human study. Rutten et al. (2007) showed that single-strand breaks accumulate in the mouse brain with age. Sen et al. (2007) showed that DNA damages which block the polymerase chain reaction in rat brain accumulate with age. Swain and Rao (2011) observed marked increases in several types of DNA damages in ageing rat brain, including single-strand breaks, double-strand breaks and modified bases (8-OHdG and uracil). Wolf et al. (2005) also showed that the oxidative DNA damage 8-OHdG accumulates in rat brain with age. Similarly, it was shown that as humans age from 48–97 years, 8-OHdG accumulates in the brain (Mecocci et al., 1993).

Decrements in function were noted in ageing human brain, where transcription of a set of evaluated genes declines with age from 40 to 106 years (Lu et al., 2004). These genes play central roles in synaptic plasticity, vesicular transport and mitochondrial function. In the brain, promoters of genes with reduced expression have markedly increased DNA damage (Lu et al., 2004). In cultured human neurons, these gene promoters are selectively damaged by oxidative stress. Thus Lu et al. (2004) concluded that DNA damage may reduce the expression of selectively vulnerable genes involved in learning, memory and neuronal survival, initiating a program of brain ageing that starts early in adult life.

Muscle

Muscle strength, and stamina for sustained physical effort, have decrements in function with age in humans and other species. Skeletal muscle is a tissue composed largely of multinucleated myofibres, elements that arise from the fusion of mononucleated myoblasts. Accumulation of DNA damage with age in mammalian muscle has been reported in at least 18 studies (Bernstein et al., in press 2008) since 1971. We will mention here only two of the more recent studies in rodents plus one in humans. Hamilton et al. (2001) reported that the oxidative DNA damage 8-OHdG accumulates in heart and skeletal muscle (as well as in brain, kidney and liver) of both mouse and rat with age. In humans, increases in 8-OHdG with age were reported for skeletal muscle (Mecocci et al., 1999). Catalase is an enzyme that removes hydrogen peroxide, a reactive oxygen species, and thus limits oxidative DNA damage. In mice, when catalase expression is increased specifically in mitochondria, oxidative DNA damage (8-OHdG) in skeletal muscle is decreased and lifespan is increased by about 20% (Schriner et al., 2005; Linford et al., 2006). These findings suggest that mitochondria are a significant source of the oxidative damages contributing to ageing.

Protein synthesis and protein degradation decline with age in skeletal and heart muscle, as would be expected, since DNA damage blocks gene transcription. In a recent study (Piec et al., 2005) found numerous changes in protein expression in rat skeletal muscle with age, including lower levels of several proteins related to myosin and actin. Force is generated in striated muscle by the interactions between myosin thick filaments and actin thin filaments.

Liver

Liver hepatocytes do not ordinarily divide and appear to be terminally differentiated, but they retain the ability to proliferate when injured. With age, the mass of the liver decreases, blood flow is reduced, metabolism is impaired, and alterations in microcirculation occur. At least 21 studies (Bernstein et al., in press 2008) have reported an increase in DNA damage with age in liver. For instance, Helbock et al. (1998) estimated that the steady state level of oxidative DNA base alterations increased from 24,000 per cell in the liver of young rats to 66,000 per cell in the liver of old rats.

Kidney

In kidney, changes with age include reduction in both renal blood flow and glomerular filtration rate, and impairment in the ability to concentrate urine and to conserve sodium and water. DNA damages, particularly oxidative DNA damages, increase with age (at least 8 studies)(Bernstein et al., in press 2008). For instance Hashimoto et al. (2007) showed that 8-OHdG accumulates in rat kidney DNA with age.

Long-lived Stem Cells

Tissue-specific stem cells produce differentiated cells through a series of increasingly more committed progenitor intermediates. In hematopoiesis (blood cell formation), the process begins with long-term hematopoietic stem cells that self-renew and also produce progeny cells that upon further replication go through a series of stages leading to differentiated cells without self-renewal capacity. In mice, deficiencies in DNA repair appear to limit the capacity of hematopoietic stem cells to proliferate and self-renew with age (Rossi et al., 2007). Sharpless and Depinho (2007) reviewed evidence that hematopoietic stem cells, as well as stem cells in other tissues, undergo intrinsic ageing. They speculated that stem cells grow old, in part, as a result of DNA damage. DNA damage may trigger signalling pathways, such as apoptosis, that contribute to depletion of stem cell stocks. This has been observed in several cases of accelerated ageing and may occur in normal ageing too (Freitas and de Magalhaes, 2011).

Mutation Theories of Ageing

A popular idea, that has failed to gain significant experimental support, is the idea that mutation, as distinct from DNA damage, is the primary cause of ageing. As discussed above, mutations tend to arise in frequently replicating cells as a result of errors of DNA synthesis when template DNA is damaged, and can give rise to cancer. However, in mice there is no increase in mutation in the brain with ageing (Dolle et al., 1997; Stuart et al., 2000; Hille et al., 2005). Mice defective in a gene (Pms2) that ordinarily corrects base mispairs in DNA have about a 100-fold elevated mutation frequency in all tissues, but do not appear to age more rapidly (Narayanan et al., 1997). On the other hand, mice defective in one particular DNA repair pathway show clear premature ageing, but do not have elevated mutation (Dolle et al., 2006).

One variation of the idea that mutation is the basis of ageing, that has received much attention, is that mutations specifically in mitochondrial DNA are the cause of ageing. Several studies have shown that mutations accumulate in mitochondrial DNA in infrequently replicating cells with age. DNA polymerase gamma is the enzyme that replicates mitochondrial DNA. A mouse mutant with a defect in this DNA polymerase is only able to replicate its mitochondrial DNA inaccurately, so that the mutation rate is 500-fold higher than in normal mice. Yet these mice showed no obvious features of rapidly accelerated ageing (Vermulst et al., 2007). The probable explanation for the apparent lack of effect of the additional mutations in mitochondrial DNA is that, within a typical cell, there are large numbers of mitochondria and each mitochondrion can have multiple copies of mitochondrial DNA. Since most mutations are recessive, any particular deleterious mutation would not be expected to have a pronounced effect when many copies of the correct DNA sequence are present in the same and in other mitochondria in the cell. Overall, the observations discussed in this section indicate that mutations are not the primary cause of ageing.

Dietary Restriction

In rodents, caloric restriction slows ageing and extends lifespan. At least 4 studies have shown that caloric restriction reduces 8-OHdG damages in various organs of rodents. One of these studies (Hamilton et al., 2001) showed that caloric restriction reduced accumulation of 8-

OHdG with age in rat brain, heart and skeletal muscle, and in mouse brain, heart, kidney and liver. More recently, Wolf et al. (2005) showed that dietary restriction reduced accumulation of 8-OHdG with age in rat brain, heart, skeletal muscle, and liver. Thus reduction of oxidative DNA damage is associated with a slower rate of ageing and increased lifespan.

Inherited Defects that Cause Premature Ageing

If DNA damage is the underlying cause of ageing, it would be expected that humans with inherited defects in the ability to repair DNA damages should age at a faster pace than persons without such a defect. Numerous examples of rare inherited conditions with DNA repair defects are known. Several of these show multiple striking features of premature ageing, and others have fewer such features. Perhaps the most striking premature ageing conditions are Werner syndrome (mean lifespan 47 years), Huchinson-Gilford Progeria (mean lifespan 13 years), and Cockayne syndrome (mean lifespan 13 years). Werner syndrome is due to an inherited defect in an enzyme (a helicase and exonuclease) that acts in base excision repair of DNA (e.g. Harrigan et al., 2006). Hutchinson-Guilford Progeria is due to a defect in Lamin A protein which forms a scaffolding within the cell nucleus to organise chromatin and is needed for repair of double-strand breaks in DNA (Liu et al., 2007). Cockayne Syndrome is due to a defect in a protein necessary for the repair process, transcription coupled nucleotide excision repair, which can remove damages, particularly oxidative DNA damages, that block transcription (D'Errico et al., 2007). In addition to these three conditions, several other human syndromes, that also have defective DNA repair, show several features of premature ageing. These include ataxia telangiectasia, Nijmegen breakage syndrome, some subgroups of xeroderma pigmentosum, trichothiodystrophy, Fanconi anemia, Bloom syndrome and Rothmund-Thomson syndrome.

In addition to human inherited syndromes, experimental mouse models with genetic defects in DNA repair show features of premature ageing and reduced lifespan (e.g. Vogel et al., 1999; Niedernhoffer et al., 2006; Mostoslavsky et al., 2006).

Lifespan in Different Mammalian Species

Studies comparing DNA repair capacity in different mammalian species have shown that repair capacity correlates with lifespan. The initial study of this type, by Hart and Setlow (1974), showed that the ability of skin fibroblasts of seven mammalian species to perform DNA repair after exposure to a DNA damaging agent correlated with lifespan of the species. The species studied were shrew, mouse, rat, hamster, cow, elephant and human. This initial study stimulated many additional studies involving a wide variety of mammalian species, and the correlation between repair capacity and lifespan generally held up. In one of the more recent studies, Burkle et al. (2005) studied the level of a particular enzyme, poly(ADP-ribose) polymerase, which is involved in repair of single-strand breaks in DNA. They found that the lifespan of 13 mammalian species correlated with the activity of this enzyme. In addition, they found that humans who lived past 100 years had a significantly higher activity of this enzyme than younger individuals.

Conclusions

Numerous studies have shown that DNA damage accumulates in brain, muscle, liver, kidney, and in long-lived stem cell. These accumulated DNA damages are the likely cause of the decline in gene expression and loss of functional capacity observed with increasing age. On the other hand, accumulation of mutations, as distinct from DNA damages, is not a plausible candidate as the primary cause of ageing. A calorie-restricted diet in mammals improves lifespan, and this improvement is associated with a decrease in oxidative DNA damage. Several inherited genetic defects in ability to repair DNA damage give rise to premature ageing suggesting a causal relationship between DNA damage and ageing. In comparisons of different mammalian species that differ in lifespan, DNA repair capacity is found to correlate with lifespan. The principal source of the DNA damages leading to normal ageing appears to be reactive oxygen species, produced as byproducts of normal cellular metabolism.

Reliability Theory of Ageing and Longevity

Reliability theory of ageing and longevity is a scientific approach aimed to gain theoretical insights into mechanisms of biological ageing and species survival patterns by applying a general theory of systems failure, known as reliability theory.

Overview

Reliability theory allows researchers to predict the age-related failure kinetics for a system of given architecture (reliability structure) and given reliability of its components. Applications of reliability-theory approach to the problem of biological ageing and species longevity lead to the following conclusions:

1. Redundancy is a key for understanding ageing and the systemic nature of ageing in particular. Systems, which are redundant

in numbers of irreplaceable elements, do deteriorate (that is, age) over time, even if they are built of non-ageing elements.

2. Paradoxically, the apparent ageing rate or expression of ageing (measured as relative differences in failure rates between compared age groups) is *higher* for systems with higher redundancy levels.
3. Redundancy exhaustion over the life course explains the observed 'compensation law of mortality' (mortality convergence at later life, when death rates are becoming relatively similar at advanced ages for different populations of the same biological species), as well as the observed late-life mortality deceleration, leveling-off, and mortality plateaus.
4. Living organisms seem to be formed with a high initial load of damage (HIDL hypothesis), and therefore their lifespan and ageing patterns may be sensitive to early-life conditions that determine this initial damage load during early development. The idea of early-life programming of ageing and longevity may have important practical implications for developing early-life interventions promoting health and longevity.
5. Reliability theory explains why mortality rates increase exponentially with age (the Gompertz law) in many species, by taking into account the initial flaws (defects) in newly formed systems. It also explains why organisms "prefer" to die according to the Gompertz law, while technical devices usually fail according to the Weibull (power) law. Theoretical conditions are specified when organisms die according to the Weibull law: organisms should be relatively free of initial flaws and defects. The theory makes it possible to find a general failure law applicable to all adult and extreme old ages, where the Gompertz and the Weibull laws are just special cases of this more general failure law.
6. Reliability theory helps evolutionary theories to explain how the age of onset of deleterious mutations could be postponed during evolution, which could be easily achieved by a simple increase in initial redundancy levels. From the reliability perspective, the increase in initial redundancy levels is the simplest way to improve survival at particularly early reproductive ages (with gains fading at older ages). This matches exactly with the higher fitness priority of early reproductive ages emphasized by evolutionary theories. Evolutionary and reliability ideas also help in understanding why organisms seem

to "choose" a simple but short-term solution of the survival problem through enhancing the systems' redundancy, instead of a more permanent but complicated solution based on rigorous repair (with the potential of achieving negligible senescence). Thus there are promising opportunities for merging the reliability and evolutionary theories of ageing.

Overall, the reliability theory provides a parsimonious explanation for many important ageing-related phenomena and suggests a number of interesting testable predictions. Therefore, reliability theory seems to be a promising approach for developing a comprehensive theory of ageing and longevity integrating mathematical methods with specific biological knowledge and evolutionary ideas. Reliability theory of ageing provides an optimistic perspective on the opportunities for healthy life-extension. According to reliability theory, human lifespan is not fixed, and it could be further increased through better body maintenance, repair, and replacement of the failed body parts in the future.

Free-radical Theory of Ageing

The free radical theory of ageing (FRTA) states that organisms age because cells accumulate free radical damage over time. A free radical is any atom or molecule that has a single unpaired electron in an outer shell. While a few free radicals such as melanin are not chemically reactive, most biologically-relevant free radicals are highly reactive. For most biological structures, free radical damage is closely associated with oxidative damage. Antioxidants are reducing agents, and limit oxidative damage to biological structures by passivating them from free radicals. Strictly speaking, the free radical theory is only concerned with free radicals such as superoxide (O_2^-), but it has since been expanded to encompass oxidative damage from other reactive oxygen species such as hydrogen peroxide (H_2O_2), or peroxynitrite ($OONO^-$).

Denham Harman first proposed the free radical theory of ageing in the 1950s, and in the 1970s extended the idea to implicate mitochondrial production of reactive oxygen species.

In some model organisms, such as yeast and *Drosophila*, there is evidence that reducing oxidative damage can extend lifespan. In mice, interventions that enhance oxidative damage generally shorten lifespan. However, in roundworms (*Caenorhabditis elegans*), blocking the production of the naturally occurring antioxidant superoxide dismutase has recently been shown to *increase* lifespan. Whether reducing oxidative damage below normal levels is sufficient to extend lifespan remains an open and controversial question.

Background

The free radical theory of ageing was conceived by Denham Harman in the 1950s, when prevailing scientific opinion held that free radicals were too unstable to exist in biological systems. This was also before anyone invoked free radicals as a cause of degenerative diseases. Two sources inspired Harman: 1) the rate of living theory, which holds that lifespan is an inverse function of metabolic rate which in turn is proportional to oxygen consumption, and 2) Rebbeca Gershman's observation that hyperbaric oxygen toxicity and radiation toxicity could be explained by the same underlying phenomenon: oxygen free radicals. Noting that radiation causes "mutation, cancer and ageing", Harman argued that oxygen free radicals produced during normal respiration would cause cumulative damage which would eventually lead to organismal loss of functionality, and ultimately death.

In later years, the free radical theory was expanded to include not only ageing *per se*, but also age-related diseases. Free radical damage within cells has been linked to a range of disorders including cancer, arthritis, atherosclerosis, Alzheimer's disease, and diabetes. There has been some evidence to suggest that free radicals and some reactive nitrogen species trigger and increase cell death mechanisms within the body such as apoptosis and in extreme cases necrosis.

In 1972, Harman modified his original theory to what became known as the mitochondrial theory of ageing. In its current form, this theory proposes that reactive oxygen species that are produced in the mitochondria, causes damage to certain macromolecules including lipids, proteins and most importantly mitochondrial DNA. This damage then causes mutations which leads to an increase of ROS production and greatly enhances the accumulation of free radicals within cells. This mitochondrial theory has been more widely accepted that it could play a major role in contributing to the ageing process.

Since Harman first proposed the free radical theory of ageing, there have been continual modifications and extensions to his original theory.

Processes

Free radicals are atoms or molecules containing unpaired electrons. Electrons normally exist in pairs in specific orbitals in atoms or molecules. Free radicals, which contain only a single electron in any orbital, are usually unstable toward losing or picking up an extra electron, so that all electrons in the atom or molecule will be paired.

Note that the unpaired electron does not imply charge - free radicals can be positively charged, negatively charged, or neutral.

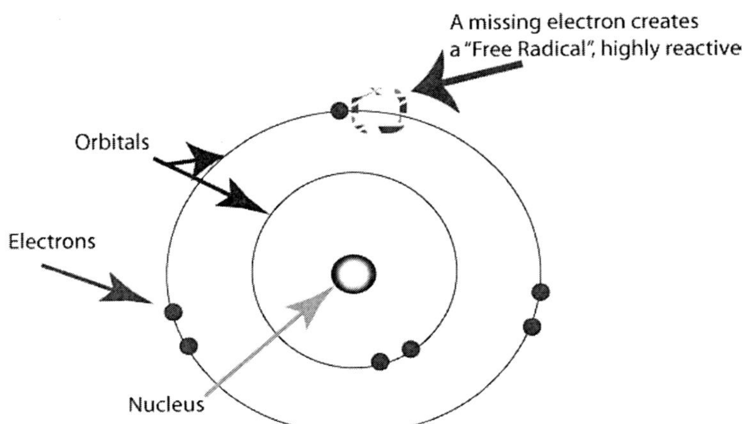

Figure: *In chemistry, a free radical is any atom, molecule, or ion with an unpaired valence electron*

Damage occurs when the free radical encounters another molecule and seeks to find another electron to pair its unpaired electron. The free radical often pulls an electron off a neighbouring molecule, causing the affected molecule to become a free radical itself. The new free radical can then pull an electron off the next molecule, and a chemical chain reaction of radical production occurs. The free radicals produced in such reactions often terminate by removing an electron from a molecule which becomes changed or cannot function without it, especially in biology. Such an event causes damage to the molecule, and thus to the cell that contains it (since the molecule often becomes dysfunctional).

The chain reaction caused by free radicals can lead to cross-linking of atomic structures. In cases where the free radical-induced chain reaction involves base pair molecules in a strand of DNA, the DNA can become cross-linked.

DNA cross-linking can in turn lead to various effects of ageing, especially cancer. Other cross-linking can occur between fat and protein molecules, which leads to wrinkles. Free radicals can oxidize LDL, and this is a key event in the formation of plaque in arteries, leading to heart disease and stroke. These are examples of how the free-radical theory of ageing has been used to neatly "explain" the origin of many chronic diseases. Free radicals that are thought to be involved in the process of ageing include superoxide and nitric oxide. Specifically, an increase in superoxide affects ageing whereas a decrease in nitric oxide formation, or its bioavailability, does the same.

Antioxidants are helpful in reducing and preventing damage from free radical reactions because of their ability to donate electrons which neutralize the radical without forming another. Ascorbic acid, for example, can lose an electron to a free radical and remain stable itself by passing its unstable electron around the antioxidant molecule.

This has led to the hypothesis that large amounts of antioxidants, with their ability to decrease the numbers of free radicals, might lessen the radical damage causing chronic diseases, and even radical damage responsible for ageing.

Evidence

Numerous studies have demonstrated a role for free radicals in the ageing process and thus tentatively support the free radical theory of ageing. Studies have shown a significant increase in superoxide radical (SOR) formation and lipid peroxidation in ageing rats. Chung et al. suggest ROS production increases with age and indicated the conversion of XDH to XOD may be an important contributing factor. This was supported by a study that showed superoxide production by xanthine oxidase and NO synthase in mesenteric arteries was higher in older rats than young ones.

Hamilton et al. examined the similarities in impaired endothelial function in hypertension and ageing in humans and found a significant overproduction of superoxide in both. This finding is supported by a 2007 study which found that endothelial oxidative stress develops with ageing in healthy men and is related to reductions in endothelium-dependant dilation. Furthermore, a study using cultured smooth muscle cells displayed increased reactive oxygen species (ROS) in cells derived from older mice. These findings were supported by a second study using Leydig cells isolated from the testes of young and old rats.

The Choksi et al. experiment with Ames dwarf (DW) mice suggests the lower levels of endogenous ROS production in DW mice may be a factor in their resistance to oxidative stress and long life. Lener et al. suggest Nox4 activity increases oxidative damage in human umbilical vein endothelial cells via superoxide overproduction. Furthermore, Rodriguez-Manas et al. found endothelial dysfunction in human vessels is due to the collective effect of vascular inflammation and oxidative stress.

Sasaki et al. reported superoxide-dependent chemiluminescence was inversely proportionate to maximum lifespan in mice, Wistar rats, and pigeons. They suggest ROS signalling may be a determinant in the ageing process. Mendoza-Nunez et al. propose an age of 60 years or older may be linked with increased oxidative stress. Miyazawa found mitochondrial superoxide anion production can lead to organ atrophy and dysfunction via mitochondrial- mediated apoptosis. In addition, they suggest mitochondrial superoxide anion plays an essential part in ageing. Lund et al. demonstrated the role of endogenous extracellular superoxide dismutase in protecting against endothelial dysfunction during the ageing process using mice.

Modifications of the free Radical Theory of Ageing

One of the main criticisms of the free radical theory of ageing is the idea free radicals are responsible for the damage of biomolecules resulting in changes to the biology of the cell and thus organismal ageing. Thus several modifications have been proposed to integrate current research into the overall theory.

Mitochondrial Theory of Ageing

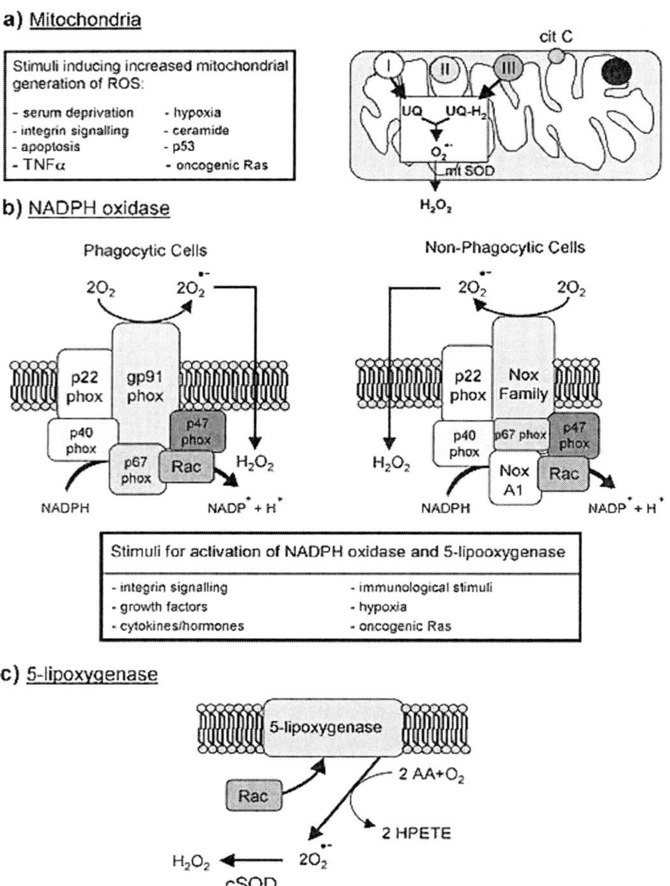

Figure: *Major sources of Reactive oxygen species in living systems*

Mitochondrial theory of ageing was first proposed in 1978, and shortly thereafter the Mitochondrial free radical theory of ageing was introduced in 1980. The theory implicates the mitochondria as the chief target of radical damage, since there is a known chemical mechanism by which mitochondria can produce Reactive oxygen species (ROS), mitochondrial components such as mtDNA are not as well protected as nuclear DNA, and by studies comparing damage to nuclear and mtDNA that demonstrate higher levels of radical damage on the mitochondrial molecules. Electrons may escape from metabolic processes in the mitochondria like the Electron transport chain, and these electrons may in turn react with water to form ROS such as the superoxide radical, or via an indirect route the hydroxyl radical. These radicals then damage the mitochondria's DNA and proteins, and these damage components in turn are more liable to produce ROS byproducts. Thus a positive feedback loop of oxidative stress is established that, over time, can lead to the deterioration of cells and later organs and the entire body.

This theory has been widely debated and it is still unclear how ROS induced mtDNA mutations develop. Conte et al. suggest iron-substituted zinc fingers may generate free radicals due the zinc finger proximity to DNA and thus lead to DNA damage.

Afanas'ev suggests the superoxide dismutation activity of CuZnSOD demonstrates an important link between life span and free radicals. The link between CuZnSOD and life span was demonstrated by Perez et al. who indicated mice life span was affected by the deletion of the Sod1 gene which encodes CuZnSOD.

Contrary to the usually observed association between mitochondrial ROS (mtROS) and a decline in longevity, Yee et al. recently observed increased longevity mediated by mtROS signalling in an apoptosis pathway. This serves to support the possibility that observed correlations between ROS damage and ageing are not necessarily indicative of the causal involvement of ROS in the ageing process but are more likely due to their modulating signal transduction pathways that are part of cellular responses to the ageing process.

Epigenetic Oxidative Redox Shift (EORS) Theory of Ageing

Brewer proposed a theory which integrates the free radical theory of ageing with the insulin signalling effects in ageing. Brewer's theory suggests "sedentary behaviour associated with age triggers an oxidized redox shift and impaired mitochondrial function". This mitochondrial impairment leads to more sedentary behaviour and accelerated ageing.

Metabolic Stability Theory of Ageing

The metabolic stability theory of ageing suggests it is the cells ability to maintain stable concentration of ROS which is the primary determinant of lifespan. This theory criticizes the free radical theory because it ignores that ROS are specific signalling molecules which are necessary for maintaining normal cell functions.

Mitohormesis

Oxidative stress may promote life expectancy of *Caenorhabditis elegans* by inducing a secondary response to initially increased levels of reactive oxygen species. This observation was initially named mitohormesis, or mitochondrial hormesis on a purely hypothetical basis. In mammals, the question of the net effect of reactive oxygen species on ageing is even less clear. Recent epidemiological findings support the process of mitohormesis in humans, and even suggest that the intake of exogenous antioxidants may increase disease prevalence in humans (according to the theory, because they prevent the stimulation of the organism's natural response to the oxidant compounds which not only neutralizes them but provides other benefits as well).

Effects of Calorie Restriction

Studies have demonstrated that calorie restriction displays positive effects on the lifespan of organisms even though it is accompanied by increases in oxidative stress. Many studies suggest this may be due to anti-oxidative action, oxidative stress suppression, or oxidative stress resistance which occurs in calorie restriction. Fontana et al. suggest calorie restriction influenced numerous signal pathways through the reduction of insulin-like growth factor I (IGF-1). Additionally they suggest antioxidant SOD and catalase are involved in the inhibition of this nutrient signalling pathway.

The increase in life expectancy observed during some calorie restriction studies which can occur with lack of decreases or even increases in O2 consumption is often inferred as opposing the mitochondrial free radical theory of ageing. However, Barja showed significant decreases in mitochondrial oxygen radical production (per unit of O2 consumed) occur during dietary restriction, aerobic exercise, chronic exercise, and hyperthyroidism. Additionally, mitochondrial oxygen radical generation is lower in long-lived birds than in short-lived mammals of comparable body size and metabolic rate. Thus, mitochondrial ROS production must be regulated independently of O2 consumption in a variety of species, tissues and physiologic states.

Antioxidant Therapy

The free radical theory of ageing implies that antioxidants such as vitamin A, vitamin C, vitamin E (alpha-tocopherol), beta-carotene and Superoxide dismutase will slow the process of ageing by preventing free radicals from oxidizing sensitive biological molecules or reducing the formation of free radicals. The antioxidant chemicals found in many foods are frequently cited as the basis of claims for the benefits of a high intake of vegetables and fruits in the diet.

Nonetheless, some recent studies tend to show that antioxidant therapy have no effect and can even increase mortality.

Since many different substances operate synergistically in antioxidant defence, its complicated process may require more sophisticated approaches to determine if antioxidant therapy may benefit the ageing process.

Proponents of the theory claim that this phenomenon can be explained by hormesis: The addition of antioxidants can lead to a decrease of normal biological response to free radicals and lead to a more sensitive environment to oxidation. Furthermore, a recent study tracking the eating habits of 478,000 Europeans suggests that consuming lots of fruits and vegetables has little if any effect on preventing cancer.

Network Theory of Ageing

The network theory of ageing supports the idea that multiple connected processes contribute to the biology of ageing. Kirkwood and Kowald helped to establish the first model of this kind by connecting theories and predict specific mechanisms. In departure of investigating a single mechanistic cause or single molecules that lead to senescence, the network theory of ageing takes a systems biology view to integrate theories in conjunction with computational models and quantitative data related to the biology of ageing.

Implications

- The free radical theory, describing the reactions of free radicals, antioxidants and proteolytic enzymes, was computationally connected with the protein error theory to describe the error propagation loops within the cellular translation machinery.
- The study of gene networks revealed proteins associated with ageing to have significantly higher connectivity than expected by chance.

- Investigation of ageing on multiple levels of biological organisation contributed to a physiome view, from genes to organisms, predicting lifespans based on scaling laws, fractal supply networks and metabolism as well as ageing related molecular networks.
- The network theory of ageing has encouraged the development of data bases related to human ageing. Proteomic network maps suggest a relationship between the genetics of development and the genetics of ageing.

Stem Cell Theory of Ageing

The stem cell theory of ageing is a new theory which was recently formulated by several scientists and which postulates that the ageing process is the result of the inability of various types of stem cells to continue to replenish the tissues of an organism with functional differentiated cells capable of maintaining that tissue (or organ) original function. Damage and error accumulation in genetic material is always a problem for systems regardless of the age. The number of stem cells in young people is very much higher than older people and this cause a better and more efficient replacement mechanism in the young contrary to the old. In other words ageing is not a matter of the increase of damage, but a matter of failure to replace it due to decreased number of stem cells. They decrease in number and tend to lose the ability to differentiate into progenies or lymphoid lineages and myeloid lineages.

Maintaining the dynamic balance of stem cell pools requires several conditions. Balancing proliferation and quiescence along with homing and self-renewal of hematopoietic stem cells are favouring elements of stem cell pool maintenance while differentiation, mobilization and senescence are detrimental elements. These detrimental effects will eventually cause apoptosis.

There are also several challenges when it comes to therapeutic use of stem cells and their ability to replenish organs and tissues. First, different cells may have different life spans even though they are originated from the same stem cells. Also, continual effort to replace the somatic cells may cause exhaustion of stem cells.

Research

Some of the proponents of this theory have been Norman E. Sharpless, Ronald A. DePinho, Huber Warner, Alessandro Testori and others. Dr Warner came to this conclusion after analyzing human case of Hutchinson's Guilford Syndrome and mouse models of accelerated ageing. Stem cells divide more than non stem cells so the tendency of accumulating damage is greater. Although they have protective mechanisms, they still age and lose function. In fact *Matthew R. Wallenfang*, *Renuka Nayak* and *Stephen DiNardo* showed this in their study. According to their findings, it is possible to track male GSCs labelled with lacZ gene in *Drosophila* model by inducing recombination with heat shock and observe the decrease in GSC number with ageing. In order to mark GSCs with lacZ gene, flip recombinase (Flp)-mediated recombination is used to combine a ubiquitously active tubulin promoter followed by an FRT (flip recombinase target) site with a promotorless lacZ ORF (open reading frame) preceded by an FRT site. Heat shock is used to induce Flp recombinase marker gene expression is activated in dividing cells due to recombination. Consequently, all clone of cells derived from GSC are marked with a functional lacZ gene. By tracking the marked cells, they were able to show that GSCs do age.

Another study in a mouse model shows that stem cells do age and their ageing can lead to heart failure. Findings of the study indicate that diabetes leads to premature myocyte senescence and death and together they result in the development of cardiomyopathy due to decreased muscle mass.

Evidence Against the Stem Cell Theory of Ageing

Diseases such as Alzheimer's disease, end-stage renal failure or heart disease are caused by different mechanisms that are not related with stem cells. Also, when it comes to some diseases related to hematopoietic system such as aplastic anemia and complete bone marrow failure, they are not especially age-dependent. Moreover, a dog study published by *Zaucha J.M, Yu C.* and *Mathioudakis G., et al.* also shows evidence against the stem cell theory. Experimental comparison of the engraftment properties of young and old marrow in a mammal model, the dog, failed to show any decrement in stem cell function with age.

Miscellanea

Biological clocks, which objectively measure the biological age of cells and tissues, may become useful for testing different biological ageing theories.

A set of rare hereditary (genetic) disorders, each called progeria, has been known for some time. Sufferers exhibit symptoms resembling accelerated ageing, including wrinkled skin. The cause of Hutchinson–Gilford progeria syndrome was reported in the journal *Nature* in May 2003. This report suggests that DNA damage, not oxidative stress, is the cause of this form of accelerated ageing. Recently, a kind of early senescence has been alleged to be a possible unintended outcome of early cloning experiments. The issue was raised in the case of Dolly the sheep, following her death from a contagious lung disease. The claim that Dolly's early death involved premature senescence has been vigorously contested, and Dolly's creator, Dr. Ian Wilmut has expressed the view that her illness and death were probably unrelated to the fact that she was a clone.

Effects of Ageing

Steady decline in many cognitive processes is seen across the lifespan, accelerating from the twenties or even thirties. Research has focused in particular on memory and ageing and has found decline in many types of memory with ageing, but not in semantic memory or general knowledge such as vocabulary definitions, which typically increases or remains steady until the late adulthood. Early studies on changes in cognition with age generally found declines in intelligence in the elderly, but studies were cross-sectional rather than longitudinal and thus results may be an artefact of cohort rather than a true example of decline. However, longitudinal studies could be confounded due to prior test experience. Intelligence may decline with age, though the rate may vary depending on the type and may in fact remain steady throughout most of the lifespan, dropping suddenly only as people near the end of their lives. Individual variations in rate of cognitive decline may therefore be explained in terms of people having different lengths of life. There are changes to the brain: though neuron loss is minor after 20 years of age there is a 10% reduction each decade in the total length of the brain's myelinated axons.

Ageing in Communication

Healthy Ageing

Healthy ageing implies optimal well-being in spite of barriers resulting from age.

The global population is ageing and will continue to have communication inabilities unless barriers of communication with the elderly are more highly promoted.

Barriers to Communication in Ageing:

Sensory impairments include hearing and vision deficits, which can cause communication barriers. Changes in cognition, hearing, and vision are easily associated with healthy ageing and can causes problems when diagnosing dementia and aphasia due to the similarities.

Hearing Loss

Hearing loss is a common condition among ageing adults. Common conditions that can increase the risk of hearing loss in elderly people are high blood pressure, diabetes or the use of certain medications harmful to the ear. Hearing aids are commonly referred to as personal amplifying systems, which can generally improve hearing by about 50%.

Hearing loss among the aged community lessens elders ability to compensate for other age related social and/or physical problems. Mechanical problems including translation of ideas into linguistic representations, the expression of linguistic representations, the perception of linguistic stimuli and the derivation of an idea from a given unit of disclosure, have the greatest affect on the communication ability of older adults. Changes in these mechanical problems are more important than changes in linguistic knowledge. The main goal of hearing aids is to improve communication and quality of life, not just to restore hearing. Presbycusis is an example of a hearing deficit that cannot be corrected by hearing aids. Presbycusis, the alteration of hearing sensitivity associated with normal hearing loss, is caused by the decreased amount of hair cells of the inner ear. This is normally caused by long periods of distressing noise that diminish the hair cells which with increasing age will not grow back. Presbycusis and other such hearing related problems promote social withdrawal, as individuals begin to lose touch with the world around them. Hearing loss among the aged community lessens elder's ability to compensate for other age related social and/or physical problems. This impairment can cause elders to lose touch of social skills because in conversation they may have trouble keeping up with fast paced or hearing different pitched voices in conversation.

Visual Impairment

The interpretation of facial expressions and mouthing can be difficult to understand when an individual has a visual impairment. Such problems hinder the ability of people to understand stimuli and translate information pertaining to perception with their brain for analysis. Non-verbal communication is important in effective communication and elders with vision loss are more likely to misinterpret or read the other persons actions in a wrong way. Visual impairments also cause a loss in positive perceptions of the environment around them. This can lead to isolation and possible depression in elderly people. Macular degeneration is a common of vision loss problem in elderly people. It diminishes the macula of the eye, which is responsible for clear vision. It causes progressive loss of central vision and possible colour loss in vision. The cause of this degeneration is due to systemic changes in the circulation of waste products and growth of abnormal vessels around the retina causing the photoreceptors not to receive proper images. Though ageing almost always causes this, other possible effects and risk factors include smoking, obesity, family history and excessive sunlight exposure.

Strategies for Communicating with Ageing Individuals:

- Allow more time for conversation and conduct conversation in a quiet place.
- Be honest if you do not understand what is being said.
- Repeat back what is being said to make sure you understand.
- Do not cover mouth when speaking and squarely face the speaker.
- Use open-ended questions.
- Use familiar terms when speaking to the individual.

Cultural Variations

The age of an adult human is commonly measured in whole years since the day of birth. Fractional years, months or even weeks may be used to describe the age of children and infants for finer resolution. The time of day the birth occurred is not commonly considered. In some cultures there are other ways to express age: by counting years with or without including current year. For example, it could be said for the same person that he is twenty years old or that he is in the twenty-first year of his life.

In Russian the former expression is generally used, the latter one has restricted usage: it is used for age of a deceased person in obituaries and for the age of an adult when it is desired to show him/her older than he/she is. (Psychologically, a woman *in her 20th year* seems older than one who is *19 years old.*)

Depending on cultural and personal philosophy, ageing can be seen as an undesirable phenomenon, reducing beauty and bringing one closer to death; or as an accumulation of wisdom, mark of survival and a status worthy of respect. In some cases numerical age is important (whether good or bad), whereas others find the stage in life that one has reached (adulthood, independence, marriage, retirement, career success) to be more important.

East Asian age reckoning is different from that found in Western culture. Traditional Chinese culture uses a different ageing method, called *Xusui* ([†rk) with respect to common ageing which is called

Zhousui (hTrk). In the *Xusui* method, people are born at age 1, not age 0, possibly because conception is already considered to be the start of the life span and possibly because the number '0' was not historically present in Ancient China, and another difference is the ageing day: *Xusui* grows up at the Spring Festival (aka. Chinese New Year's Day), while *Zhousui* grows up at one's birthday. In parts of Tibet, age is counted from conception i.e. one is usually 9 months old when one is born.

Age in prenatal development is normally measured in gestational age, taking the last menstruation of the mother as a point of beginning. Alternatively, fertilisation age, beginning from fertilisation can be taken.

Society

Legal

Figure: *An elderly man*

There are variations in many countries as to what age a person legally becomes an adult. Most legal systems define a specific age for when an individual is allowed or obliged to do particular activities. These age specifications include voting age, drinking age, age of consent, age of majority, age of criminal responsibility, marriageable age, age of candidacy, and mandatory retirement age. Admission to a movie for instance, may depend on age according to a motion picture rating system. A bus fare might be discounted for the young or old.

Similarly, in many countries in jurisprudence, the defence of infancy is a form of defence by which a defendant argues that, at the time a law was broken, they were not liable for their actions and thus should not be held liable for a crime.

Many courts recognise that defendants who are considered to be juveniles may avoid criminal prosecution on account of their age and in borderline cases the age of the offender is often held to be a mitigating circumstance.

Economics

As life expectancy rises and birth rates decline in developed countries, the median age itself rises accordingly. According to the United Nations, this process is taking place in nearly every country in the world. A rising median age can have significant social and economic implications, as the workforce gets progressively older and the number of old workers and retirees grows relative to the number of young workers. Older people generally incur more health-related costs than do younger people in the workplace and can also cost more in worker's compensation and pension liabilities. In most developed countries an older workforce is somewhat inevitable. In the United States for instance, the Bureau of Labour Statistics estimates that one in four American workers will be 55 or older by 2020.

Health Care Demand

Many societies in Western Europe and Japan have ageing populations. While the effects on society are complex, there is a concern about the impact on health care demand. The large number of suggestions in the literature for specific interventions to cope with the expected increase in demand for long-term care in ageing societies can be organised under four headings: improve system performance; redesign service delivery; support informal caregivers; and shift demographic parameters.

However, the annual growth in national health spending is not mainly due to increasing demand from ageing populations, but rather has been driven by rising incomes, costly new medical technology, a shortage of health care workers and informational asymmetries between providers and patients. A number of health problems become more prevalent as people get older. These include mental health problems as well as physical health problems, especially dementia.

Even so, it has been estimated that population ageing only explains 0.2 percentage points of the annual growth rate in medical spending of 4.3 percent since 1970. In addition, certain reforms to the Medicare system in the United States decreased elderly spending on home health care by 12.5 percent per year between 1996 and 2000. This would suggest that the impact of ageing populations on health care costs is not inevitable. In United States prisons, medical costs for an ageing inmate could be above $100 per day as of July 2007, while typical inmates cost $33 per day. Most State DOCs report spending more than 10 percent of the annual budget on elderly care. That is expected to rise over the next 10–20 years. Some states have talked about releasing ageing inmates early.

Coping and Well-Being

Psychologists have examined coping skills in the elderly. Various factors, such as social support, religion and spirituality, active engagement with life and having an internal locus of control have been proposed as being beneficial in helping people to cope with stressful life events in later life. Social support and personal control are possibly the two most important factors that predict well-being, morbidity and mortality in adults.

Other factors that may link to well-being and quality of life in the elderly include social relationships (possibly relationships with pets as well as humans), and health.

Individuals in different wings in the same retirement home have demonstrated a lower risk of mortality and higher alertness and self-rated health in the wing where residents had greater control over their environment, though personal control may have less impact on specific measures of health. Social control, perceptions of how much influence one has over one's social relationships, shows support as a moderator variable for the relationship between social support and perceived health in the elderly and may positively influence coping in the elderly.

Religion

Religion is an important factor used by the elderly in coping with the demands of later life and appears more often than other forms of coping later in life. Religiosity is a multidimensional variable; while participation in religious activities in the sense of participation in formal and organised rituals may decline, it may become a more informal, but still important aspect of life such as through personal or private prayer.

Self-Rated Health

Self-ratings of health, the beliefs in one's own health as excellent, fair or poor, has been correlated with well-being and mortality in the elderly; positive ratings are linked to high well-being and reduced mortality. Various reasons have been proposed for this association; people who are objectively healthy may naturally rate their health better than that of their ill counterparts, though this link has been observed even in studies which have controlled for socioeconomic status, psychological functioning and health status. This finding is generally stronger for men than women, though the pattern between genders is not universal across all studies and some results suggest sex-based differences only appear in certain age groups, for certain causes of mortality and within a specific sub-set of self-ratings of health.

Paradox of Ageing

Seniors' subjective health remains relatively stable while objective health worsens with age. Furthermore, it seems that the perceived health improves with age when objective health is controlled in the equation. This phenomenon is known as the paradox of ageing. People's expectations concerning health co-evolve with the health norms surrounding one's age. Elderly people often associate their functional and physical decline with the normal ageing process. The elderly may actually enhance their perception of their own health through social comparison; for instance, the older people get, the more they may consider themselves in better health than their same-aged peers. Hence, the older a person becomes and the more their actual health declines, the greater the potential role is for social comparison processes to create a gap between a person's objective and subjective health.

Retirement

Retirement, a common transition faced by the elderly, may have both positive and negative consequences.

Political Struggle against Ageing

Though many scientists state that radical life extension, delaying and stopping ageing are achievable, there are still no international or national programmes focused on stopping ageing or on radical life extension. There are political forces staying for and against life extension. In 2012 the Longevity political parties started in Russia, then in the USA, Israel and the Netherlands. These parties aim to provide political support to anti-ageing and radical life extension research and technologies and want to ensure the fastest possible and at the same time the softest societal transition to the next step: radical life extension and life without ageing, that will make it possible to provide the access to such technologies to the most of the currently living people.

Successful Ageing

Successful ageing (American English) or successful ageing (British English) refers to physical, mental and social well-being in older age. The concept of successful ageing can be traced back to the 1950s, and was popularized in the 1980s. It reflects changing view on ageing in Western countries, where a stigma associated with old age has led to considering older people as a burden on society. Consequently, in the past most of the scientists have been focusing on negative aspects of ageing or preventing the decline of youth.

Research on successful ageing, however, acknowledges the fact that there is a growing number of older adults functioning at a high level and contributing to the society. Scientists working in this area seek to define what differentiates successful from usual ageing in order to design effective strategies and medical interventions to protect health and well-being from ageing.

Definitions

Definitions Focusing on Successful Emotional and Cognitive Ageing: Recent studies emphasize the importance of adaptation and emotional well-being in successful ageing. New data suggests that for most senior citizens, subjective quality of life is more important than the absence of disease and other objective measures relating to physical and mental health. In two recent studies the vast majority of older people rated themselves as ageing successfully, even when they did not meet all objective physical and mental criteria for successful ageing. Studies which incorporated the perspectives of older adults into the model of successful ageing found that optimism, effective coping styles, and social and community involvement are more important to ageing successfully than traditional measures of health and wellness. Additionally, recent studies have shown that for most senior citizens, subjective quality of life is strongly tied with psychosocial protective traits such as resilience, optimism, and mental and emotional status.

Early Definitions: Traditional definitions of successful ageing have emphasized absence of physical and cognitive disabilities. In their 1987 article, Rowe and Kahn characterized successful ageing as involving three components:

a) freedom from disease and disability,

b) high cognitive and physical functioning, and

c) social and productive engagement.

Recently, many scientists have argued that the early definitions are overly restrictive and limit successful ageing to an objective judgment made by others, thereby ignoring the seniors' perception. Others have pointed out that definitions focusing on physical functioning and freedom from disability are misleading and may lead to the conclusion that a large majority of individuals are getting older unsuccessfully, given the high incidence and prevalence of diseases that are common in later life.

Genetics of Successful Ageing

A number of studies indicate that there are genetic influences on successful ageing - beyond those that influence longevity alone.

Evidence suggests that successful ageing is a multifactorial trait influenced by numerous genes and environmental factors, each making a small contribution to the phenotype. Specifically, genes such as APOE, GSTT1, IL6, IL10, PON1, and SIRT3 may to have individual effects on the likelihood of ageing successfully.

Additionally, the genes contributing to successful ageing can be grouped in several main categories (ontologies):

- Genes involved in the maintenance of cholesterol, lipid or lipoprotein levels. Their ability to metabolize and transport molecules such as cholesterol relates to cardiovascular health, which could directly influence physical activity levels and longevity.
- Genes related to cytokines, which influence inflammation and immune responses. These genes could influence successful ageing by regulating cellular senescence, determining susceptibility to age-related cancers, or other mechanisms.
- Genes involved in drug metabolism and insulin signalling.
- Genes related to age-associated pathological processes (e.g., Alzheimer's disease.)

Recently, successful ageing has been also linked to expression levels of genes and length of chromosomal telomeres.

Ageing-Associated Wisdom

In has been found that mental and psychosocial functioning often improve with age, even if physical health, and some elements of memory decline. Physicians, psychologists and gerontologists argue that age-related wisdom might serve to compensate for the biological losses in old age, thereby enabling older adults to better utilise their remaining resources and age successfully. Age-associated wisdom may help to overcome the negative effects of diseases and stressors that are common in late life and lead to improved mental health and psychosocial functioning. Neurological research has demonstrated that brain growth and development continue into old age – the concept known as neuroplasticity of ageing.

Cultural Differences

Components of successful ageing differ across cultures. In a 2004 survey, Japanese older adults were more likely to endorse social belonging as more important, whereas European American ranked independence as more important.

Strategies to Enhance Successful Ageing

The idea of successful ageing is a social construct which aids in our acceptance of the apparent inevatibility and pain associated with the ageing process. As successful ageing tends to be more dependent on behaviour, attitude and environment than to the hereditary traits, researchers and clinicians are developing strategies to enhance ageing well. Current strategies include restricting calories intake, exercising, quitting smoking and substance use, obtaining appropriate health care, and eating healthy. Seeking help for mental illnesses such as depression is critical, as these conditions interfere with nearly all determinants of successful ageing. Additionally, it is considered important to develop cognitive and psychological strategies such as positive attitude, resilience, and reducing stress. Cognitive and emotional adaptation to chronic illnesses that often impact older adults is also an important aspect. Finally, social strategies, such as seeking and giving social support through volunteering, working in a group, learning a new skill, or mentoring younger individuals, have been found to promote successful ageing.

Although many dietary supplements on the market and advertised as having anti-ageing effects, there is a general lack of evidence as for their impact on ageing, and some researchers even point to several possible health risks. Currently most of these supplements are not categorized as drugs by the U.S. Food and Drug Administration.

Disengagement Theory

The disengagement theory of ageing states that "ageing is an inevitable, mutual withdrawal or disengagement, resulting in decreased interaction between the ageing person and others in the social system he belongs to". The theory claims that it is natural and acceptable for older adults to withdraw from society. The theory was formulated by Cumming and Henry in 1961 in the book *Growing Old*, and it was the first theory of ageing that social scientists developed. Thus, this theory has historical significance in gerontology. Since then, it has faced strong criticism since the theory was proposed as innate, universal, and unidirectional. The disengagement theory is one of three major psychosocial theories which describe how people develop in old age. The other two major psychosocial theories are the activity theory and the continuity theory, and the disengagement theory comes to odds with both.

Postulates

Cumming and Henry provided the following nine postulates for the "process of disengagement":

- Postulate 1: Everyone expects death, and one's abilities will likely deteriorate over time. As a result, every person will lose ties to others in his or her society.
- Postulate 2: Because individual interactions between people strengthen norms, an individual who has fewer varieties of interactions has greater freedom from the norms imposed by interaction. Consequently, this form of disengagement becomes a circular or self-perpetuating process.
- Postulate 3: Because men have a centrally instrumental role in America, and women a socioemotional one, disengagement differs between men and women.
- Postulate 4: The individual's life is punctuated by ego changes. For example, ageing, a form of ego change, causes knowledge and skill to deteriorate. However, success in an industrialized society demands certain knowledge and skill. To satisfy these demands, age-grading ensures that the young possess sufficient knowledge and skill to assume authority and the old retire before they lose their skills. This kind of disengagement is effected by the individual, prompted by either ego changes or the organisation—which is bound to organisational imperatives—or both.
- Postulate 5: When both the individual and society are ready for disengagement, complete disengagement results. When neither is ready, continuing engagement results. When the individual is ready and society is not, a disjunction between the expectations of the individual and of the members of this social systems results, but engagement usually continues. When society is ready and the individual is not, the result of the disjunction is usually disengagement.
- Postulate 6: Man's central role is work, and woman's is marriage and family. If individuals abandon their central roles, they drastically lose social life space, and so suffer crisis and demoralisation unless they assume the different roles required by the disengaged state.
- Postulate 7: This postulate contains two main concepts.
    - o (a) Readiness for disengagement occurs if:
        - An individual is aware of the shortness of life and scarcity of time.
        - Individuals perceive their life space decreasing.
        - A person loses ego energy.

- o (b) Each level of society grants individuals permission to disengage because of the following:
  - Requirements of the rational-legal occupational system in an affluent society
  - The nature of the nuclear family
  - The differential death rate
- Postulate 8: Fewer interactions and disengagement from central roles lead to the relationships in the remaining roles changing. In turn, relational rewards become more diverse, and vertical solidarities are transformed to horizontal ones.
- Postulate 9: Disengagement theory is independent of culture, but the form it takes is bound by culture.

Activity Theory (Ageing)

The activity theory, also known as the implicit theory of ageing, normal theory of ageing, and lay theory of ageing, proposes that successful ageing occurs when older adults stay active and maintain social interactions. It takes the view that the ageing process is delayed and the quality of life is enhanced when old people remain socially active. The activity theory rose in opposing response to the disengagement theory. The activity theory and the disengagement theory were the two major theories that outlined successful ageing in the early 1960s. The theory was developed by Robert J. Havighurst in 1961. In 1964, Bernice Neugarten asserted that satisfaction in old age depended on active maintenance of personal relationships and endeavors.

The theory assumes that a positive relationship between activity and life satisfaction. One author suggests that activity enables older adults adjust to retirement and is named “the busy ethic”.

The critics of the activity theory state that it overlooks inequalities in health and economics that hinders the ability for older people to engage in such activities. Also, some older adults do not desire to engage in new challenges.

Activity theory reflects the functionalist perspective that the equilibrium that an individual develops in middle age should be maintained in later years. The theory predicts that older adults that face role loss will substitute former roles with other alternatives.

The activity theory is one of three major psychosocial theories which describe how people develop in old age. The other two psychosocial theories are the disengagement theory, with which the activity comes to odds, and the continuity theory which modifies and elaborates upon the activity theory. Though in recent years the acceptance activity theory has diminished, it is still used as a standard to compare observed activity and life satisfaction patterns.

Continuity Theory

The continuity theory of normal ageing states that older adults will usually maintain the same activities, behaviours, personalities, and relationships as they did in their earlier years of life. According to this theory, older adults try to maintain this continuity of lifestyle by adapting strategies that are connected to their past experiences.

The continuity theory is one of three major psychosocial theories which describe how people develop in old age. The other two psychosocial theories are the disengagement theory, with which the continuity theory comes to odds, and the activity theory upon which the continuity theory modifies and elaborates. Unlike the other two theories, the continuity theory uses a life course perspective to define normal ageing.

The continuity theory can be classified as a micro-level theory because it pertains to the individual, and more specifically it can be viewed from the functionalist perspective in which the individual and society try to obtain a state of equilibrium.

History

The continuity theory originated in the observation that a large proportion of older adults show consistency in their activities, personalities, and relationships despite their changing physical, mental, and social status. In 1968, George L. Maddox gave an empirical description of the theory in a chapter of the book *Middle Age and Ageing: A Reader in Social Psychology* called "Persistence of life style among the elderly: A longitudinal study of patterns of social activity in relation to life satisfaction". The continuity theory was formerly proposed in 1971 by Robert Atchley in his article "Retirement and Leisure Participation: Continuity or Crisis?" in the journal *The Gerontologist*. Later, in 1989, he published another article entitled "A Continuity Theory of Normal Ageing, in *The Gerontologist* in which he substantially developed the theory. In this article, he expanded the continuity theory to explain the development of internal and external structures of continuity. In 1999, Richard Atchley continued to strengthen his theory in his book *Continuity and Adaptation in Ageing: Creating Positive Experiences*.

Elements

The theory deals with the internal structure and the external structure of continuity to describe how people adapt to their situation and set their goals. The internal structure of an individual such as personality, ideas, and beliefs remain constant throughout the life course. This provides the individual a way to make future decisions based on their internal foundation of the past. The external structure of an individual such as relationships and social roles provides a support for maintaining a stable self-concept and lifestyle.

Criticisms and Weaknesses

The major criticism for the theory is its definition of normal ageing. The theory distinguishes normal ageing from pathological ageing, neglecting the older adults with chronic illness.

The feminist theories also attack the continuity theory for defining normal ageing around a male model.

One weakness of the theory is that it fails to demonstrate how social institutions impact the individuals and the way they age.

Prevention and Reversal

Since ageing is regarded as cause or major risk factor of the age related diseases and many other causes of mortality there are growing effort in ageing research and stopping ageing thus extending healthy lifespan. There are several prizes for extending lifespan and slowing ageing in mammals such as Mprize of Methuselah Foundation, Palo Alto Longevity Prize and others. Several companies and organisations, such as Google Calico, Human Longevity, Inc of Craig Venter, Quantum Pharmaceuticals, SENS Research Foundation Science against ageing foundation, declared stoping or delaying ageing as their goal.

Many scientists who study the biology of ageing believe that the development of interventions which slow ageing is inevitable. Several drugs and food supplements have been shown to retard or reverse the biological effects of ageing in animal models, but none has yet been proven to do so in humans.

There are three main signalling pathways which influence the rate of ageing: caloric restriction, the insulin/IGF-1-like signalling pathway, and the activity levels of the electron transport chain.

The US National Institute on Ageing currently funds an intervention testing program, whereby investigators nominate compounds (based on specific molecular ageing theories) to have evaluated with respect to their effects on lifespan and age-related biomarkers in outbred mice. Previous age-related testing in mammals has proved largely irreproducible, because of small numbers of animals and lax mouse husbandry conditions. The intervention testing program aims to address this by conducting parallel experiments at three internationally recognised mouse ageing-centres, the Barshop Institute at UTHSCSA, the University of Michigan at Ann Arbor and the Jackson Laboratory.

Ronald A. DePinho, a cancer geneticist at the Dana-Farber Cancer Institute and Harvard Medical School, published a paper in Nature magazine in November 2010 which indicated that the organs of genetically altered mice, designed to activate telomerase after feeding them with a chemical, were rejuvenated. Shrivelled testes grew back to normal and the animals regained their fertility. Other organs, such as the spleen, liver, intestines and brain, recuperated from their degenerated state. In this experiment mice were engineered to not produce telomerase naturally but after a chemical "switch" the system would then restore telomerase. Importantly, this chemical does not have the ability to produce telomerase in animals that are not genetically altered. Moreover, telomerase activation is also associated with the growth of cancerous tumours which could prevent anti-ageing treatments using this discovery.

mTOR inhibition and the frequent activation of autophagy has been shown to increase longevity in model organisms such as yeast, flies and mice. mTor inhibition and autophagy have also been linked to insulin sensitivity and the reduction of reactive oxygen species (ROS) damage, which is another major proposed cause to ageing. It has become clear that autophagy activation in the body by mTOR inhibition increases longevity. mTOR inhibition reduces ROS damage by activating autophagy, which will recycle the damaged parts of cells and re use them for functioning parts. This process reduces ROS damage to a reasonable amount, therefore increasing longevity. mTOR inhibition has also been linked to other major ageing diseases. mTOR inhibition has helped treat neurodegenerative diseases like Alzheimer's in mice. It has also been used to reduce tumor growth in several cancers including renal, breast and several other rare cancers. Finally mTOR inhibition is also linked to reducing obesity and increasing immune function. The mTOR inhibition reduces the likelihood of diet induced and age induced obesity in mice, but in some cases led to glucose intolerance. Caloric restriction and exercise are two ways to activate autophagy and inhibit mTOR which can help resolve all of these common age related health issues.

The cellular balance between energy generation and consumption (energy homeostasis) requires tight regulation during ageing. In 2011, it was demonstrated that acetylation levels of AMP-activated protein kinase change with age in yeast and that preventing this change slows yeast ageing.

Caloric restriction substantially affects lifespan in many animals, including the ability to delay or prevent many age-related diseases. Evidence in both animals and humans suggests that resveratrol may be a caloric restriction mimetic.

Most known genetic interventions in C. elegans increase lifespan by 1.5 to 2.5-fold. As of 2009, the record for lifespan extension in C. elegans is a single-gene mutation which increases adult survival by tenfold. The strong conservation of some of the mechanisms of ageing discovered in model organisms imply that they may be useful in the enhancement of human survival. However, the benefits may not be proportional; longevity gains are typically greater in C. elegans than fruit flies, and greater in fruit flies than in mammals. One explanation for this is that mammals, being much longer-lived, already have many traits which promote lifespan. However, there are still opportunities for healthy human life to be extended beyond its current levels by pharmacological interventions.

Life Extension

Life extension science, also known as anti-ageing medicine, indefinite life extension, experimental gerontology, and biomedical gerontology, is the study of slowing down or reversing the processes of ageing to extend both the maximum and average lifespan. Some researchers in this area, and "life extensionists", "immortalists" or "longevists" (those who wish to achieve longer lives themselves), believe that future breakthroughs in tissue rejuvenation, stem cells, regenerative medicine, molecular repair, pharmaceuticals, and organ replacement (such as with artificial organs or xenotransplantations) will eventually enable humans to have indefinite lifespans (agerasia) through complete rejuvenation to a healthy youthful condition.

The sale of putative anti-ageing products such as nutrition, physical fitness, skin care, hormone replacements, vitamins, supplements and herbs is a lucrative global industry, with the US market generating about $50 billion of revenue each year. Some medical experts state that the use of such products has not been proven to affect the ageing process and many claims regarding the efficacy of these marketed products have been roundly criticized by medical experts, including the American Medical Association. However, it has not been shown that the goal of indefinite human lifespans itself is necessarily unfeasible; some animals such as hydra, planarian flatworms, and certain sponges, corals, and jellyfish do not die of old age and exhibit potential immortality. The ethical ramifications of life extension are debated by bioethicists.

Public Opinion

Life extension is a controversial topic due to fear of overpopulation and possible effects on society. Religious people are no more likely to oppose life extension than the unaffiliated, though some variation exists between religious denominations. Blacks and Hispanics are more likely to support life extension than white people. Biogerontologist Aubrey De Grey counters the overpopulation critique by pointing out that the therapy could postpone or eliminate menopause, allowing women to space out their pregnancies over more years and thus *decreasing* the yearly population growth rate. Moreover, the philosopher and futurist Max More argues that, given the fact the worldwide population growth rate is slowing down and is projected to eventually stabilize and begin falling, superlongevity would be unlikely to contribute to overpopulation.

A Spring 2013 Pew Research poll in the United States found that 38% of Americans would want life extension treatments, and 56% would reject it. However, it also found that 68% believed most people would want it and that only 4% consider an "ideal lifespan" to be more than 120 years. The median "ideal lifespan" was 91 years of age and the majority of the public (63%) viewed medical advances aimed at prolonging life as generally good. 41% of Americans believed that radical life extension would be good for society, while 51% said they believed it would be bad for society. One possibility for why 56% of Americans claim they would reject life extension treatments may be due to the cultural perception that living longer would result in a longer period of decrepitude, and that the elderly in our current society are unhealthy.

Average and Maximum Lifespans

During the process of ageing, an organism accumulates damage to its macromolecules, cells, tissues and organs. Specifically, ageing is characterized as and thought to be caused by "genomic instability, telomere attrition, epigenetic alterations, loss of proteostasis, deregulated nutrient sensing, mitochondrial dysfunction, cellular senescence, stem cell exhaustion, and altered intercellular communication." Oxidation damage to cellular contents caused by free radicals is believed to contribute to ageing as well.

The longest a human has ever been proven to live is 122 years, the case of Jeanne Calment who was born in 1875 and died in 1997, whereas the maximum lifespan of a wildtype mouse, commonly used as a model in research on ageing, is about three years. Genetic differences between humans and mice that may account for these different ageing rates include differences in efficiency of DNA repair, antioxidant defences, energy metabolism, proteostasis maintenance, and recycling mechanisms such as autophagy.

Average lifespan in a population is lowered by infant and child mortality, which are frequently linked to infectious diseases or nutrition problems. Later in life, vulnerability to accidents and age-related chronic disease such as cancer or cardiovascular disease play an increasing role in mortality. Extension of expected lifespan can often be achieved by access to improved medical care, vaccinations, good diet, exercise and avoidance of hazards such as smoking.

Maximum lifespan is determined by the rate of ageing for a species inherent in its genes and by environmental factors. Widely recognised methods of extending maximum lifespan in model organisms such as nematodes, fruit flies, and mice include caloric restriction, gene manipulation, and administration of pharmaceuticals. Another technique uses evolutionary pressures such as breeding from only older members or altering levels of extrinsic mortality.

Theoretically, extension of maximum lifespan in humans could be achieved by reducing the rate of ageing damage by periodic replacement of damaged tissues, molecular repair or rejuvenation of deteriorated cells and tissues, reversal of harmful epigenetic changes, or the enhancement of telomerase enzyme activity. Research geared towards life extension strategies in various organisms is currently under way at a number of academic and private institutions.

Current Anti-ageing Strategies and Issues

Diets and Supplements

Much life extension research focuses on nutrition—diets or supplements—as a means to extend lifespan, although few of these have been systematically tested for significant longevity effects. The many diets promoted by anti-ageing advocates are often contradictory. A dietary pattern with some support from scientific research is caloric restriction.

Preliminary studies of caloric restriction on humans using surrogate measurements have provided evidence that caloric restriction may have powerful protective effect against secondary ageing in humans. Caloric restriction in humans may reduce the risk of developing Type 2 diabetes and atherosclerosis. More research is needed.

The free-radical theory of ageing suggests that antioxidant supplements, such as Vitamin C, Vitamin E, Q_{10}, lipoic acid, carnosine, and N-acetylcysteine, might extend human life. However, combined evidence from several clinical trials suggest that â-Carotene supplements and high doses of Vitamin E increase mortality rates. Other substances proposed to extend lifespan include oxytocin, insulin, human chorionic gonadotropin (hCG), and erythropoietin (EPO). Resveratrol is a sirtuin stimulant that appears to extend lifespan in simple organisms such as nematodes and short-lived fish.

Some supplements, including the minerals selenium or zinc have been reported to extend the lifespan of rats and mice, though none have been proven to do so in humans, and significant toxic effects were observed. Metformin may also extend life span in mice.

There are many traditional herbs purportedly used to extend the health-span, including a Chinese tea called Jiaogulan (Gynostemma pentaphyllum), dubbed "China's Immortality Herb." Ayurveda, the traditional Indian system of medicine, describes a class of longevity herbs called rasayanas, including Bacopa monnieri, Ocimum sanctum, Curcuma longa, Centella asiatica, Phyllanthus emblica, Withania somnifera and many others. Along with their Chinese counterparts (called superior or tonic herbs), Indian rasayanas demonstrate preliminary positive results in animal models.

Hormone Treatments

The anti-ageing industry offers several hormone therapies. Some of these have been criticized for possible dangers to the patient and a lack of proven effect. For example, the American Medical Association has been critical of some anti-ageing hormone therapies.

Although some recent clinical studies have shown that low-dose growth hormone (GH) treatment for adults with GH deficiency changes the body composition by increasing muscle mass, decreasing fat mass, increasing bone density and muscle strength, improves cardiovascular parameters (i.e. decrease of LDL cholesterol), and affects the quality of life without significant side effects, the evidence for use of growth hormone as an anti-ageing therapy is mixed and based on animal studies. An early study suggested that supplementation of mice with growth hormone increased average life expectancy. Additional animal experiments have suggested that growth hormone may generally act to shorten maximum lifespan; knockout mice lacking the receptor for growth hormone live especially long. Furthermore, mouse models lacking the insulin-like growth factor also live especially long and have low levels of growth hormone.

Insulin Like Growth Factor (IGF-1) Restriction

People suffering from a rare condition known as Laron syndrome have a mutation in the gene that makes the receptor for growth hormone. It is theorised that this mutation may hold a key to life extension.

Longo said that some level of IGF-1 was necessary to protect against heart disease, but that lowering the level might be beneficial. A drug that does this is already on the market for treatment of acromegaly, a thickening of the bones caused by excessive growth hormone. "Our underlying hypothesis is that this drug would prolong life span," Longo said. He said he was not taking the drug, called pegvisomant or Somavert, which is very hard to obtain.

Scientific Controversy Regarding Anti-ageing Nutritional Supplementation and Medicine

Some critics dispute the portrayal of ageing as a disease. For example, Leonard Hayflick, who determined that fibroblasts are limited to around 50 cell divisions, reasons that ageing is an unavoidable consequence of entropy. Hayflick and fellow biogerontologists Jay Olshansky and Bruce Carnes have strongly criticized the anti-ageing industry in response to what they see as unscrupulous profiteering from the sale of unproven anti-ageing supplements.

Ethics and Politics of Anti-ageing Nutritional Supplementation and Medicine

Politics relevant to the substances of life extension pertain mostly to communications and availability.

In the United States, product claims on food and drug labels are strictly regulated. The First Amendment (freedom of speech) protects third-party publishers' rights to distribute fact, opinion and speculation on life extension practices. Manufacturers and suppliers also provide informational publications, but because they market the substances, they are subject to monitoring and enforcement by the Federal Trade Commission (FTC), which polices claims by marketers. What constitutes the difference between truthful and false claims is hotly debated and is a central controversy in this arena.

Consumer Motivations for Using Anti-ageing Products

Research by Sobh and Martin (2011) suggests that people buy anti-ageing products to obtain a hoped-for self (e.g., keeping a youthful skin) or to avoid a feared-self (e.g., looking old). The research shows that when consumers pursue a hoped-for self, it is expectations of success that most strongly drive their motivation to use the product. The research also shows why doing badly when trying to avoid a feared self is more motivating than doing well. Interestingly, when product use is seen to fail it is more motivating than success when consumers seek to avoid a feared-self.

Proposed Strategies of Life Extension

Anti-ageing Drugs

There are a number of drugs intended to slow the ageing process currently being researched. One type of research is related to the observed effects a calorie restriction diet, which has been shown to extend lifespan in some animals Based on that research, there have been attempts to develop drugs that will have the same effect on the ageing process as a caloric restriction diet, which are known as Caloric restriction mimetic drugs. Drugs that have been studied for possible longevity effects on laboratory animals because of a possible CR-mimic effect include Rapamycin, Metformin, and Resveratrol. Two drugs that may have potential benefits of combating age-related maladies are Resveratrol and Rapamycin. These drugs are considered to be the forefront drugs in anti-ageing research. Before these drugs had been tested, the best-characterized anti-ageing therapy was and still is, calorie restriction or CR. In some studies calorie restriction has been shown to extend the life of mice, yeast, and rhesus monkeys significantly. However, a more recent study has shown that in contrast, calorie restriction has not improved the survival rate in rhesus monkeys. Long-term human trials of CR are now being done. It is the hope of the anti-ageing researchers that Resveratrol and Rapamycin may act as CR mimetics to increase the life span of humans.

Resveratrol was first thought to be an activator of sirtuins, a family of deacetylases, that would promote anti ageing effects without having to restrict caloric intake. However, recent replication studies have failed to show that Resveratrol increases the life span in yeast or mice and that Resveratrol may not activate sirtuins that are biologically beneficial to age reduction. Another study was done showing that Resveratrol activates or inhibits fifteen or more different enzymes. Of those enzymes, one stands out with potential for reducing age-related disease. AMP-activated protein kinase (AMPK) has shown to increase life span of nematodes and prevent obesity in mice. Although Resveratrol has not been proven to extend the life-span of mammals at the current doses tested, Resveratrol could be used to access some of the same molecular pathways that CR does. Several examples would include diet induced obesity, some cancers, cardiovascular disease, and neurodegenerative diseases.

While Resveratrol has not been proven to increase life span, Rapamycin has shown much more promise. Rapamycin is shown to increase longevity by inhibiting the target of rapamycin kinase (TOR) the same way CR does. Study systems including yeast, nematodes, flies, and mammals, have shown that reduction of TOR signalling will result in an increased life span. Additionally, Rapamycin has similar effects of Resveratrol in protecting against several cancers, cardiovascular, and neurodegenerative diseases. Rapamycin also has been shown to act as an immunosuppressant, however more testing is needed to show if the life extending dose comes at the cost of an impaired immune system.

Resveratrol and Rapamycin have both shown protection against cancers, cardiovascular disease, and neurodegenerative diseases in multiple study systems. Rapamycin looks to have more potential in life span extension than Resveratrol, but may come at a price of immune system impairment. Clinical trials are now being performed to see if Rapamycin or Resveratrol will have anti-ageing effects in humans.

Other attempts to create anti-ageing drugs have taken different research paths. One notable direction of research has been research into the possibility of using the enzyme telomerase in order to counter the process of telomere shortening. However, there are potential dangers in this, since some research has also linked telomerase to cancer and to tumor growth and formation.

Nanotechnology

Future advances in nanomedicine could give rise to life extension through the repair of many processes thought to be responsible for ageing. K. Eric Drexler, one of the founders of nanotechnology, postulated cell repair machines, including ones operating within cells and utilising as yet hypothetical molecular computers, in his 1986 book Engines of Creation. Raymond Kurzweil, a futurist and transhumanist, stated in his book *The Singularity Is Near* that he believes that advanced medical nanorobotics could completely remedy the effects of ageing by 2030.

Cloning and Body Part Replacement

Some life extensionists suggest that therapeutic cloning and stem cell research could one day provide a way to generate cells, body parts, or even entire bodies (generally referred to as reproductive cloning) that would be genetically identical to a prospective patient. Recently, the US Department of Defence initiated a program to research the possibility of growing human body parts on mice. Complex biological structures, such as mammalian joints and limbs, have not yet been replicated. Dog and primate brain transplantation experiments were conducted in the mid-20th century but failed due to rejection and the inability to restore nerve connections. As of 2006, the implantation of bio-engineered bladders grown from patients' own cells has proven to be a viable treatment for bladder disease. Proponents of body part replacement and cloning contend that the required biotechnologies are likely to appear earlier than other life-extension technologies.

The use of human stem cells, particularly embryonic stem cells, is controversial. Opponents' objections generally are based on interpretations of religious teachings or ethical considerations. Proponents of stem cell research point out that cells are routinely formed and destroyed in a variety of contexts. Use of stem cells taken from the umbilical cord or parts of the adult body may not provoke controversy.

The controversies over cloning are similar, except general public opinion in most countries stands in opposition to reproductive cloning. Some proponents of therapeutic cloning predict the production of whole bodies, lacking consciousness, for eventual brain transplantation.

Cyborgs

Replacement of biological (susceptible on diseases) organs with mechanical ones could extend life. This is the goal of 2045 Initiative.

Cryonics

For cryonicists (advocates of cryopreservation), storing the body at low temperatures after death may provide an "ambulance" into a future in which advanced medical technologies may allow resuscitation and repair. They speculate cryogenic temperatures will minimize changes in biological tissue for many years, giving the medical community ample time to cure all disease, rejuvenate the aged and repair any damage that is caused by the cryopreservation process.

Many cryonicists do not believe that legal death is "real death" because stoppage of heartbeat and breathing—the usual medical criteria for legal death—occur before biological death of cells and tissues of the body. Even at room temperature, cells may take hours to die and days to decompose. Although neurological damage occurs within 4–6 minutes of cardiac arrest, the irreversible neurodegenerative processes do not manifest for hours. Cryonicists state that rapid cooling and cardio-pulmonary support applied immediately after certification of death can preserve cells and tissues for long-term preservation at cryogenic temperatures. People, particularly children, have survived up to an hour without heartbeat after submersion in ice water. In one case, full recovery was reported after 45 minutes underwater. To facilitate rapid preservation of cells and tissue, cryonics "standby teams" are available to wait by the bedside of patients who are to be cryopreserved to apply cooling and cardio-pulmonary support as soon as possible after declaration of death.

No mammal has been successfully cryopreserved and brought back to life, with the exception of frozen human embryos. Resuscitation of a postembryonic human from cryonics is not possible with current science. Some scientists still support the idea based on their expectations of the capabilities of future science.

Strategies for Engineered Negligible Senescence (SENS)

Another proposed life extension technology would combine existing and predicted future biochemical and genetic techniques. SENS proposes that rejuvenation may be obtained by removing ageing damage via the use of stem cells and tissue engineering, removal of telomere-lengthening machinery, allotopic expression of mitochondrial proteins, targeted ablation of cells, immunotherapeutic clearance, and novel lysosomal hydrolases. While many biogerontologists find these ideas "worthy of discussion" and SENS conferences feature important research in the field, some contend that the alleged benefits are too speculative given the current state of technology, referring to it as "fantasy rather than science".

Genetic Modification

Gene therapy, in which nucleic acid polymers are delivered as a drug and are either expressed as proteins, interfere with the expression of proteins, or correct genetic mutations, has been proposed as a future strategy to prevent ageing. A large array of genetic modifications have been found to increase lifespan in model organisms such as yeast, nematode worms, fruit flies, and mice. As of 2013, the longest extension of life caused by a single gene manipulation was roughly 150% in mice and 10-fold in nematode worms.

Fooling Genes

In *The Selfish Gene*, Richard Dawkins describes an approach to life-extension that involves "fooling genes" into thinking the body is young. Dawkins attributes inspiration for this idea to Peter Medawar. The basic idea is that our bodies are composed of genes that activate throughout our lifetimes, some when we are young and others when we are older. Presumably, these genes are activated by environmental factors, and the changes caused by these genes activating can be lethal. It is a statistical certainty that we possess more lethal genes that activate in later life than in early life.

Therefore, to extend life, we should be able to prevent these genes from switching on, and we should be able to do so by "identifying changes in the internal chemical environment of a body that take place during ageing... and by simulating the superficial chemical properties of a young body".

Reversal of Informational Entropy

According to some lines of thinking, the ageing process is routed into a basic reduction of biological complexity, and thus loss of information. In order to reverse this loss, gerontologist Marios Kyriazis suggested that it is necessary to increase input of actionable and meaningful information both individually (into individual brains), and collectively (into societal systems).

This technique enhances overall biological function through up-regulation of immune, hormonal, antioxidant and other parameters, resulting in improved age-repair mechanisms. Working in parallel with natural evolutionary mechanisms that can facilitate survival through increased fitness, Kyriazis claims that the technique may lead to a reduction of the rate of death as a function of age, i.e. indefinite lifespan.

Mind Uploading

One hypothetical future strategy that, as some suggest, "eliminates" the complications related to a physical body, involves the copying or transferring (e.g. by progressive replacing neurons with transistors) of a conscious mind from a biological brain to a non-biological computer system or computational device. The basic idea is to scan the structure of a particular brain in detail, and then construct a software model of it that is so faithful to the original that, when run on appropriate hardware, it will behave in essentially the same way as the original brain. Whether or not an exact copy of one's mind constitutes actual life extension is matter of debate.

History of the Life Extension Movement

In 1970, the American Ageing Association was formed under the impetus of Denham Harman, originator of the free radical theory of ageing. Harman wanted an organisation of biogerontologists that was devoted to research and to the sharing of information among scientists interested in extending human lifespan.

In 1976, futurists Joel Kurtzman and Philip Gordon wrote *No More Dying. The Conquest Of Ageing And The Extension Of Human Life*, (ISBN 0-440-36247-4) the first popular book on research to extend human lifespan. Subsequently, Kurtzman was invited to testify before the House Select Committee on Ageing, chaired by Claude Pepper of Florida, to discuss the impact of life extension on the Social Security system.

Saul Kent published *The Life Extension Revolution* (ISBN 0-688-03580-9) in 1980 and created a nutraceutical firm called the Life Extension Foundation, a non-profit organisation that promotes dietary supplements. The Life Extension Foundation publishes a periodical called *Life Extension Magazine*. The 1982 best-selling book *Life Extension: A Practical Scientific Approach* (ISBN 0-446-51229-X) by Durk Pearson and Sandy Shaw further popularized the phrase “life extension”.

In 1983, Roy Walford, a life-extensionist and gerontologist, published a popular book called *Maximum Lifespan*. In 1988, Walford and his student Richard Weindruch summarized their research into the ability of calorie restriction to extend the lifespan of rodents in *The Retardation of Ageing and Disease by Dietary Restriction* (ISBN 0-398-05496-7). It had been known since the work of Clive McCay in the 1930s that calorie restriction can extend the maximum lifespan of rodents. But it was the work of Walford and Weindruch that gave detailed scientific grounding to that knowledge. Walford's personal interest in life extension motivated his scientific work and he practiced calorie restriction himself. Walford died at the age of 80 from complications caused by amyotrophic lateral sclerosis.

Money generated by the non-profit Life Extension Foundation allowed Saul Kent to finance the Alcor Life Extension Foundation, the world's largest cryonics organisation. The cryonics movement had been launched in 1962 by Robert Ettinger's book, *The Prospect of Immortality*. In the 1960s, Saul Kent had been a co-founder of the Cryonics Society of New York. Alcor gained national prominence when baseball star Ted Williams was cryonically preserved by Alcor in 2002 and a family dispute arose as to whether Williams had really wanted to be cryopreserved.

Regulatory and legal struggles between the Food and Drug Administration (FDA) and the Life Extension Foundation included seizure of merchandise and court action. In 1991, Saul Kent and Bill Faloon, the principals of the Foundation, were jailed. The LEF accused the FDA of perpetrating a "Holocaust" and "seeking gestapo-like power" through its regulation of drugs and marketing claims.

In 2003, Doubleday published "The Immortal Cell: One Scientist's Quest to Solve the Mystery of Human Ageing," by Michael D. West. West emphasised the potential role of embryonic stem cells in life extension.

Scientific Research

In 1991, the American Academy of Anti-Ageing Medicine (A4M) was formed as a non-profit organisation to create what it considered an anti-ageing medical speciality distinct from geriatrics, and to hold trade shows for physicians interested in anti-ageing medicine. The A4M trains doctors in anti-ageing medicine and publicly promotes the field of anti-ageing research. It has about 26,000 members, of whom about 97% are doctors and scientists. The American Board of Medical Specialities recognises neither anti-ageing medicine nor the A4M's professional standing.

In 2003, Aubrey de Grey and David Gobel formed the Methuselah Foundation, which gives financial grants to anti-ageing research projects. In 2009, de Grey and several others founded the SENS Research Foundation, a California-based scientific research organisation which conducts research into ageing and funds other anti-ageing research projects at various universities. In 2013, Google announced Calico, a new company based in San Francisco that will harness new technologies to increase scientific understanding of the biology of ageing. It is led by Arthur D. Levinson, and its research team includes scientists such as Hal V. Barron, David Botstein, and Cynthia Kenyon. In 2014, biologist Craig Venter founded Human Longevity Inc., a company dedicated to scientific research to end ageing through genomics and cell therapy. It subsequently began building the a human genotype, microbiome, and phenotype database in the world to aid in its research.

Aside from private initiatives, ageing research is being conducted in university laboratories, and includes universities such as Harvard and UCLA. University researchers have made a number of breakthroughs in extending the lives of mice and insects by reversing certain aspects of ageing.

Ethics and Politics of Life Extension

Though many scientists state that life extension and radical life extension are possible, there are still no international or national programs focused on radical life extension. There are political forces staying for and against life extension. By 2012, in Russia, the United States, Israel, and the Netherlands, the Longevity political parties started. They aimed to provide political support to radical life extension research and technologies, and ensure the fastest possible and at the same time soft transition of society to the next step - life without ageing and with radical life extension, and to provide access to such technologies to most currently living people.

Leon Kass (chairman of the US President's Council on Bioethics from 2001 to 2005) has questioned whether potential exacerbation of overpopulation problems would make life extension unethical. He states his opposition to life extension with the words:

"simply to covet a prolonged life span for ourselves is both a sign and a cause of our failure to open ourselves to procreation and to any higher purpose ... [The] desire to prolong youthfulness is not only a childish desire to eat one's life and keep it; it is also an expression of a childish and narcissistic wish incompatible with devotion to posterity."

John Harris, former editor-in-chief of the Journal of Medical Ethics, argues that as long as life is worth living, according to the person himself, we have a powerful moral imperative to save the life and thus to develop and offer life extension therapies to those who want them.

Transhumanist philosopher Nick Bostrom has argued that any technological advances in life extension must be equitably distributed and not restricted to a privileged few. In an extended metaphor entitled "The Fable of the Dragon-Tyrant", Bostrom envisions death as a monstrous dragon who demands human sacrifices. In the fable, after a lengthy debate between those who believe the dragon is a fact of life and those who believe the dragon can and should be destroyed, the dragon is finally killed. Bostrom argues that political inaction allowed many preventable human deaths to occur.

Ageing as a Disease

Most mainstream medical organisations and practitioners do not consider ageing to be a disease. David Sinclair says: "I don't see ageing as a disease, but as a collection of quite predictable diseases caused by the deterioration of the body". The two main arguments used are that ageing is both inevitable and universal while diseases are not. However not everyone agrees. Harry R. Moody, Director of Academic Affairs for

AARP, notes that what is normal and what is disease strongly depends on a historical context. David Gems, Assistant Director of the Institute of Healthy Ageing, strongly argues that ageing should be viewed as a disease. In response to the universality of ageing, David Gems notes that it is as misleading as arguing that Basenji are not dogs because they do not bark. Because of the universality of ageing he calls it a 'special sort of disease'. Robert M. Perlman, coined the terms 'ageing syndrome' and 'disease complex' in 1954 to describe ageing.

The discussion whether ageing should be viewed as a disease or not has important implications. It would stimulate pharmaceutical companies to develop life extension therapies and in the United States of America, it would also increase the regulation of the anti-ageing market by the FDA. Anti-ageing now falls under the regulations for cosmetic medicine which are less tight than those for drugs.

Anti-ageing Movement

The anti-ageing movement is a social movement of physicians and other health providers and patients devoted to reducing the effects of and reversing ageing. A substantial portion of the attention of the movement is on the possibilities for life extension, but there is also interest in techniques such as cosmetic surgery which ameliorate the effects of ageing rather than delay or defeat it.

Two popular proponents of the anti-ageing movement include Ray Kurzweil, who thinks humanity can defeat ageing through the advance of technology, and Aubrey De Grey, who thinks the human body is a very complicated machine and thus, can be repaired indefinitely. Other scientists and significant contributors to the movement include molecular biologists, geneticists, and biomedical gerontologists such as Gary Ruvkun, Cynthia Kenyon, and Arthur D. Levinson.

Anti-ageing Medicine

Anti-ageing medicine has become a budding and rapidly growing medical speciality as physicians who initially sought treatment for themselves have received training and certification in its practice by organisations such as the American Academy of Anti-Ageing Medicine (A4M). Presently there are few if any medicines proven to slow ageing, however in the near future, it is likely that organ replacement, nanotechnology and other advancements will change this.

Human Growth Hormone

Some recent clinical studies have shown that low-dose GH treatment for adults with GH deficiency changes the body composition by increasing muscle mass, decreasing fat mass, increasing bone density and muscle strength, improves cardiovascular parameters (i.e. decrease of LDL cholesterol), and affects the quality of life without significant side effects. Central to anti-ageing medicine is administration of human growth hormone (HGH), It has the effect, in adults, of increasing muscle mass, reducing fat, and increasing energy. It also has dangerous side-effects.

But anti-ageing practitioners claim it is safe at low dosage. It is not approved for use in healthy ageing patients. That restriction is sidestepped by means of a diagnosis of some injury or organic condition, adult growth hormone deficiency, which supposedly has resulted in reduced secretion of the hormone.

Menopausal Hormone Drugs

Administration of Estrogen and other hormones such as progestin were popularized by the 1966 book, *Feminine Forever* by Robert A. Wilson. However, the increase of the use of estrogen was shown to be associated with an increased risk of cancer. Later, in 2002, research into the long-term effects of estrogen on post-menopausal women, the Women's Health Initiative, produced evidence that there were serious side effects. Physicians who prescribe the hormones now prescribe low doses of the drugs. Research into the long-term effects of HRT are continuing, with a 2009 Cochrane review concluding that long-term use may decrease the risk of bone fractures, but increase the risk of stroke, heart attacks and breast cancer.

Annual World Congress on Anti-ageing Medicine & Regenerative Biomedical Technologies

An annual conference is held which in addition to presentations by the American Academy of Anti-Ageing Medicine (A4M), offers booths and presentations by manufactures of products and providers of services. The 17th annual conference was held December 9–12, 2009 at the THE hotel at Mandalay Bay in Las Vegas, Nevada. According to the A4M website key conference topics:

- Alternative cancer therapies
- Sleep disorders
- Bioidentical hormone replacement therapy
- Facial rejuvenation
- Weight Management including non-invasive procedures for obesity
- DNA mitochondrial repair

- Infectious disease and restoring the immune system
- Exercise physiology for seniors
- Metabolic-cellular detoxification
- Hormone restoration in men and women
- IV parenteral mutrition

Scientific Approaches

Biogerontology

Biogerontology is a scientific discipline which has the same area of interest, but as a branch of Gerontology, takes a more conservative approach.

Age Management Medicine

Age Management Medicine distinguishes itself from anti-ageing by being a more evidence based, proactive, preventative approach to healthcare for an ageing population focused on preservation of optimum human function and quality of life making every effort to modulate the process of ageing prior to the onset of degenerative ageing. Led by the Age Management

Medicine Group (AMMG), which provides education and information on the speciality of Age Management Medicine to physicians and healthcare professionals through evidence-based continuing medical education conferences, workshops, seminars, certifications, publications and web media.

Mass Movement

A substantial fraction of older people, taking their cue from alternative medicine, purchase and use herbal supplements and other products which promise relief from the incidents and dangers of ageing. These products are nearly always useless and sometimes are harmful.

Realistic and Modest Appraisal

There is a great deal of over-heated rhetoric in use with respect to life extension with over-optimistic projections on the part of its advocates. There is little evidence that any significant break through has been made, or is on the horizon, however, this is largely due to a current lack of funding or interest in the issue.

A study of the common supplements and hormone treatments used published in 2006 in the *Cleveland Clinic Journal of Medicine* showed that none of them are effective with respect to extending life.

Criticism

Though there is no scientific reason to think curing ageing is impossible, there are some criticisms of both the time frame life extensionists envision (the first, perhaps somewhat crude, treatments within the next several decades, or at least before the beginning of the 22nd century) and of whether curing ageing is even desirable.

Common criticisms of the idea of life extension are fears it will cause the world to be more overpopulated; however De Grey counters that by saying that since menopause would also be delayed, women could wait longer to have children and thus, the rate of growth would actually *decline* as a result.

Also, the slowly growing population would buy centuries of time to figure out new places to live, such as space colonies.

Chapter 3

Sociological Perspectives on Ageing

Sociological perspectives on ageing emphasize the importance of group membership and the effects of historical events on the experiences of later life. Consider a seventy year old woman being admitted for psychological evaluation. What if anything can we know about her based solely on her age and personal experiences? Is turning seventy a significant milestone or a common occurrence? Is she likely to be in good health? What avenues are available to her for financial support? Is she embedded in a social network? What opportunities were available to her over the life course? What historical events on a societal level shaped her life? What more do we know about her if we have information on her ethnicity, social class and education level?

Situating individuals in social contexts is essential if we want to understand the lives of older people. Many scholars acknowledge this, but may not recognise how it applies at a broad societal and historical level. It is all too easy to stereotype older people from the perspective of our own class background and the current historical period. When we recognise the importance of broad-level social contexts, we can better understand the diversity of experiences of ageing across time and location.

While there are many types of sociological approaches that can be used to understand ageing, we will focus here on family, work, the state, and religion - four significant contexts which have changed greatly over the past century. By understanding these changing contexts, professionals can better understand the lives of older individuals.

Social Structures

Individuals live and interact in social contexts that affect their everyday lives. These contexts can be understood as social structures—large scale patterns of behaviour that are ordered across time and location and reflect accepted patterns of values and beliefs. Social structures can operate at two levels: those of whole societies and those representing integral components of society (Connell, 1987). At the latter level, commonly recognised social structures include family, work, the state, religion, the legal system, and education.

Social structures shape individual practices in marked ways through the establishment of social rules - norms - and the distribution of resources - power. These rules and resources govern practices such as entry into school, the timing of marriage, exit from the paid labour force, and receipt of government-sponsored health care. Through rituals, individuals celebrate these accepted life transitions and use them to give meaning to their lives.

At the same time, people shape change in social structures in direct and indirect ways. Individuals and groups can challenge social structures directly through organised resistance to dominant ideology and indirectly through non-adherence to social norms. The interplay between individuals and social structures provides the vital force that brings about social change.

The pace of change between individual lives and social structures is often uneven. Because of the routinized nature of social structures, structural norms are slow to change. In contrast, people can change their lives very rapidly to meet their individual needs. Thus, social structures "lag behind" individual lives (Riley, Kahn & Foner, 1994). When individuals are faced with an increasingly out of date social structure, they sometimes develop creative adaptations for their personal lives and may challenge the social structure itself. For example, in the past few decades, middle aged women from the middle and upper classes have returned to school when caregiving responsibilities have lessened in the home. These women directly challenged notions of "student" and "experienced" worker by adapting their unpaid homeworking skills for use in the paid labour force.

The goal of this chapter is to highlight selected social structures which influence the lives of ageing individuals and to describe these changing contexts as we approach the 21st century. We have chosen to focus on the social structures of family, work, state, and religion because of their widespread significance in older people's lives.

Family

The boundaries of "family" are hotly contested by politicians, academics and the public (Stacey, 1996). Family can be thought of in several ways; its meaning has changed over time, across cultures, and differs by context within cultures. How "family" is defined legally has implications far beyond the home - for insurance coverage eligibility, tax bracket status, pension levels and distribution, child custody decisions, probate outcomes, decisions about medical intervention, and immigration options (Weston, 1991). In this section we will focus on family as a social structure. Next, we will examine

(1) historical change in family structures and definitions,

(2) increased diversity in the experiences of family, and how these shape the lives of older individuals.

Family as a Social Structure

As a social structure, families represent a symbolic context in which individuals' needs for love and support are met and reciprocated. Family members exchange significant levels of help and support throughout the life course (Cicerelli, 1990; Silverstein, Parrott & Bengtson, 1995). They help each other in many ways, providing assistance with regular tasks, financial support and advice. They share companionship, love and leisure time. They experience shared history that comes from long term relationships with kin who recognise their multiple facets. Many experience pride in seeing the continuation of their family lines in younger generations.

Here we mainly emphasize the positive potentials of family life, and it is important to add that family conflict can play a real and serious role in the lives of older people. While conflict, disagreement and competition can coexist with affection and support in families (Bengtson, Rosenthal, & Burton, 1996), it can also lead to negative memories and decreased willingness to help in times of need (Whitbeck, Hoyt, & Huck, 1994). Thus, while we acknowledge that families' interactions reflect the imperfections of their members, we emphasize that despite this, the social structure of family remains powerfully important.

Children of Ageing Parents

Familial responsibilities often go beyond emotional and social support. Sometimes, one must investigate outside resources and possibilities for a loved one. While this can seem overwhelming, often it is merely a matter of knowing where to turn for information.

Historical Change in Family Structures and Definitions

One of the most profound changes that has influenced our understanding of family over the last century is the lengthening of average life expectancy. Improved sanitary conditions, better nutrition, and medical advances have lowered levels of infant and child mortality and increased average life expectancy at birth. In 1900, the average life expectancy of a child born in the United States was 47 years. Ninety years later it was 75.4 years (Treas, 1995). For older individuals, having longer lives means having increased time in family roles. For example, the average duration of relationships between parents and children has increased dramatically. On average adult children today experience twice as much shared time with a living parent as their counterparts in 1800, and triple the amount of time with both parents living (Watkins, Menken & Bongaarts, 1987). This means that adult children have more potential for contact and support from parents, but they may also have more responsibility for ageing parents throughout the life course. Beyond parent-child relationships, higher average life spans have increased the potential for extended intergenerational relationships. Grandparenting and great-grandparenting, which were less common in 1900, have become enduring life roles for many as we approach the year 2000. Many grandparents have a lot to offer to younger generations, and this interaction can also provide older individuals with an increased sense of purpose (Robertson, 1995).

Ambiguous Relationships

Looking back at both Examples 2 and 3 of Genograms, what might be some of the "ambiguous" relationships that could occur? The tenuousness of marriage and the increased visibility of alternative partnerships lead to several implications for older individuals. One is that while older individuals today may not experience the same high levels of divorce, cohabitation, and publicly open homosexuality as their younger counterparts, they are affected by these practices in their children and other younger relatives. They will need to make decisions about how to negotiate their changing kinship networks. A second implication for older individuals is that more in the future are likely to enter old age while divorced or in short term remarriages/ cohabitations. Ex- and short-term spouses may not be as likely to provide the depth of personal care that long term spouses typically gave in the past. As a result, it may fall more to children, siblings and other long term family members to supplement relatively weak spousal support systems. Older men who are divorced may also lose contact or closeness with intergenerational kin, since they are less likely to enact strong kinkeeping roles than women (Hagestad, 1986). Older women who are divorced may face compounded economic problems with ageing, since many have only been in the paid labour force sporadically, and their retirement incomes are only a fraction of men's. As new forms of chosen partnerships are becoming socially acceptable, the meanings of family life have become increasingly diverse. It is this phenomenon that we will explore next.

Diversity in Experiences of Family

Many researchers are now recognising what much of the public already knows - that family and kinship are often not bounded by marriage, adoption, or biology. This has been stated in the past about specific subgroups such as African Americans (Stack, 1970), but is increasingly acknowledged for the majority of society. Regardless of family form, adult intergenerational relationships are structurally diverse (Bengtson, Rosenthal & Burton, 1990; Silverstein & Bengtson, 1997). Widespread changes in structural family forms and lived family lives have many important implications for ageing individuals. Riley and Riley (1993) describe an emerging kinship structure they call a "latent matrix" of kin connections. This matrix consists of a large and complex network of kin relationships, that are flexible/voluntary, not constrained by age or generation in closeness and support, and latent in quality until they are called upon (Riley & Riley, 1993). The Rileys conceptualize the latent matrix as a network of kin that is continually shifting, allowing for the activation and intensification of close kin relationships. Boundaries are wide to encompass several degrees of stepkin and in-laws, single- parent families, cohabitation-related, adopted and other "relatives" chosen from outside the family.

This type of socially constructed family or opportune family (Johnson, 1995) includes individuals who are selectively accumulated through marriage, divorce and remarriage. These relationships are variable and negotiable for those of all ages, adding complexity to many family relationships. This complexity has influenced the role of grandparents (Giarrusso, Silverstein & Bengtson, 1996). For example, Johnson and Barer (1987) examined four different ways divorce or remarriage among family members altered kinship networks for grandparents:

(1) when relationships with relatives of a child's divorce were retained, while new relatives were added with a child's remarriage;

(2) when the divorces and remarriages of multiple children created several subsets of relatives;

(3) when the divorces and remarriages of the grandparents added another set of step and in-law relations; and

(4) when they retained relationships with former children-in-law after these children remarried.

Nearly half of the grandparents in Johnson and Barer's study experienced kinship expansion fitting the above criteria, during the three years following a child's marital separation. Those grandmothers who severed relations with former in-laws after their children divorced experienced a temporary contraction in the kinship system, which expanded again if the children remarried. Johnson and Barer's (1987) research highlights the voluntary aspect of relationships formed after divorce and remarriage.

Like the grandparents in their study, a great number of individuals of all ages do and will face choices about kinship expansion and reduction throughout their lives. We can no longer assume that help and support are exchanged across only certain family structures.

The structural changes described above and the diversity of decisions people might make about them can bring a great deal of ambiguity into the lives of older individuals. Boss and Greenberg (1984) describe a state of boundary ambiguity, in which individuals can feel a lack of clarity about who is in or out of a family system at any given time. Steprelatives, cohabiting partners of relatives, and even biological relatives may be seen as physically present but psychologically absent, or as psychologically present but physically absent.

In these cases, the family boundaries are ambiguous, contributing to confusion over the roles and tasks individuals perform. Should stepgrandchildren living with biological grandchildren be invited for the holidays and given comparable gifts? Should a child's cohabiting partner be included in a family portrait? Should former stepchildren be called on for assistance in times of need?

These and many other everyday decisions shape whether ambiguously-related family members are treated as integral, peripheral or negligible to a larger family system. Family members may disagree about who should be included and the level of inclusion or exclusion. This kind of conflict may be bewildering for older individuals, many of whom grew up during a time when family boundaries were perceived as more clear. While negotiable kinship provides more potential for emotional and financial support, it can also leave ageing individuals in a precarious situation, since obligations between family members may also become more ambiguous.

Work

The relationship between work, careers, and ageing is changing. The 19th Century notion of work did not include retirement. People worked until they died or were physically disabled. By the end of the 20th Century retirement has become something that most workers expect to experience; yet changes in the structure of labour markets, economies, and societal attitudes have led to differential experiences of work. In this section we begin by discussing work as a social structure. We then explore how trajectories and transitions in work careers vary due to two main factors;

(1) changes over historical time in labour markets and economies, and

(2) diversity in the experience of work.

Work as a Social Structure

The social structure of work provides an opportunity structure of available occupations, norms about appropriate people for these occupations, and a reward structure related to these occupations. Like family, work can be thought of in a multitude of ways. It can incorporate many types and situations of labour. This labour can be physical or mental. It can be paid or unpaid. It may take place in the public sphere or inside a private home. Work can take the form of a recognised position in an established labour market or can be a marginal position in the underground economy. Workers can work full-time or part-time, they can be paid in salaries, hourly wages, by the job, or in exchange for other goods and services.

Here we focus on the context of the paid labour force and older people's relationships with it. Our understanding of work is based on patterns established in the paid labour force. Even with this caveat, the meaning and experience of work is extremely complex. Transitions in and out of work are not clearly delineated at any stage of life. For instance, many contemporary entry-level jobs require high levels of education. As a result, many young people are spending more years in education, and delaying entry into the paid work force. Similarly, the process of exiting the paid labour force is not simple. It involves not only individual choices but overall opportunity structures. Though retirement can be viewed as a separate social structure (Atchley, 1993), the boundaries between retirement and work are becoming increasingly permeable. The transition between work and retirement is blurred (Mutchler, Burr, Pienta & Massagli, 1997) and decisions to retire may not be final (Hayward, Grady & McLaughlin, 1988). Although the decision to exit or remain in the labour force is a very personal one, larger societal factors play a role by either pushing older workers out of work or pulling them into the labour force (Kohli, 1994).

Historical Changes in Labour Markets and Economies

As labour markets change, work opportunities for older adults also change. A major indication of this is the changes to the overall availability of certain types of jobs. Service and high tech positions have replaced the large number of agricultural and manufacturing jobs available in the early 1900s. As the labour market has shifted to a post- industrial, service based economy, the types of jobs available are less likely to be the career jobs that contemporary elderly (middle class men) entered into as young adults. In the United States, corporate downsizing and restructuring in the past decade have also reduced the demand for senior workers. Instead the jobs available to many older workers are "contingent jobs" with no promise of lifetime employment or company loyalty (Henretta, 1994). Many of the skills of contemporary older workers are obsolete in today's marketplace, which emphasizes advanced technological skills.

Another component of the changing workplace is that certain types of people are funnelled into certain jobs. For instance, only when the demand for labour is high, such as during World War II, have concerted efforts been made to retrain older workers (Kohli, 1994). Partly because of these factors, there has been a downward trend in labour force participation among men over 55 (Easterlin, Crimmins & Ohanian, 1984; Treas, 1995). This reflects a pattern of early retirement among a significant proportion of the male work force. This pattern has stabilized during the last quarter century, especially since the 1980's. Retirement trends for older women are more varied than for men - while some women fit the male pattern, others are entering the paid labour force in later life for the first time (Quinn & Burkhauser, 1994).

In addition, the size and skills of the available pool of younger workers influences the job opportunities open to ageing individuals. When the size of younger cohorts is smaller, there may be more demand for older workers. Nevertheless, many employers will hire supplemental workers from the pool of women and immigrants before they will approach older workers (Kohli, 1994). In contrast, a rise in unemployment among younger workers can increase the push toward early exit for older workers.

Changes in economies can result in changes in the value of income. The more people depended on work for their preretirement income, instead of assets or savings, the more likely they are to return to work if their pensions and savings decrease in value (Hayward, Grady & McLaughlin, 1988). Part-time and self employment are increasingly common among older workers, the majority of whom are working part time by choice. “Bridge jobs,” which are the part time jobs that workers obtain between careers and retirement, are becoming more prevalent among older workers (Quinn & Kozy, 1996).

Diversity in Experiences of Work

The work history of individuals influences their subsequent opportunities as they age. Diversity in careers by gender, race, and class can lead to differences in opportunities and marketability in later life. The establishment of seniority both within and between occupations is also diverse (Henretta, 1994). The type or prestige of an occupation influences individual decisions to remain in the labour force. For instance, high prestige jobs that focus on mental work may retain older workers who continue to find their work gratifying and whose expertise continues to be highly valued. For menial labourers, the situation is reversed. Remaining in a job may be less desirable for older workers whose skills are devalued. Ironically, these workers are more likely to be in need of additional income in old age.

Opportunity structures during primary working years affect opportunities and access to resources during retirement (Calasanti, 1993). For workers with a career of manual and low-paying jobs, exit from the workforce is often more about health issues and disability than gaining leisure time. Hayward, Friedman, and Chin (1996) found that in the United States, African Americans' unequal footing in the labour force persisted into retirement years with significantly higher rates of disability.

Women's work trajectories reflect the opportunities available to them in society, and deeply held beliefs about gender roles. Most occupations in the US remain sex-segregated, and most women continue to hold low-status, female-typed, dead-end jobs, earning much lower wages than men (Blum, 1991). Because women are more likely to spend time outside the paid labour force, they are even less marketable in later life.

Industrialization and workplace patterns encourage lives that are structured around age norms. Many Western notions of appropriate life activities have come to be organised around work (Kohli, 1986). Work has become more individualized historically, as it has been pulled away from community and family life.

The State

The state - or government - shapes older people's lives in profound ways. First, we want to provide a sociological perspective on the state as a social structure and how it influences the lives of ageing individuals. Next, we will highlight how states/governments act as both (1) providers for the well being of older individuals; and (2) regulators of life course activities.

The State as a Social Structure

The state is the largest social structure and wields incredible power over individual lives. As a social structure, the state manages collective resources and maintains social order. Toward these ends, the state privileges some groups over others, and its programs and policies reflect the ideologies of those in control.

The state can be defined as a combination of "executive, legislative and judicial branches of government, the military, the criminal justice system, educational institutions, and public health and welfare institutions" (Estes, Linkins & Binney, 1996, p. 347). Our perspective draws from the work of political economists who emphasize the social construction and value-laden nature of state activities (Estes, Linkins & Binney, 1996; Minkler & Estes, 1991).

As societies have become more industrialized, states have become increasingly complex in order to meet the needs of individuals. Through legislation, states establish rules about citizenship, employment, health care and many other things. Through funding, states facilitate research and development in the fields of science and technology.

State activities have played a major role in constructing what people think of as "old age". Since the 1930's in the US, "older people" were designated as all people over age 65. This was the age limit required for receipt of full Social Security benefits. Sixty-five as an age marker originated in Germany in the 1880s (Myles, 1984) with the introduction of the first social insurance program. Today, certain segments of society provide benefits for "seniors" at a range of ages. The US government has pushed the old age eligibility marker of 65 upward, with the planned increase in the retirement age from 65 to 67 (Torres-Gil, 1992).

Most people don't have a good idea of how their Social Security benefits will be figured upon retirement. The Social Security Administration offers all individuals the opportunity to request a Personal Earnings and Benefit Statement. The Statement estimates your benefits based on information you supply; for example, current and expected salary, planned retirement date etc. Go to Social Security Administration's web site above and read about Social Security benefits.

In its functions as manager of resources and maintainer of social order, the state shapes the lives of older individuals in two key ways. It provides for later life social welfare through programs such as Social Security and Medicare, and regulates activities at all stages of the life course.

The State as Provider

The term "welfare state" refers to government entitlement programs that distribute income, health care and social services (Myles, 1984; Schulz, 1996). It is this aspect of the state that most concerns us here, since states have taken on significant responsibilities for the economic maintenance of older people (Myles, 1984). As a result, older people depend on state policies more than people of other age groups (Estes, 1991a).

In recent decades across the industrialized world, government programs benefiting the elderly have expanded (Jacobs, 1990; Mayer & Schoepflin, 1989; Myles, 1984). Some describe the years 1930-1990 as the era of "Modern Ageing", in which governments took on a major role in the provision of services and benefits for older people (Torres-Gil, 1992). This expansion has made the practice of retirement more accessible (Quadagno & Myles, 1991) and has led to an increase in independent living for those over 65 (Jacobs, 1990).

Nations differ from each other and across time in their provision of social welfare programs for the elderly. Cross-national variations can be linked to levels of industrialization, economic development, and political culture and values (Binstock & Day, 1996). For example, the U.S. is set apart from other nations in its focus on individualism and its resistance to government action (Binstock & Day, 1996; Parrott, Reynolds & Bengtson, 1997). As a result, only in the US is health care a part of the politics of old age (Estes, 1991b). Other capitalistic Western nations have health care for people of all ages.

While welfare state expansion has contributed to the economic well being of older people in general, certain groups of elderly remain at-risk under current systems. Disadvantaged groups include women, minorities, the poor, the frail, and those in rural areas (Torres-Gil, 1992). This can be explained in part by policies that benefit certain groups over others. For example, the application of Social Security in the US is not gender- neutral. Benefits based on spousal wages reinforce women's dependence on men. Women's prior economic dependence (resulting from societal norms of women providing the bulk of unpaid home care) has led to gender inequality in retirement income for men and women. Single women are particularly impoverished (Estes, Linkins & Binney, 1996).

Another issue is that the needs of older people exceed the programs available to fill those needs. Governments expect that much of the care that older people need will be provided by family members and other loved ones. But care is compromised when primary caregivers, often women, are unable to "do it all", and dependent elderly are shifted off into impersonal institutionalized forms of care, such as day care and nursing homes (Hochschild, 1995). Even if paid workers strive to give high quality care, it is doubtful that state provided care offers the same level of mental, emotional and physical attention to well being that someone with a long term emotional bond would give (Hochschild, 1995).

The size and scope of welfare state activities, including entitlement programs for older people, continue to be a matter of public debate. The state is now being framed as a social structure unable to handle the increasing needs of the elderly. Social policy discussions have shifted from a focus on improvement to one of crisis and budget cutting (Estes, 1991b). Three long-term developments challenge whether elderly income security can be maintained at current levels: (1) the accelerated rate of population ageing; (2) anticipated rises in public expenditures; and (3) the trend toward early retirement (Quadagno & Myles, 1991). A basic question comes up again and again: "What should be the role of the public sector in caring for citizens in later life?" (Jacobs, 1990, p. 358). Although this question will continue to be a major one facing policymakers in upcoming decades, many argue that it is unlikely that there will be dramatic changes in governmental policies toward the aged in the near future (Parrott, Reynolds & Bengtson, 1997).

The State as Regulator of the Life Course

State policies regulate many aspects of life, including the structure of schooling, the legal marriage age, and the age of pension eligibility (Mayer & Schoepflin, 1989). In these and other ways, the state provides a structure for people to fit into as they live their lives.

One aspect of this regulation occurs as a by-product of welfare state provision. By providing age-based transfer incomes, states decrease older people's dependency on others and allow for decision making that might otherwise be impossible (Mayer & Schoepflin, 1989). For instance, in the past when people reached retirement age in the

US, they forfeited income if they delayed retirement, since public pensions did not increase if receipt was delayed. This provided a strong incentive to stop working at age 65 for financial reasons. Age-based eligibility contributes to sharp life transitions that are arbitrarily and universally applied, rather than based on need (Neugarten & Neugarten, 1986) or individual preferences (Mayer & Schoepflin, 1989). "Whenever the state establishes rules, provides services, or offers monetary incentives, it is functionally rational for individuals to make use of such opportunities" (Mayer & Schoepflin, 1989, p. 202).

Other regulation of older people occurs through general legislation that shapes decision-making. Certain laws have a particularly strong impact on older people. One example is "right to die" regulation. This has become an issue in many industrialized countries, and encompasses various forms of euthanasia and assisted suicide (Glick & Smith, 1993).

Another example of regulation that is extremely relevant to older people is legislation surrounding "autonomy" and "competency". When an individual becomes unable to make his or her own decisions about medical treatment or health care, others must be brought in to help make these decisions. A variety of options exist in this realm, depending on the specifics of the situation (Wilber & Reynolds, 1995). States are involved in regulating the practices of surrogacy and guardianship, which in turn affect health care and financial outcomes in the lives of older people who have become incapacitated.

Due to state involvement, ageing individuals experience a context that promotes transitions that are ordered yet are not individually motivated (Mayer & Schoepflin, 1989). This is a powerful force that students may want to consider - that externally and universally applied rules are shaping the lives of older individuals. Further, these rules do not evolve in a vacuum but in specific historical and political contexts.

Some groups, including gerontologists, have challenged the necessity of a life course segmented by age, arguing instead for an "age-integrated" society, in which individuals of all ages can move between educational, occupational, unpaid work, and leisure activities (Riley, Kahn & Foner, 1994). They argue that there is a lack of productive and meaningful role opportunities for the rising numbers of strong, healthy, and capable older people (Riley, Kahn & Foner, 1994). States may encourage continued productive roles in the future by raising the eligibility age of public pensions (Burkhauser & Quinn, 1994).

In sum, states, with their entitlement programs, age-based rules, and general legislation, act as major providers and regulators in the lives of older people. Their policies do not have an equal impact on all individuals—some are privileged and others disadvantaged under current systems. It is important to guard against seeing this as "natural"— states have developed over time and location within specific historical contexts. They enable and constrict the lives of older people. They make some preferred decisions possible and others unattainable.

Religion

Organised religion plays a major role in the lives of billions of people worldwide. Taken collectively, the major world religions - Christianity, Judaism, Islam, Buddhism, Hinduism, Confucianism, and Taoism - condition the lives and belief structures of people of all ages. These religions have varying influences at multiple levels - some shape government policy and societal norms, while others have an influence primarily at a personal and small group level. This section will focus on 1) the role of religion in articulating a system of beliefs and values, and 2) religious institutions as locations of social interaction and support for older people.

Religion as a Social Structure

Religious organisations transmit values and beliefs to members of society. As mentioned above, they have varying influences on people's lives. Nevertheless, viewing religion as a social structure allows us to see how at a broad societal level, religion offers a context in which individual and collective needs for meanings are met through established beliefs and rituals.

Religion, in Articulating a System of Beliefs & Values

Religion seeks to define the spiritual world and give meaning to events that are difficult to explain or understand. Religious values, beliefs and rituals can integrate members of a community and provide a source of strength in difficult times. Religion can facilitate the process of older people making sense of their lives by providing hope, emotional strength, and coping strategies for dealing with death and suffering (Johnson, 1995; Koenig, 1994; Ellison, 1994). These can serve as resources for older individuals, even in the absence of tangible social support (Payne and McFadden, 1994). Religion acts as a source of continuity for many older individuals, but it can also be a source of conflict. Religious beliefs and meanings may clash with other aspects of people's lives, such as conventional medical practices, legal rights, and expectations at the workplace (O'Connell, 1994). Other times people's beliefs clash with the beliefs of others, leading to social conflict. This can result in generational conflict as younger members of a religious community seek to adapt rituals and values to contemporary society. On a more personal level, individuals might feel that they have not lived up to the expectations of their religion, leading to a sense of guilt or a fear of damnation, which may have an effect on psychological well-being (Moberg, 1983). Others may feel let down by a religion that could not prevent sorrow and loss of loved ones.

As Facilitator of Social Interaction and Support for Elderly

Religion provides a meeting ground for its members. These meeting grounds can be physical spaces such as temples and shrines or social spaces such as prayer groups and religious festivals. Older individuals who are lonely or depressed may be particularly comforted by the social opportunity provided by religious participation. Religious communities enable the creations of social networks and the exchange of support in times of need (Ellison, 1994). Since people of older ages are currently more likely to be involved in religion than those of younger ages (Payne and McFadden, 1994), religious activities may provide important sites for peer interaction among older individuals and comfort in the face of losses of family and friends. The interaction and support provided by religion also affords additional benefits. Increased social support and stronger social networks provided by religious involvement are correlated with better health. Religion promotes a sense of intimacy and a feeling of belonging among older individuals (Johnson, 1995). The mental health benefits of religious involvement are consistent over the life course (Levin, Chatters and Taylor, 1995). Recently researchers have been careful to point out that health benefits are not simply due to religious participation, but are a result of related factors such as social support (Atchley, 1997). In the U.S., African American churches have been shown to provide the kind of social and psychological support that links older people with health communities (Levin, Chatters and Taylor, 1995). While the support and interaction that comes with religion can be a major support for older individuals, it can also have some negative effects. Non-compliance with religious norms may lead to social stigma within a religious community, or meddling on the part of "well-meaning" religious members.

Implications for Professionals Who Work with Elderly

Understanding ageing individuals in the context of social structures is important for professionals because social contexts define and shape the lives of the elderly. As Mills (1959) stated in The Sociological Imagination, "neither the life of an individual nor the history of a society can be understood without understanding both" (p. 3). Older people who benefit from the services of professionals are living in an increasingly complex world. Social contexts condition the opportunities and social support available to them. The rapid changes to social institutions that have occurred across the 20th century can be hard to continually adapt to, and older people may find themselves increasingly alienated, confused, and even estranged from the society in which they live. By recognising the historically changing structural diversity of their clients' lives, professionals can adapt their services to best fit clients' particular life situations.

Older people have many needs and a variety of professionals play a critical role in helping them adjust to the changes of later life. Many of these changes can be linked to broader trends in society that vary across time and location. Recognition of these broad trends enables professionals to anticipate issues and to develop programs to better meet the needs of the older people they serve. In addition, geroprofessionals can influence the social context in which their clients live by sharing their expertise with the larger community. For instance, by serving on civic, educational or religious organisations, professionals can help their community adapt to the needs of older individuals. By recognising and incorporating the structural contexts discussed in this chapter, geroprofessionals can develop services that help older individuals cope with their changing worlds.

Each social structure discussed in this chapter has been linked to the lives of ageing individuals. The changing family context can lead to ambiguity in terms of older family members' responsibility toward younger family members. By providing older individuals with information on (grand)child custody and visitation, estate planning, and strategies to manage family conflict, those who work with the elderly can empower the lives of ageing individuals negotiating family relationships. The changing work context can place older people, especially women, in precarious financial circumstances. Professionals can address these needs by creating programs which focus on job retraining, strategies for re-entering the work force, and retirement planning. The changing context of the state structures the lives of ageing individuals. By developing services for them which emphasize political action, interpret new laws and regulations, and negotiate the health care system, professionals can help ageing individuals recognise their own agency in dealing with the monolithic structure of the state. The changing context of religion can leave older individuals isolated from like-minded peers. Professionals can address these needs by encouraging religious organisations to reach out to the elderly population and by providing information to older clients about diverse religious communities that service elders.

Conclusions

It is all too easy to think of the elderly in individualistic terms. While this is important, it is incomplete because it ignores structural constraints and the power of social norms. The main thrust of this chapter has been to show the importance of four societal contexts to the lives of ageing individuals. These four contexts - family, work, the state, and religion - are in constant flux, and a change in one area can precipitate changes in each of the others, which affects individual lives. A recognition of these broad level contexts enhances the understanding of behaviour, and will contribute to a fuller understanding of the lives of older individuals.

Gerontology

Gerontology is the study of the social, psychological and biological aspects of ageing. It is distinguished from geriatrics, which is the branch of medicine that studies the diseases of older adults. Gerontologists include researchers and practitioners in the fields of biology, nursing, medicine, criminology, dentistry, social work, physical and occupational therapy, psychology, psychiatry, sociology, economics, political science, architecture, geography, pharmacy, public health, housing, and anthropology.

Gerontology encompasses the following:

- studying physical, mental, and social changes in people as they age
- investigating the ageing process itself (biogerontology)
- investigating the social and psychosocial impacts of ageing (sociogerontology)
- investigating the psychological effects on ageing (psychogerontology)
- investigating the interface of normal ageing and age-related disease (geroscience)
- investigating the effects of an ageing population on society
- applying this knowledge to policies and programs, including the macroscopic (for example, government planning) and microscopic (for example, running a nursing home) perspectives.

The multidisciplinary nature of gerontology means that there are a number of subfields, as well as associated fields such as psychology and sociology that overlap with gerontology. Gerontologists view ageing in terms of four distinct processes: chronological ageing, biological ageing, psychological ageing, and social ageing. Chronological ageing is the definition of ageing based on a person's years lived from birth. Biological ageing refers to the physical changes that reduce the efficiency of organ systems. Psychological ageing includes the changes that occur in sensory and perceptual processes, cognitive abilities, adaptive capacity, and personality. Social ageing refers to an individual's changing roles and relationships with family, friends, and other informal supports, productive roles and within organisations.

History

In the medieval Islamic world, several physicians wrote on issues related to Gerontology. Avicenna's *The Canon of Medicine* (1025) offered instruction for the care of the aged, including diet and remedies for problems including constipation. Arabic physician Ibn Al-Jazzar Al-Qayrawani (Algizar, c. 898–980) wrote on the aches and conditions of the elderly (Ammar 1998, p. 4). His scholarly work covers sleep disorders, forgetfulness, how to strengthen memory and causes of mortality Ishaq ibn Hunayn (died 910) also wrote works on the treatments for forgetfulness (U.S. National Library of Medicine, 1994).

While the number of aged humans, and the maximum life span, tended to increase in every century since the 14th, society tended to consider caring for an elderly relative as a family issue. It was not until the coming of the Industrial Revolution that ideas shifted in favour of a societal care-system. Care homes for the aged emerged in the 19th century.

Some early pioneers, such as Michel Eugène Chevreul, who himself lived to be 102, believed that ageing itself should be a science to be studied. Élie Metchnikoff coined the term "gerontology" c. 1903

It was not until the 1940s, however, that pioneers like James Birren began organising gerontology into its own field. Recognising that there were experts in many fields all dealing with the older population, it became apparent that a group like the Gerontological Society of America (founded in 1945) was needed. Two decades later, James Birren was appointed as the founding director of the first academic research centre devoted exclusively to the study of ageing, the Ethel Percy Andrus Gerontology Centre at the University of Southern California. The Baltimore Longitudinal Studies of Ageing began in 1958 in order to study physiological changes in healthy middle-aged and older men living in the community by testing them every two years on numerous physiological parameters. In 1967, the University of South Florida and the University of North Texas (formerly North Texas State University) received Older Americans Act training grants from the U.S. Administration on Ageing to launch the nation's first degree programs in gerontology, at the master's level. In 1975, the University of Southern California's Leonard Davis School of Gerontology, with Birren as its founding dean, became the country's first school of gerontology within a university and, later, offered the first PhD in Gerontology degree. Since that time, a number of other universities have formed departments or schools of gerontology or ageing studies.

More generally, gerontological education has flourished in the United States since 1967 and degrees at all academic levels are now offered by a number of colleges and universities. One of the pioneering gerontologists, Robert Neil Butler, has pushed for care and respect of the elderly. Butler won a Pulitzer Prize for his book titled, *Why Survive? Being Old in America*, where he discusses how the elderly are overlooked, mistreated, and sometimes even abused. His book argues that we as a society must modify our behaviour toward the elderly. Several university-based centres on ageing have been founded such as the Duke University Centre on Ageing, the University of Georgia Institute of Gerontology, the Centre of Ageing at the University of Chicago, and the Stanford Centre on Longevity. Relatively few universities offer a PhD in gerontology. Currently, PhD programs in gerontology are available at Miami University, the University of Kansas, University of Kentucky, University of Maryland Baltimore, University of Massachusetts Boston, and the University of Southern California. The substantial increase in the ageing population in post-industrial Western nations has led to this becoming one of the most rapidly growing fields.

From the 1950s to the 1970s, the field was mainly social and concerned with issues such as nursing homes and health care. However, research by Leonard Hayflick in the 1960s (showing that a cell line culture will only divide about 50 times) helped lead to a separate branch, biogerontology. It became apparent that simply treating ageing was not enough. Developing an understanding of the ageing process, and what could be done about it, became an issue.

Biogerontology was also bolstered when research by Cynthia Kenyon and others demonstrated that life extension was possible in lower life forms such as fruit flies, worms, and yeast. So far, however, nothing more than incremental (marginal) increases in life span have been seen in any mammalian species.

Ageing Demographics

Rapid ageing populations are expected worldwide. In 1900, there were 3.1 million people aged 65 years and older living in the United States. However, this population continued to grow throughout the 20th century and reached 31.2, 35, and 40.3 million people in 1990, 2000, and 2010, respectively. Notably, in the United States, the "baby boomer" generation began to turn 65 in 2011. Recently, the population aged 65 years and older has grown at a faster rate than the total population in the United States. The total population increased by 9.7%, from 281.4 million to 308.7 million, between 2000 and 2010. However, the population aged 65 years and older increased by 15.1% during the same period. It has been estimated that 25% of the population in the United States and Canada will be aged 65 years and older by 2025. Moreover, by 2050, it is predicted that, for the first time in United States history, the number of individuals aged 60 years and older will be greater than the number of children aged 0 to 14 years. Those aged 85 years and older (oldest-old) are projected to increase from 5.3 million to 21 million by 2050. Adults aged 85–89 years constituted the greatest segment of the oldest-old in 1990, 2000, and 2010. However, the largest percentage point increase among the oldest-old occurred in the 90- to 94-year-old age group, which increased from 25.0% in 1990 to 26.4% in 2010. With the rapid growth of the ageing population, social work education and training specialised in older adults and practitioners interested in working with older adults are increasingly in demand In the last decade, geriatric social work education, practice, and research have received substantial support from foundations such as the John. A Hartford Foundation, Robert Wood Johnson Foundation, and Atlantic Philanthropies.

Of the roughly 150,000 people who die each day across the globe, about two thirds—100,000 per day—die of age-related causes; In industrialized nations, the proportion is much higher, reaching 90%.

Gender Differences with Age

There has been a considerable disparity between the number of men and women in the older population in the United States. In both 2000 and 2010, women outnumbered men in the older population at every single year of age (e.g., 65 to 100 years and over). The sex ratio, which is a measure used to indicate the balance of males to females in a population, is calculated by taking the number of males divided by the number of females, and multiplying by 100. Therefore, the sex ratio is the number of males per 100 females. In 2010, there were 90.5 males per 100 females in the 65-year-old population. However, this represented an increase from 1990 when there were 82.7 males per 100 females, and from 2000 when the sex ratio was 88.1. Although the gender gap between men and women has narrowed, women continue to have a greater life expectancy and lower mortality rates at older ages relative to men. For example, the Census 2010 reported that there were approximately twice as many women as men living in the United States at 89 years of age (361,309 versus 176,689, respectively). The age-related changes males experience is likely to progress faster than the age-related changes in which females experience. Neural systems associated with behavioural domains identify age effects on behaviour and brain parameters, which indicate more pronounced age-related changes in men than in women. Research and studies have found strong evidence of ovarian hormones playing a key role in mediating behaviour and brain function.

Geographic Distribution of Older Adults

The number and percentage of older adults living in the United States vary across the four different regions (Northeast, Midwest, West, and South) defined by the United States census. In 2010, the South contained the greatest number of people aged 65 years and older and 85 years and older. However, proportionately, the Northeast contains the largest percentage of adults aged 65 years and older (14.1%), followed by the Midwest (13.5%), the South (13.0%), and the West (11.9%). Relative to the Census 2000, all geographic regions demonstrated positive growth in the population of adults aged 65 years and older and 85 years and older. The most rapid growth in the population of adults aged 65 years and older was evident in the West (23.5%), which showed an increase from 6.9 million in 2000 to 8.5 million in 2010. Likewise, in the population aged 85 years and older, the West (42.8%) also showed the fastest growth and increased from 806,000 in 2000 to 1.2 million in 2010. It is worth highlighting that Rhode Island was the only state that experienced a reduction in the number of people aged 65 years and older, and declined from 152,402 in 2000 to 151,881 in 2010. Conversely, all states exhibited an increase in the population of adults aged 85 years and older from 2000 to 2010.

Biogerontology

Biogerontology is the sub-field of gerontology concerned with the biological processes of ageing and their evolutionary origins. It involves interdisciplinary research on biological aging's causes, effects, and mechanisms. Conservative biogerontologists such as Leonard Hayflick have predicted that the human life expectancy will peak at about 92 years old, although the consensus now is that the numbers will continue to rise.

Biomedical gerontology, also known as experimental gerontology and life extension, is a sub-discipline of biogerontology that endeavors to slow, prevent, and even reverse ageing in both humans and animals. Approaches include curing age-related diseases and slowing down the underlying processes of ageing. Most "life extensionists" believe the human life span can be increased within the next century, if not sooner. Optimists such as Aubrey de Grey estimate that the first person to live to a thousand years may have already been born. Some biogerontologists take an intermediate position, emphasizing the study of the ageing process as a means of mitigating ageing-associated diseases, while either claiming that maximum life span cannot be altered or that it is undesirable to try.

As with biogerontology, geriatrics studies the biological causes and effects of ageing. Both fields are considered by many scientists to be the most important frontiers in ageing research.

Biological Theories of Ageing

Theories of ageing are numerous and no one theory has been accepted. There is a wide spectrum of the types of theories for the causes of ageing with programmed theories on one extreme and error theories on the other. Regardless of the theory, a commonality is that as humans age, functions of the body decline.

Wear and Tear

Wear and tear theories of ageing suggest that as an individual ages, body parts such as cells and organs wear out from continued use. Wearing of the body can be attributable to internal or external causes that eventually lead to an accumulation of insults which surpasses the capacity for repair. Due to these internal and external insults, cells lose their ability to regenerate, which ultimately leads to mechanical and chemical exhaustion. Some insults include chemicals in the air, food, or smoke. Other insults may be things such as viruses, trauma, free radicals, cross-linking, and high body temperature.

Genetic

Genetic theories of ageing propose that ageing is programmed within each individual's genes. According to this theory, genes dictate cellular longevity. Programmed cell death, or apoptosis, is determined by a "biological clock" via genetic information in the nucleus of the cell. Genes responsible for apoptosis provide an explanation for cell death, but are less applicable to death of an entire organism. An increase in cellular apoptosis may correlate to ageing, but is not a 'cause of death'.

Environmental factors and genetic mutations can influence gene expression and accelerate ageing. More recently epigenetics have been explored as a contributing factor. The epigenetic clock, which objectively measures the biological age of cells and tissues, may become useful for testing different biological ageing theories.

General Imbalance

General imbalance theories of ageing suggest that body systems, such as the endocrine, nervous, and immune systems, gradually decline and ultimately fail to function. The rate of failure varies system by system.

Accumulation

Accumulation theories of ageing suggest that ageing is bodily decline that results from an accumulation of elements. Elements can be foreign and introduced to the body from the environment. Other elements can be the natural result of cell metabolism. An example of an accumulation theory is the Free Radical Theory of Ageing. According to this theory, byproducts of regular cell metabolism called free radicals interact with cellular components such as the cell membrane and DNA and cause irreversible damage. A more recent and comprehensive accumulation theory by Dr. Aubrey de Grey posits that ageing is the consequence of the accumulation of 7 types of 'damage' at the molecular, cellular and intracellular levels.

The Free Radical Theory of Ageing

The idea that free radicals are toxic agents was first proposed by Rebeca Gerschman and colleagues. In 1956, Denham Harman proposed the free-radical theory of ageing and even demonstrated that free radical reactions contribute to the degradation of biological systems. Oxidative damage of many types accumulate with age, such as oxidative stress that oxygen-free radicals, because the free radical theory of ageing argues that ageing results from the damage generated by reactive oxygen species (ROS). ROS are small, highly reactive, oxygen-containing molecules that can damage a complex of cellular components such as fat, proteins, or from DNA, they are naturally generated in small amounts during the body's metabolic reactions. These conditions become more common as we age, including diseases related to ageing, such as dementia, cancer and heart disease. The Free Radical Theory of Ageing is not accepted by everyone because we cannot determine if the free-radicals or the ageing came first and if it is why the human body ages. Reasonably, the damage done by free radical may only begin after the ageing process does. Future research must be conducted to see if one of the solutions to stabilize the free-radicals may postpone ageing.

The DNA Damage Theory of Ageing

DNA damage has been one of the many causes in diseases related to ageing. The stability of the genome is defined by the cells machinery of repair, damage tolerance, and checkpoint pathways that counteracts DNA damage. One hypothesis proposed by Gioacchino Failla in 1958 is that damage accumulation to the DNA causes ageing. The hypothesis was developed soon by physicist Leó Szilárd. This theory has changed over the years as new research has discovered new types of DNA damage and mutations, and several theories of ageing argue that DNA damage with or without mutations causes ageing. If DNA damage and other stressors can be conserved, the anticancer and survival responses from cells may boost defences that maintain the integrity of the cell. This may improve health and extend the lifespan. The importance of DNA damage and the genome maintenance in relation to ageing can be investigated further more for treatment.

Social Gerontology

Social gerontology is a multi-disciplinary sub-field that specialises in studying or working with older adults.

Social gerontologists may have degrees or training in social work, nursing, psychology, sociology, demography, gerontology, or other social science disciplines. Social gerontologists are responsible for educating, researching, and advancing the broader causes of older people.

Because issues of life span and life extension need numbers to quantify them, there is an overlap with demography. Those who study the demography of the human life span differ from those who study the social demographics of ageing.

Social Work with Older Adults

Social work with older adults, known as geriatric social work practice, is considered to be both a macro and micro practice with individuals over the age of 60 or 65, their families and communities, ageing related policy, and ageing research. Geriatric social workers typically provide counselling, direct services, care coordination, community planning, and advocacy in an array of agencies and organisations including private practice, in home, neighbourhoods, hospitals, senior congregate living, hospice/end of life care, senior centres, oncology centres and residential long term care facilities such as nursing facilities. At the macro level, geriatric social workers work within state departments of health, adult protective services, and at universities and colleges, as well as Administration on Ageing offices on a federal level in the United States.

Social Theories of Ageing

According to Dannefer, ageing is an interactive process where the individual is affected by the environment while also influencing the environment in which he/she ages. Several theories of ageing are developed to observed the ageing process of older adults in society as well as how these processes are interpreted by men and women as they age.

Activity Theory

Activity theory was developed and elaborated by Cavan, Havighurst, and Albrecht. According to this theory, older adults' self-concept depends on social interactions. In order for older adults to maintain morale in old age, substitutions must be made for lost roles. Examples of lost roles include retirement from a job or loss of a spouse.

Activity is preferable to inactivity because it facilitates well-being on multiple levels. Because of improved general health and prosperity in the older population, remaining active is more feasible now than when this theory was first proposed by Havighurst nearly six decades ago. The activity theory is applicable for a stable, post-industrial society, which offers its older members many opportunities for meaningful participation. Weakness: Some ageing persons cannot maintain a middle-aged lifestyle, due to functional limitations, lack of income, or lack of a desire to do so. Many older adults lack the resources to maintain active roles in society. On the flip side, some elders may insist on continuing activities in late life that pose a danger to themselves and others, such as driving at night with low visual acuity or doing maintenance work to the house while climbing with severely arthritic knees. In doing so, they are denying their limitations and engaging in unsafe behaviours.

Disengagement Theory

Disengagement theory was developed by Cumming and Henry. According to this theory, older adults and society engage in a mutual separation from each other. An example of mutual separation is retirement from the workforce. A key assumption of this theory is that older adults lose "ego-energy" and become increasingly self-absorbed. Additionally, disengagement leads to higher morale maintenance than if older adults try to maintain social involvement. This theory is heavily criticized for having an escape clause - namely, that older adults who remain engaged in society are unsuccessful adjusters to old age.

Gradual withdrawal from society and relationships preserves social equilibrium and promotes self-reflection for elders who are freed from societal roles. It furnishes an orderly means for the transfer of knowledge, capital, and power from the older generation to the young. It makes it possible for society to continue functioning after valuable older members die. Weakness: There is no base of evidence or research to support this theory. Additionally, many older people desire to remain occupied and involved with society. Imposed withdrawal from society may be harmful to elders and society alike. This theory has been largely discounted by gerontologists.

Continuity Theory

Continuity theory is an elusive concept. On the one hand, to exhibit continuity can mean to remain the same, to be uniform, homogeneous, unchanging, even humdrum. This static view of continuity is not very applicable to human ageing. On the other hand, a dynamic view of continuity starts with the idea of a basic structure which persists over time, but it allows for a variety of changes to occur within the context provided by the basic structure. The basic structure is coherent: It has an orderly or logical relation of parts that is recognisably unique and that allows us to differentiate that structure from others. With the introduction of the concept of time, ideas such as direction, sequence, character development, and story line enter into the concept of continuity as it is applied to the evolution of a human being. In this paper, a dynamic concept of continuity is developed and applied to the issue of adaptation to normal ageing.

A central premise of continuity theory is that, in making adaptive choices, middle-aged and older adults attempt to preserve and maintain existing internal and external structures and that they prefer to accomplish this objective by using continuity (i.e., applying familiar strategies in familiar arenas of life). In middle and later life, adults are drawn by the weight of past experience to use continuity as a primary adaptive strategy for dealing with changes associated with normal ageing. To the extent that change builds upon, and has links to, the person's past, change is a part of continuity. As a result of both their own perceptions and pressures from the social environment, individuals who are adapting to normal ageing are both predisposed and motivated toward inner psychological continuity as well as outward continuity of social behaviour and circumstances.

Continuity theory views both internal and external continuity as robust adaptive strategies that are supported by both individual preference and social sanctions. Continuity theory consists of general adaptive principles that people who are normally ageing could be expected to follow, explanations of how these principles work, and a specification of general areas of life in which these principles could be expected to apply. Accordingly, continuity theory has enormous potential as a general theory of adaptation to individual ageing.

Age Stratification Theory

According to this theory, older adults born during different time periods form cohorts that define "age strata". There are two differences among strata: chronological age and historical experience. This theory makes two arguments.

1. Age is a mechanism for regulating behaviour and as a result determines access to positions of power.
2. Birth cohorts play an influential role in the process of social change.

Life Course Theory

According to this theory, which stems from the Life Course Perspective (Bengston and Allen, 1993), ageing occurs from birth to death. Ageing involves social, psychological, and biological processes. Additionally, ageing experiences are shaped by cohort and period effects. Also reflecting the life course focus, consider the implications for how societies might function when age-based norms vanish—a consequence of the deinstitutionalization of the life course— and suggest that these implications pose new challenges for theorizing ageing and the life course in postindustrial societies. Dramatic reductions in mortality, morbidity, and fertility over the past several decades have so shaken up the organisation of the life course and the nature of educational, work, family, and leisure experiences that it is now possible for individuals to become old in new ways. The configurations and content of other life stages are being altered as well, especially for women. In consequence, theories of age and ageing will need to be reconceptualized.

Cumulative Advantage/Disadvantage Theory

According to this theory, which was developed beginning in the 1960s by Derek Price and Robert Merton and elaborated on by several researchers such as Dale Dannefer, inequalities have a tendency to become more pronounced throughout the ageing process. A paradigm of this theory can be expressed in the adage "the rich get richer and the poor get poorer". Advantages and disadvantages in early life stages have a profound effect throughout the life span. However, advantages and disadvantages in middle adulthood have a direct influence on economic and health status in later life.

Constructionist Theories

A spectrum of theorizing in gerontology has emerged that is "anti-theoretical" in the sense that its common point of departure is to set aside or "bracket" taken-for-granted realities such as activity, disengagement, the life course, continuity, cumulative advantage, and the like, in order to foreground their construction, use, institutional articulations, and experiential consequences in everyday life. A decided interest in subjectivity, agency, discourses, and their ordinary practices leads the way. The goal is to document how members of speech communities theorize realities in their own terms and how this relates to communicative context. Meaning-making, performativity, categorization, agency, narrativity, discourse, practice, and structuration are leading concepts. Constructionist approaches range from the ideas and conceptual proclivities of European cultural gerontologists, to the growing international network of narrative gerontologists, and longstanding programs of research on selves, social interaction, and meaning-making. Important contributors are Sara Arber, Bill Bytheway, Jaber Gubrium, Haim Hazan, Stephen Katz, Sharon Kaufman, Gary Kenyon, Marc Luborsky, Sara Matthews, William Randall, Robert Rubinstein, Andrea Sankar, Christine Swane, and Julia Twigg, among many others.

Environmental Gerontology

The environmental gerontology is a knowledge area which aims Gerontology understand, analyze, modify and optimize the relationship between the ageing person and their physical and social environment, from interdisciplinary perspectives and approaches, covering different disciplines like psychogerontology, geography, urban planning, architecture and urban design, social policy, social work, sociology and other sciences at the end. In the 1930s (USA, Canada, UK and Germany), begin to emerge the first studies on Behavioural and Social Gerontology, and associated with deterministic explanations of the relationship between ageing and environment from genetic parameters and biological. In the 1970s and 1980s, theories of different researchers, as Kurt Lewin (living space model as a function of the person and the environment) and, mainly, M. Powell Lawton (1923-2001) (ecological adaptation model), based on the influence of the interactions between the older person and their environment (adaptation - ambient pressure), confirm the importance of the physical and social environment (objective and subjective) in the understanding of the ageing population and the possibility of improving the quality of life in old age. Environmental Gerontology strives to understand the socio-spatial implications of ageing and its complex relationship with the environment, from analysis at different scales : micro scales (home and family) and macro scales (neighbourhood, city, region), to enable social and environmental policies that enable successful ageing. Among the main contributions of the discipline are the contributions to ageing at home (ageing in place), and that older people prefer to age in their immediate environment (housing), where aspects such as spatial experience and place attachment are important for understanding the process.

Researchers Examples of Environmental Gerontology, interdisciplinarity discipline, leading researchers emphasize, as the psychologist and gerontologist M. Powell Lawton (1923-2001) and the architect and gerontologist Paul Gordon Windley PhD. (1941-2007). The latter was one of the pioneers of this field, which showed that a good architectural design can encourage independence and competence of the elderly with their environment. Windley was interested to know the implications of the built environment on ageing, highlighting the importance of encouraging a design built integrator. Between late 1970 and 1980 PG. Windley led an interdisciplinary team of architects and psychologists to examine how physical and social characteristics of small rural Kansas towns affected the quality of life of older people. Also noteworthy is the contribution of Graham D. Rowles, PhD. (1946-), one of the social geographers recognised worldwide for his contributions to the geography of ageing and environmental gerontology. Graham D. Rowles has been interested in the changing relationship between the elderly and their environment, first in rural (Appalachian Region) and later in urban areas, with special regard to the variety of residential and institutional environments. It is expected that in coming years the ageing population worldwide incrementantará interest in environmental gerontology studies, due to social, economic, cultural and environmental factors associated with this phenomenon in cities, mainly in countries development.

Theorising Social Gerontology: The case of Social Philosophies of Age

There has been an unprecedented rise and consolidation of theoretical publications relating to age and ageing that has cut right across and through social and human sciences (Bury 1995). Social Gerontology is multidisciplinary and is the principal instrument of orthodox theorising about old age particularly in US, UK and Australasian academies (Phillipson 1998; Biggs and Powell 2001).

Turner (1989) and Phillipson (1998) both acknowledge that social theory must be brought into the frame of analysing old age. This paper faces up to this challenge and is concerned with highlighting the major theoretical ideas which have informed social understanding of age and ageing in recent years. The analysis of the major theoretical ideas which have influenced understanding of social gerontology in recent years: functionalism, marxism, feminism and postmodernism. It is important to illuminate the contrasting theories of age and ageing, as research papers in mainstream social gerontology have not attempted to review these theories in an attempt to understand the philosophical dimensions of human experience.

Social Theory and the Rise of Functionalist Accounts of Age and Ageing

The broad pedigree of social theories of age can be located to the early post-war years with the concern about the consequences of demographic change and the potential shortage of 'younger' workers in USA and UK. Social gerontology emerged as a field of study which attempted to respond to the social policy implications of demographic change (Vincent 1996). Such disciplines were shaped by significant external forces. First, by state intervention to achieve specific outcomes in health and social policy; secondly, by a political and economic environment which viewed an ageing population as creating a 'social problem' for society (Jones, 1993). This impinged mainly upon the creation of functionalist accounts of age and ageing primarily in US academies. Functionalist sociology dominated the sociological landscape in the USA from the 1930's up until 1960s (Blaikie 1999). Talcott Parsons was a key exponent of general functionalist thought and argued that society needed certain functions in order to maintain its well-being: the stability of the family; circulation of elites in education drawing from a "pool of talent" (Giddens 1993). Society was seen as akin to a biological organism – all the parts (education/family/religion/government) in the system working together in order for society to function with equilibrium (Giddens 1993).

The important point to note is that theories often mirror the norms and values of their creators and their social times, reflecting culturally dominant views of what should be the appropriate way to analyse social phenomena. The two theories which dominated American gerontology in the 1950s of Disengagement and Activity theory follow this normative pattern. Both disengagement and activity theories postulate not only how individual behaviour changes with ageing, but also imply how it should change.

This was seen in the United States via the dominance of the structural-functionalist school via the work of 'disengagement theorists' (Phillipson 1998). Such major protagonists of disengagement theory was Cumming and Henry (1961) who looked at how older people should disengage from work roles and prepare for the ultimate disengagement: death (Powell 2000). There are two broad schools of thought within the functionalist umbrella theory: Disengagement theory and Activity theory. The former is the most controversial. Disengagement theory is associated with Cumming and Henry (1961) and proposes that gradual withdrawal of older people from work roles and social relationships is both an inevitable and natural process:

> *'...withdrawal may be accompanied from the outset by an increased preoccupation with himself: certain institutions may make it easy for him' (Cumming and Henry 1961: 14).*

For this variant of functionalism, this process benefits society, since it means that the death of individual society members does not prevent the ongoing functioning of the social system. Cumming and Henry (1961) further propose that the process of disengagement is inevitable, rewarding and universal process of mutual withdrawal of the individual and society from each other with advancing age – was normal and to be expected. This theory argued that it was beneficial for both the ageing individual and society that such disengagement takes place in order to minimise the social disruption caused at an ageing person's eventual death (Neurgarten 1998).

Retirement is a good illustration of disengagement process, enabling the ageing person to be freed of the responsibilities of an occupation and to pursue other roles not necessarily aligned to full-pay of economic generation. Through disengagement, Cumming and Henry argued, society anticipated the loss of ageing people through death and brought "new blood" into full participation within the social world (cited in Katz 1996). Bronley (1966: 136) further portends 'in old age, the individual is normally disengaged from the main streams of economic and community activity'. Not surprisingly for Bromley (1966 quoted in Bond and Coleman 1993: 44)) 'The (disengagement) process is graded to suit the declining biological and psychological capacities of the individual and the needs of society'.

A number of critiques exist: firstly, this theory condones indifference towards 'old age' and social problems (Bond & Coleman 1993). Secondly, disengagement theory underplays the cultural and economic structures have in creating, with intentional consequences of, withdrawal. This theory engages in sociological reductionism in presupposing that 'old age' is bound up with the explanation of 'disengagement' and engages in 'functional teleology' (Giddens 1993) in attempting to explain old age in terms of its effects or 'death'. Also, Kastenbaum (1993) claims disengagement theory represented a threat to the promotion of a positive and involved lifestyle for ageing persons across the lifecourse.

Both advocate a retired old age as a 'natural' period of transition. In order to legitimise its generalisations, disengagement theory self-praised itself to objective and value-free rigour of research methods: survey and questionnaire methods of gerontological inquiry. In a sense, by arguing for 'disengagement' from work roles under the guise of objectivity is a very powerful argument for governments to legitimise boundaries of who can work and who cannot based on age (Powell 1999).

Activity theory is a counterpoint to disengagement theory, since it claims a successful 'old age' is can be achieved by maintaining roles and relationships. Activity theory actually pre-dates disengagement theory. In the 1950s Havighurst and Albrecht (1953 cited in Katz 1996) insisted ageing can be lively and creative experience. Any loss of roles, activities or relationships within old age, should be replaced by new roles or activities to ensure happiness, value consensus and well-being. For activity theorists, disengagement is not a natural process as advocated by Cumming and Henry. For activity theorists, disengagement theory is inherently ageist and does not promote in any shape or form 'positive ageing'. Thus, "activity" was seen as an ethical and academic response to the disengagement thesis which re-casted retirement as joyous and mobile.

Nevertheless, Activity theory neglects issues of power, inequality and conflict between age groups. An apparent 'value consensus' may reflect the interests of powerful and dominant groups within society who find it advantageous to have age power relations organised in such a way. Whilst Phillipson (1998) sees such functionalist schools as important in shaping social theory responses to them, such functionalist theories 'impose' a sense of causality on ageing by implying you will either 'disengage' or will be 'active'.

This can be argued to be a form of 'academic imperialism' where the activities of ageing people are dictated to and from theoretical models which reconstruct age and ageing along lines of enforced experiences. They are very macro orientated and fail to resolve tensions within age-group relations which impinge upon the inter-connection of 'race', class and gender with age.

Political Economy

As an intellectual backdrop against such functionalist theoretical dominance, Political Economy of Old Age emerged as a fashionable theory in both sides of the Atlantic, drawing from Marxian insights in analysing the capitalist complexity of modern society and how old age was socially constructed to foster the needs of the economy (Estes 1979). This critical branch of Marxist gerontology grew as a direct response to the hegemonic dominance of structural functionalism in the form of disengagement theory, the biomedical paradigm and world economic crises of the 1970s. As Phillipson (1998) points out in the UK huge forms of social expenditure were allocated to older people. Consequently, not only were older people viewed in medical terms but in resource terms by governments. This brought a new perception to attitudes to age and ageing. As Phillipson (1998: 17) teases out:

'Older people came to be viewed as a burden on western economies, with demographic change... seen as creating intolerable pressures on public expenditure'.

A major concern of 'political economy of old age' was to challenge both the theoretical dominance of functionalist thought and biomedical models of age and ageing. The political economy approach wanted to have an understanding of the character and significance of variations in the treatment of the aged, and to relates these to polity, economy and society in advanced capitalist society.

The major focus is an interpretation of the relationship between ageing and the economic structure. In the USA, Political Economy theory was pioneered via the work of Estes (1979), and Estes, Swan and Gerard (1982). Similarly, in the UK, the work of Walker (1981), Townsend (1981) and Phillipson (1982) added a critical sociological dimension to understanding age and ageing in advanced capitalist societies. For Estes, Swan and Gerard (1982) in the U.S.A, the class structure is perceived as the major determinant of the socio-economic position of older people in advanced capitalist society. For Estes (1979) political economy challenges the ideology of older people as belonging to a homogenous group unaffected by dominant structures in society. Estes (1979) claims political economy focuses upon an analysis of the state in contemporary societal formations. Here, we can see how Marxism is inter-connected to this theory. Estes looks to how the state decides and dictates who is allocated resources and who is not. This impinges upon retirement and subsequent pension schemes. As Phillipson (1982) points out, the retirement experience is linked to the timing of economic reduction of wages and enforced withdrawal from work has made many older people in the UK in a financially insecure position. Hence, the state can make and break the fortunes of its populace. Consequently, current governmental discourses of cutting public expenditure on pensions and increasingly calling for private provision legitimises ideological mystification stereotypes of "burden" groups and populations. In the USA, Estes, Swann and Gerard (1982) claims that the state is using its power to transfer responsibility of welfare provision from the state and onto individuals. Indeed, blaming people for non-provision of own savings obscures and mystifies that real economic problems derive from the capitalist mode of production and political decisions (Powell 1999).

American Political Economy then is a 'grand' theory drawing from Marxian historiography, locates the determining explanatory factors in the structure of society and focuses upon welfare and its contribution to the institutional decommodification of retired older people. Negative attitudes towards older people and impoverished position are best explained by the latter's loss of social worth brought about by their loss of a productive role in American society that puts premium on production (Estes et al. 1982).

Similarly, this is an argument reiterated by critical gerontological writers in the U.K on the social position of older people. In particular, Townsend (1981) observes that society creates the social problems of old age through 'structured dependency' embedded in institutional agism through lack of material resources via poverty, retirement policies, negative consequences of residential care, and passive forms of community care services. Townsend focuses on a 'structural' perspective of 'rules and resources' governing older people in advanced capitalism and wider social system. Importantly, Townsend claims is approach as:

'one whereby society is held to create the framework of institutions and rules within which the general problem of the elderly emerge or, indeed, "manufactured". In the everyday management of the economy and the administration and development of social institutions the position of the elderly subtly changed and shaped'. (Townsend 1981: 9)

Similarly, Walker (1981) argued for a 'political economy of old age' in order to understand the position of older people. In particular, Walker (1981: 77) paid attention to the 'social creation of dependency' and how social structure and relations espoused by the mode of production which helps intensify structural class marginalisation. In a similar vein, Phillipson (1982, 1986) considers how capitalism helps socially construct the social marginality of older people in key areas such as welfare delivery. The important argument to be made is that inequalities in the distribution of resources should be understood in relation to the distribution of power within society, rather than in terms of individual variation.

Feminist Gerontology

Coupled with this, there has been an acceleration of Feminist insights into understanding age and gender as key identity variables of analysis (Arber & Ginn 1991 and 1995). There are two important issues: first, power imbalances shape theoretical construction; second, a group's place within the social structure influences theoretical attention they are afforded. Henceforth, because older women tend to occupy a position of lower class status, especially in terms of economic status than men of all ages and younger women, they are given less theoretical attention. According to Acker (1988 cited in Arber and Ginn 1991) in all known societies the relations of distribution and production are influenced by gender and thus take on a gendered meaning. Gender relations of distribution in capitalist society are historically rooted and are transformed as the means of production change. Similarly, age relations are linked to the capitalist mode of production and relations of distribution. "Wages" take on a specific meaning depending on age. For example, teenagers work for less money than adults, who in turn work for less money than middle-aged adults. Further, young children rely on personal relations with family figures such as parents. Many older people rely on resources distributed by the state.

There is a "double standard of ageing" with age in women having particularly strong negative connotations. Older women are viewed as unworthy of respect or consideration (Arber and Ginn 1991).

Catherine Itzin sees the double standard of ageing as arising from the sets of conventional expectations as to age-pertinent attitudes and roles for each sex which apply in patriarchal society. These are defined by Itzin as a male and a female 'chronology', socially defined and sanctioned so that the experience of prescribed roles is sanctioned by disapproval. Male chronology hinges on employment, but a woman's age status is defined in terms of events in the reproductive cycle.

Arguably, Arber & Ginn (1991) claim because women's value is exercised the awareness of a loss of a youthful appearance brings social devaluation; vulnerability to pressure is penetrated by cosmeticisation. Daly (cited in Arber and Ginn 1991) draws a mirror image between western cosmetic surgery and the genital mutilation carried out in some African societies: both cultured practices demonstrate the pressure on women to comply with male standards of desirability and the extent of male domination. For older black women, the ideal of 'beauty' portrayed by white male culture was doubly distant and alienating, until growing black consciousness subverted disparaging language and argued 'black is beautiful'.

Arber and Ginn (1991) claim patriarchal society exercises power through the chronologies of employment and reproduction, and through the sexualised promotion of a 'youthful' appearance in women. As a result, many older women suffer from a 'double jeopardy' thesis through age and sexual discrimination.

Postmodern Gerontology

In addition to these broad and macro based theories, there has been a vast interest in Postmodern perspectives of age and ageing identity underpinned by discourses of "better lifestyles" and increased leisure opportunities for older people due to healthier lifestyles and increased use of bio-technologies to facilitate the longevity of human experiences (Blaikie 1999; Featherstone & Hepworth 1993, Featherstone & Wernick 1995 and Powell & Biggs 2002). The intellectual roots of 'postmodern gerontology' derive from Jaber F. Gubrium's (1975) sociological analysis of the discovery and conceptual elaboration of Alzheimer's disease in the USA and the establishment of boundaries between 'normal' and pathological ageing, old age is seen as a "mask" which conceals the essential identity of the person beneath. The view of the ageing process as a mask/disguise concealing the essentially youthful self beneath is one which appears to be a popular argument (Featherstone & Hepworth 1989, 1993). When asked at the age of 79 to describe what it felt like to be old, the author J.B. Priestley replied:

'It is as though, walking down Shaftesbury Avenue as a fairly young man, I was suddenly kidnapped, rushed into a theatre and made to don the grey hair, the wrinkles and the other attributes of age, then wheeled on stage. Behind the appearance of age I am the same person, with the same thoughts, as when I was younger' (Puner 1978: 7).

There are two underlying issues for Featherstone and Hepworth (1993) which should be understood as the basis for understanding postmodern gerontology. Firstly, the image of the mask alerts social gerontologists to the possibility that a tension exists between the external appearance of the body and face and functional capacities and the internal or subjective sense of experience of personal identity which is likely to become prominent as ageing traverses through the lifecourse.

Secondly, older people are usually 'fixed' to roles without resources which does not do justice to the richness of their individual experiences and multi-facets of their personalities. Idealistically, Featherstone and Hepworth argue that a postmodern perspective would deconstruct such realities and age should be viewed as fluid with possibilities not constrained by medical model decline discourses.

According to Powell and Biggs (2000) the direct use of new technologies to either modify the appearance or performance of ageing identity is symptomatic of postmodern times. To paraphrase Morris (1998) technologies here hold out the promise of 'utopian bodies'. Indeed, Haraway's (1991) (cited in Powell and Biggs 2002) original reference to cyborgic fusion of biological and machine entities has been enthusiastically taken up by postmodern gerontology. The list of technologies available extends beyond traditional prosthesis to include virtual identities created by and reflected in the growing number of 'silver surfers' using the Internet as a free-floating form of identity management. Thus Featherstone and Wernick (1995: 3) trill that it is now possible to' Re-code the body itself 'as biomedical and information technologies make available' the capacity to alter not just the meaning, but the very material infrastructure of the body. Bodies can be re-shaped, remade, fused with machines, empowered through technological devices and extensions'.

Coupled with this, the control of the ageing body had been enhanced by external constraining virtue of the corset, contemporary shaping has involved active working, through exercise and diet. The multiplication of magazine articles, self-help manuals, diet and exercise clubs, extending through midlife and beyond also bear witness to the popularity of attempts to work on the self in this way.

The use of diet and exercise as techniques specifically related to later adulthood, is closely related to the growth of leisure and a lifestyle approach to the creation of late life identities (Turner 1989; Powell & Biggs 2000 and 2002). It therefore resonates beyond the simple fuelling and repair of the bodily machine to include a continual re-creation of the self within a particular social discourse. This discourse closely associates the construction of a healthy lifestyle with positive self-identity.

Indeed, closely related to postmodern gerontology is also a small body of knowledge pertaining to 'Foucauldian gerontology' deriving in Canadian (Katz 1996; Frank 1998) and UK (Biggs & Powell 1999 and 2000; Powell & Biggs 2000, 2002; Powell & Cook 2000; Wahidin & Powell 2001) academies. This Foucauldian theoretical development attempts to understand age and ageing through conceptual exploration of power/knowledge and how surveillance practices from professionals such as 'medics' or 'social workers' further marginalize, normalize and provide shape to the experiences of older people (Powell & Biggs 2000).

Conclusion

These theories have been at the forefront of understanding old age in US, UK and Australasian academies. Taken together, these theoretical currents have been influential in providing social gerontology with a rich social dimension. Such social theories have been used also to analyse pressing social issues such as, elder abuse, the gendered nature of age, the politics of power relations between older people and state/society and community care. The purpose of this paper has been to amalgamate the key ideas of social theories of age in order to stress the importance of social philosophy to understanding age and ageing.

Social Demography

The word demography was used for the first time by A.Guillard a Frenchman in his book Elements de Statistique Humanine. It is a statistical study of population composition, distribution and trends. It is the analysis of population variables which includes stock and flow. The national census is the source of stock variable which is carried out periodically in most of the countries. The flow variables are the components of population change which include birth and death registrations.

Migration

The movement of people from one place to the other to stay on for a considerable period of time for various reasons is known as migration. It is one of the three components of the population change the other two being mortality and fertility. Migration is associated with the socio-economic development of the country. In India one of the side-effects of unprecedented population growth is industrialization and economic development which helped in a rapid increase in internal migratory movements. M.S.A Rao has written about different types of migration.

Internal Migration: The movement of people from one region to another within the country. In internal migration there are different forms of migration such as " Rural-to-rural " Urban-to-urban migration " Rural to urban migration " Urban to rural migration. International migration: Migration from one country to another country.

Emigration: It refers to the movement out of the particular country.

Immigration: It refers to the movement into a particular country.

Out Migration: It is the movement out of a particular territory within a country.

In Migration: It is the movement into a particular region within a country.

Migration Stream: It refers to the total number of moves made during a given migration interval which have a common area of origin and common area of destination.

Gross and Net Migration: It is the total number of arrivals of migrants and departures of emigrants is known as gross migration. Net migration is the difference between the total number of persons who arrive and the total number of persons who leave.

Theories of Demography

Malthus

The essay on the principle of population an important work of Malthus is a landmark in the history of population studies. The theme of the Essay was mainly to argue that the tendency of the population to grow faster in relation to its means of subsistence has led to human misery and placed several obstacles in the path of human progress. In 1803, Malthus published the second edition of his essay, a much expanded and changed edition which can't really be called a re print of the 1797 essay, for in the new edition the emphasis was more on arguments against the poor laws than on country arguments against the opinions of Condorcet and Godwin.

Neo- Maltusian Theory

Neo-Malthusians maintain that although the gloomy predictions of Malthus may have been pre-mature they are basically correct.

According to Anti Malthusians' world's resources are adequate for a much larger population. Exploitation not over population is the basic cause of world hunger.

Demographic Transition Theory

Two different interpretations have been given for this theory. One by Frank Notestein says that every country passes through three stages of population growth; 1. High birth rate and high death rate ii.High birth rate and low death rate (population explosion) iii.Low birth rate and low death rate. In western nations the desire for high standard of living led to the reductions in the birthrate.These nations are approaching a new equilibrium with both birthrates and death rates quite low and little population growth. This is explained by the theory of demographic transition -the theory that industrial and commercial development first cuts the death rate but creates a desire for smaller families and eventually cuts the birthrate.

The other theory is given by C.P Blacker.There are five phrases in this theory.

i. High stationary phase marked by high fertility and mortality rate.
ii. Early expanding phase marked by high fertility and high but declining mortality.
iii. Late Expanding phase with declining fertility but mortality declining more rapidly.
iv. Low stationary phase with low fertility and equally low mortality.
v. Declining phase with low mortality, low fertility and an excess of deaths over births.

Optimum Population Theory

According to Canan the propounder of this theory population must grow upto certain desired level after which further growth is harmful. The two important principles of this theory are:

1. When there is an increase in population than the ratio between the total population and the working population remains almost constant.
2. When at a point of time the population of a country increases the natural resources capital and technical know how do not change with the result that after sometime the law of diminishing returns begins to operate. This law provides that for maximum production all the sources of production should be combined in that proper ratio than it shall not be possible to have maximum production.

Population Policy

A policy is a plan of action, statement of aims and ideals especially one made by a government, a political party, a business company etc. Population policy is an effort to affect the size, structure and distribution or characteristics of population. In its broader range it includes efforts to regulate economic and social conditions which are likely to have demographic consequences.

National Population Policy

The immediate objective of this new policy is to address the unmet needs of contraception, health infrastructure, health personnel and to provide integrated service delivery for basic reproductive and child health care. The medium term objective is to bring the total fertility rated to replacement level by 2010. The long term objective is to achieve a stable population by 2045. In pursuance of these objectives 14 National Socio- Demographic goals are formulated to be achieved by 2010. The important goals are:

1. Making school education compulsory and to reduce the dropouts.
2. Reduce infant-mortality rate to 30 per 1000 live births.
3. Reduce maternal mortality rate to below 100 per 100000 live births.
4. Promote delayed marriage.
5. Achieve 80% institutional deliveries.
6. Prevent and control communicable diseases.
7. Promote vigorously the small family norm to achieve replacement levels of Total Fertility Rate.

The policy speaks about the formation of National Commission of Population under the chairmanship of the Prime -Minister to monitor and implement population policy and to guide planning implementations. The policy also suggests some promotional and motivational measures to promote adoption of the small family norm. The main features of the policy are

1. Reward panchayats and Zila Parishads for promoting small family norms.
2. Incentives to adopt two child norms.
3. Couples below poverty line, having sterilization with not more than two living children will be eligible for health insurance plan.
4. Strengthening abortion facility scheme.

Chapter 4

Population Ageing

Population ageing is a phenomenon that occurs when the median age of a country or region rises due to rising life expectancy and/or declining birth rates. There has been, initially in the more economically developed countries (MEDC) but also more recently in less economically developed countries (LEDC), an increase in life expectancy which causes the ageing of populations. This is the case for every country in the world except the 18 countries designated as "demographic outliers" by the UN. For the entirety of recorded human history, the world has never seen as aged a population as currently exists globally.

The UN predicts the rate of population ageing in the 21st century will exceed that of the previous century. Countries vary significantly in terms of the degree, and the pace, of these changes, and the UN expects populations that began ageing later to have less time to adapt to the many implications of these changes.

Overview

Population ageing is a shift in the distribution of a country's population towards older ages. This is usually reflected in an increase in the population's mean and median ages, a decline in the proportion of the population composed of children, and a rise in the proportion of the population that is elderly.

Population ageing is widespread across the world. It is most advanced in the most highly developed countries. The Oxford Institute of Population Ageing, however, concluded that population ageing has slowed considerably in Europe and will have the greatest future impact in Asia, especially as Asia is in stage five of the demographic transition model.

Among the countries currently classified by the United Nations as more developed (with a total population of 1.2 billion in 2005), the overall median age rose from 29.0 in 1950 to 37.3 in 2000, and is forecast to rise to 45.5 by 2050. The corresponding figures for the world as a whole are 23.9 in 1950, 26.8 in 2000, and 37.8 in 2050. In Japan, one of the world's most quickly ageing countries, in 1950 there were 9.3 people under 20 for every person over 65. By 2025 this ratio is forecast to be 0.59 people under 20 for every person over 65.

Population ageing arises from two (possibly related) demographic effects: increasing longevity and declining fertility. An increase in longevity raises the average age of the population by increasing the numbers of surviving older people. A decline in fertility reduces the number of babies, and as the effect continues, the numbers of younger people in general also reduce.

Of these two forces, it is declining fertility that is the largest contributor to population ageing in the world today. More specifically, it is the large decline in the overall fertility rate over the last half century that is primarily responsible for the population ageing in the world's most developed countries. Because many developing countries are going through faster fertility transitions, they will experience even faster population ageing than the currently developed countries in the future.

The rate at which the population ages is likely to increase over the next three decades; however, few countries know whether their older populations are living the extra years of life in good or poor health. A "compression of morbidity" would imply reduced disability in old age, whereas an expansion would see an increase in poor health with increased longevity. Another option has been posed for a situation of "dynamic equilibrium". This is crucial information for governments if the limits of lifespan continue to increase indefinitely, as some researchers believe it will. The World Health Organisation's suite of household health studies is working to provide the needed health and well-being evidence, including, for example the World Health Survey, and the Study on Global Ageing and Adult Health (SAGE). These surveys cover 308,000 respondents aged 18+ years and 81,000 aged 50+ years from 70 countries.

The Global Ageing Survey, exploring attitudes, expectations and behaviours towards later life and retirement, directed by George Leeson, and covering 44,000 people aged 40–80 in 24 countries from across the globe has revealed that many people are now fully aware of the ageing of the world's population and the implications which this will have for their lives and the lives of their children and grandchildren.

Canada has the highest per capita immigration rate in the world, partly to counter population ageing. The C. D. Howe Institute, a conservative think tank, has suggested that immigration cannot be used as a viable mean for countering population ageing. This conclusion is also seen in the work of other scholars. Demographers Peter McDonald and Rebecca Kippen comment, "[a]s fertility sinks further below replacement level, increasingly higher levels of annual net migration will be required to maintain a target of even zero population growth".

Ageing Around the World

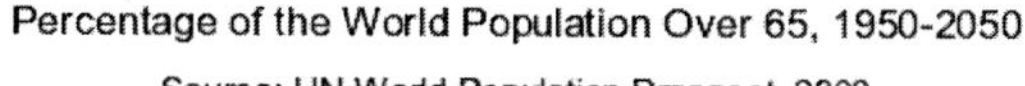

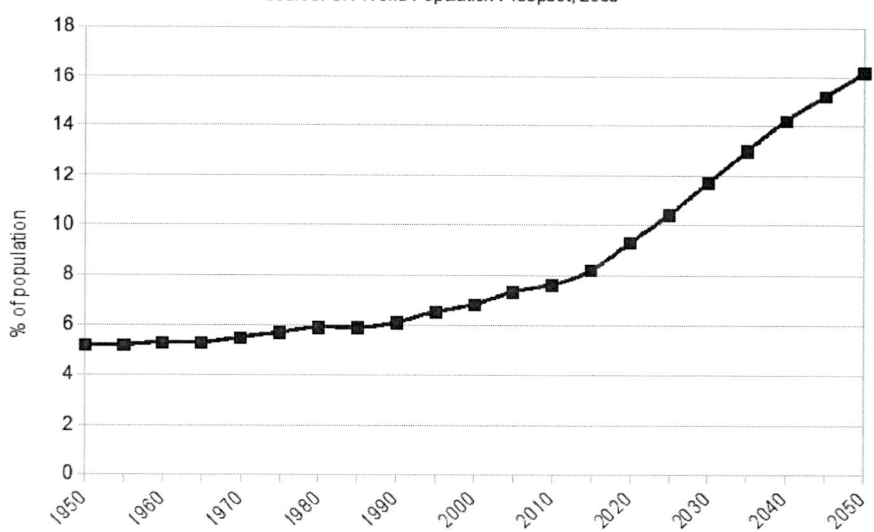

Figure: *Percentage of world population over 65*

Asia and Europe are the two regions where a significant number of countries face population ageing in the near future. In these regions within twenty years many countries will face a situation where the largest population cohort will be those over 65 and average age approach 50 years old.

The Oxford Institute of Ageing is an institution looking at global population ageing. Its research reveals that many of the views of global ageing are based on myths and that there will be considerable opportunities for the world as its population matures. The Institute's Director, Professor Sarah Harper highlights in her book Ageing Societies the implications for work, families, health, education, and technology of the ageing of the world's population.

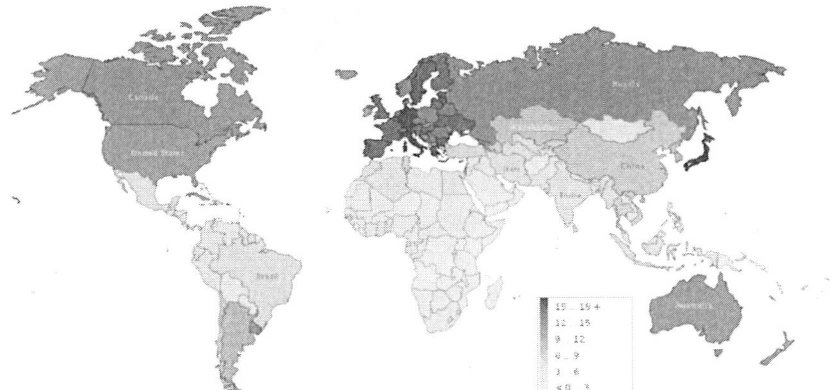

Figure: *This map illustrates global trends in ageing by depicting the percentage of each country's population that is over the age of 65. The more developed countries also have older populations as their citizens live longer. Less developed countries have much younger populations. An interactive version of the map is available here.*

Most of the developed world (with the notable exception of the United States) now has sub-replacement fertility levels, and population growth now depends largely on immigration together with population momentum which arises from previous large generations now enjoying longer life expectancy.

Of the roughly 150,000 people who die each day across the globe, about two thirds—100,000 per day—die of age-related causes. In industrialized nations, the proportion is much higher, reaching 90%.

Well-Being and Social Policies

The economic effects of an ageing population are considerable. Older people have higher accumulated savings per head than younger people, but spend less on consumer goods. Depending on the age ranges at which the changes occur, an ageing population may thus result in lower interest rates and the economic benefits of lower inflation. Some economists (Japan) see advantages in such changes, notably the opportunity to progress automation and technological development without causing unemployment. They emphasize a shift from GDP to personal well-being.

However population ageing also increases some categories of expenditure, including some met from public finances. The largest area of expenditure in many countries is now health care, whose cost is likely to increase dramatically as populations age. This would present governments with hard choices between higher taxes, including a possible reweighing of tax from earnings to consumption, and a reduced government role in providing health care. However, recent studies in some countries demonstrate the dramatic rising costs of health care are more attributable to rising drug and doctor costs, and higher use of diagnostic testing by all age groups, and not by the ageing population as is often claimed.

The second-largest expenditure of most governments is education and these expenses will tend to fall with an ageing population, especially as fewer young people would probably continue into tertiary education as they would be in demand as part of the work force.

Social security systems have also begun to experience problems. Earlier defined benefit pension systems are experiencing sustainability problems due to the increased longevity. The extension of the pension period was not paired with an extension of the active labour period or a rise in pension contributions, resulting in a decline of replacement ratios. In recent years, many countries have adopted policies to strengthen the financial sustainability of pension systems, although the challenges regarding pension adequacy remain.

Ageing in the American Workforce

The ageing workforce (also The Silver Tsunami) refers to the rise in the median age of the United States workforce, to levels unseen since the passage of the Social Security Act of 1935. It is projected that by the year 2020, about 25% of the U.S. workforce will be composed of older workers (ages 55 and over). While many factors contribute to the ageing workforce, the Post-World War II baby boom created an unusually large birth cohort for the U.S. population, resulting in a large ageing population today. This phenomena has many short-term and long-term implications, affecting many areas, including the U.S. economy, society and public health.

Projections

According to the Bureau of Labour Statistics, as of April 2014, the labour force participation rate was 62.8%. The overall labour force participation rate is expected to decline for the remainder of the decade, projected to fall to 62.5% in 2020. By the year 2020, the subpopulation of older adults in the United States is expected to reach 97.8 million people, comprising 28.7% percent of the entire U.S. population, a rise from the 24.7% in 2010. This increase in proportion of older adults can be attributed to the entire Baby Boomer cohort joining the older adult population (ages 55+) by 2020.

It is projected that by 2020, the proportion of the U.S. labour force that is composed of older adults will be 25.2%. This continues a trend in increasing rates of older adults remaining in the workforce, as the rates were 13.1% in 2000 and 19.5% in 2010. A complementary trend that follows this is the increasing median age of the U.S. workforce. By 2020, the workforce is expected to have a median age of 42.8, which will be an increase from 39.3 in 2000 and 41.7 in 2010.

A further factor contributing to an ageing workforce is the fact that employment rates among older workers are increasing. The rate of people who continue working after they are 65 is relatively high in the US, if compared to other developed countries. For example, in 2011, 16.7% among people aged 65 and over and 29.9% among 65-69 were employed in the US, while the corresponding rates in the EU were only 4.8 and 10.5%.

Impacts

With continuing trends of an ageing American workforce and a declining labour force participation rate, there may be many consequences arising from this phenomena. The impending repercussions from a large ageing workforce entering retirement has led some to call this situation "The Silver Tsunami." The Silver Tsunami can have a profound effect on many areas of life.

Economy

Due to a declining labour participation rate, there is expected to be a shortage of workers in the U.S. workforce. Projections show that the demand for labour needed now is not being fulfilled, and the gap between labour needed and labour available will continue to expand over the future. Owing to the differences in population size between the Baby Boomers and the following younger generations, there has been negative growth in the working age population. The retirement of members of the ageing workforce could also possibly result in shortages of skilled labour. A majority of experienced utility workers and hospital caregivers, for example, will be eligible for retirement.

Social Security Benefits

The U.S. federal social security system functions through the taxation of large numbers of young workers, in order to support smaller numbers of older dependents. A diminishing workforce, coupled with growing numbers of longer-living elderly can deplete the social security system. The Social Security Administration estimates that the old age dependency ratio (people ages 65+ divided by people ages 20–64) in 2080 will be over 40%, compared to the 20% old age dependency ratio in 2005. Increasing life expectancies of the older population will not only result in decreases in Social Security Benefits, but also devalues private and public pension programs. The dearth of funds supplying programs such as social security and Medicare may be a contributing factor for adults to delay retirement and to continue working.

Occupational Safety and Health

Because of the many older adults opting to remain in the U.S. workforce, many studies have been done to investigate whether the older workers are at greater risk of occupational injury than their younger counterparts. Due to the physical declines associated with ageing, older adults tend to exhibit losses in eyesight, hearing and physical strength. Data shows that older adults have low overall injury rates compared to all age groups, but are more likely to suffer from fatal and more severe occupational injuries. Of all fatal occupational injuries in 2005, older workers accounted for 26.4%, despite only comprising 16.4% of the workforce at the time. Age increases in fatality rates in occupational injury are more pronounced for workers over the age of 65. The return to work for older workers is also extended; older workers experience a greater median number of lost work days and longer recovery times than younger workers. Some common occupational injuries and illnesses for older workers include arthritis and fractures. Among older workers, hip fractures are a large concern, given the severity of these injuries.

Health Care

With larger numbers of older adults, there will be an increased need for geriatric care. Older adults will have to deal with more chronic diseases; older adults who have worked in the construction industry have shown high rates of chronic diseases. Experts suggest that the number of geriatricians will have to triple to meet the demands of the rising elderly. There is expected be a similarly increased demand in other healthcare professionals, such as nurses, physical therapists and dentists. In addition, there is expected to be an increasing demand over common geriatric care consumption needs, such as medications, joint replacements and cardiovascular operations.

Society

The Silver Tsunami can potentially change American society as a whole. Many companies use an antiquated system, in which older, tenured workers get raises and benefits over time, eventually hitting retirement. With larger numbers of older workers in the workforce, this model is possibly unsustainable. In addition, perceptions of older adults in society will change, as the elderly are living longer lives and more active than before. Some state that society faces a cultural ageism in the perceptions about older adults, which will change over time.

Demographic Transition

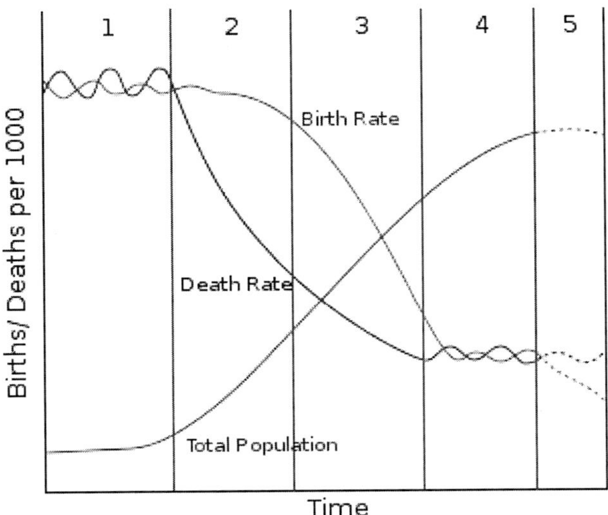

Figure: *A plot of the demographic transition model, including stage 5*

Demographic transition (DT) refers to the transition from high birth and death rates to low birth and death rates as a country develops from a pre-industrial to an industrialized economic system. This is typically demonstrated through a demographic transition model (DTM). The theory is based on an interpretation of demographic history developed in 1929 by the American demographer Warren Thompson (1887–1973). Thompson observed changes, or transitions, in birth and death rates in industrialized societies over the previous 200 years. Most developed countries are in stage 3 or 4 of the model; the majority of developing countries have reached stage 2 or stage 3. The major (relative) exceptions are some poor countries, mainly in sub-Saharan Africa and some Middle Eastern countries, which are poor or affected by government policy or civil strife, notably Pakistan, Palestinian Territories, Yemen and Afghanistan.

Although this model predicts ever decreasing fertility rates, recent data show that beyond a certain level of development fertility rates increase again.

A correlation matching the demographic transition has been established; however, it is not certain whether industrialization and higher incomes lead to lower population or if lower populations lead to industrialization and higher incomes. In countries that are now developed this demographic transition began in the 18th century and continues today. In less developed countries, this demographic transition started later and is still at an earlier stage.

Summary of the Theory

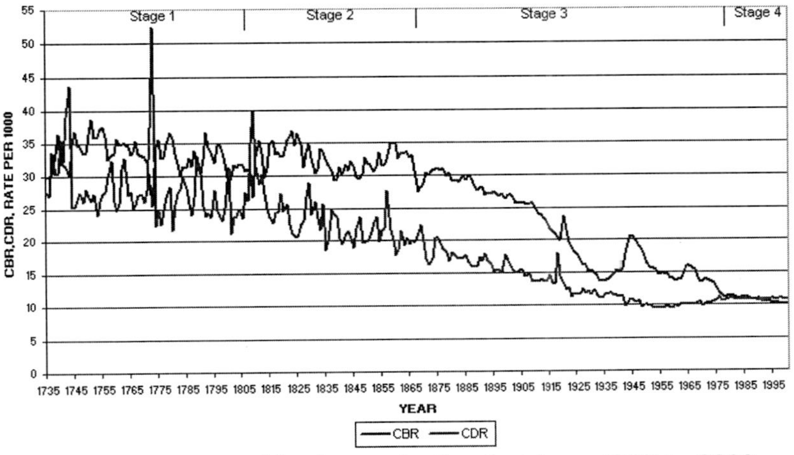

Figure: *Demographic change in Sweden from 1735 to 2000.*

Red line: crude death rate (CDR), blue line: (crude) birth rate (CBR)

The Transition Involves Four Stages, or Possibly Five.

- In stage one, pre-industrial society, death rates and birth rates are high and roughly in balance. All human populations are believed to have had this balance until the late 18th century, when this balance ended in Western Europe. In fact, growth rates were less than 0.05% at least since the Agricultural Revolution over 10,000 years ago. Birth and death rates both tend to be very high in this stage. Because both rates are approximately in balance, population growth is typically very slow in stage one.
- In stage two, that of a developing country, the death rates drop rapidly due to improvements in food supply and sanitation, which increase life spans and reduce disease. The improvements specific to food supply typically include selective breeding and crop rotation and farming techniques. Other improvements generally include access to technology, basic healthcare, and education. For example, numerous improvements in public health reduce mortality, especially childhood mortality. Prior

to the mid-20th century, these improvements in public health were primarily in the areas of food handling, water supply, sewage, and personal hygiene. One of the variables often cited is the increase in female literacy combined with public health education programs which emerged in the late 19th and early 20th centuries. In Europe, the death rate decline started in the late 18th century in northwestern Europe and spread to the south and east over approximately the next 100 years. Without a corresponding fall in birth rates this produces an imbalance, and the countries in this stage experience a large increase in population.

- In stage three, birth rates fall due to access to contraception, increases in wages, urbanization, a reduction in subsistence agriculture, an increase in the status and education of women, a reduction in the value of children's work, an increase in parental investment in the education of children and other social changes. Population growth begins to level off. The birth rate decline in developed countries started in the late 19th century in northern Europe. While improvements in contraception do play a role in birth rate decline, it should be noted that contraceptives were not generally available nor widely used in the 19th century and as a result likely did not play a significant role in the decline then. It is important to note that birth rate decline is caused also by a transition in values; not just because of the availability of contraceptives.
- During stage four there are both low birth rates and low death rates. Birth rates may drop to well below replacement level as has happened in countries like Germany, Italy, and Japan, leading to a shrinking population, a threat to many industries that rely on population growth. As the large group born during stage two ages, it creates an economic burden on the shrinking working population. Death rates may remain consistently low or increase slightly due to increases in lifestyle diseases due to low exercise levels and high obesity and an ageing population in developed countries. By the late 20th century, birth rates and death rates in developed countries leveled off at lower rates.

As with all models, this is an idealized picture of population change in these countries. The model is a generalization that applies to these countries as a group and may not accurately describe all individual cases. The extent to which it applies to less-developed societies today remains to be seen. Many countries such as China, Brazil and Thailand have passed through the Demographic Transition Model (DTM) very quickly due to fast social and economic change. Some countries, particularly African countries, appear to be stalled in the second stage due to stagnant development and the effect of AIDS.

Stage One

In pre-industrial society, death rates and birth rates were both high and fluctuated rapidly according to natural events, such as drought and disease, to produce a relatively constant and young population. Family planning and contraception were virtually nonexistent; therefore, birth rates were essentially only limited by the ability of women to bear children. Emigration depressed death rates in some special cases (for example, Europe and particularly the Eastern United States during the 19th century), but, overall, death rates tended to match birth rates, often exceeding 40 per 1000 per year. Children contributed to the economy of the household from an early age by carrying water, firewood, and messages, caring for younger siblings, sweeping, washing dishes, preparing food, and working in the fields. Raising a child cost little more than feeding him or her; there were no education or entertainment expenses. Thus, the total cost of raising children barely exceeded their contribution to the household. In addition, as they became adults they become a major input to the family business, mainly farming, and were the primary form of insurance for adults in old age. In India, an adult son was all that prevented a widow from falling into destitution. While death rates remained high there was no question as to the need for children, even if the means to prevent them had existed.

During this stage, the society evolves in accordance with Malthusian paradigm, with population essentially determined by the food supply. Any fluctuations in food supply (either positive, for example, due to technology improvements, or negative, due to droughts and pest invasions) tend to translate directly into population fluctuations. Famines resulting in significant mortality are frequent. Overall, the population dynamics during stage one is highly reminiscent of that commonly observed in animals.

Stage Two

This stage leads to a fall in death rates and an increase in population. The changes leading to this stage in Europe were initiated in the Agricultural Revolution of the 18th century and were initially quite slow. In the 20th century, the falls in death rates in developing countries tended to be substantially faster. Countries in this stage include Yemen, Afghanistan, the Palestinian territories, Bhutan and Laos and much of Sub-Saharan Africa (but do not include South Africa, Zimbabwe, Botswana, Swaziland, Lesotho, Namibia, Kenya and Ghana, which have begun to move into stage 3).

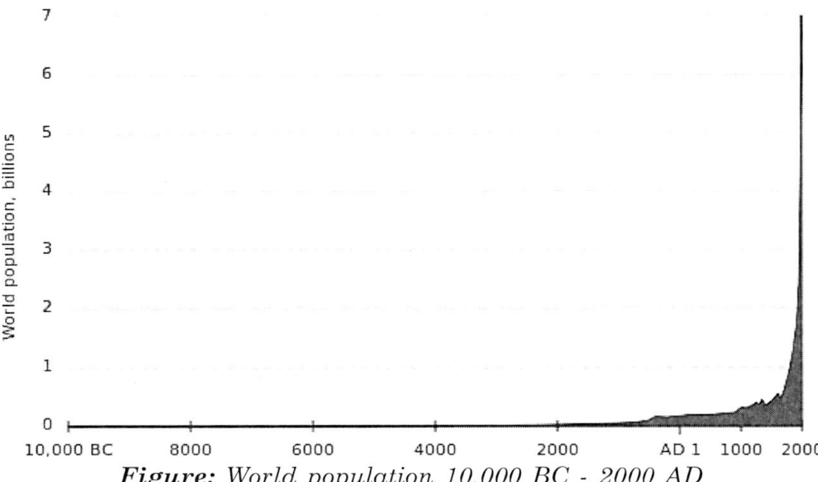

Figure: *World population 10,000 BC - 2000 AD*

The decline in the death rate is due initially to two factors:

- First, improvements in the food supply brought about by higher yields in agricultural practices and better transportation prevent death due to starvation and lack of water. Agricultural improvements included crop rotation, selective breeding, and seed drill technology.
- Second, significant improvements in public health reduce mortality, particularly in childhood. These are not so many medical breakthroughs (Europe passed through stage two before the advances of the mid-20th century, although there was significant medical progress in the 19th century, such as the development of vaccination) as they are improvements in water supply, sewerage, food handling, and general personal hygiene following from growing scientific knowledge of the causes of disease and the improved education and social status of mothers.

A consequence of the decline in mortality in Stage Two is an increasingly rapid rise in population growth (a "population explosion") as the gap between deaths and births grows wider. Note that this growth is not due to an increase in fertility (or birth rates) but to a decline in deaths. This change in population occurred in north-western Europe during the 19th century due to the Industrial Revolution. During the second half of the 20th century less-developed countries entered Stage Two, creating the worldwide population explosion that has demographers concerned today. In this stage of DT, countries are vulnerable to become failed states in the absence of progressive governments.

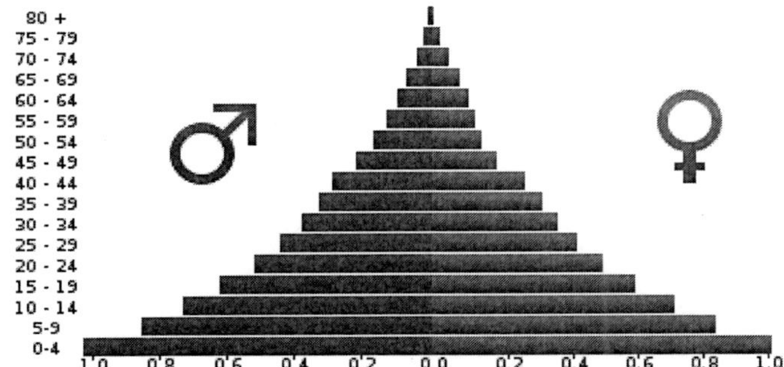

Figure: *Population pyramid of Angola 2005*

Another characteristic of Stage Two of the demographic transition is a change in the age structure of the population. In Stage One, the majority of deaths are concentrated in the first 5–10 years of life. Therefore, more than anything else, the decline in death rates in Stage Two entails the increasing survival of children and a growing population. Hence, the age structure of the population becomes increasingly youthful and more of these children enter the reproductive cycle of their lives while maintaining the high fertility rates of their parents. The bottom of the "age pyramid" widens first, accelerating population growth. The age structure of such a population is illustrated by using an example from the Third World today.

Stage Three

Stage Three moves the population towards stability through a decline in the birth rate. Several factors contribute to this eventual decline, although some of them remain speculative:

- In rural areas continued decline in childhood death means that at some point parents realise they need not require so many children to be born to ensure a comfortable old age. As childhood death continues to fall and incomes increase parents can become increasingly confident that fewer children will suffice to help in family business and care for them in old age.
- Increasing urbanization changes the traditional values placed upon fertility and the value of children in rural society. Urban living also raises the cost of dependent children to a family. A

recent theory suggests that urbanization also contributes to reducing the birth rate because it disrupts optimal mating patterns. A 2008 study in Iceland found that the most fecund marriages are between distant cousins. Genetic incompatibilities inherent in more distant outbreeding makes reproduction harder.

- In both rural and urban areas, the cost of children to parents is exacerbated by the introduction of compulsory education acts and the increased need to educate children so they can take up a respected position in society. Children are increasingly prohibited under law from working outside the household and make an increasingly limited contribution to the household, as school children are increasingly exempted from the expectation of making a significant contribution to domestic work. Even in equatorial Africa, children now need to be clothed, and may even require school uniforms. Parents begin to consider it a duty to buy children books and toys. Partly due to education and access to family planning, people begin to reassess their need for children and their ability to raise them.
- Increasing female literacy and employment lowers the uncritical acceptance of childbearing and motherhood as measures of the status of women. Working women have less time to raise children; this is particularly an issue where fathers traditionally make little or no contribution to child-raising, such as southern Europe or Japan. Valuation of women beyond childbearing and motherhood becomes important.
- Improvements in contraceptive technology are now a major factor. Fertility decline is caused as much by changes in values about children and sex as by the availability of contraceptives and knowledge of how to use them.

The resulting changes in the age structure of the population include a reduction in the youth dependency ratio and eventually population ageing. The population structure becomes less triangular and more like an elongated balloon. During the period between the decline in youth dependency and rise in old age dependency there is a demographic window of opportunity that can potentially produce economic growth through an increase in the ratio of working age to dependent population; the demographic dividend.

However, unless factors such as those listed above are allowed to work, a society's birth rates may not drop to a low level in due time, which means that the society cannot proceed to Stage Four and is locked in what is called a demographic trap.

Countries that have experienced a fertility decline of over 40% from their pre-transition levels include: Costa Rica, El Salvador, Panama, Jamaica, Mexico, Colombia, Ecuador, Guyana, Philippines, Indonesia, Malaysia, Sri Lanka, Turkey, Azerbaijan, Turkmenistan, Uzbekistan, Egypt, Tunisia, Algeria, Morocco, Lebanon, South Africa, India, Saudi Arabia, and many Pacific islands.

Countries that have experienced a fertility decline of 25-40% include: Honduras, Guatemala, Nicaragua, Paraguay, Bolivia, Vietnam, Myanmar, Bangladesh, Tajikistan, Jordan, Qatar, Albania, United Arab Emirates, Zimbabwe, and Botswana.

Countries that have experienced a fertility decline of 10-25% include: Haiti, Papua New Guinea, Nepal, Pakistan, Syria, Iraq, Libya, Sudan, Kenya, Ghana and Senegal.

Stage Four

This occurs where birth and death rates are both low, leading to a total population which is high and stable. Death rates are low for a number of reasons, primarily lower rates of diseases and higher production of food. The birth rate is low because people have more opportunities to choose if they want children; this is made possible by improvements in contraception or women gaining more independence and work opportunities. Some theorists consider there are only 4 stages and that the population of a country will remain at this level. The DTM is only a suggestion about the future population levels of a country, not a prediction.

Countries that are at this stage (Total Fertility Rate of less than 2.5 in 1997) include: United States, Canada, Argentina, Australia, New Zealand, most of Europe, Bahamas, Puerto Rico, Trinidad and Tobago, Brazil, Sri Lanka, South Korea, Singapore, Iran, China, Turkey, Thailand and Mauritius.

Stage Five and/or Six

The original Demographic Transition model has just four stages, but additional stages have been proposed. Both more-fertile and less-fertile futures have been claimed as a Stage Five.

Some countries have sub-replacement fertility (that is, below 2.1 children per woman). Replacement fertility is typically 2.1 because this replaces the two parents and adds population to compensate for deaths (i.e. members of the population who die without reproducing) with the additional 0.1. Many European and East Asian countries now have higher death rates than birth rates. Population ageing and population decline may eventually occur, assuming that the fertility rate does not change and sustained mass immigration does not occur.

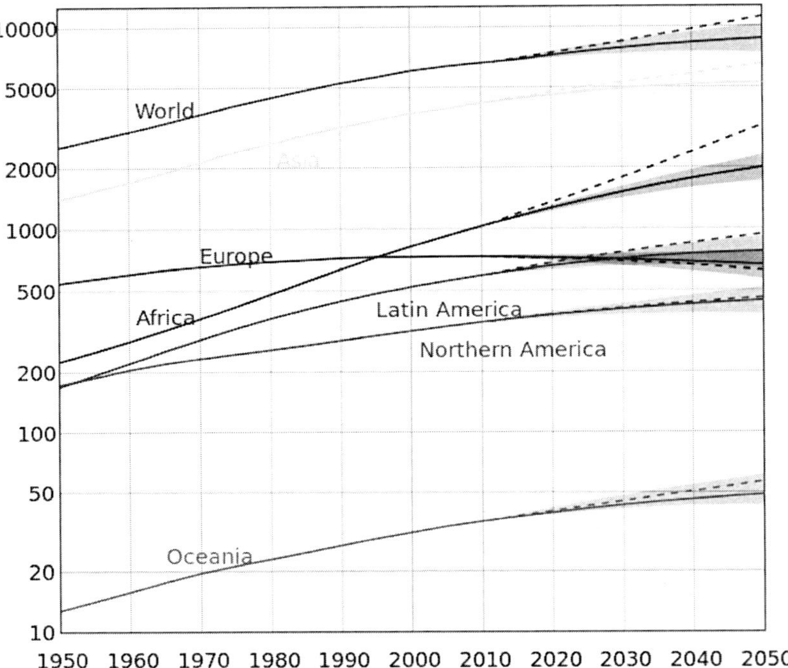

Figure: *United Nation's population projections by location.*

In an article in the August 2009 issue of *Nature*, Myrskyla, Kohler and Billari show that the previously negative relationship between national wealth (as measured by the Human Development Index (HDI)) and birth rates has become J-shaped. Development promotes fertility decline at low and medium HDI levels, but advanced HDI promotes a rebound in fertility. In many countries with very high levels of development fertility rates are now approaching two children per woman — although there are exceptions, notably Germany, Italy, Japan.

In the current century, most developed countries have increased fertility. From the point of view of evolutionary biology, richer people having fewer children is unexpected, as natural selection would be expected to favour individuals who are willing and able to convert plentiful resources into plentiful fertile descendants.

Effects on Age Structure

The decline in death rate and birth rate that occurs during the demographic transition leads to a radical transformation of the age structure. When the death rate declines during the second stage of the transition, the result is primarily an increase in the child population. The reason is that when the death rate is high (stage one), the infant mortality rate is very high, often above 200 deaths per 1000 children born. When the death rate falls or improves, this, in general, results in a significantly lower infant mortality rate and, hence, increased child survival. Over time, as cohorts increased by higher survival rates get older, there will also be an increase in the number of older children, teenagers, and young adults. This implies that there is an increase in the fertile population which, with constant fertility rates, will lead to an increase in the number of children born. This will further increase the growth of the child population. The second stage of the demographic transition, therefore, implies a rise in child dependency.

Historical Studies

Britain

Between 1750 and 1975 England experienced the transition from high levels of both mortality and fertility, to low levels. A major factor was the sharp decline in the death rate for infectious diseases, which has fallen from about 11 per 1,000 to less than 1 per 1,000. By contrast, the death rate from other causes was 12 per 1,000 in 1850 and has not declined markedly. The agricultural revolution and the development of transport, initiated by the construction of canals, led to greater availability of food and coal, and enabled the Industrial Revolution to improve the standard of living. Scientific discoveries and medical breakthroughs did not, in general, contribute importantly to the early major decline in infectious disease mortality, and the decline in fertility occurred before efficient contraception became available.

Ireland

In the 1980s and early 1990s, the Irish demographic status converged to the European norm. Mortality rose above the European Community average, and in 1991 Irish fertility fell to replacement level. The peculiarities of Ireland's past demography and its recent rapid changes challenge established theory. The recent changes have mirrored inward changes in Irish society, with respect to family planning, women in the work force, the sharply declining power of the Catholic Church, and the emigration factor.

France

France displays real divergences from the standard model of Western demographic evolution. The uniqueness of the French case arises from its specific demographic history, its historic cultural values, and its internal regional dynamics. France's demographic transition was unusual in that the mortality and the natality decreased at the same time, thus there was no demographic boom in the 19th century.

France's demographic profile is similar to its European neighbours and to developed countries in general, yet it seems to be staving off the population decline of Western countries. With 62.9 million inhabitants in 2006, it is the second most populous country in the European Union, and it displays a certain demographic dynamism, with a growth rate of 2.4% between 2000 and 2005, above the European average. More than two-thirds of that growth can be ascribed to a natural increase resulting from high fertility and birthrates. In contrast, France is one of the developed nations whose migratory balance is rather weak, which is an original feature at the European level. Several interrelated reasons account for such singularities, in particular the impact of pro-family policies accompanied by greater unmarried households and out-of-wedlock births. These general demographic trends parallel equally important changes in regional demographics. Since 1982 the same significant tendencies have occurred throughout mainland France: demographic stagnation in the least-populated rural regions and industrial regions in the northwest, with strong growth in the southwest and along the Atlantic coast, plus dynamism in metropolitan areas. Shifts in population between regions account for most of the differences in growth. The varying demographic evolution regions can be analyzed though the filter of several parameters, including residential facilities, economic growth, and urban dynamism, which yield several distinct regional profiles. The distribution of the French population therefore seems increasingly defined not only by inter-regional mobility but also by the residential preferences of individual households. These challenges, linked to configurations of population and the dynamics of distribution, inevitably raise the issue of town and country planning. The most recent census figures show that an outpouring of the urban population means that fewer rural areas are continuing to register a negative migratory flow - two-thirds of rural communities have shown some since 2000. The spatial demographic expansion of large cities amplifies the process of peri-urbanization yet is also accompanied by movement of selective residential flow, social selection, and sociospatial segregation based on income.

Asia

McNicoll (2006) examines the common features behind the striking changes in health and fertility in East and Southeast Asia in the 1960s–

1990s, focusing on seven countries: Taiwan and South Korea ("tiger" economies), Thailand, Malaysia, and Indonesia ("second wave" countries), and China and Vietnam ("market-Leninist" economies). Demographic change can be seen as a byproduct of social and economic development together with, in some cases, strong governmental pressures. The transition sequence entailed the establishment of an effective, typically authoritarian, system of local administration, providing a framework for promotion and service delivery in health, education, and family planning. Subsequent economic liberalization offered new opportunities for upward mobility — and risks of backsliding —, accompanied by the erosion of social capital and the breakdown or privatization of service programs.

India

As of year 2013, India is in later half of third stage demographic transition with 1.23 billion population. It is nearly 40 years behind in demographic transition process compared to EU countries, Japan, etc. The present demographic transition stage of India along with its higher population base will yield rich demographic dividend in future decades.

Korea

Cha (2007) analyzes a panel data set to explore how industrial revolution, demographic transition, and human capital accumulation interacted in Korea from 1916–38. Income growth and public investment in health caused mortality to fall, which suppressed fertility and promoted education. Industrialization, skill premium, and closing gender wage gap further induced parents to opt for child quality. Expanding demand for education was accommodated by an active public school building program. The interwar agricultural depression aggravated traditional income inequality, raising fertility and impeding the spread of mass schooling. Landlordism collapsed in the wake of de-colonization, and the consequent reduction in inequality accelerated human and physical capital accumulation, hence leading to growth in South Korea.

Africa

Campbell has studied the demography of 19th-century Madagascar in the light of demographic transition theory. Both supporters and critics of the theory hold to an intrinsic opposition between human and "natural" factors, such as climate, famine, and disease, influencing demography. They also suppose a sharp chronological divide between the precolonial and colonial eras, arguing that whereas "natural" demographic influences were of greater importance in the former period, human factors predominated thereafter. Campbell argues that in 19th-century Madagascar the human factor, in the form of the Merina state, was the predominant demographic influence. However, the impact of the state was felt through natural forces, and it varied over time. In the late 18th and early 19th centuries Merina state policies stimulated agricultural production, which helped to create a larger and healthier population and laid the foundation for Merina military and economic expansion within Madagascar. From 1820, the cost of such expansionism led the state to increase its exploitation of forced labour at the expense of agricultural production and thus transformed it into a negative demographic force. Infertility and infant mortality, which were probably more significant influences on overall population levels than the adult mortality rate, increased from 1820 due to disease, malnutrition, and stress, all of which stemmed from state forced labour policies. Available estimates indicate little if any population growth for Madagascar between 1820 and 1895. The demographic "crisis" in Africa, ascribed by critics of the demographic transition theory to the colonial era, stemmed in Madagascar from the policies of the imperial Merina regime, which in this sense formed a link to the French regime of the colonial era. Campbell thus questions the underlying assumptions governing the debate about historical demography in Africa and suggests that the demographic impact of political forces be re-evaluated in terms of their changing interaction with "natural" demographic influences.

Russia

Figure: *Russian male and female life expectancy since 1950.*

In the 1980s and 1990s Russia underwent a unique demographic transition; observers call it a "demographic catastrophe": the number of deaths exceeded the number of births, life expectancy fell sharply (especially for males) and the number of suicides increased. From 1992 through 2011, the number of deaths exceeded the number of births.

United States

Greenwood and Seshadri (2002) show that from 1800 to 1940 there was a demographic shift from a mostly rural US population with high fertility, with an average of seven children born per white woman, to a minority (43%) rural population with low fertility, with an average of two births per white woman. This shift resulted from technological progress. A sixfold increase in real wages made children more expensive in terms of forgone opportunities to work and increases in agricultural productivity reduced rural demand for labour, a substantial portion of which traditionally had been performed by children in farm families.

A simplification of the DTM theory proposes an initial decline in mortality followed by a later drop in fertility. The changing demographics of the U.S. in the last two centuries did not parallel this model. Beginning around 1800, there was a sharp fertility decline; at this time, an average woman usually produced seven births per lifetime, but by 1900 this number had dropped to nearly four. A mortality decline was not observed in the U.S. until almost 1900—a hundred years following the drop in fertility.

However, this late decline occurred from a very low initial level. It's been estimated that the crude death rate in 17th century rural New England was already as low as 20 deaths per 1000 residents per year (levels of up to 40 per 1000 being typical during stages one and two). The phenomenon is explained by the pattern of colonization of the United States: high death rates unavoidably had to match high birth rates in densely populated Europe, whereas in the United States, westward expansion of the frontier into sparsely populated interior allowed ample room to absorb all the excess people, resulting in exponential population growth (from less than 4 million people in 1790, to 23 million in 1850, to 76 million in 1900.)

Today, the U.S. is recognised as having both low fertility and mortality rates. Specifically, birth rates stand at 14 per 1000 per year and death rates at 8 per 1000 per year.

Critical Evaluation

It has to be remembered that the DTM is only a model and cannot necessarily predict the future. It does however give an indication of what the future birth and death rates may be for an underdeveloped country, together with the total population size. Most particularly, of course, the DTM makes no comment on change in population due to migration. It is not applicable for high levels of development, as it has been shown that after a HDI of 0.9 the fertility increases again.

Non-Applicability to Less-Developed Countries

DTM has a questionable applicability to less economically developed countries (LEDCs), where wealth and information access are limited. For example, the DTM has been validated primarily in Europe, Japan and North America where demographic data exists over centuries, whereas high quality demographic data for most LEDCs did not become widely available until the mid-20th century. DTM does not account for recent phenomena such as AIDS; in these areas HIV has become the leading source of mortality. Some trends in waterborne bacterial infant mortality are also disturbing in countries like Malawi, Sudan and Nigeria; for example, progress in the DTM clearly arrested and reversed between 1975 and 2005. The DTM did not include government interventions (population control e.g. one child policy of China).

Economic Development not Sufficient Cause to Affect Demographic Change

DTM assumes that population changes are induced by industrial changes and increased wealth, without taking into account the role of social change in determining birth rates, e.g., the education of women. In recent decades more work has been done on developing the social mechanisms behind it.

DTM assumes that the birth rate is independent of the death rate. Nevertheless, demographers maintain that there is no historical evidence for society-wide fertility rates rising significantly after high mortality events. Notably, some historic populations have taken many years to replace lives after events such as the Black Death.

Some have claimed that DTM does not explain the early fertility declines in much of Asia in the second half of the 20th century or the delays in fertility decline in parts of the Middle East. Nevertheless, the demographer John C Caldwell has suggested that the reason for the rapid decline in fertility in some developing countries compared to Western Europe, the United States of America, Canada, Australia and New Zealand is mainly due to government programs and a massive investment in education both by governments and parents.

Ageing, Social Relationships, and Health among Older Immigrants

The United States and other Western countries have seen a steady increase in the number of immigrants since the 1970s. A recent report from the U.S. Census Bureau indicates that close to 13 percent of the U.S. population is foreign-born, and about 12 percent of the immigrant population are ages 65 and older (Grieco et al., 2012). A majority of recent immigrants are from Latin America and Asia, and Latino adults, particularly of Mexican origin, represent a growing segment of the ageing population.

Immigrants, especially from developing countries, may benefit from the improved living conditions and better healthcare of their destination country. But migration has often been considered a major stressful life event because it entails a dramatic change in living arrangements, employment, and cultural opportunities, and, the topic of this article, social relationships (Friis, Yngve, and Persson, 1998; Markides and Gerst, 2011).

Social relationships encompass the nature and type of social networks, as well as the support perceived or received from friends, family, or the community at large. The existence of supportive social connections and relationships may help immigrants acclimate to their new living situations, benefitting health. However, immigrants' ability to make friends and maintain social relationships varies by such contextual factors as age at migration and acculturation level.

Research on immigration, social relationships, and health is limited, but a majority of the extant literature suggests that older adult immigrants are more dependent than are native-born elders on smaller, close-knit social networks for support and care in later life. Below, we provide an overview of immigration, social relationships, and health, with particular attention paid to older immigrants from Latin America, especially Mexico. We focus on the roles of neighbourhood context, religious involvement, family, and friendship networks.

Immigration's Impact on Health

In the United States, foreign-born persons live longer and tend to be healthier than their native-born counterparts (Cho et al., 2004; Markides and Eschbach, 2005; Mehta, Sudharsanan, and Elo, 2014; Rogers, Hummer, and Nam, 2000; Ronellenfitsch et al., 2006; Singh and Hiatt, 2006). Markides and Coreil (1986) suggested such a "healthy migrant" or "migration selection" effect might explain the relatively low mortality rates and good health of Mexican Americans living in the Southwestern United States. They used the term "epidemiologic paradox" because Mexican Americans shared similar socioeconomic characteristics and conditions with African Americans, yet their mortality and health conditions were similar to the more advantaged non-Hispanic whites.

Immigration typically involves younger and healthier individuals. Most people immigrate for employment, which requires a relatively good level of health. And Western countries typically require medical screenings by prospective immigrants. Plus, people who immigrate tend to have a positive outlook on their lives and futures, which is consistent with good health (Markides and Gerst, 2011). However, as immigrants live in their destination country longer and become more acculturated, their physical and mental health status often begins to mirror that of their native-born counterparts (Antecol and Bedard, 2006).

This mirroring has been attributed to lifestyle factors such as poor diet, increased alcohol and cigarette use, and reduced physical activity, which can contribute to adverse health outcomes (Friis, Yngve, and Persson, 1998; Singh et al., 2011). For some, linguistic and economic barriers, encounters with discrimination, and less access to healthcare can have an adverse effect on health. Immigrants are less likely to have insurance and a regular source of care than are native-born adults in the United States, are less satisfied with their care, and report more discrimination in healthcare settings (Derose et al., 2009). The more rapid health decline observed for foreign-born adults in the United States in later life has also been attributed to the erosion of social and familial ties that arises from acculturative processes (Mehta, Sudharsanan, and Elo, 2014). Yet, a majority of older adult immigrants rely heavily on their social networks for financial, social, and emotional support.

Neighbourhood Context

The neighbourhood environment can affect health depending upon how well it provides resources and safety to its inhabitants. Immigrants, on average, have lower levels of educational attainment and are more likely to live in poverty than the native born (Greico et al., 2012). Older immigrant health, more so than younger immigrant health, may be influenced by neighbourhood context because of restricted mobility in later life (Yen, Michael, and Perdue, 2009). Specifically, older immigrants tend to be concentrated in poor neighbourhoods with few resources (Iceland, 2009). Poor neighbourhoods compromise health because of poor housing quality, close proximity to environmental toxins (including poor air and water quality), higher crime rates, and overall lack of resources (Hill and Maimon, 2013).

Older foreign-born adults, however, tend to live in homogenous neighbourhoods, which may provide sociocultural benefits that protect against health decline (Markides, Angel, and Peek, 2013). For example, Eschbach and colleagues (2004) found that older Mexican Americans living in the Southwestern United States in high-density immigrant areas tend to have more favourable health profiles and a slower health decline over time than those in low-density areas.

Sociocultural resources, such as the perception or ability to rely on neighbours for help and feelings of neighbourhood solidarity may provide benefits to psychological well-being and, consequently, physical health. Almeida and colleagues (2009) found some support for the notion that those who live in high immigrant–density areas report more supportive and expansive social networks. Neighbours in high immigrant–density areas tend to speak the same language, which can facilitate close personal friendships. Neighbours may also help one another in a number of capacities that allow older adults to remain in the community, including assistance with instrumental activities of daily living such as providing transportation to the grocery store, and help with housework or yard work. Overall, neighbourhoods provide the structural basis that allows for supportive relationships and exchanges, and neighbours may be key purveyors of help and assistance for older immigrants. Similar to neighbourhoods, religious communities can also facilitate social connectedness.

Religious Involvement

Religious attendance is an indicator of social engagement, and can help with the trauma of relocating to a new country. In terms of age, older immigrants tend to report more frequent religious participation than younger immigrants (Van Tubergen, 2006). In general, older adults who attend religious services on a regular basis tend to have lower risks of premature mortality, psychological distress, and cognitive impairment (Ellison et al., 2000; Hill et al., 2005; Hill et al., 2006; Krause, 2006; Reyes-Ortiz et al., 2008) and less fear of falling (Reyes-Ortiz et al., 2006).

Religious organisations may also serve to preserve customs and help immigrants adapt to new living situations. Many religious organisations provide social services to their congregants with direct assistance for food, clothing, and housing, and provide the opportunities for integration into social networks that lead to work opportunities and civic engagement (Cadge and Ecklund, 2007).

Past research also demonstrates that older immigrants derive more emotional benefits from religious participation than native-born older adults (Hao and Johnson, 2000). The benefits of attending religious services may be especially protective for immigrants who arrive earlier in life, because this allows them to develop and maintain strong social ties. Several mechanisms linking religious attendance to health have been described in previous research, namely, social support, social control of health-compromising behaviours such as heavy drinking or smoking, and a sense of control (Hill, Burdette, and Idler, 2011; Koenig, King, and Carson, 2012; Rote, Hill, and Ellison, 2013). Often, attending religious services is a family activity and families are a key source of social support for older immigrants.

Living with Family

A majority of immigrants live with other family members for financial and sociocultural reasons (Angel, Angel, and Markides, 2000). Specifically, Mexican-born adults living in the United States are more likely to live with family members than native-born adults (Angel et al., 1996). This is largely due to economic constraints, preferences for ageing in place with loved ones, as well as health decline in later life. There is also evidence that Mexican-origin immigrants who immigrated in late rather than early life are more likely to live with children (Angel, Angel, and Markides, 2000; Angel et al., 1996). Those who immigrate later also report more expectations for social support from their family (Taylor et al., 2004), tend to have lower socioeconomic standing, and face more language barriers than those who immigrated earlier in life. Common late-life transitions, such as widowhood, often spur intergenerational co-residence.

About half of all current immigrants living in the United States are married (Grieco et al., 2012). Marriage results in better health through shared resources and income, shared support, and also social control of health behaviours. Spouses often help one another in times of need and provide assistance to one another in terms of financial, social, emotional, and tangible support (i.e., helping with activities of daily living such as dressing, bathing, preparing meals, etc.). Using data on older Mexican American couples, researchers have found high levels of spousal health concordance on blood pressure, hypertension, diabetes, arthritics, and cancer (Peek and Markides, 2003; Stimpson and Peek, 2005). Following widowhood, which results in losing such social and economic resources, and is more commonly experienced among women, many widows move in with adult children.

Older immigrants are especially likely to live with their adult children. However, there tends to be a high degree of reciprocity between the oldest generation and their middle-aged children because older adults may provide childcare for grandchildren or even some financial assistance to their children (Markides, Boldt, and Ray, 1986).

More attention needs to be paid to the types of support and help that older family members provide to their adult children. If the older family member is contributing time, money, and support to their children or grandchildren, this may be burdensome, however, it also may instill a sense of duty and feelings of reciprocity, which may be advantageous to elder immigrants' mental well-being.

Also, immigrant elders often maintain transnational ties in later life, especially immigrants who left their country of origin in late life. They may send money and exchange emotional support, as well as maintain a sense of belonging through telephone conversations with family members living abroad (Viruell-Fuentes and Schulz, 2009). Technology that helps older immigrants maintain connections with their family and friends abroad is likely to aid in maintaining these transnational ties.

Moving Near Friends

Immigrants also tend to relocate to areas of the United States in which they have existing social ties. Immigrants may rely on their social network more so than their native-born counterparts, which helps instill a sense of belonging and community (Almeida et al., 2009; Viruell-Fuentes and Schulz, 2009). Viruell-Fuentes and Schulz (2009), however, reviewed extant literature and found that few studies reported more social support among immigrants relative to their native-born counterparts, with some studies reporting significantly lower levels of social support and integration. Their in-depth interviews revealed that first-generation Latino immigrants tend to have small social networks with two to five close friends. Therefore, if one of the links or friendships is broken, foreign-born adults may be especially vulnerable to loneliness and isolation. Also, these networks can become overburdened if the older adult is highly dependent upon their social network for basic functions.

Timing of immigration is also an important consideration for social network ties. Those who immigrate earlier in life have more time and more settings (e.g., work, school, etc.) in which to develop and maintain social ties earlier on. Additionally, later-life immigrants who may have recently experienced functional decline or spousal loss often relocate to live with adult children. Those who immigrate in later life have smaller social networks than those who immigrated earlier in the life course (Weeks and Cuellar, 1983).

Social Isolation and Loneliness

Older immigrants may experience social isolation or loneliness when physical health limits their ability to leave the house or drive, especially in areas with inadequate public transportation. Even in conditions of good health, language barriers prevent some older adults from navigating the transportation system (Gentry, 2010), leaving them confined to their houses.

When living with adult children, the children may be preoccupied with work and other family demands, and unable to devote much time to providing companionship to their ageing family members (Treas and Mazumdar, 2002). Older immigrants may be out of the workforce and unable to make ties through work settings. This may be especially evident among those who immigrated in late life. Loneliness is linked to depression, anxiety, and biological risk (Friedman, 2012).

Conclusion: Social Relationships Ease the Stress of Immigration

The United States has seen a dramatic increase in the number of immigrants over the past forty years. Prior research finds an immigrant health advantage, but longer stays in the United States often lead to a more rapid health decline over time. This has largely been attributed to the (on average) lower socioeconomic standing of immigrants. Adjustment to life following immigration and language barriers in healthcare and school settings pose hurdles to many immigrants.

Translating health and educational material to help immigrants understand health conditions, providing access to human services providers who speak native languages, and the use of community-based approaches are all important for older immigrant health (Gentry, 2010). Immigrants also tend to live in neighbourhoods with fewer economic resources. However, close family networks are the foundation for supportive exchange processes for many immigrants who also lack access to aspects of the U.S. social safety net, especially in later life.

It is important for practitioners to incorporate close family members, especially middleaged children of ageing parents who typically serve as caregivers, and be mindful that how old someone is when they immigrate affects social relationships and health.

Assessing the daily lives and functioning of social relationships of elderly immigrants also is important to understand vulnerability to disease and disability in late life.

Overall, adjustment to immigration often is a stressful experience, but social relationships can help ease the burden and improve health.

Relationships Among the Elderly: The Effects on One's Health and Psychosocial Well Being

Advances in medicine are allowing many adults to live longer lives than previous generations. In fact, the elderly population is becoming one of the largest growing sectors of the present population. Recently, researchers have begun studying what factors contribute to successful ageing. These studies are showing that the impact of family and social relationships plays an important part in one's health and psychosocial well being.

The Pennsylvania Department of Ageing (2008) defines an elderly person as one who is age 65 or older. Those age 85 and above are considered to be the oldest old and are predicted to increase 44% in number by 2020 (PA Department of Ageing). As one reaches these once unfathomable ages researchers are interested in analyzing their psychosocial and health dispositions as to what these elderly adults ascribe to their longevity.

Older adults attribute successful ageing to quality of life (Reichstadt, Sengupta, Depp, Palinkas, and Jeste, 2010). Flood, Nies, and Seo (2010) define successful ageing as one's ability to successfully adapt to their physical and social surroundings. This satisfaction can be all encompassing contributing to an overall sense of a purposeful life (Flood et al.). Many older adults noted that a "feeling that somebody cares" played an important role in this sense of well being (Reichstadt et al.). Social interaction and support with spouses, family and friends can provide one with an acceptance of self and lend to a decrease in mortality (Antonucci, Birditt, and Webster, 2010).

There are many different types of relationships such as social, marital, and family. Each of these relationships can have a negative or positive influence on the individual. Trudel, Boyer, Villeneuve, Anderson, Pilon, and Bounader (2007) note that a positive relationship with a spouse can be one of the greatest buffers against physical and psychosocial problems. This relationship has the most impact on one's sense of purpose and mental disposition (Trudel et al.).

A study by David Sbarra (2009) found that C-reactive protein (CRP) levels in older married men were lower than in their single counterparts. He attributes this finding to one of the health benefits a quality marriage can offer (Sbarra). An article in the Harvard Women's Health Watch (2010) notes that stress levels are decreased for older couples in strong relationships. The sharing of experiences and closeness may have a far greater impact on one's health than previously realised (Gerstorf, Hoppmann, Kadlec, and McArdle 2009).

Antonucci et al. (2010) find that the negative effects of a marital relationship may actually improve health while contributing to depression. These negative may be real or perceived as the older individual can interpret demands made on them as smothering or pressuring (Antonucci et al.). Other negative effects such as declining physical or cognitive functions of a spouse have been found to increase one's depressive symptoms (Gerstorf et al., 2009). It is interesting to note that wives with depressive symptoms were more likely to have an impact on their spouse's cognitive decline as well as their own (Gerstorf et al.).

Older adult relationships with children or other family members did not carry the importance of a spousal relationship unless the person is unmarried (Antonucci et al., 2010). Positive interaction with family did not show the decrease in mortality that one might expect (Antonucci et al.). It has been suggested that as one ages their family ties often remain intact as opposed to other relationships since family are thought to be a greater source of support, care, and emotional well being than a social relationship (Shaw, Krause, Liang, and Bennett, 2007). Antonucci et al. suggest that families of those nearer to death may choose to hide any troubles and focus on the positive.

Many elderly report that social involvement contributes to a positive self attitude and self acceptance (Reichstadt et al., 2010). Shaw et al., (2007) note that social support is directly linked to decreased mortality and offers positive health benefits. One reason for this may be that social relationships as opposed to family and marital are chosen by the elderly person (Antonucci et al., 2010). This allows the individual to surround himself with an effective support system. A study by Shaw et al. (2007) finds that elderly women are often the ones providing and receiving more support than elderly men. However, the study also notes that men are happier with their support systems overall (Shaw et al.).

Interviews conducted among the elderly by Reichstadt et al.(2010) note that those who found a meaningful way to stay active in society by working, volunteering or interacting socially expressed a greater sense of happiness. Self acceptance and a realistic approach to one's present circumstances greatly contributed to psychosocial well being and a better quality of life (Reichstadt et al). Murray and Crummett (2010) find that participating in social activities can lead to a positive physical and mental state.

Loneliness and isolation on the other hand have been shown to lead to health disparities and depressive symptoms (Shiovitz and Leitsch, 2010). Mauk notes that 38% of older women and 19% of older men lived alone as of 2005. A study by Sato, Kishi, Suzukawa,

Horikawa, Saijo, and Yoshioka (2007) found that lacking a sense of worth may contribute to increased mortality. Some of the elderly interviewed by Shiovitz and Leitsch reported feeling forgotten by their community and were noted to have higher systolic blood pressure readings and cardiovascular issues. Harvard Women's Health Watch (2010) reports that premature death was found to increase by 50% in those without social or family ties.

It is interesting to note that some of those that experience loneliness do not live alone (Shiovitz and Leitsch). According to Mauk (2009) these older adults may being dealing with depression that family or friends misconstrue as a normal part of ageing. Some may be dealing with mistreatment or neglect at the hands of a caregiver. Shiovitz and Leitsch (2010) note that some relationships are harmful and detrimental to the individual.

In conclusion, it is noted that positive relationships with spouse, family or friends are a significant factor in the overall health and well being of the elderly person (Antonucci et al., 2010). As one ages support systems tend to decrease and it is important for one to remain socially active (Antonucci et al.). Positive marital relationships seem to provide the greatest means of protection from health and mental disparities (Trudel et al., 2007). As Reichstadt et al. (2010) note, those that give of themselves to others, cherish each day, possess a positive self attitude, and maintain a social support system are key evidence as to how one can age successfully.

Chapter 5

Socioemotional Selectivity Theory

Socioemotional selectivity theory (developed by Stanford psychologist, Laura Carstensen) is a life-span theory of motivation. The theory maintains that as time horizons shrink, as they typically do with age, people become increasingly selective, investing greater resources in emotionally meaningful goals and activities. According to the theory, motivational shifts also influence cognitive processing. Ageing is associated with a relative preference for positive over negative information in attention and memory (called the "positivity effect").

Because they place a high value on emotional satisfaction, older adults often spend more time with familiar individuals with whom they have had rewarding relationships. This selective narrowing of social interaction maximizes positive emotional experiences and minimizes emotional risks as individuals become older. According to this theory, older adults systematically hone their social networks so that available social partners satisfy their emotional needs.

The theory also focuses on the types of goals that individuals are motivated to achieve. Knowledge-related goals aim at knowledge acquisition, career planning, the development of new social relationships and other endeavors that will pay off in the future. Emotion-related goals are aimed at emotion regulation, the pursuit of emotionally gratifying interactions with social partners and other pursuits whose benefits can be realised in the present.

When people perceive their future as open ended, they tend to focus on future-oriented/knowledge-related goals, but when they feel that time is running out, their focus tends to shift towards present-oriented/emotion-related goals. Research on this theory often compares age groups (i.e., young and old adulthood) but the shift in goal priorities is a gradual process that begins in early adulthood. Importantly, the theory contends that the cause of these goal shifts is not age itself, *i.e.*, not the passage of time itself, but rather an age-associated shift in time perspective. This justified shift in perspective is the rational equivalent of the psychological perceptual disorder known as "foreshortened future," in which an individual, usually a young and physically healthy individual, unreasonably believes (either consciously or unconsciously) that his/her time horizons are more limited than they actually are, with the effect that the individual undervalues long-term goals and long-run pleasure and instead disproportionately pursues short-term goals and pleasure, thereby diverting resources from investment for the future and often even actively reduce his/her long-term prospects.

Cross-Cultural Incidence

Researchers have found that across diverse samples – ranging from Norwegians to Catholic nuns to African-Americans to Chinese Americans to European-Americans – older adults report better control of their emotions and fewer negative emotions than do younger adults. At the same time, culture seems to colour how ageing-related effects impact one's emotional life: Whereas older Americans were shown to de-emphasize negative experiences more than younger Americans, no such effect has been observed in Japan. Instead, older Japanese were shown to assign a greater value to positive aspects of otherwise negative experiences than younger Japanese, whereas no such effect has been observed in the U.S.

Affective Events Theory

Affective events theory (AET) is a model developed by organisational psychologists Howard M. Weiss (Purdue University) and Russell Cropanzano (University of Colorado) to explain how emotions and moods influence job performance and job satisfaction. The model explains the linkages between employees' internal influences (e.g., cognitions, emotions, mental states) and their reactions to incidents that occur in their work environment that affect their performance, organisational commitment, and job satisfaction. The theory proposes that affective work behaviours are explained by employee mood and emotions, while cognitive-based behaviours are the best predictors of job satisfaction. The theory proposes that positive-inducing (e.g., uplifts) as well as negative-inducing (e.g., hassles) emotional incidents at work are distinguishable and have a significant psychological impact upon workers' job satisfaction.

This results in lasting internal (e.g., cognition, emotions, mental states) and external affective reactions exhibited through job performance, job satisfaction, and organisational commitment.

Alternatively, some research suggests that job satisfaction mediates the relationship between various antecedent variables such as dispositions, workplace events, job characteristics, job opportunities, and employee behaviour exhibited while on the job (e.g., organisational citizenship behaviours, counter-productive work behaviours, and job withdrawal). To that end, when workers experience uplifts (e.g., completing a goal, receiving an award) or hassles (e.g., dealing with a difficult client, reacting to an updated deadline), their intention to continue or quit depends upon the emotions, moods, and thoughts associated with the satisfaction they derive from their jobs.

Other research has demonstrated that the relationship between job satisfaction and turnover is fully mediated by intention to quit; workers who report low job satisfaction are likely to engage in planned quitting. However, this relationship does not account for employees who report high job satisfaction, but quit unexpectedly. Although extrinsic rewards, such as better job offers outside their current organisation, may influence their decisions, employees' personality factors may also impact their decisions to exit early from otherwise ideal jobs under ideal working conditions.

Recipients often refer to specific events in exit interviews when voluntarily leaving their current jobs. Minor events with subtle emotional effects also have a cumulative impact on job satisfaction, particularly when they occur acutely with high frequency. For example, perceived stressful events at work are often positively associated with high job strain on the day that they occur and negatively associated with strain the day after, resulting in an accumulation of perceived job-related stress over time. This is consistent with the general understanding in vocational psychology that job satisfaction is a distal, long-term outcome that is mediated by perceived job stress.

Factors Affecting Employee Experience at Work

The relationships between components associated with work (e.g., tasks, autonomy, job demands, and emotional labour) and their impact on job outcomes support AET. Tasks that are considered challenging, rewarding, or that provide an opportunity to develop new skills induce positive affect and increase job satisfaction. Alternatively, tasks that are rated as routine, boring, or overwhelming are associated with negative affect (e.g., low self-esteem, low self-confidence) and concerns over job evaluations. This may lead workers to engage in planned quitting behaviours.

The degree of autonomy workers have in their jobs affects their productivity, satisfaction, and intention to quit. Research shows that the ability to make decisions and influence what happens on the job has the greatest impact on job satisfaction, particularly among young male workers. Job autonomy even trumps income's effect on job satisfaction. Alternatively, work overload significantly reduces job satisfaction among middle-aged women and men but does not significantly impact job satisfaction among young male workers. These differences between the age and gender of workers indicate differences in career phase, where young (male) workers are more likely to put up with or expect work overload, while middle-aged workers tend to be approaching their peak and may expect some concessions (e.g., based on track record, merit, or currency to the organisation).

Likewise, work flexibility affects job satisfaction. In fact, the flexibility to decide when work is performed ranks number one among women and number two or three among men in determining the characteristics of a satisfying job. Similar to job autonomy, job flexibility is more important than income when evaluating job satisfaction. Flexibility to determine one's work schedule is an important contributor to job satisfaction across the spectrum of low- and high-income jobs. Work flexibility empowers employees by reducing the incidence of work-family conflicts and engagement in planned quitting to improve overall quality of life. Positive affect is a fringe benefit of work flexibility that pays rich dividends to both employees and their employers, empowering the former and improving the ability of the latter to retain workers.

Past research has suggested that workplace affect was a state-oriented construct (like emotions and mood) that depended upon the work environment or situations encountered at work. However, more recent research describes affect as a dispositional trait that is dependent upon the individual. Although workplace events have a significant impact on employees, their mood largely determines the intensity of their reaction to events experienced at work. This emotional response intensity tends to affect job performance and satisfaction. Other employment variables, like effort, leaving, deviance, commitment, and citizenship, are also affected by positive and negative perceptions of events experienced at work.

General cognitive ability (also known as 'g') and personality also influence job performance. Emotion and cognition help to explain Organisational Citizenship Behaviours (OCB). For example, emotions about one's job (i.e., job affect) are strongly associated with OCBs directed at individuals, while one's thoughts or job cognitions are reportedly more strongly associated with OCBs directed at the organisation. The outcome of how satisfied an individual employee is with her/his job within the organisation may depend upon how s/he perceives an incident experienced at work. Job satisfaction also depends upon the emotions and thoughts associated with that perception, as well as the social support provided by co-workers and the organisation as a whole.

Five Factor Model of Personality and AET

Personality research on the Five Factor Model (FFM) supports AET. The FFM is a parsimonious model that distinguishes between differences among individuals' dispositions. This is done on the basis of five factors, each of which contains six underlying facets. Self-reported measures of conscientiousness, agreeableness, neuroticism, openness to experience, and extraversion consistently predict affect and outcome from events experienced at work. There is some evidence that other personality factors predict, explain, and describe how employees may react to affective events experienced at work. For instance, maladaptive traits derived from the Diagnostic and Statistical Manual correlate with work-related affect, but the incremental validity that these traits explain is minimal beyond the FFM.

Conscientiousness

In general, conscientiousness concerns delayed gratification. As a personality trait, conscientiousness involves regulating impulsiveness by following methodically determined plans to achieve non-immediate goals. Of the five factors, conscientiousness is considered the best predictor of training and job performance and occupational attainment. Conscientiousness is demonstrated through employee industriousness, self-initiative, self-discipline, orderliness, and time management. It positively predicts intrinsic (i.e., job satisfaction) and extrinsic (i.e., compensation and benefit) career success. Accomplishment of complex tasks is correlated with high conscientiousness and general cognitive ability. Intention to leave an organisation is less influenced by extrinsic reward than perceived procedural fairness, which is highly important to conscientious workers

Perceptions of the conscientiousness of others may also influence intention to provide assistance at work. Investigations examining the impact of the interaction between low performing members' g and conscientiousness on team-level prosocial behaviour demonstrates that other team members are likely to exhibit high prosocial behaviour when the poor performer is perceived to have low g and high conscientiousness or high g and high conscientiousness. Team members exhibit moderate levels of prosocial behaviour when the poor performer exhibits low g and low conscientiousness. When the poor performer is perceived to have high g and low conscientiousness, other team members exhibit the least amount of prosocial behaviour.

Conscientiousness and emotional stability predict low employee turnover and high job performance, indicating that these personality traits are robust and should be assessed during personnel selection in subsequent validation and utility analysis. Conscientiousness is considered to account for possible moral, ethical, and contractual obligations that may lead to employee turnover. In this mental state, employees high in conscientiousness may decide to demonstrate high organisational commitment due to transactional fairness in accordance with the norms of reciprocity, as long as a perceived debt exists. Highly religious and conscientious workers may believe that quitting goes against their work-oriented beliefs (e.g., the Protestant work ethic), with any volition to carry through with quitting, a sign of poor character.

Agreeableness

Individuals who are high in agreeableness exhibit prosocial behaviours, are cooperative, compassionate, and polite, and show sincere concern for the welfare and rights of others. Research links agreeableness with empathy and theory of mind to explain the emotions, intentions, and mental states of others. Agreeable workers are valued employees; their agreeableness is a key factor in maintaining their social relationships. Their tendency to strive toward integration, inclusion, and solidarity with others supports group cohesion. They tend to be helpful and concerned for the welfare of others. Agreeable workers also tend to experience high job satisfaction compared to less agreeable workers. Workers high in agreeableness tend to rate themselves as high in intrinsic motivation, particularly when work performed on behalf of others or an organisation is considered. Heterogeneity of personality is important in team productivity, particularly where agreeableness is involved; having complete agreeableness among all members of a team is negatively related to performance as it tends to lead to groupthink.

The relationship between agreeableness and job satisfaction is most apparent in exchange-oriented or transactional work environments. When workers who are low in agreeableness are satisfied with their work environment and those they are required to interact with, they are likely to engage in prosocial organisational citizenship behaviours. Low-agreeable workers are likely to disengage in such behaviours when they find the work environment less favourable.

Highly agreeable workers, on the other hand, are likely to engage in prosocial organisational citizenship behaviours regardless of the work climate, environment, or disposition of others they are required to work with, since they tend to focus more on the needs of others and the organisation as opposed to keeping track of transactions. Further, deviant behaviour is higher among workers low in agreeableness, particularly when organisational support is low.

Agreeableness and Conscientiousness have been consistently linked to organisational citizenship behaviour, although this relationship is weak. Recent research suggests that agreeableness acts as a moderator that affects workers' experienced states of citizenship behaviour. These two personality traits are also negatively correlated with employee turnover. Workers who self-report as low on agreeableness are likely to engage in unplanned quitting, leading to a condition known as the "Hobo Syndrome" (i.e., habitual job quitting).

Neuroticism

Individual sensitivity to punishment is at the core of neuroticism. Numerous findings show that neuroticism is related to the tendency to experience negative affect at work and other social environments. Neurotic individuals exhibit irritability, anxiety, impulsiveness, and self-consciousness that seems to underlie a general sensitivity to threat and punishment. The authors of the NEO-PI-R indicate that poor emotion regulation, low self-esteem, and excessive rumination are common among neurotic individuals.

The underlying anxiety implied by neuroticism is linked to emotional instability, which is typically important in predicting employees' intentions to quit. Low emotional stability is also linked with intention to quit for reasons other than job dissatisfaction or poor job performance. Neuroticism is the best predictor among the Big Five personality traits of negative job satisfaction. For example, neuroticism negatively predicts extrinsic (i.e., compensation and benefit) success. This is why conscientiousness (a great predictor of positive job performance and job satisfaction) and neuroticism (the best predictor of negative job satisfaction) are regularly used in personnel selection and personnel psychology. Neuroticism explains significant variation in mood and job satisfaction among workers.

Openness to Experience

Openness to experience is exhibited through mental abstraction and flexibility in perception. Non-linear thinking is enabled through the use of imagination, intellectual curiosity, and an appreciation for aesthetics, all of which are core facets of this personality factor. Employees assessed as high in openness to experience generally score high on tests of general cognitive ability and demonstrate high abilities in information processing, working memory, abstract reasoning, and focused attention.

Workers high in openness to experience are more likely to engage in unplanned quitting. However, this finding may have little to do with affect derived from events experienced at work. Individuals who self-report as high in openness to experience may be impulsive, but their decisions to suddenly quit may be due to the value placed on job diversity, need for change, exploration of other interests, intolerance for routine and boredom, and an underlying sense of curiosity. Openness to experience does not appear to predict or explain job satisfaction.

Extraversion

Extraversion is considered to be responsible for individual sensitivity to reward. It is extraversion's underlying facets of assertiveness, sociability, and talkativeness that are reported to be related to approach tendencies within individuals toward either intrinsic or extrinsic rewards. Like most human activity, the currency of the world of work involves rewards. High sensitivity to reward seems to be synonymous with extraversion, making workers who exhibit high extraversion likely to be highly motivated and highly productive in independent and collaborative work. This is particularly heightened when work involves supervision of others, management of resources, or leadership.

Extraverts tend to experience more positive affect, perceive themselves more positively, and recall more positive than negative work events compared to introverts. Intention to quit among extraverts is less dependent upon procedural fairness within the organisation, particularly when the opportunity for social rewards at work is perceived as high. Conscientiousness and extraversion are the best predictors of positive job satisfaction.

Mood and AET

Workers' mood influences their job performance and job satisfaction. Hedonic tone explains most of the variation in how an event at work affects a worker's internal state (i.e., mood) and how this state is expressed to others. Even though positive events are reported three to five times more often, negative events have approximately five times the impact on mood. An inverse relationship exists between hedonic tone and work affect, with hedonic tone negatively-related to work performance and positively-related to work withdrawal. Workers are likely be selfless and more altruistic when positive events occur, such as compliments, open acknowledgement of a job well-done, and promotions (which, in turn, seem to improve job performance). Negative events at work, however, are likely to cause negative mood in employees, resulting in negative work behaviours such as work slowdowns, work withdrawal, and absenteeism.

Mood may be moderated by organisational commitment which, in turn, may affect workers' decisions to stay or quit. For example, workers may suppress their true feelings and choose to dissociate their mood at work if they are high in continuance organisational commitment (i.e., committed due to social or economic costs of leaving). The same may be true for workers who are high in affective organisational commitment, which is typically the case for workers who are highly affiliated with their organisations (e.g., workers who have a family history of working for the same organisation or who believe deeply in the organisation's values or cause). Similarly, workers who are high in normative organisational commitment feel they *have* to put up with less-than-favourable work environmental conditions because of contractual obligations.

Research demonstrates that employee mood is a strong predictor of job satisfaction. Neuroticism and extraversion explain a lot of the variation in individual differences in job satisfaction, with variation in mood and job satisfaction accurately predicting an individual worker's level of neuroticism. There is also some indication that individuals may be predisposed to perceive events that occur at work as either negative or positive. The effect of positive events on job satisfaction is weaker among workers with high negative mood predisposition than those with low negative mood predisposition.

This predisposition to either be optimistic or pessimistic about job satisfaction may frame the job even before positive or negative events occur at work. To rule out the possibility of hiring personnel who come to the job with a negative outlook, the personality of potential employees should be evaluated through the use of standardized self-report personality inventories (e.g., NEO-PI-R) during the hiring process. Highly conscientious, agreeable, or extraverted personnel tend to be more satisfied with their jobs and, by extension, tend to stay longer in organisations. Alternatively, organisations may develop their own structured interview questions with behaviourally anchored rating scales (BARS) that provide further convergent validity on critical predictors of job performance (e.g., neuroticism). Such inventories, interviews, and tests must be reliable and valid in order to demonstrate their utility and legal defencibility in support of the selection and hiring process.

Mitigating Negative Affect Experienced from Work-related Events

The intensity of negative affect experienced at work often leads to workwithdrawal,absenteeism,vandalism,andearlyexit.Organisations continuallyseektoselect,train,andretainemployeesthroughincentives, compensation, benefits, and advancement. Such mechanisms influence theorganisationalcommitmentdemonstratedbyemployees.Organisational commitment suggests that employees self-identify with their employers; themoreindividualsidentifywiththeiremployingorganisations,themore likely they are to support the organisation and act in its best interest. Of the three components of organisational commitment (i.e., affective, continuance, and normative), affective organisational commitment is correlatedwithexperiencingmorepositiveaffectatwork.Thisorganisational commitmentstylehasagreaterimpactonaffectthanindividualpersonality factors and traits.

This finding supports organisational psychological findings indicating that employee identification with the organisation is based upon their affective commitment. In fact, there is a stronger correlation between positive emotions and affective commitment than between positive emotions and job satisfaction. The decision to continue working for an organisation, however, does not seem to be dependent upon negative affect. Other factors, such as debt, pension implications, and future job prospects outside of the organisation, must also be considered. Negative affect experienced through events at work may be related to changes in work performance, such as work withdrawal and absenteeism, as well as job satisfaction, but it does not seem to be the deciding factor on whether or not an employee will leave the organisation.

Psychosomatic Complaint and Health Concerns Due to Emotions Experienced at Work

Research suggests that poor physical, mental, and emotional health can result from negative emotions experienced at work. This may be due to perfectionist dispositional tendencies that interact with daily hassels manifested through psychosomatic complaints. Workers who experience frequent thoughts of needing to be perfect tend to report more psychosomatic complaint. Psychosomatic complaint may also occur as a response to emotional dissonance caused by the need to suppress one's true feelings toward co-workers and more so toward patients, students, customers, or clients. Emotional labour or emotion work is required to achieve the effect required by the organisation. As a consequence, workers may 'act' as oppose to 'feel' positive or negative emotions at work to remain compliant with an organisational code of conduct. However, adherence to such organisational norms may belie the true internal state of the individual worker. Authenticity and emotional harmony in such situations, may yield to dissonance and negatively impact on workers' health.

The resulting emotional dissonance may lead to increased stress symptoms and a general decrease in overall health.

Job satisfaction is negatively correlated with the need to suppress negative emotions on the job.

Emotions at Work

Emotions play an important role in how co-workers respond to poor performers. Emotions have a stronger influence than either expectancies or attributions in predicting behavioural intentions toward poor performing team members at work. In turn, this could spread to affect the emotions of other team members toward poor performance through contagion. Emotional outcomes have been shown to be depend upon whether workers are promotion- or protection-focused at work. Promotion-focused workers tend to exhibit eager risk-taking toward opportunities to demonstrate competence in order to accumulate gains, whereas protection-focused workers are inclined to show emotions that are more vigilant toward defending against erosion of their perceived credibility. Feeling good about one's job is not as strongly associated with overall job satisfaction as the need to work as a function of one's continuance commitment.

Feedback and Motivation

Performance feedback has an important influence on employee affect. Regular performance reviews are a well-established occurrence in most medium- to large-scale organisations. The type of performance feedback provided by supervisors and managers can affect subsequent employee performance and job satisfaction. Employees tend to rate a leader's effectiveness as low when leaders provide failure feedback with negative affect in feedback sessions. Similarly, team members tend to provide lower quality performance ratings on their collective tasks when negative affect accompanies failure feedback by leaders.

Family Health & Caring for Elderly Parents

Care of the elderly is a major concern of nursing, gerontology and policy makers as needs of ageing societies continue to increase in dramatic proportions (Brubaker & Brubaker, 1992; Tennstedt, 1999). Eighty percent of all care to elders in the United States is provided by family members (Westbrook, 1989), primarily by the spouse or adult daughters (Brody, 1985; Reece, Walz, & Hageboeck, 1983; Montgomery, Gonyea, & Hooyman, 1983; Stone, Cafferata, & Sangl, 1987).

There is no doubt that the illness of any family member is stressful, and this review focuses on how taking care of elderly parents affects the health of the family. The consensus in the literature, built on a strong foundation of empirical evidence, is that caregiving of the elderly can be hazardous to the caregiver's health (Grunfeld, Glossop, McDowell, & Danbrook, 1997; Schulz & Beach, 1999; Schulz, Visintainer, & Williamson, 1990). However, the health effects on others in the caregiver's family—such as spouse, siblings, or children—are relatively unknown (Leiberman & Fisher, 1995).

Research on family caregiving of the elderly has concentrated on the "primary caregiver," or the person who provides the most care to the patient, or who has the principal responsibility for the patient's care. This approach tends to obscure the involvement of—and consequences to—other family members or the family unit. In one of few studies that broach this gap, Lieberman and Fischer (1995) reported negative effects on both mental and physical health of the caregiver's spouse and offspring. Due to the scarcity of direct evidence, inferences for the health of the caregiver's family will be derived in this article from a review of the effects of caregiving on the primary caregiver.

The empirics of family care of the elderly have been built on the general stress model, which contributes to the casting of family caregiving as primarily a negative event, or "burden" (Warnes, 1993). In this review, current thought on the benefits of caregiving will be included to offset negativity. In addition, a life course perspective for individual and family development will counterbalance the negative potential of caregiving that is emphasized in the literature, as well as provide the structure of an action plan for health professionals.

Definition of Family Health

For the purpose of this review, family health is defined as the collective emotional and physical health of a family. A life course perspective on parent care is foundational to understanding family health over time (Bengtson & Allen, 1993). Families denote groups of individuals connected across the lifespan, in which energies are often shifted to address new demands, for example, childcare or major illness. In times of any caregiving demand, family health is the balanced comfort level of a family unit, in which the needs of the care recipient can be met without deleterious consequences to other family members.

A significant caregiving event is by necessity a shared family event, and the roles and experiences of all players need to be considered in balancing the resources of the family unit to solve the crisis or needs of one particular family member. Extending the definition of health to include family members automatically complicates the picture. When focusing on one person, it is easier to evaluate benefits and risks of actions to that individual. But when the health of the family is considered, it is much more difficult to tally the total impact.

For the purpose of this review, it is assumed that principal costs or risks to the family unit can be calculated as the personal consequences to the primary caregiver, especially emotional and physical, as well as financial. These costs to the primary caregiver can be extended to the family unit. While it seems likely that family members would react negatively to the loss of attention from the primary caregiver, such effects have not been studied. Relatively little is known about the role or reactions of the caregiver's spouse. Adult children report feeling the loss of the parents' previous support (Ziemba, 2002), but is in unclear to what degree others in the caregiver's family experience similar losses. Nonetheless, it makes intuitive sense that grandchildren might suffer the loss of their parents' attentions as well as the loss of the grandparents.

Family Caregiving & Cultural Diversity

Family roles and expectations are shaped by cultural values (Burr et al. 1979), with varying degrees of prescriptive custom. For example, in contrast to the U. S., many societies clearly designate the particular child in the family who has primary responsibility for the care of parents (Sokolovsky, 1990). Cultural heritage could constitute either an additional stressor or a mitigating resource for families of various backgrounds seeking care in the United States.

America is a large, complicated and diverse nation, and is typically classified as a unique culture with historical connections to western European traditions. Family participation in care of the elderly is further complicated in American culture, which, driven by values of autonomy and informed choice, tends to focus on the preferences and perspectives of the patient, with little systematic accommodation for the needs and views of other involved family members (Collopy, Dubler, & Zuckerman, 1990; Hardwig, 1990; High, 1991).

Despite differing racial and ethnic preferences or customs, the following common issues transcend cultures and families and may affect relationships between health care providers and patients' families:

1. Variations of family structure and degrees of family cohesiveness (or collectivism)
2. Gender roles and relationships with authority figures
3. Family structures for decision making
4. Desired degree of family presence in health care situations
5. Extended families and available social support
6. The interface with the health care delivery system and the predominant cultural group.

Health of the Primary Caregiver

Psychological Health

Because of the burgeoning demands for care represented by an increased number of frail elderly in American society, much has been written since the 1960s about the experiences of family caregivers of the elderly. The majority of research studies have been conducted from the perspective of the general stress model (Barer & Johnson, 1990; Given & Given, 1991). As a result of the demands or stressors, caregivers of the elderly are at risk for "burnout," depression, lost income, and isolation (Sayles-Cross, 1992; Tennstedt, 1999; Wright, Clipp, & George, 1993). Family caregiving commonly results in psychological distress and increased risk for clinical depression (Mellins, Blum, Boyd-Davis, & Gatz, 1993; Reese, Gross, Smalley, & Messer, 1994; Schulz et al., 1990; Skaff & Pearlin, 1992). Schulz, Visintainer, and Williamson (1990) reviewed over thirty studies on family caregivers and reported that a majority contained evidence of demoralization, and a higher rate of depressive symptoms. Indeed, despite a wide variety of measurement and selection issues, the finding of depression and depressive symptoms among caregivers is robust.

In order to effectively help caregivers of the elderly adjust over the long haul it is important to distinguish clinical depression from shock, loss, and grief. Daughters have consistently reported that one of the hardest parts of taking care of elderly parents was dealing with emotions—their parents' as well as their own (Given & Given, 1991). It is important to keep in mind that the parents may be depressed or traumatized by the changes in health and independence, and such moods will affect those who care for them. Grief and loss are dominant themes in narratives about caregiving and are to be expected (Hausman, 1979; McCarty, 1996; Shaw, 1987; Ziemba, 2002). Adult children are likely to report guilt, anger, depression, and role reversal (Bowers, 1987; Fischer, 1985). In one study, daughters used the term "role reversal" to define the experience of losing the prior support of the parent, in combination with the new demand to provide the safety net for the parents (Ziemba, 2002).

While empirical investigation is lacking, it is likely that others close to the caregiver could be affected by the caregiver's depressive symptoms, depression, and grief. Other family members might be a source of support and mitigate the negative impact on the primary caregiver, but could also be another source of conflict or a stressor for the primary caregiver due to their own distressed or negative reactions to the situation.

Social Ties

The social effects of caregiving include isolation (Aneshensel, Pearlin, & Schuler, 1993; Given & Given, 1991; Jepson, McCorkle, Adler, Nuamah, & Lusk, 1999) and disrupted relationships with other family members (Mellins et al., 1993), including conflict with one's own children (Franks & Stephens, 1996; Pruchno, Peters, & Burant, 1995).

Parent care has been proposed as a developmental task of the sibling network (Cicirelli, 1994; Goetting, 1986), but siblings are often a source of conflict for adult children taking care of elderly parents (Brody, Hoffman, Kleban, & Schoonover, 1989; Hausman, 1979; Suitor & Pillemer, 1993). Parent care can revive sibling rivalries and other long-standing family issues. Forty percent of adult children in one study reported conflict with another family member, usually a sibling who was not helping as expected (Strawbridge & Wallhagen, 1991). However, siblings are also likely to be identified as a major source of instrumental support (Suitor & Pillemer, 1996).

Often it is assumed that people from different ethnic or minority backgrounds enjoy the added assistance that comes from large, extended families, and values of family collectivism. However, such assumptions may lead to false security among health care professionals that the needs of family caregivers are being met. For example, the majority of studies reviewed by Dilworth-Anderson and colleagues (2002) that examined social support and culture indicated that non-Hispanic whites have a less diverse set of extended helpers than do minority caregivers. However, the studies did not support the common assumption that minority caregivers receive more informal social support. For example, when other factors were controlled, it was more likely that African Americans were sole providers of care and in greater need of formal support services.

Thus, family and extended family could be actual or potential resources to the primary caregiver, but could also represent additional sources of strain. Caregiving itself could lead to decreased socialization and isolation for the caregiver.

Work & Other Roles

Balancing multiple roles—including work—is a common and central task for family caregivers (McCarty, 1996). The typical caregiver of elderly parents is female, married, and employed full-time. Adult children may fill many other social roles, such as raising their own children, and pursuing a career. Work roles may be a source of added stress for some, but may provide others with information and referral, as well as an escape from caregiving by means of distraction and socialization (Barnes, Given, & Given, 1995; Reece et al., 1983). However, caregivers often make adjustments in employment status to facilitate caregiving, such as reducing or quitting work, or taking an early retirement (Guberman, Maheu, & Maille, 1992; Kingson & O' Grady-LeShane, 1993; Pohl, Given, Collins, & Given, 1994).

Another strategy to address the care needs of the ageing parent is for the parent or child to move in with the other (Tennstedt, 1999; Ziemba, 2002). This has implications for other people in the household and typically requires adjustment to the new living arrangements. Thus, multiple roles—including work roles or childcare—may provide respite, distraction, or resources that offset the demands of caregiving. However, the constellation of benefits and conflicting demands of multiple roles will depend on the situation, and caregivers and their families may face difficult choices or periods of adjustment.

Physical Health

In contrast to the large volume of studies on the psychosocial effects of caregiving, there is less certainty as to the risks for physical health (Reese et al., 1994; Schulz et al., 1990) but caution is warranted. Health problems could result from the deleterious effects of stress on the immune system, resulting in less resistance to acute or chronic disease. Shulz and Beach (1999) found a 63% higher death rate in caregivers who reported role strain. The family could be at risk for "double trouble" if the caregiver's health is affected by caregiving demands.

Other Risks over the Lifespan

In addition to health risks, caregiving can threaten financial well-being. In the short run, there may be additional costs of hired help, which can be very expensive (Grunfeld et al., 1997; Levine, 1999). Tennstedt (1999) reported analyses by Harrow et al. (1995), using a market value approach that estimated family care contributions at $9,552 per year.

Caregivers face other expenses when replacement costs of providing direct care services are considered. In the long run, many caregivers reduce work hours to provide care, take early retirement, or pass up promotions or career changes (Guberman et al., 1992; Kingson & O'Grady-LeShane, 1993). For women pursuing careers, the disruption caused by family caregiving could decrease total earning power, and divert energy and funds from the development of the caregivers' own retirement prospects (Grunfeld et al., 1997; Kingson & O' Grady-LeShane, 1993). In addition, care demands can disrupt work schedules, concentration, and productivity, thus placing the caregiver at risk of losing a job (Gottlieb, Kelloway, & Fraboni, 1994; Neal et al., 1993).

The Beneficial Effects of Caregiving

Most of the research to date has emphasized harmful consequences on caregivers of the elderly. Belief in the benefits of family caregiving helps to build a strong platform of support for caregivers as a result of a more positive outlook, and thus promotes family health (Louderback, 2000). Many caregivers do not report role strain or other negative consequences (Tennstedt, 1999). In life-span developmental approaches, care of elderly parents is often viewed as a developmental task of middle- to late-life through which the adult child gains maturity and wisdom for their own later years (e. g, Blenkner, 1965).

While caregiving has potential risks, real costs, and serious implications, it is simply unavoidable for many families when the call comes. As part of the human experience integral to family relationships, family caregiving is often not an option, but a certainty. Adult children feel their duty, and parent care is often assumed out of obligation.

Rewards of Caregiving

The most obvious benefit to family health is protection of the well being of the care recipient and the satisfaction of knowing that a parent was well cared for (NAC & AARP, 1997; Riedel, Fredman, & Langenberg, 1998). In a national survey, the majority of family caregivers (57%) described their experiences positively, using terms such as "rewarding" or "enjoyable" (NAC & AARP, 1997), and identified additional benefits of pride in doing a good deed, of making the care recipient happy, and of earning the care recipient's gratitude. Other common themes were fulfilling family obligations, and repaying parents.

Such rewards and benefits of caregiving accrue not only during the time spent caregiving, but increase in value long after the parent's death. A life course or developmental model suggests latent benefits for caregivers since they avoid guilt and find comfort in rewarding memories. A good resolution of the "filial crisis" means that adult children attain greater maturity and are better prepared for their own ageing (Blenkner, 1965).

Greater emphasis on the ultimate or "spiritual" meaning of being a caregiver may be a more fruitful approach than focusing on costs. McLeod (1999) asserts that accepting the difficult aspects of caregiving is a realistic approach, and that for caregivers to grow from the event they must internalize the experience in terms of life goals and the importance of human, caring relationships.

Improved Family Relationships

The most salient and persistent influence on all aspects of caregiver burden is the quality of the relationship between caregiver and care recipient (Tennstedt, 1999). Caregiving can stress relationships, but it can also improve them. About a third of caregivers in one study reported an improvement in their relationships as a result of assuming a caregiver role (Ziemba, 2002). Spending time with the care recipient is another reward of caregiving (NAC & AARP, 1997). Likewise, whereas 40% of adult children named their siblings as a major source of conflict, 60% reported no such problems and some took pride in how siblings matured, and worked together to meet the parents' needs (Strawbridge & Wallhagen, 1991).

Action Plan for Health Professionals

The role of the health care professional is aimed primarily at helping the caregiver cope with the increased demands, and to help caregivers balance responsibilities to the care recipient, to themselves, and to other family members. Health professionals may find it helpful to choose from the many lifespan developmental and family systems frameworks to guide therapeutic interactions with adults involved in parent care (e. g., Bengtson & Allen, 1993; Blenkner, 1965; Kramer, 1993; Worthington, 1987). While general stress models highlight the hazards of caregiving, developmental and family systems theories are useful in that parent care is acknowledged as an important and temporary challenge to the family, and thus redirect emphasis to long-term benefits of caregiving as well as draw attention to the roles and needs of other family members.

It is helpful to distinguish between stress and a state of crisis. Caregiving can be viewed as normal family stress but with the potential to cause deleterious health effects on the caregiver and other family members if a state of crisis persists. The need for care can arise suddenly and dramatically, or can build gradually over many years. Or, sudden death of the parent may preclude the need for caregiving, but not for griefwork.

Health professionals with middle-aged clients or family practices need to be alert to the likelihood of caregiving of elderly parents as an emergent or future stressor on the adult child, with potential effects on the caregiver's health especially at midlife and beyond. Health care professionals also need to recognise that adult children may be responsible for the care of both parents, either at once, or sequentially. As a result, some adult children face cumulative loss and strain (Ziemba, 2002).

Adopt "Family-Friendly" Policies

Concerned health care professionals should invite family participation and assess family concerns. Respect for cultural diversity and family preferences mandates assessment of patient preferences for the presence and involvement of family members, especially concerning the procedures and roles of family members in major decisions. Policies supportive of cultural diversity also include awareness of gender roles and patterns of interaction with authority figures (such as with parents, or with health care professionals). Assessment of the family structure can potentially strengthen resources for the primary caregiver as well as open avenues to understanding the effects of the elder's illness on others in the family.

Strategies can be implemented to help patients and their families discuss caregiving concerns and to make health-related decisions. Studies suggest that caregivers in general fail to prepare, plan, or anticipate events associated with caregiving (Archbold, Stewart, Greenlick, & Harvath, 1990; Archbold et al., 1995; Horowitz, 1985; Pohl et al., 1994; Tennstedt, 1999). Health professionals can start by encouraging either the care recipient or the caregiver to formulate anticipatory strategies, such as Living Wills.

It takes an adjustment for many elderly parents to accept help from their children, for fear of becoming a burden to them, or from fear of losing independence, control, and privacy (Brakman, 1994;

McCullough, Wilson, Teasdale, Kolpakchi, & Skelly, 1993; Motenko & Greenberg, 1995; Strandberg, Norberg, & Jansson, 2000). Adult children may be overprotective or conversely, might need to take charge in the presence of unsafe situations. Parents may even hide their infirmities from their children (Ziemba, 2002).

Adult children may have negative memories of their own upbringing, and parent and child may not necessarily get along. Despite interpersonal conflict, adult children are often compelled by obligation to persist as caregivers. Therefore, health care professionals need to be sensitive to the perceptions and needs of care recipients and caregivers, in order to help both parties negotiate new roles and behaviours, and attain healthier outcomes for all involved.

Caregivers may be so concerned about their parents that they might be overlooking signs of trouble for other important family members. Health care professionals can inquire about the potential effects on others in the family, such as children who might be feeling ignored or left out.

Respect, Comfort & Counsel

The number one need of caregivers is to be appreciated for what they do and how they are feeling (Levine, 1999). Recognise and respect the significance of the caregivers' loss and emotions, including grief. Caregiving represents painful realities experienced amid a host of heavy emotions such as guilt, anxiety, worry, and frustration. These are normal reactions and it will take time to resolve them.

Inform & Guide

Caregivers often report a need for information (Levine, 1999; NAC, 1998). Learning needs may be simple or complex. Acquiring a sense of mastery can ease caregiving (Tennstedt, 1999). Caregivers may need help to access information and services. The health care system itself is often a source of frustration and stress for caregivers, due to gaps in the continuum of care and barriers to information. This problem could be especially intimidating to families with language barriers or cultural values prohibiting the questioning of authority figures.

Caregivers need to be persistent in tracking down information and services that work for them. Good places for caregivers to start their search are the local Area Agency on Ageing; social work departments in health care agencies; the Visiting Nurses Association or other home care provider; and libraries and bookstores. Ethnic, religious, and alternative communities often provide services and direction to their members.

Promote Balancing Acts & Caregiver Self Care

Achieving and maintaining balance are important and central tasks of adult caregivers (Shyu, 2000). Help caregivers to evaluate options, set limits to their involvement, and dash the cherished myth of being all things to all people. Assist caregivers to recognise the importance of maintaining their own health and peace of mind to the greatest extent possible. Encourage opportunities for caregivers to reflect on the deeper meaning of caregiving and to maintain their spiritual health (McLeod, 1999).

Some of the adult "children" of the elderly are themselves elderly and at risk for health problems. Encourage caregivers to maintain check-ups and screening such as mammograms, etc. Explore and encourage the recruitment of other family members, friends and services to provide respite so that caregivers can renew their energies and outlook.

Build in Support for the Long Term

While there can be a great variation in the duration, intensity, and sequelae of the caregiving trajectory, the average length of time as a caregiver is four to five years (NAC & AARP, 1997; Strawbridge & Wallhagen, 1991). Be aware of the major transitions that caregivers may face, from combining households with the parent, to changing work status. Be alert to the potential for caregiver engulfment, burnout, and depression (Skaff & Pearlin, 1992). Caregivers may avoid seeking additional help because of beliefs that the problem will be quickly resolved, from unrealistic expectations of themselves, or from a simple lack of awareness of available services. Caregivers involved in individual or family counselling face better outcomes (Whitlatch, Zarit, & Eye, 1991).

Since caregivers find it helpful to talk with others who have been through similar problems (Suitor & Pillemer, 1996), encourage them and their family members to join caregiver support groups. There are many resources on caregiving, including support groups at local agencies, a wide range of self-help books in bookstores, and numerous virtual communities.

Encourage Quality Family Time

Encourage opportunities for "quality family time," that is, recreational time with the care recipient, and don't leave out the grandchildren. Despite caregiving's bad reputation in the literature, this time can also be one of great meaning and enjoyment. Interventions aimed at family enrichment (e. g., Archbold et al., 1990; Archbold et al., 1995) enhance the caregiving experience and contribute to the ultimate aim of pleasant memories of time well spent.

Respite, Advocacy & the Health Care System

Last, but perhaps most important, engage in critical self evaluation of services provided to the elderly and their families. Advocate for family-friendly policies and procedures such as family conferences, flexible scheduling for office visits, house calls for frail elderly, workplace support for caregivers, and reduction of barriers to information and services. In addition, meeting the needs of caregivers requires improvement in the continuum of respite services and long-term care options available in the community.

Conclusion

In summary, taking care of elderly parents is an important event to adult children and their families. Health care professionals can enable adult children as caregivers through supportive and family-focused strategies. While health risks and benefits to other family members are not as well delineated as those for the primary caregiver, cautious inquiry is advisable in order to prevent secondary harm to the family unit. Involvement and recognition of the potential contributions of other family members may help to reduce the deleterious effects on the primary caregiver as well as to promote growth of other individuals in the family. Such concern and intervention can help families through a difficult time, strengthen family bonds, and promote comforting memories of their time together as a family.

Families and Elder Care in the Twenty-First Century

For most of the nation's history, caring for the elderly was a family affair carried out largely by women in the home. As the twenty-first century unfolds, however, elder care in the United States is an increasingly complex enterprise, with much personal care "outsourced" to paid nonfamily caregivers.

Today elder care is a multisector undertaking with six key stakeholder groups—health care providers, nongovernmental community-based service agencies, employers, government, families, and elders themselves.

The six groups, however, often work separately, or even at cross-purposes. They must be better integrated and resourced to ensure that seniors can age with dignity, families can receive appropriate supports, and society can manage the costs associated with geriatric health care and elder economic security.

Changing Demographics

With the numbers of older Americans rapidly growing ever larger, the landscape of elder care in the United States is changing. During the past century, the population of Americans aged sixty-five and older increased elevenfold. According to the 2010 census, 13 percent of the population, or 40.3 million individuals, were sixty-five or older. The population share of those aged eighty-five and older, sometimes called the "oldest old," was 1.1 percent. By 2030 approximately 80 million Americans, or 20 percent of the population, are projected to be sixty-five or older, and 2.3 percent of the population will be eighty-five and older.

In addition to its increasing numbers over the coming decades, the elderly population will change in a variety of ways—more people will live longer and healthier lives, the number of older males will grow, and the group's racial and ethnic diversity will increase. But not all trends are positive. Although the poverty rate among the elderly fell from 25 percent in 1970 to 13 percent in 1992, as the real median income of both males and females increased, in 2009, approximately 12.9 percent of people 65 and older still had incomes at the poverty level. The Great Recession that began in 2007 eroded the economic status of moderate-income and middle-class elders, many of whom saw their pensions and 401(k)s decrease, the value of their homes decline, and their other financial investments lose value.

Clearly these changes in the nation's elderly population will present challenges to family members who help provide elder care. And other national demographic shifts—delayed marriage and childbearing for young adults, decreased family size, and changes in family composition and structure—are complicating that challenge. Increased longevity among elders not only extends the years of caregiving by their adult children but may require their grandchildren to become caregivers as well. Married couples may have as many as four elderly parents living; in fact, they may have more parents or relatives in need of care than they have children living at home or on their own. In the past, research on elder care focused on the challenges facing working adults who were caring for both children and elderly parents—the so-called sandwich generation—a term coined by sociologist Dorothy Miller to refer to specific generational inequalities in the exchange of resources and support. Miller's research highlighted the stress on the middle generation of employees who are caring for two groups of dependents while receiving little support. The sandwich metaphor, however, is outmoded in several respects: it does not convey that more than one generation may provide elder care or that members of any generational cohort can be both caregivers and care receivers. Nor does the image of static layers do justice to the dynamic interaction between generations, such as transfers of financial aid, sharing residential space, or exchanging personal and emotional care.

Today researchers are increasingly finding that adults may spend more years caring for their parents than caring for their children. And because families today tend to be small, middle-aged adults may have smaller sibling networks to share elder care responsibilities. In short, elder care in the United States is a demanding task, and caregivers, especially the almost 60 percent of family caregivers who are employed, are finding it harder to undertake that task alone.

Care Work and the Dimensions of Elder Caregiving

There is an extensive body of research on family "care work" dating back to the 1960s with a study that challenged the "myth of the abandoned elderly" and showed that families were still caring for elders, but that changes in external conditions in the family, the workplace, and the community were making caregiving more challenging.

One of the contributions of recent care work research is to draw attention to the "work" aspects of caregiving. This framing contradicts personal and cultural ideas about why families care for elders and makes two related arguments: the first is that because family caregiving is largely done by women and is unpaid, it is often devalued; the second is that despite this devaluing, unpaid care work adds huge value to U.S. society in providing much needed care and "services" to the most vulnerable in the nation's population. Some scholars have tried to calculate the monetary value of unpaid care work to strengthen the argument about its value. Estimates vary from $196 billion a year, calculated in 1997, to $257 billion a year based on a subsequent study by the United Hospital Fund in 2004. In either case, the numbers far exceed what the United States spends on home health care and nursing home care, underscoring the importance of family care.

To differentiate the work families provide from the work that professionals and paraprofessionals provide, many studies of caregiving use the terms "informal care" to refer to the care provided by families and "formal care" to refer to that provided by trained health and social service staff. The distinction creates a sharp line between the informal care that is unpaid and takes place in private homes and the formal care that is paid and takes place in institutional and community settings. The distinction, however, has been challenged by some elder care scholars who find that family caregivers of elders provide care in hospitals, rehabilitation facilities, outpatient clinics, and community agencies. Family caregivers are a "shadow workforce" in the geriatric health care system. Some states are piloting "cash and counselling" programs to pay families for the elder care they do, so the paid-unpaid distinction is being challenged in public policies. Elder care entails a variety of supports and responsibilities, many of which can change in intensity and complexity over time. Cultural differences unique to elders and their families shape their views on what ageing, health, and end of life mean and thus affect expectations about who provides care and what is provided. The variations in elder care are numerous, as the following eight dimensions illustrate.

Time Dimension

Elder care takes three forms: short-term, intermittent, and long-term. Elderly parents may, for example, have surgery that immobilizes them temporarily, but restores them to a high level of daily functioning. In such cases the care needed may be fairly intense but of short duration, and so it disrupts the caregiver's job, family, and personal life, but only temporarily. In contrast, the seven in ten care recipients who have chronic health conditions may require intermittent care that entails regular trips to one or more specialists, medication management, and adjustments to household and personal routines. In such cases, the caregiver is needed frequently over a longer period and may be hard pressed to integrate caregiving demands with paid work. In other cases elder care may be long-term, lasting for months or years. Such caregiving may be required on a daily basis and can seriously complicate the caregiver's ability to maintain a job, provide care for other family members, and maintain personal and community involvement.

Since 1987 the American Association of Retired Persons (now called AARP) and the National Alliance for Caregiving (NAC) have conducted several national surveys tracking the time Americans invest in elder care. The most recent survey, in 2009, found intermittent elder care to be the type most commonly provided. Caregivers surveyed in that poll report providing such care for an average of 4.6 years; 31 percent report giving such care for more than five years. Half of all of caregivers spend eight hours or less a week, while 12 percent spend more than forty hours. Short-term or intermittent care may evolve into long-term care as an elder's physical or mental function, or both, deteriorates.

Geographic Dimension

The distance between an elder's place of residence and that of the caregiver has a major effect on the type and frequency of care. Because some American families are mobile—about 16 percent of families move each year—adult children sometimes live in different cities, states, or even regions from their elderly parents. According to the most recent AARP-NAC survey data, 23 percent of caregivers live with the elder for whom they are caring (co-residence is particularly common among low-income caregivers) and 51 percent live twenty minutes away.

Long-distance caregiving, however, has been on the rise over the past fifteen years. One study by MetLife finds that at least 5 million caregivers live an hour or more away from the elder for whom they care. Of this group, about 75 percent provide help with daily activities, such as shopping, transportation, and managing household finances. Most long-distance caregivers share responsibilities with siblings or paid caregivers, or both. Several studies document that adult children who live near an elderly relative are most likely to provide the majority of elder care, underscoring the importance of geographic location.

Residential Dimension

To move, or not to move? Many elders struggle with this question, and often turn to family caregivers for help with the answer. Most elders want to live in their own homes and neighbourhoods; for some, safety and accessibility require home renovations. Family caregivers may plan, organise, and finance adaptations in an elder's living space. Not all elders and all caregivers are homeowners (some are renters), which can pose particular challenges for all parties. When it is not feasible for elders to adapt their dwelling, moving becomes necessary. In that case, caregivers often research, plan, and organise the move. Some elders move to continuing care retirement communities that provide different types of units for residents of different abilities. Although such communities have grown in popularity, and may relieve families of some responsibilities, the units are expensive to buy, and monthly maintenance fees are costly, thus making this option unaffordable for most elders.

A small share of elders lives in rehabilitation facilities, usually on a short-term basis. Between 5 and 6 percent of elders live in a long-term-care facility or nursing home, with caregivers making regular or intermittent trips to visit and monitor the care being provided. Most elders live in their own homes, which must be constantly assessed for safety and the availability of community services such as transportation, social services, and recreational opportunities. Nongovernmental organisations (NGOs) help maintain more than 10 million elders a day with long-term care supports and services so they can continue to live in their homes independently. To help caregivers assess what is required for independent living, researchers have developed tools that can aid in choosing appropriate housing and support services.

Financial Dimension

The economic resources available to caregiving families vary widely. Upper-middle-class and affluent families usually have adequate funds to pay for elder care services, while poor families are usually eligible for a variety of subsidized services, such as home health care. The hardest-hit families are the working poor and those with moderate incomes, who are too "rich" to qualify for subsidized services but unable to pay for care themselves. Many families caring for elderly relatives encounter this type of "middle-class squeeze."

Researchers who explore the financial dimension of elder care find that cross-generational transfers are fairly common. In a 2005 study, percent of baby boomers provided financial assistance to a parent in the previous year, while about a fifth received financial support from a parent. A recent nationally representative survey of elders over sixty-five offers a slightly different picture: half of these elders say they have given money to their adult children, while about a third say they help their adult children with child care, errands, housework, and home repairs. When asked what their adult children give them, more than 40 percent report receiving help with errands and rides to appointments; about a third, help with housework and home repairs; and about a fifth, help with bill paying and direct financial support. What is striking is that care, time, and money are being exchanged between the generations, going both ways.

Health Dimension

Some caregivers provide help in a short-term acute health care crisis, others care for elders with one or more chronic diseases, and a third group cares for elders with long-term incurable or progressive diseases. Families are a critical resource for the nation's health care system when they care for a relative with a debilitating disease, such as dementia or Alzheimer's, for which paid care is very expensive. Giving such care, however, is a major burden on these families, who frequently find that caregiver training—both how to manage the behaviour and symptoms of the elder and how to cope with their own feelings—is often not available.

The health status of an elder determines the extent of a caregiver's involvement with personal care, often referred to as activities of daily living, such as eating, bathing, toileting, and dressing, or as instrumental activities of daily living, such as cooking, shopping, and bill paying. The health status of the elder also shapes the extent of caregivers' involvement in medical tasks such as giving medications; dressing wounds after surgery; checking weight, blood pressure, and blood sugar levels; and monitoring medical equipment. A national survey of caregivers found that more than 40 percent helped with one or more medical tasks, even though only one-third reported that they had the training to do so. That finding underscores the "medicalization" of the care work that families are providing for elders.

One elderly cohort that is growing is "frail elders," defined as those sixty-five and older who do not live in nursing homes, but have difficulty with at least one aspect of independent living or are severely disabled, or both. This group numbered about 10.7 million people in 2002. Analyses of a national data set showed that two-thirds of frail elders receive help—an average of 177 hours a month—with personal care from an unpaid family caregiver. More than half of that help comes from their daughters, most of whom are working.

Legal and Ethical Dimension

When significant declines in physical and mental health compromise elders' ability to manage their own affairs, it is usually the family caregiver who assumes some level of control, decision-making power, and ultimately legal authority such as power of attorney. Studies on the legal issues of elders often focus, particularly when financial resources are involved, on the caregiver as a source of interfamilial conflict and even elder abuse. A recent study of financial elder abuse, however, found that only 16.9 percent of the perpetrators were family members.

Legal issues may also require caregivers to take on complex health-related roles, such as acting as health care proxy or setting up an advance directive or DNR (do not resuscitate) order. These steps can involve complex ethical questions and decisions, such as when to discontinue life supports for a terminally ill parent. Studies on elders at the end of life show the critical role that family caregivers play once palliative care is chosen, including assisting elders with daily living, handling medications, and making medical decisions. Using ethnographic data, a study of one elderly mother and her daughter documents how this family navigated the health care system and brought their own cultural meaning to end-of-life care. Other studies emphasize the high degree of stress on families with terminally ill elders, showing the unresponsiveness of some health care systems, as well as the ways in which community services can ease stress.

Emotional, Moral, and Spiritual Dimension

Much of the research on elder care explores the practical daily routines involved in personal care, health care, and housing. The emotional care that families provide, although essential to the well-being of elders, is less studied and is difficult to define. The medical anthropologist Arthur Kleinman, a caregiver for his wife with Alzheimer's, argues that the emotional part of caregiving is in essence a moral act—"an existential quality of what it is to be a human being."

Attending to the spiritual needs of elders for whom religious experience, practice, and faith have been important is also critical to sustaining their physical and mental health and longevity. For these elders, caregivers' tasks include: spiritual and well-being assessments; using a reminiscence-and-life-review approach; identifying and facilitating contact with religious services, organisations, and clergy; and discussing end-of-life issues. Tailoring these tasks to an individual elder's particular faith tradition is both time-consuming and extremely meaningful.

Outsourcing Elder Care and Care Coordination

When family members cannot provide care, particularly if they are full-time workers or long-distance caregivers, or both, their job is to find an agency close to where the elder lives that will provide services for a fee. It takes time and effort to find an appropriate multiservice or ageing service agency, to provide the agency with detailed personal and health information about the elder to ensure a good "client-provider fit," and to monitor services to be sure that needs are met and the elder is comfortable with the provider. Carrying out all these tasks to find just one type of service is difficult enough; if an elder needs multiple services, the work for the family can be significant.

Many studies have documented the fragmentation in the geriatric health care and social services system, and others have called for greater care coordination to support caregivers. The handoffs between hospitals and families, or between rehabilitation facilities and families, can often be unsafe and unsatisfying, and the need for improved communication is widely documented. Given the cross-institutional complexities, some caregivers hire a geriatric care manager—often a trained social worker—to identify, monitor, and coordinate services. Hiring a care manager requires research by the family caregiver, as well as ongoing monitoring and extensive communication. The work of care coordination is a significant, often unnoticed, aspect of care many families do themselves, either because they cannot afford to hire a geriatric care manager or because they prefer to keep an eye on things themselves.

Elder Caregiving and Diversity

Most studies on ageing and elder care treat elders and their caregivers as monolithic groups. But as the nation has become more diverse, so too has the population of elders. Elder caregiving varies by gender, race, and socioeconomic status, and families from African American, Latino, Asian, Native American, and other groups bring their own strengths and needs to the caregiving experience. Although gender, race, and socioeconomic status are treated separately below, it is important to note that these variables often intersect in powerful and important ways in the lives of caregivers. An "intersectionality" approach shows how unequal opportunity over the life course shapes trajectories of advantage and disadvantage for elders and the families who care for them. Future research must explore multiple aspects of diversity in order to develop new policies that address the interaction between socioeconomic inequality and differences based on gender, race, and culture.

Gender and Elder Care

Elderly women live longer than do elderly men, and despite a lifetime of providing care to others, they are more likely than men to live alone, live in poverty, and lack care themselves when they are elderly. Research on gender and caregiving has two major themes. First, the majority (67 percent) of family caregivers are women, with wives providing care to spouses and adult daughters providing the majority of care to elderly parents. Second, given the persistence of gender inequality in the workforce, including the gender gap in wages, women caregivers are more likely than men to cut back on work hours or quit their jobs because of their caregiving duties and are thus left with less income, small savings, and reduced pensions.

Although women in the general population have greater elder care responsibilities than do men, recent studies reveal that employed women and employed men provide care in roughly equal numbers. But gender differences persist nonetheless: employed women are more likely than employed men to provide family care on a regular basis, they spend more hours providing care, and they spend more time providing direct care such as meal preparation, household work, physical care, and transportation. This finding is consistent with other evidence on gender trends in elder care showing that women tend to perform household and personal care tasks that are physically draining and likely to interrupt daily activities, while men tend to give periodic assistance. Both working and nonworking male caregivers receive more assistance with their caregiving efforts than do women; they also tend to delegate their tasks to others and to seek paid assistance to alleviate some of their caregiving responsibilities.

Despite the growing number of men balancing work and elder care responsibilities, women are particularly vulnerable to negative work-related consequences. Women who are caring for elders generally reduce their work hours, leave the workforce, or make other adjustments that have negative financial or career implications. Some refuse overtime and pass up promotions, training, assignments that are more lucrative, jobs requiring travel, and other challenging but time-consuming job opportunities. Many low-income women and women of colour who are employed do not have sufficient flexibility or autonomy in their jobs to be able to take an elderly parent to the doctor or attend to other needs.

Despite feelings of satisfaction from their care, caregivers can sometimes feel burdened, socially isolated, strained, and hopeless. A recent MetLife study of working caregivers, based on a large corporate employer's health risk appraisal database of roughly 17,000 respondents, found that employed women are significantly more likely than employed men caregivers to self-report negative effects on personal well-being. Caregivers in general report more physical and mental health problems than noncaregivers, and more female caregivers (58 percent) report negative health effects than male caregivers (42 percent). In a study assessing gender differences in caregiver health, Martin Pinquart and Silvia SÃ¶renson found that women had lower scores for subjective well-being and perceived physical health, as well as higher scores for burden and depression than men. The effects for women caregivers indicated a positive and statistically significant relationship.

Race, Ethnicity, and Elder Care

The growing diversity of the United States makes it important for researchers to consider how race and ethnicity—both socially constructed categories—shape ageing and the caregiving experience. The nation's legacy of racial oppression and structural inequality has created socioeconomic inequities in education, health, housing, income, and wealth. Many low-income men and women of colour enter old age after a lifetime of cumulative disadvantage, during which limited access to economic opportunity has obstructed efforts to accumulate savings for retirement and limited access to health care has led to poorer health.

Few families from racial and ethnic minority groups use paid or outsourced care, and those who do can sometimes face structural barriers in accessing them. Although most Americans refrain from putting their elderly kin in nursing homes, Latinos, African Americans, and Asians are least likely to do so. Even elders of colour with greater care needs, such as those afflicted with dementia or chronic illnesses, are more likely than whites to receive care from their children and live in the community with them.

Many studies show that families of colour rely on extended kin networks and friends for financial assistance, material goods, domestic duties, and other supports. African Americans, especially, rely on networks of neighbours, friends, and fellow congregants. Language and cultural barriers often lead Chinese American and Puerto Rican caregivers to use ethnically oriented organisations in their communities for support. Extensive social support may partially explain why racial and ethnic minority groups tend to have more favourable attitudes toward caregiving and higher caregiving satisfaction. Studies suggest that many groups of colour value mutual exchange, reciprocity, filial responsibility, and interdependence, whereas Western European and white ethnic groups value self-reliance and independence. Using well-established positive appraisal scales and coping questionnaires, several studies find a significant "race" effect, with caregivers of colour such as African Americans and Latinos showing the highest appraisals of positive aspects of caregiving and higher scores on well-being measures.

Among some Latino groups, the extended family is expected to provide care to older relatives, and Native Americans strongly value giving back to those who have provided for them, reinforcing the value of reciprocity in their culture. White caregivers report greater depression and view caregiving as more stressful than do caregivers of colour. Studies that have addressed racial and ethnic differences among caregivers generally have not focused on working caregivers. One that does finds that employed white caregivers report significantly higher work demand and strain than Latino and black working caregivers.

Although research consistently reveals significant differences in caregiver outcomes by race, findings may vary because of differences in recruitment strategies, in criteria for inclusion and exclusion, in construct measurement, in research instruments, and in statistical techniques. The studies also vary in sample size and sampling strategy and rarely use random assignment or national probability sampling to posit any causal relationships between variables. To strengthen generalizability, accuracy of statistical findings, and comparability across studies, researchers will have to use more diverse and random sampling strategies as well as experimental and mixed qualitative and quantitative methodologies.

Socioeconomic Status and Elder Care

Although researchers do not often explore the implications of socioeconomic status— defined by education, occupational status, family income, net worth, and financial assets—for elder care, it can nevertheless have important effects on elders' quality of life and the kind of care their families can provide.

In the first place, many low-income elders have insufficient resources. More than half of all senior households (54 percent) cannot meet their expenses even using their combined financial net worth, Social Security benefits, and pension incomes. Among older persons reporting income in 2008, 20.3 percent had less than $10,000. Such economic challenges often increase the financial burden, hardship, and strain on their families. Many studies do show that families with higher socioeconomic status tend not to provide physical care themselves, and instead tend to purchase elder care services, provide financial gifts, buy alternative lodging, and remodel homes to accommodate an elder.

A scarcity of resources makes working poor and working-class caregivers more likely to provide direct care themselves rather than to hire professional care managers. When low income families do purchase formal services, they use them only for short periods. Middleclass and higher-income caregivers hire elder care assistance for longer periods or until their resources run out.

Responses from Employers and Government

Researchers have also investigated how employers and government are responding to the challenges families face in providing elder care. Are employers, for example, providing working caregivers of elders with "familyfriendly" benefits and policies? Are federal, state, and local governments meeting the needs of elders and caregivers with public policies? We explore the adequacy of their responses to the needs of both elders and family caregivers to gain insight into what policy changes may be needed in the future.

Responses from Employers

Given the ageing of the population and the high rate of female labour force participation, the share of elder caregivers who are employed has been growing over the past thirty years and is expected to continue, nearing the percentage of employees with child care responsibilities. One of the earliest national estimates, based on data from the 1982 National Long-Term Care Survey and its companion National Informal Caregivers Survey, was that 15.8 percent of elder caregivers were employed, 9 percent had quit their jobs because of elder care responsibilities, and 20 percent were experiencing conflict between work and elder care. Surveys conducted in the late 1980s and 1990s found the share of employed caregivers rising significantly, up to 64 percent in 1997. One 2010 study found that six in ten family caregivers are employed; another found that considered as a group, 50 percent of employed caregivers of elders work full time, and 11 percent work part time. In the coming years, employers will need to respond to the elder care needs of their workforce lest they compromise the performance of their firms and the retention of some of their most valued employees.

Research on work and family conflict is extensive, and many studies focus on work and elder care for employees. Beyond general feelings of role conflict, working caregivers in one study report using their own sick leave or vacation hours to accommodate elder care needs (48 percent), cutting back on hours or quitting their job (37 percent), taking an additional job or increasing their hours to get funds for elder care expenses (17 percent), taking unpaid leave (15 percent), and leaving their job for a different one (14 percent). Many studies report negative health consequences for employed caregivers, including increased risk of stress and depression, diabetes, hypertension, and even premature death. If caregivers cut back work hours, take unpaid leaves, or leave their jobs, the negative effects can go beyond the individual caregivers themselves to include whole families. For example, a MetLife study documented negative financial repercussions for families from short-term income losses, long-term losses of retirement savings, and lost opportunities for career advancement.

Researchers are also examining the policies and programs of employers to address their employees' elder care needs; rough estimates are that from 25 to 50 percent of employers offer these programs. Large firms are more likely than small companies to have elder care programs, and a 2003 study estimates that 50 percent of large corporations offer such programs. For small and mid-sized firms, the estimate was 26 percent in 2006 and 22 percent in 2007. Studies on how the recent recession affected elder care programs are just now becoming available; one, for example, shows that most employers are maintaining workplace flexibility, although reduction of hours may translate into reduction in pay, so increased flexibility entails both costs and benefits.

Elder Care Assistance Programs, introduced by companies during the late 1980s, have grown in scope. The early programs— paralleling those developed to support workers with young children—included resource and referral services to locate elder care services in the elder's community, and flexible spending accounts for putting aside funds on a pre-tax basis to cover elder care expenses. During the 1990s, some companies expanded elder care benefits through Employee Assistance Programs or new "work-life programs" to include flexible work arrangements (58 percent), personal or sick leaves (16 percent), and access to short-term emergency backup care when a paid caregiver was unexpectedly absent (4 percent).

During the mid-1990s, some researchers began exploring the question of whether employees made use of elder care benefits. Early studies found that use rates were low, although the range was fairly wide—from 2 to 34 percent—with use by employees in private-sector firms lower than use by public-sector employees. Most scholars and human resource managers hypothesize that rates were low because employers had not publicized the programs that were available. A 2007 survey of human resource managers at Fortune 500 companies found that flexible work arrangements and leave programs were the most highly utilised and had the best use-to-cost ratio. Emergency short-term home care had the lowest use rates and highest cost, and thus the worst use-to-cost ratio. In open-ended questions, respondents focused on the need for better communication about elder care programs; the importance of supervisors actively encouraging the use of these programs; and the difficulty of countering negative perceptions about these programs. Although elder care benefits appear to boost employee recruitment and retention, that link has not been conclusively demonstrated.

To date, the needs of employed elder caregivers far exceed the employer response, and elder care assistance tends to be offered only by the largest employers. Some studies about "family-responsive" workplaces do not even mention elder care as a benefit needed by families, and the findings of studies that do focus on elder care have less than encouraging findings. The 2009 Age and Generations study found that employees who are caring for elders had less access to flexible work arrangements than did employees who were caring for their children or who had no dependent care responsibilities, that employees in the sandwich generation were less likely to be included in new projects based on teamwork than workers with no elder care demands, and that employees who provide elder care had lower job security than other groups. Elder care programs are still less frequently offered than child care programs, and a 2006 study found that although almost three-quarters of employers offered some child care assistance, only one-third offered elder care assistance.

What accounts for employers' lag in offering elder care assistance? And how can workplaces make elder care a key component of the work-family or work-life agenda? Elder care may have received less attention than child care because ageism and denial about ageing is deeply entrenched in U.S. culture. As Muriel Gillick, a palliative care physician, argues, "Contemporary Americans are eager to prevent, obliterate, or at least conceal old age...in keeping with the belief that we can control our destiny." This denial can lead employers to ignore or minimize the elder care needs of their workforce, using arguments about high costs and low utilisation to justify having few elder care programs.

Some work-family scholars argue that developing a family-friendly workplace is a long-term process with three distinct stages. In the first stage the goal is to promote the recognition of a particular work-family issue as a visible, legitimate need. In the second stage the goal is to implement and then refine specific programs, including effective communication and supervisor training. The third stage involves institutionalizing the new work-family programs into the culture of the workplace to heighten program reach and effectiveness. In this evolutionary paradigm, different percentages of companies are at different stages in responding to elder care. Many private-sector firms and the majority of small and mid-sized firms are still in the first stage, struggling to recognise elder care programs as a legitimate need of the workforce. Roughly a third of firms are in the second stage, starting, developing, and retaining elder care programs. Only a minority of firms—mainly large companies—are in the third stage. Making the "family-friendly workplace" an "elder-care-friendly workplace" remains an unrealised project for many employers.

Responses from Government

During the nineteenth and twentieth centuries the United States gradually transferred responsibility for elder care from the family to the government, from the private sphere to the public sphere. But despite landmark twentieth-century legislation, it can be argued that the United States lacks the full range of public policies needed to address the ageing of the population, and that families still bear the primary responsibility.

Table depicted earlier, briefly summarizes six public policies that are key to the well-being of elders and their family caregivers. Some have enhanced health and income security for elders; others have enhanced the supports available to both employed and nonemployed family caregivers. We briefly address the strengths and weaknesses of some of these policies to suggest possible areas for policy expansion.

Social Security is critical to providing a basic level of financial support and security to elders. Several issues, however, weaken its effectiveness. Initially the system strengthened intergenerational ties because those who retired—only 5.2 percent of the population was sixty-five or older in 1930—were reaping benefits based on the productivity of younger workers. But in the decades ahead, more people will be needing retirement income, and fewer young workers will be available to replenish Social Security funds, thus putting pressure on the younger generation and creating tension between generations. In addition, because Social Security is based on wages in the paid labour force, women who delayed work, interrupted work, or never entered the workforce because of family caregiving responsibilities have smaller benefits in old age than men (though at the death of her spouse, a woman is eligible to collect a "survivor" Social Security benefit).

Medicare, a second foundational piece of economic security for elders, ensures coverage of many health care costs. It, too, however, is problematic. Originally enacted to cover the costs of acute care and hospitalization, Medicare does not provide adequate insurance for chronic illnesses, those common to most elders. Medicare does not reimburse hospitals fully for the care they provide, so many hospitals have shortened patient stays, creating difficulties for caregivers when an elder is prematurely discharged to rehab or to home. Medicare will cover a stay in a skilled nursing facility only if daily nursing or rehab services are needed, and will cover ten hours a week of home care only if skilled nursing care is required. Finally, Medicare does not cover the cost of long-term care.

Medicaid, the third key government policy, is the largest source of payment for nursing home care, and it will become increasingly important as the nation's population ages. In 2008, nearly 41 percent of the nation's nursing facility care was paid by Medicaid, averaging nearly $30,000 for each beneficiary. In most states, Medicaid also pays for some long-term care services at home and in the community. Although eligibility varies from state to state, those elders who are eligible for Medicaid assistance must have limited assets and incomes below the poverty line. They also must contribute all or most of their available income toward the cost of their care. Many elderly who enter nursing homes pay for their own care initially. Once their resources have been depleted, however, they are covered by Medicaid. According to a study by Brenda Spillman and Peter Kemper, 16 percent of

Medicaid users began by paying their own way in long-term nursing facilities, exhausted their resources, and converted to Medicaid; 27

percent were covered by Medicaid when they were admitted to the nursing home. Medicaid often provides supplemental services to fill gaps left by Medicare. The Centres for Medicare and Medicaid Services estimated that Medicaid provided some additional health coverage for 8.5 million Medicare beneficiaries in 2009. In addition, Medicare and Medicaid jointly fund a model program called PACE (Program of All-Inclusive Care for the Elderly), in which an interdisciplinary team, consisting of professional and paraprofessional staff, assesses participants' needs, develops care plans, and delivers all services (including acute care services and nursing facility services when necessary), which are integrated for a seamless provision of total care. The program is available to individuals fifty-five and older who are certified by the state as nursing home eligible and meet the income and assets requirements to qualify for Medicaid.

Despite their many provisions for elder support, Medicaid and Medicare leave significant gaps in coverage. The new Patient Protection and Affordable Care Act of 2010 should ease some of the burdens by expanding drugs covered by Medicare Part D, the prescription drug program, improving prevention benefits such as free annual wellness visits, and changing the cost of Medicare Advantage plans. Mechanisms to control or reduce Medicare spending may or may not benefit elders, and a new Medicare and Medicaid Innovations Centre holds promise of testing new payment and service delivery models that could benefit elders and their families.

A fourth important policy with implications for elder care is the Older Americans Act (OAA), passed as part of Lyndon Johnson's "Great Society" reforms and the first public policy to recognise the importance of community-based NGOs in the elder care system. Although the OAA signalled a significant effort to systematize and broaden access to elder services, studies evaluating its effectiveness have had mixed findings. For example, studies of home care programs have found that although providers have had some success in managing the daily practical needs of elders, they have been less successful in dealing with emergencies or significant health issues or levels of impairment. Studies have shown that home care is more effective than inpatient care and reduces the length of hospital stays, but little data are available on how OAA programs affect measures of quality of life for elders or caregivers.

OAA's Long-Term Care Ombudsman

Program summarizes a number of issues cited in studies of other OAA programs. These include: a misalignment of resources and goals, which compromises program effectiveness; a lack of coordination between OAA programs and resources, which diminishes program effectiveness; and a lack of elder or caregiver empowerment to take control of elders' health care or make positive programs more sustainable and cost-effective.

The Family and Medical Leave Act (FMLA) is the only law that deals specifically with the challenges of working and providing elder care. A bipartisan commission that conducted two nationally representative random-sample surveys to study the impact of the FMLA on employers and employees reported to Congress in 1996 that the law was not the burden to business that some had anticipated. In terms of ease of administration and impact on productivity, profitability, and performance, the law was found either to have "no noticeable effect" or, in some cases, to produce cost savings. On the employee side, the FMLA was found to be a boon to families in their caregiving roles. Most leaves were short, and concerns that employees would abuse the law and use it for recreational time off proved unwarranted. In fact, some "leave-needers" did not take advantage of the law because they could not afford an unpaid leave. The surveys were repeated in 2000 with largely comparable results for employers and employees. The major complaint from the employer community was the difficulty of administering "intermittent leaves," although employees find that type of leave useful for chronic health problems. Between the 1995 and 2000 surveys there was a statistically significant increase in the use of FMLA for elder care.

From a policy perspective, the FMLA is like a minimum labour standard. It provides valuable protections to workers, but has limitations that hamper its effectiveness. Access to FMLA, for example, is restricted to about 55 percent of the workforce because of eligibility requirements for firms and employees. The definition of "family" is limited to parent, child, and spouse, depriving many elderly relatives such as grandparents or aunts and uncles, as well as those who are members of the lesbian, gay, bisexual, and transgendered (LGBT) community or who are not legally married, of coverage. And because the leave provided is unpaid, it is difficult for low-income workers to use. Recently two states, California and New Jersey, passed laws to establish paid leave programs, and a new study of the California law yields useful information about the applicability of these models for other states. These new state policies are contemporary examples of the historical research of sociologist Theda Skocpol, who showed that federal policy is often driven by demands from local citizen associations and the actions of state legislatures.

Finally, the National Family Caregiver Support Program (NFCSP) is the first federal law to acknowledge fully the needs of caregivers regardless of their employment status. Preliminary studies have shown that the program is expanding caregivers' access to elder care information and providing needs assessments, support groups, and stress reduction programs. Although NFCSP offers many excellent services, such as respite care, counselling, and training for family caregivers, the funds available to deliver them are limited, particularly in the area of respite care. As with many OAA programs, the goals of the statute are not matched by the resources needed for nongovernmental agencies to carry them out. Although the NFCSP has brought greater attention and supports to families caring for elders, particularly resources to promote caregiver health and prevent caregiver burnout, inadequate resources impair its effectiveness. Proposals for tax-based supports for caregivers or programs to pay family caregivers are appearing in state legislatures, but have yet to gain traction in Congress.

When government and employers cannot provide adequate support for elder care, family caregivers often rely on nongovernmental organisations, such as health care providers and community-based ageing service agencies. Although NGOs are often created and funded by government, they are not direct policy-making organisations, and their role is beyond the scope of this article. Caregivers do, however, receive significant support, information, and services from these groups, including faith-based organisations, neighbourhood centres in communities of colour, LGBT advocacy organisations, and educational organisations. Because so many elder caregivers are employed, NGOs that provide services for elders and their caregivers must take the needs of employees into account.

Creating an Ageing-Friendly Society

The challenges faced today by elders and their family caregivers are enormous and will continue to increase during the twenty-first century as the population ages. Families alone cannot provide elder care, employers alone cannot provide all the supports employed caregivers need, and the government alone cannot provide or fund all the elder policies required. A large-scale, cross-sector initiative is needed to coordinate efforts at the national, state, and local level and to support all citizens from diverse cultures and income levels as they age.

Public policies must move in a universal direction, like Social Security and Medicare, to help transform U.S. communities and make housing, transportation, and open space accessible to all elders. There is a pressing need to better integrate nongovernmental organisations in the health care and social service sectors and to ensure they are culturally responsive. Employers must be encouraged to give employees in both professional and hourly jobs access to flexible work arrangements including part-time work, paid leave policies, paid sick days, and other "elder-friendly" workplace benefits. Overall, these groups must work together to create a culture in which ageing is seen as a natural part of the life course and caregiving is seen as a multigenerational enterprise of great value to children, adults, elders, and society.

Elders themselves and their family caregivers, as well as the public and private sectors, must build support for social investment in the next generation. Today's children will be the workers, citizens, and family caregivers who will care for the growing U.S. elderly population tomorrow. Focusing on children's healthy development and education will build their capacity to provide supportive care for the elders of future generations.

Later Life Families

Similar to their younger counterparts, families in later life experience both change and continuity. In addition to *retirement, grandparenthood,* and changing *intergenerational relationships,* members of later life families experience marital transitions, the onset of health problems, and changes in marital satisfaction and sexual relationships as well as emerging needs for the caregiving of older family members. Race, ethnicity, class, country of origin, age, and sexual orientation combine to further augment the diversity of experience within the family in later life.

Defining Later Life Families

Timothy Brubaker (1983; 1990) suggests that later life families are delineated by the fact that they have completed the child-rearing stage. In contrast, Ingrid Connidis (2001) asserts that definitions of the later life family should allow for the diversity of individual experience by focusing on familial relationships rather than a particular life-course stage or chronological age. Connidis (2001) points out that older childless couples do not fit Brubaker's definition of the later life family. Similarly, age is not always an accurate means of defining later life families as individuals may become grandparents in their twenties and thirties (Burton and Bengtson 1985). Undoubtedly, the term *family* implies a different set of meanings and relationships for each individual (Holstein and Gubrium 1999). Victoria Bedford and Rosemary Blieszner (1997) offer the most helpful means of defining later life familial relationships as they state:

A family is a set of relationships determined by biology, adoption, marriage, and, in some societies, social designation and existing even in the absence of contact or affective involvement, and, in some cases, even after the death of certain members (526). Thus, familial relationships derive from biologically and socially defined relationships that transcend the finality of death and the exclusiveness of blood and marital kinship relationships.

Characteristics of Later Life Families

Brubaker (1990) notes that later life families are characterized by the presence of three, four, and even five generations. Family structures with four or five generations but relatively few people in each generation are referred to as *beanpole families* (Bengtson, Rosenthal, and Burton 1990). Families in which successive generations have children at an earlier age, resulting in smaller age differences between the generations, are referred to as *agecondensed families.* In contrast, families in which successive generations delay childbearing, resulting in larger age differences between the generations, are referred to as *age-gapped families.* The number of individuals in each generation—as well as the age differences between the generations—influences familial relationships in later life. For example, the beanpole family structure is associated with the concept of the *sandwich generation,* in which the middle generation, particularly women, experiences simultaneous demands to care for ageing relatives and dependent children. The burden experienced by the sandwich generation is augmented by the lack of family members with whom caregiving tasks may be shared. Although it is thought to be the most common family form, Peter Uhlenberg (1993) states that the prevalence of the beanpole family structure has been exaggerated. Carolyn Rosenthal (2000) points out that relatively few women experience being sandwiched between the competing demands of their parents and children. Rosenthal (2000) asserts that daughters are more likely to be providing active help to their aged parents when they themselves are older and their children have been launched, thus there is a decreased likelihood of having conflicting roles. Nevertheless, smaller or larger age differences between the generations may influence the nature and duration of intergenerational relationships as well as the type and extent of help and care exchanged between the generations.

At the same time, family structures in later life vary as a result of social, demographic, and cultural differences. Although longevity continues to increase around the world, there are notable distinctions between developed and developing countries as well as between men and women. For example, the World Health Organisation (2000) reports that healthy life-expectancy rates range from approximately 75 years in Japan to less than 26 years in Sierra Leone. Women tend to outlive men by seven or eight years in developed countries, whereas men and women have similar life expectancy rates in developing countries (World Health Organisation 2000). Life-expectancy differences have an impact on later life familial relationships such that in some countries three- and four-generation families are more common than in others. With increasing longevity, later life becomes a normative life-course stage. In contrast, in some developing countries low life expectancy renders the experience of later life less common and the definition of *old age* is much younger than in developed countries (Albert and Cattell 1994). Moreover, differing cultural values lead to diversity in norms surrounding old age and intergenerational relations. In some countries, such as Japan and China, older relatives hold a special place of honour in the family and there are strong social norms that dictate that adult children provide care and shelter for aged family members (Thorson 2000).

Despite differences in family structure, later life families tend to share another characteristic identified by Timothy Brubaker (1990), namely family history. Brubaker (1990) points out that later life families have a long and rich "reservoir of experience." As well as having well-established patterns of interactions, later life families may also be characterized by "unfinished business or tensions" (Brubaker 1990, p. 16) arising from events that happened earlier in the family's history.

Couple Relationships in Later Life

With increased longevity and barring divorce or separation, married and common-law couples can expect to be together into their later years. Relatively few older adults are either never married or divorced (Choi 1996). Although they are becoming increasingly visible and socially accepted, older lesbian and gay couples are also a minority. In contrast, most older adults are either currently married or widowed. Marriage has been found to have positive effects on the well-being of individuals in later life. Indeed, married individuals report greater well-being than never-married, divorced, separated, or widowed individuals (Mastekaasa 1994). However, at all stages of the marital relationship, men report higher levels of satisfaction and a greater sense of well-being than women.

In addition to gender differences, there are also differences in marital satisfaction in later life related to race, ethnicity, and nationality. For example, one study found that in the United States, African-American adults tend to report lower levels of marital satisfaction across the life-course than white adults (Adelmann, Chadwick, and Baerger 1996). In another study, Mexican-American women experienced greater declines in marital satisfaction over the life-course than did Mexican-American men (Markides et al. 1999). Ed Diener, Carol Gohm, Eunkook Suh, and Shigehiro Oishi (2000) compared marital satisfaction across forty-two different countries. They define *collectivist countries,* such as China, South Korea, and Nigeria, as nations that tend to have strong norms about marriage, conformity, and supporting in-group members. *Individualist countries,* such as the United States, Great Britain, and the Netherlands, place greater emphasis on individual rights, attitudes, and choices. Diener and his colleagues (2000) found that although individuals derive greater satisfaction from marriage than cohabitation in collectivist countries, the relationship between marital status and subjective well-being is relatively similar cross-nationally.

Couples in later life experience a number of transitions as children leave home, individuals retire, and grandchildren are born. Previous research has suggested that marital satisfaction tends to follow a U-shaped curve with the highest levels of marital satisfaction reported in the beginning and later stages of the relationship and declines in marital satisfaction during the middle (and usually parental) years. Following the launching of adult children, couples may have more time to spend with each other, more privacy, and more financial resources. The bond between couples in later life may be enhanced by a lifetime of shared history and experiences. Some researchers have found that increased marital satisfaction in later life is largely explained by decreases in parenting and work responsibilities stemming from the launching of adult children and the transition to retirement (Orbuch et al. 1996). Similarly, Barbara Mitchell and Ellen Gee (1996) note that the return of adult children to the home following initial launching has a potentially negative impact on marital satisfaction. The presence of adult children in the home may augment existing marital tensions, particularly in the case where the parents are in a second marriage or in poor health. Returning adult children may also result in decreased marital satisfaction in cases where the adult child has made three or more departures from and returns to the family home. However, Mitchell and Gee (1996) found that strong relationships between mothers and adult children are associated with fewer declines in marital satisfaction following the return of the adult child.

Later research on the U-shaped pattern of marital satisfaction across the life-course has generated conflicting findings. One longitudinal study found that marital satisfaction tends to decline over time "with the steepest declines in marital happiness occurring during the earliest and latest years of marriage" (VanLaningham, Johnson, and Amato 2001, p. 1313). In other words, they did not find any evidence of increases in marital satisfaction following the launching of adult children or the transition to retirement. Defining a lack of success in terms of marriages that ended in divorce or that were reported as being less than happy, Norval Glen's (1998) study of marital success also rebutted the U-shaped model of marital satisfaction. Glen's (1998) research suggests that differences in marital success across the life-course are due to cohort differences. Glen also contends that declines in marital success may be due to personal and health characteristics that occur over time and that serve to make couples less compatible or less well-matched.

Another way of examining marital satisfaction and marital quality in later life is in terms of conflict. Older couples have been found to have a decreased potential for marital conflict and an increased potential for deriving pleasure from their children and grandchildren, from shared activities, and from shared aspirations and vacations (Levensen, Carstensen, and Gottman 1993). In addition, older couples tend to be less emotionally negative and more affectionate in their resolution of conflict than their middle-aged counterparts (Carstensen, Gottman, and Levensen 1995). Thus, older couples may have developed strategies for avoiding conflict as well as resolving differences in a more amiable manner. Older couples' shared and long-term histories may serve to further strengthen their bonds as well as buffering the negative impact of marital tension and conflict.

Retirement and Couple Relationships

Retirement is one of the most significant changes that face later life families. As has been stated above, the U-shaped pattern of marital satisfaction suggests that retirement may enhance satisfaction with the marital relationship. However, the process of transition from employment to retirement may pose a difficult challenge to many couples. During the transition stage, both husbands and wives tend to describe losses in marital quality (Moen, Kim, and Hofmeister 2001). The timing of retirement may be a source of marital conflict as well as the result of negotiation between the spouses. Deborah Smith and Phyllis Moen (1998) report that the husband's decision to retire is more likely to influence the timing of the wife's retirement than the other way round. Couples in which one partner retires while the other continues to work tend to experience greater marital discord, regardless of gender (Moen, Kim, and Hofmeister 2001).

Upon retirement, couples may spend more time together, which will either enhance the marital relationship or lead to increased conflict. There are gender differences in the perception of marital conflict and satisfaction following retirement. Maximiliane Szinovacz and Anne Schaffer (2000) state that husbands—but not wives—tend to perceive a decrease in the number of "heated arguments" following the retirement of the wife. The retirement of the husband is associated with an increase in calm discussions about conflictual issues in relationships where the spouses are strongly attached to the marriage. In contrast, the retirement of the husband may culminate in a decrease in calm discussions where one or both of the spouses are not strongly attached to the marriage.

Unlike their younger counterparts, the majority of today's older women did not work outside the home. Thus, the retirement of the husband and his increased presence in the home may result in a wife's sense that she has lost personal freedom and autonomy (Rosenthal and Gladstone 1994). The retirement of one or both spouses may necessitate the negotiation of personal space and domestic duties. Although the wife may have been primarily responsible for domestic tasks, following retirement there is often a lessening of a traditional gendered division of labour (Szinovacz 2000). In addition to increasing the amount of time spent on their own chores, retired spouses tend to spend more time doing tasks formerly designated the responsibility of the other spouse. Nevertheless, wives continue to spend a significantly greater amount of time on household labour than do husbands. The division of domestic labour following retirement has been found to be related to marital satisfaction. Couples who divide household chores more equitably tend to report higher levels of marital satisfaction than couples who adhere to more traditional definitions of gender roles and behaviour (Rosenthal and Gladstone 1994).

Sexuality in Later Life

Benjamin Schlesinger (1996) asserts that older adults are often perceived as being a sexual. Indeed, the sexual behaviour of older adults is frequently assumed to be nonexistent, funny, physically risky, embarrassing, or less satisfying and exciting. In reality, sexuality continues to be an important part of couple relationships in later life. However, sexual activity tends to decline with age as a result of changing health levels, the loss of partners, the declining interest of husbands, and the effects of prescription medications. At the same time, definitions of sexual behaviour in later life expand beyond sexual intercourse as older adults refer to "kissing, touching, caressing, holding hands, and hugging" (Neugebauer-Visano 1995, p. 22) as important elements of sexual activity. In this way, sexual intercourse is only one facet of the sexual expression of couples in later life.

Sexual interest and activity have been found to be contributors to marital satisfaction and wellbeing in later life (Ade-Ridder 1995). Couples who report higher levels of sexual activity tend to describe their marriages as being happier than those in which sexual activity has declined. Levels of sexual activity in later life vary by gender, education, age, and marital status (Matthias et al. 1997). Older men report higher levels of sexual activity than older women. The strongest predictors of being sexually active for men are being younger and well-educated. In contrast, the strongest predictor of being sexually active among older women is marital status: married women tend to report higher levels of sexual activity than single older women.

Grandparenthood

Grandparenthood is a role that most people will experience in their lifetimes. Maximiliane Szinovacz (1998) notes that most people become grandparents in middle age rather than in later life. Thus, grandparents in later life will tend to have grandchildren who are in their teenage and young adult years (Connidis 2001). Women and members of ethnic minorities tend to become grandparents at earlier stages in their lives than men and Caucasians (Thorson 2000). Due to differences in life expectancy, the length of relationships between grandparents and grandchildren vary between developed and developing countries (Albert and Cat-tell 1994). Although grandparenthood is a lengthy life-course stage in developed countries, lower life expectancies in developing countries mean that grandparents and grandchildren will share fewer years together. Similarly, the longer life expectancies of women as compared to men result in grandchildren being more likely to have living grandmothers, particularly maternal grandmothers, than living grandfathers (Thorson 2000). With the growing rates of divorce both among the middle and later generations, step-grandparenthood is becoming increasingly common and roughly one-quarter of all grandparents will become step-grandparents (Thorson 2000). Finally, great-grandparenthood is becoming increasingly common and approximately one-quarter of older men and one-third of older women will have great-grandchildren (Rosenthal and Gladstone 1994).

The relationships that grandparents share with their grandchildren vary by age and gender (Connidis 2001). When grandchildren are younger, grandparents tend to be more involved in their lives. Contact between grandparents and grandchildren tends to decrease once the grandchildren reach their teenage years. Similarly, grandmothers tend to provide more emotional support, whereas grandfathers tend to give their grandchildren more instrumental support such as advice and financial assistance. Although they participate in relatively few activities with either of their grandparents, adult grandchildren spend more time with their grandmothers than with their grandfathers (Roberto and Stroes 1995). Grandmothers tend to report greater satisfaction with their relationships with their grandchildren than do grandfathers (Thomas 1995). Moreover, grandparents tend to perceive their relationships with grandchildren as being closer than do grandchildren (Connidis 2001). Regardless of the differences deriving from age and gender, grandparents play a stabilizing role in the family as they provide a sense of continuity for the younger generations.

Marital Transitions: Widowhood, Divorce and Remarriage

Among today's older adults, the death of a spouse is the typical way a marital relationship ends. Given that women tend to outlive men and to marry men who are the same age or older than themselves, women continue to be much more likely than men to be widowed (Connidis 2001). Approximately two-thirds of women aged 80 and over are widowed. In contrast, the majority of men aged 80 and over is married.

The loss of a spouse is among the most stressful life events that an individual will experience (Martin-Matthews 1991). Although widowhood is an "expectable life event" for older women, "the duration of the spouse's final illness and forewarning of the death" (Martin-Matthews 1991, p. 21) shape a widow's experience of the loss of her husband. Widowhood tends to be preceded by a period of time in which men and women provide care for their ailing spouse, usually the wife caring for the husband (Wells and Kendig 1997). Undoubtedly, the stress and anguish associated with the care of a failing spouse may account for the declines in marital satisfaction in later life (VanLaningham, Johnson, and Amato 2001). At the same time, Helena Lopata (2000) notes that an individual's experience of widowhood is shaped by the cultural importance given to marriage. In developing countries where women have less power and access to resources and where they derive social status and security from their husbands, widows may face financial and social adversity in addition to profound feelings of grief and loss.

Although remarriage following the death of a spouse in later life is uncommon, more men remarry than do women. Carolyn Rosenthal and James Gladstone (1994) suggest that the primary motivations for remarrying in later life are the desire for companionship and the wish to feel useful and able to contribute to another person's happiness. The higher remarriage rates of men may be due to the greater number of potential marriage partners (O'Bryant and Hansson 1995). Similarly, the overall low rates of remarriage among older men and women are due to fears of social disapproval, financial concerns, and the opposition of other family members (O'Bryant and Hansson 1995). Maria Talbott's (1998) study of attitudes towards remarriage reveals that older women are reluctant to remarry because they do not want to give up their freedom, they are not interested in establishing a new sexual relationship, they do not want to go through the loss of another husband, they fear the reactions of their children, they feel that it would be disloyal to their deceased husband, and/or they do not want to take on additional domestic responsibilities.

Divorce among later life couples continues to be rare, although the rates are increasing. Laurie Hatch (2000) notes that divorce in later life may be more disruptive to an individual's life than widowhood. Unlike widowhood, divorce in later life is unexpected and is often accompanied by a sense of social stigma. Charles Hennon (1995) states that divorced older adults report lower life satisfaction and physical well-being than do their widowed counterparts. William Aquilino (1994) reports that couples who divorce in later life tend to have less contact and poorer quality relationships with their adult children. The relationships between adult children and fathers tend to be more negatively impacted by later life divorce than the relationships between adult children and mothers.

Although later life divorce is rare, divorce among the younger generations is not uncommon. Older adults whose children divorce may feel caught in the middle between their biological offspring and their sons- and daughters-in-law. Depending upon custody arrangements, grandparents may have increased or decreased access to their grandchildren following the divorce of the middle generation. For example, should the grandchildren be placed in the primary custody of their mother, the paternal grandparents may see their grandchildren less often.

Conclusion

Later life families experience both change and continuity through marital, familial, social, and work transitions. At the same time, each individual's experience and definition of what constitutes the later life family and familial relationships varies. Despite the differences that derive from gender, race, class, country of origin, and the numerous transitions they encounter, families in later life are both adaptive and resilient.

Old Age

Old age consists of ages nearing or surpassing the life expectancy of human beings, and thus the end of the human life cycle. Euphemisms and terms for old people include, old people (worldwide usage), seniors (American usage), senior citizens (British and American usage), older adults (in the social sciences), the elderly, and elders (in many cultures including the cultures of aboriginal people).

Old people often have limited regenerative abilities and are more prone to disease, syndromes, and sickness than younger adults. The organic process of ageing is called senescence, the medical study of the ageing process is gerontology, and the study of diseases that afflict the elderly is geriatrics. The elderly also face other social issues such as retirement, loneliness, and ageism.

The chronological age denoted as "old age" varies culturally and historically. Thus, old age is "a social construct" rather than a definite "biological stage".

Definitions

Definitions of old age include official definitions, popular definitions, sub-group definitions, and four dimensions as follows.

Official Definitions

Old age comprises "the later part of life; the period of life after youth and middle age. . . , usually with reference to deterioration" In the 4th century BC, Plato divided the human lifespan into six phases, the last two constituting "Old Age" (the ages of 62-79) and "Advanced Age" (80-). The last phase, he noted, "is one that, fortunately, few attain."

When old age begins cannot be universally defined because it shifts according to the context. The United Nations has agreed that 60+ years may be usually denoted as old age, and this is the first attempt at an international definition of old age. However, for its study of old age in Africa, the World Health Organisation (WHO) set 50 as the beginning of old age. At the same time, the WHO recognised that the developing world often defines old age, not by years, but by new roles, loss of previous roles, or inability to make active contribution to society.

Most developed Western countries set the age of 60 to 65 for retirement and old-age social programs eligibility. However, various countries and societies reckon the onset of old age as anywhere from the mid-40s to the 70s. Furthermore, the fact that life expectancy beyond 80 has become widespread has shifted definitions of old age.

Popular Definitions

A Pew Research Centre study of 2,929 Americans, age 18+, found that they hold very different definitions of old age. Respondents under 30 said that old age begins at 60, but respondents 65+ said 74.

Most Britons define old age as starting at 59 according to a survey of 2,200 people in the UK. The under 25s reckon 54 as the beginning of old age. The 80+ define old age as starting at 68. Another survey concluded that most Britons define the onset of old age as almost 70. Europeans on average set the start of old age at 62.

Sub-group Definitions

Gerontologists have recognised the very different conditions that people experience as they grow older within the years defined as old age. In developed countries, most people in their 60s and early 70s are still fit, active, and able to care for themselves. However, after 75, they will become increasingly frail, a condition marked by serious mental and physical debilitation.

Therefore, rather than lumping together all people who have been defined as old, some gerontologists have recognised the diversity of old age by defining sub-groups. One study distinguishes the young old (60 to 69), the middle old (70 to 79), and the very old (80+). Another study's sub-grouping is young-old (65 to 74), middle-old (75–84), and oldest-old (85+). A third sub-grouping is "young old" (65-74), "old" (74-84), and "old-old" (85+). Delineating sub-groups in the 65+ population enables a more accurate portrayal of significant life changes.

Four Dimensions

Old age comprises the four dimensions: chronological, biological, psychological, and social. Chronological age may differ considerably from a person's functional age. The distinguishing marks of old age normally occur in all five senses at different times and different rates for different persons. In addition to chronological age, people can be considered old because of the other three dimensions of old age. For example, people may be considered old when they become grandparents or when they begin to do less or different work in retirement.

Marks of Old Age

The distinguishing marks associated with old age comprise both physical and mental characteristics. The marks of old age are so unlike the marks of middle age that it has been suggested that, as an individual transitions into old age, he/she might well be thought of as different persons "time-sharing" the same identity.

These marks do not occur at the same chronological age for everyone. Also, they occur at different rates and order for different people. Because each person is unique, marks of old age vary between people, even those of the same chronological age.

A basic mark of old age that affects both body and mind is "slowness of behaviour." This "slowing down principle" finds a correlation between advancing age and slowness of reaction and task performance, both physical and mental.

Physical Marks of Old Age

Physical marks of old age include the following:

- Bone and joint. Old bones are marked by "thinning and shrinkage." This results in a loss of height (about two inches by age 80), a stooping posture in many people, and a greater susceptibility to bone and joint diseases such as osteoarthritis and osteoporosis.
- Chronic diseases. Most older persons have at least one chronic condition and many have multiple conditions. In 2007-2009, the most frequently occurring conditions among older persons in the United States were uncontrolled hypertension (34%), diagnosed arthritis (50%), and heart disease (32%).
- Dental problems. Less saliva and less ability for oral hygiene in old age increases the chance of tooth decay and infection.
- Digestive system. About 40% of the time, old age is marked by digestive disorders such as difficulty in swallowing, inability to eat enough and to absorb nutrition, constipation and bleeding.
- Eyesight. Diminished eyesight makes it more difficult to read in low lighting and in smaller print. Speed with which an individual reads and the ability to locate objects may also be impaired.
- Falls. Old age spells risk for injury from falls that might not cause injury to a younger person. Every year, about one-third of those 65 years old and over half of those 80 years old fall. Falls are the leading cause of injury and death for old people.
- Hair usually becomes thinner and grayer.
- Hearing. By age 75 and older, 48% of men and 37% of women encounter impairments in hearing. Of the 26.7 million people over age 50 with a hearing impairment, only one in seven uses a hearing aid.
- Hearts are less efficient in old age with a resulting loss of stamina. In addition, atherosclerosis can constrict blood flow.

- Immune function. Less efficient immune function (Immunosenescence) is a mark of old age.
- Lungs expand less well; thus, they provide less oxygen.
- Pain afflicts old people at least 25% of the time, increasing with age up to 80% for those in nursing homes. Most pains are rheumatological or malignant.
- Sexual activity decreases significantly with age, especially after age 60, for both women and men. Sexual drive in both men and women decreases as they age.
- Skin loses elasticity, becomes drier, and more lined and wrinkled.
- Sleep trouble holds a chronic prevalence of over 50% in old age and results in daytime sleepiness. In a study of 9,000 persons with a mean age of 74, only 12% reported no sleep complaints. By age 65, deep sleep goes down to about 5%.
- Taste buds diminish so that by age 80 taste buds are down to 50% of normal. Food becomes less appealing and nutrition can suffer.
- Urinary incontinence is often found in old age.
- Voice. In old age, vocal chords weaken and vibrate more slowly. This results in a weakened, breathy voice that is sometimes called an "old person's voice."

Mental Marks of Old Age

Mental marks of old age include the following.

- Adaptable describes most people in their old age. In spite the stressfulness of old age, they are described as "agreeable" and "accepting." However, old age dependence induces feelings of incompetence and worthlessness in a minority.
- Caution marks old age. This antipathy toward "risk-taking" stems from the fact that old people have less to gain and more to lose by taking risks than younger people.
- Depressed mood. According to Cox, Abramson, Devine, and Hollon (2012), old age is a risk factor for depression caused by prejudice (i.e., "deprejudice"). When people are prejudiced against the elderly and then become old themselves, their anti-elderly prejudice turns inward, causing depression. "People with more negative age stereotypes will likely have higher rates of depression as they get older." Old age depression results in the over-65 population having the highest suicide rate.

- Fear of crime in old age, especially among the frail, sometimes weighs more heavily than concerns about finances or health and restricts what they do. The fear persists in spite of the fact that old people are victims of crime less often than younger people.
- Mental disorders afflict about 15% of people aged 60+ according to estimates by the World Health Organisation. Another survey taken in 15 countries reported that mental disorders of adults interfered with their daily activities more than physical problems.
- Reduced mental and cognitive ability afflicts old age. Memory loss is common in old age due to the decrease in speed of information being encoded, stored, and received. It takes more time to learn new information. Dementia is a general term for memory loss and other intellectual abilities serious enough to interfere with daily life. Its prevalence increases in old age from about 10% at age 65 to about 50% over age 85. Alzheimer's disease accounts for 50 to 80 percent of dementia cases. Demented behaviour can include wandering, physical aggression, verbal outbursts, depression, and psychosis.
- Set in one's ways describes a mind set of old age. A study of over 400 distinguished men and women in old age found a "preference for the routine." Explanations include old age's toll on the "fluid intelligence" and the "more deeply entrenched" ways of the old.

Perceptions of Old Age

The literature regarding old age includes perceptions of old age from a middle-age perspective, from an old-age perspective, from society's perspective, and from a simulated perspective.

Old Age from a Middle-age Perspective

Numerous books by middle-age writers depict their perceptions of old people. One writer notices the change in his parents: they move slowly, they have lost strength, they repeat stories, their minds wander, and they fret. Another writer sees her aged parents and is bewildered: they refuse to follow her advice, they are obsessed with the past, they avoid risk, they live at a "glacial pace."

Other writers treat the perceptions of middle-age people regarding their own old age. In her *The Denial of Ageing*, Dr. Muriel R. Gillick, a baby boomer, accuses her contemporaries of believing that by proper exercise and diet they can avoid the scourges of old age and proceed from middle age to death. Studies find that many people in the 55-75 range can postpone morbidity by practicing healthy life styles. However, at about age 80, all people experience similar morbidity. Even with healthy life styles, most 85+ people will undergo extended "frailty and disability."

Old Age from an Old-age Perspective

Early old age is a pleasant time: children are grown, retirement from work, time to pursue interests. In contrast, perceptions of old age by writers 80+ years old, "old age in the real meaning of the term" tend to be negative.

Lillian Rubin, active in her 80s as an author, sociologist, and psychotherapist, opens her book *60 on Up: The Truth about Ageing in America* with "getting old sucks. It always has, it always will." Dr. Rubin contrasts the "real old age" with the "rosy pictures" painted by middle-age writers.

Writing at the age of 87, Mary C. Morrison delineates the heroism required by old age: to live through the disintegration of one's own body or that of someone you love. Morrison concludes, "old age is not for the fainthearted." In the book *Life Beyond 85 Years*, the 150 interviewees had to cope with physical and mental debilitation and with losses of loved ones. One interviewee described living in old age as "pure hell."

Old Age from Society's Perspective

Historical periods reveal a mixed picture of the "position and status" of old people, but there has never been a "golden age of ageing." Studies have disproved the popular belief that in the past old people were venerated by society and cared for by their families. Veneration for and antagonism toward the aged have coexisted in complex relationships throughout history.

In ancient times, the very few people who lived beyond 35 physically and mentally healthy, especially those of social status and wealth, were treated with "respect and awe." In contrast, those who were frail were seen as a burden and ignored or in extreme cases killed. People were defined as "old" because of their inability to perform useful tasks rather than their years.

In Greek and Roman cultures, old age was denigrated as a time "decline and decrepitude."

In the Classical period, "beauty and strength" were esteemed and old age was viewed as defiling and ugly. The Medieval and Renaissance periods depicted old age as "cruel or weak." In the Modern period, the "cultural status" of old people has declined in many cultures.

Research on age attitudes consistently finds that negative attitudes exceed positive attitudes toward old people because of their looks and behaviour. In his study *Ageing and Old Age*, Posner discovers "resentment and disdain of older people" in American society.

Harvard University's Implicit-association test measures implicit "attitudes and beliefs" about Young vis a vis Old. *Blind Spot: Hidden Biases of Good People*, a book about the test, reports that 80% of Americans have an "automatic preference for the young over old" and that attitude is true worldwide. The young are "consistent in their negative attitude" toward the old. *Ageism* documents that Americans generally have "little tolerance for older persons and very few reservations about harboring negative attitudes" about them.

In spite of its prevalence, ageism is seldom the subject of public discourse.

Old Age from Simulated Perspective

Simone de Beauvoir wrote that "there is one form of experience that belongs only to those that are old – that of old age itself." Nevertheless, simulations of old age attempt to help younger people gain some understanding.

Texas A&M University offers a plan for a "Ageing Simulation" workshop. The workshop is adapted from *Sensitizing People to the Processes of Ageing*. Some of the simulations follow:

- Sight: Wearing swimmer's goggles with black paper pasted to lens with only a small hole to simulate tunnel vision,
- Hearing: Use ear plugs to dull the sound of people talking.
- Touch: Wearing thick gloves, button a shirt or buckle a belt.
- Dexterity: With tape around several fingers, unscrew a jar lid.
- Mobility and Balance: Carry packages in one hand while using a walker.

The Macklin Intergenerational Institute conducts Xtreme Ageing workshops, as depicted in the *The New York Times*. A condensed version was presented on NBC's Today Show and is available online. One exercise was to lay out 3 sets of 5 slips of paper. On set #1, write your 5 most enjoyed activities; on set #2, write your 5 most valued possessions; on set #3, write your 5 most loved people. Then "lose" them one by one, trying to feel each loss, until you have lost them all as happens in old age.

Old Age Frailty

Most people in the age range of 60-80 (the years of retirement and early old age), enjoy rich possibilities for a full life, but the condition of frailty distinguished by "bodily failure" and greater dependence becomes increasingly after that. In the United States, hospital discharge data from 2003-2011 shows that injury was the common reason for hospitalization among patient aged 65+.

Gerontologists note the lack of research regarding and the difficulty in defining frailty. However, they add that physicians recognise frailty when they see it.

A group of geriatricians proposed a general definition of frailty as "a physical state of increased vulnerability to stressors that results from decreased reserves and disregulation in multiple physiological systems."

Prevalence of Frailty

Frailty is a common condition in later old age, but different definitions of frailty produce diverse assessments of prevalence. One study placed the incidence of frailty for ages 65+ at 10.7%. Another study placed the incidence of frailty in age 65+ population at 22% for women and 15% for men. A Canadian study illustrated how frailty increases with age and calculated the prevalence for 65+ as 22.4% and for 85+ as 43.7%.

A worldwide study of "patterns of frailty" based on data from 20 nations found (a) a consistent correlation between frailty and age, (b) a higher frequency among women, and (c) more frailty in wealthier nations where greater support and medical care increases longevity.

In Norway, a 20 year longitudinal study of 400 people found that bodily failure and greater dependence became prevalent in the 80+ years. The study calls these years the "fourth age" or "old age in the real meaning of the term."

Similarly, the "Berlin Ageing Study" rated over-all functionality on four levels: good, medium, poor, and very poor. People in their 70s were mostly rated good. In the 80-90 year range, the four levels of functionality were divided equally. By the 90-100 year range, 60% would be considered frail because of very poor functionality and only 5% still possessed good functionality.

In the United States, the 85+ age group is the fastest growing, a group that is almost sure to face the "inevitable decrepitude" of survivors. (Frailty and decrepitude are synonyms.)

Markers of Frailty

Three unique markers of frailty have been proposed: (a) loss of any notion of invincibility, (b) loss of ability to do things essential to one's care, and (c) loss of possibility for a subsequent life stage.

Old age survivors on-average deteriorate from agility in their 65-80s to a period of frailty preceding death. This deterioration is gradual for some and precipitous for others. Frailty is marked by an array of chronic physical and mental problems which means that frailty is not treatable as a specific disease. These problems coupled with increased dependency in the basic activities of daily living (ADLs) required for personal care add emotional problems: depression and anxiety. In sum, frailty has been depicted as a group of "complex issues," distinct but "causally interconnected," that often include "comorbid diseases,", progressive weakness, stress, exhaustion, and depression.

Misconceptions of Frail People

Johnson and Barer did a pioneering study of *Life Beyond 85 Years* by interviews over a six year period. In talking with 85+ year olds, they found some popular conceptions about old age to be erroneous. Many studies of old age overlook the 85+ survivors so their conclusions do not apply. Such erroneous conceptions include

(1) people in old age have a least one family member for support,

(2) old age well-being requires social activity, and

(3) "successful adaptation" to age-related changes demands a continuity of self-concept.

In their interviews, Johnson and Barer found that 24% of the 85+ had no face-to-face family relationships; many have outlived their families. Second, that contrary to popular notions, the interviews revealed that the reduced activity and socializing of the over 85s does not harm their well-being; they "welcome increased detachment." Third, rather than a continuity of self-concept, as the interviewees faced new situations they changed their "cognitive and emotional processes" and reconstituted their "self–representation."

Care and Costs

Frail people require a high level of care. Medical advances have made it possible to "postpone death" for years. This added time costs many frail people "prolonged sickness, dependence, pain, and suffering."

According to a study by the Agency for Healthcare Research and Quality (AHRQ), the rate of ED visits was consistently highest among patients ages 85 years and older in 2006-2011 in the United States.

These final years are also costly in economic terms. One out of every four Medicare dollars is spent on the frail in their last year of life . . . in attempts to postpone death.

Medical treatments in the final days are not only economically costly, they are often unnecessary, even harmful. Nortin Hadler, M.D. warns against the tendency to medicalize and overtreat the frail. In her *Choosing Medical Care in Old Age*, Muriel R. Gillick M.D. argues that appropriate medical treatment for the frail is not the same as for the robust. The frail are vulnerable to "being tipped over" by any physical stress put on the system such as medical interventions.

Death and Frailty

Old age, death, and frailty are linked because approximately half the deaths in old age are preceded by months or years of frailty,

Older Adults' Views on Death is based on interviews with 109 people in the 70-90 age range, with a mean age of 80.7. Almost 20% of the people wanted to use whatever treatment that might postpone death. About the same number said that given a terminal illness, they would choose assisted suicide. Roughly half chose doing nothing except live day by day until death comes naturally without medical or other intervention designed to prolong life. This choice was coupled with a desire to receive palliative care if needed.

About half of older adults suffer multimorbidity, that is, they have three or more chronic conditions. Medical advances have made it possible to "postpone death," but in many cases this postponement adds "prolonged sickness, dependence, pain, and suffering," a time that is costly in social, psychological, economic terms.

The longitudinal interviews of 150 age 85+ people summarized in *Life Beyond 85 Years* found "progressive terminal decline" in the year prior to death: constant fatigue, much sleep, detachment from people, things, and activities, simplified lives. Most of the interviewees did not fear death; some would welcome it. One person said, "living this long is pure hell." However, nearly everyone feared a long process of dying. Some wanted to die in their sleep; others wanted to die "on their feet."

The study of *Older Adults' Views on Death* found that the more frail people were, the more "pain, suffering, and struggles" they were enduring, the more likely they were to "accept and welcome" death as a release from their misery. Their fear about the process of dying was that it would prolong their distress. Besides being a release from misery, some saw death as a way to reunion with departed loved ones. Others saw death as a way to free their caretakers from the burden of their care.

Religiosity in Old Age

At all times, old people have been more religious than young people. At the same time, wide cultural variations exist.

In the United States, 90% of old age Hispanics view themselves as very, quite, or somewhat religious. The Pew Research Centre's study of black and white old people found that 62% of those in ages 65-74 and 70% in ages 75+ asserted that religion was "very important" to them. For all 65+ people, more women (76%) than men (53%) and more blacks (87%) than whites (63%) consider religion "very important" to them. This compares to 54% in the 30-49 age range.

In a British 20-year longitudinal study, less than half of the old people surveyed said that religion was "very important" to them and one-fourth said they had become less religious in old age. The late-life rise in religiosity is stronger in Japan than in the United States, but in the Netherlands it is minimal.

In the practice of religion, a study of 60+ people found that 25% read the Bible every day and over 40% look at religious TV. Pew Research found that in the age 65+ range, 75% of whites and 87% of blacks pray daily. Participation in organised religion is not a good indicator of religiosity because transportation and health problems often hinder participation.

Demographic Changes

In the industrialized countries, life expectancy and, thus, the old age population have increased consistently over the last decades. In the United States the proportion of people aged 65 or older increased from 4% in 1900 to about 12% in 2000. In 1900, only about 3 million of the nation's citizens were 65 or older (out of 76 million total American citizens). By 2000, the number of senior citizens had increased to about 35 million (of 280 million US citizens). Population experts estimate that more than 50 million Americans—about 17 percent of the population—will be 65 or older in 2020. By 2050, it is projected that at least 400,000 Americans will be 100 or older.

The number of old people is growing around the world chiefly because of the post–World War II baby boom and increases in the provision and standards of health care. By 2050, 33% of the developed world's population and almost 20% of the less developed world's population will be over 60 years old.

The growing number of people living to their 80s and 90s in the developed world has strained public welfare systems and has also resulted in increased incidence of diseases like cancer and dementia that were rarely seen in premodern times. When the United States Social Security program was created, persons older than 65 numbered only around 5% of the population and the average life expectancy of a 65 year old in 1936 was approximately 5 years, while in 2011 it could often range from 10–20 years. Other issues that can arise from an increasing population are growing demands for health care and an increase in demand for different types of services.

Of the roughly 150,000 people who die each day across the globe, about two thirds—100,000 per day—die of age-related causes. In industrialized nations, the proportion is much higher, reaching 90%.

Psychosocial Aspects

According to Erik Erikson's "Eight Stages of Life" theory, the human personality is developed in a series of eight stages that take place from the time of birth and continue on throughout an individual's complete life. He characterises old age as a period of "Integrity vs. Despair", during which a person focuses on reflecting back on his life. Those who are unsuccessful during this phase will feel that their life has been wasted and will experience many regrets. The individual will be left with feelings of bitterness and despair. Those who feel proud of their accomplishments will feel a sense of integrity. Successfully completing this phase means looking back with few regrets and a general feeling of satisfaction. These individuals will attain wisdom, even when confronting death. Coping is a very important skill needed in the ageing process to move forward with life and not be 'stuck' in the past. The way a person adapts and copes, reflects his ageing process on a psycho-social level.

Newman & Newman proposed a ninth stage of life, Elderhood. Elderhood refers to those individuals who live past the life expectancy of their birth cohorts. There are two different types of people described in this stage of life. The "young old" are the healthy individuals who can function on their own without assistance and can complete their daily tasks independently. The "old old" are those who depend on specific services due to declining health or diseases. This period of life is characterized as a period of "immortality vs. extinction." Immortality is the belief that your life will go on past death, some examples are an afterlife or living on through one's family. Extinction refers to feeling as if life has no purpose.

Theories of Old Age

Social theories, or concepts, propose explanations for the distinctive relationships between old people and their societies.

One of the theories is the Disengagement Theory proposed in 1961. This theory proposes that in old age a mutual disengagement between people and their society occurs in anticipation of death. By becoming disengaged from work and family responsibilities, according to this concept, people are enabled to enjoy their old age without stress. This theory has been subjected to the criticism that old age disengagement is neither natural, inevitable, nor beneficial. Furthermore, disengaging from social ties in old age is not across the board: unsatisfactory ties are dropped and satisfying ones kept.

In opposition to the Disengagement Theory the Activity Theory of old age argues that disengagement in old age occurs not by desire, but by the barriers to social engagement imposed by society. This theory has been faulted for not factoring in psychological changes that occur in old age as shown by reduced activity even when available. It has also been found that happiness in old age is not proportional to activity.

According to the Continuity Theory, in spite of the inevitable differences imposed by their old age, most people try to maintain continuity in personhood, activities, and relationships with their younger days.

Socioemotional Selectivity Theory also depicts how people maintain continuity in old age. The focus of this theory is continuity sustained by social networks, albeit networks narrowed by choice and by circumstances. The choice is for more harmonious relationships. The circumstances are loss of relationships by death and distance.

Life Expectancy

Life expectancy by nation at birth in year 2011 ranged from 48 years to 82.

In most parts of the world women live, on average, longer than men; even so, the disparities vary between 12 years in Russia to no difference or higher life expectancy for men in countries such as Zimbabwe and Uganda.

The number of elderly persons worldwide began to surge in the second half of the 20th century. Up to that time (and still true in underdeveloped countries), five or less percent of the population was over 65. Few lived longer than their 70s and people who attained advanced age (i.e. their 80s) were rare enough to be a novelty and were revered as wise sages. The worldwide over 65 population in 1960 was one-third of the under 5 population. By 2013, the over 65 population had grown to equal the under 5 population. The over 65 population is projected to double the under five by 2050.

Before the surge in the over 65 population, accidents and disease claimed many people before they could attain old age, and health problems in those over 65 meant a quick death in most cases. If a person lived to an advanced age, it was due to genetic factors and/or a relatively easy lifestyle, since diseases of old age could not be treated before the 20th century.

Old Age Benefits

German chancellor Otto von Bismarck created the world's first comprehensive government social safety net in the 1880s, providing for old age pensions.

In the United States of America, and the United Kingdom, 65 (UK 60 for women) was traditionally the age of retirement with full old age benefits.

In 2003, the age at which a United States citizen became eligible for full Social Security benefits began to increase gradually, and will continue to do so until it reaches 67 in 2027. Full retirement age for Social Security benefits for people retiring in 2012 is age 66. In the United Kingdom, the state pension age for men and women will rise to 66 in 2020 with further increases scheduled after that."

Originally, the purpose of old age pensions was to prevent elderly persons from being reduced to beggary, which is still common in some underdeveloped countries, but growing life expectancies and older populations have brought into question the model under which pension systems were designed. The dominant perception of the American old age population changed from "needy" and "worthy" to "powerful" and "greedy," old people getting more than their share of the nation's resources. However, in 2011, using a Supplemental Poverty Measure (SPM), the old age American poverty rate was measured as 15.9%.

Assistance: Devices and Personal

In the USA in 2008, 11 million people aged 65+ lived alone: 5 million or 22% of ages 65–74, 4 million or 34% of ages 75–84, and 2 million or 41% of ages 85+. The 2007 gender breakdown for all people 65+ was men 19% and women 39%.

Many new assistive devices made especially for the home have enabled more old people to care for themselves activities of daily living (ADL). Able Data lists 40,000 assistive technology products in 20 categories. Some examples of devices are a medical alert and safety system, shower seat (making it so the person does not get tired in the shower and fall), a bed cane (offering support to those with unsteadiness getting in and out of bed) and an ADL cuff (used with eating utensils for people with paralysis or hand weakness).

A Swedish study found that at age 76, 46% of the subjects used assistive devices. When they reached age 86, 69% used them. The subjects were ambivalent regarding the use of the assistive devices: as "enablers" or as "disablers." People who view assistive devices as enabling greater independence accept and use them. Those who see them as symbols of disability reject them.

Even with assistive devices as of 2006, 8½ million Americans needed personal assistance because of impaired basic activities of daily living (ADLs) required for personal care or impaired instrumental activities of daily living (IADLs) required for independent living. Projections place this number at 21 million by 2030 when 40% of Americans over 70 will need assistance. There are many options for such long term care to those who require it. There is the home care in which a family member, volunteer, or trained professional will aid the person in need and help with daily activities. Another option is community services which can provide the person with transportation, meal plans, or activities in senior centres. A third option is assisted living where 24 hour round the clock supervision is given with aid in eating, bathing, dressing, etc. A final option is a nursing home which provides professional nursing care.

Elderly Care

Elderly care, or simply eldercare (also known in parts of the English speaking world as aged care), is the fulfillment of the special needs and requirements that are unique to senior citizens. This broad term encompasses such services as assisted living, adult day care, long term care, nursing homes, hospice care, and home care. Because of the wide variety of elderly care found globally, as well as differentiating cultural perspectives on elderly citizens, cannot to be limited to any one practice. For example, many countries in Asia use government-established elderly care quite infrequently, preferring the traditional methods of being cared for by younger generations of family members.

Elderly care emphasizes the social and personal requirements of senior citizens who need some assistance with daily activities and health care, but who desire to age with dignity. It is an important distinction, in that the design of housing, services, activities, employee training and such should be truly customer-centred. It is also noteworthy that a large amount of global elderly care falls under the unpaid market sector.

Cultural and Geographic Differences

The form of elderly care provided varies greatly among countries and is changing rapidly. Even within the same country, regional differences exist with respect to the care for the elderly. However, it has been observed that the global elderly consume the most health expenditures out of any other age group, an observation that shows worldwide eldercare may be very similar. We must also account for an increasingly large proportion of global elderly, especially in developing nations, as continued pressure is put on limiting fertility and decreasing family size.

Traditionally, elderly care has been the responsibility of family members and was provided within the extended family home. Increasingly in modern societies, elderly care is now being provided by state or charitable institutions. The reasons for this change include decreasing family size, the greater life expectancy of elderly people, the geographical dispersion of families, and the tendency for women to be educated and work outside the home. Although these changes have affected European and North American countries first, they are now increasingly affecting Asian countries as well.

In most western countries, elderly care facilities are residential family care homes, freestanding assisted living facilities, nursing homes, and Continuing care retirement communities (CCRCs). A family care home is a residential home with support and supervisory personnel by an agency, organisation, or individual that provides room and board, personal care and habilitation services in a family environment for at least two and no more than six persons.

Gender Discrepancies in Elderly Care

According to Family Caregiver Alliance, the majority of family caregivers are women:

"Many studies have looked at the role of women and family caregiving. Although not all have addressed gender issues and caregiving specifically, the results are still generalizable [sic] to

- Estimates of the age of family or informal caregivers who are women range from 59% to 75%.
- The average caregiver is age 46, female, married and working outside the home earning an annual income of $35,000.
- Although men also provide assistance, female caregivers may spend as much as 50% more time providing care than male caregivers."

In Developed Nations

America

According to the United States Department of Health and Human Services the older population—persons 65 years or older—numbered 39.6 million in 2009. They represented 12.9% of the U.S. population, about one in every eight Americans. By 2030, there will be about 72.1 million older persons, more than twice their number in 2000. People 65-plus years old represented 12.4% of the population in the year 2000, but that is expected to grow to be 19% of the population by 2030. This will mean more demand for elderly care facilities in the coming years. There were more than 36,000 assisted living facilities in the United States in 2009, according to the Assisted Living Federation of America in 2009. More than 1 million senior citizens are served by these assisted living facilities.

Last-year-of-life expenses represent 22% of all medical spending in the United States, 26% of all Medicare spending, 18% of all non-Medicare spending, and 25 percent of all Medicaid spending for the poor.

In the United States, most of the large multi-facility providers are publicly owned and managed as for-profit businesses. There are exceptions; the largest operator in the US is the Evangelical Lutheran Good Samaritan Society, a not-for-profit organisation that manages 6,531 beds in 22 states, according to a 1995 study by the American Health Care Association.

Given the choice, most elders would prefer to continue to live in their own homes (ageing in place). Many elderly people gradually lose functioning ability and require either additional assistance in the home or a move to an eldercare facility. The adult children of these elders often face a difficult challenge in helping their parents make the right choices. Assisted living is one option for the elderly who need assistance with everyday tasks. It costs less than nursing home care but is still considered expensive for most people. Home care services may allow seniors to live in their own home for a longer period of time.

One relatively new service in the United States that can help keep the elderly in their homes longer is respite care. This type of care allows caregivers the opportunity to go on vacation or a business trip and know that their elder has good quality temporary care, for without this help the elder might have to move permanently to an outside facility. Another unique type of care cropping in U.S. hospitals is called acute care of elder units, or ACE units, which provide "a homelike setting" within a medical centre specifically for the elderly.

Information about long term care options in the United States can be found by contacting the local Area Agency on Ageing or elder referral agencies such as Silver Living, or A Place for Mom. Furthermore, the U.S. government recommends evaluation of health care facilities through websites using data collected from sources such as Medicare records.

Canada

In Canada, such privately run for-profit and not for profit facilities also exist. Because of cost factors, some provinces operate government-funded public facilities run by each province's or territory's Ministry of Health, or the government may subidize the cost of the facility. In these care homes, elderly Canadians may pay for their care on a sliding scale based on annual income. The scale that they are charged on depends on whether they are considered "Long Term Care" or "Assisted Living." For example, commencing in January 2010 seniors living in British Columbia's government subsidized "Long Term Care" (also called "Residential Care") will pay 80% of their after tax income unless their After Tax Income is less than $16,500. The "Assisted Living" tariff is calculated more simply as 70% of the After Tax Income.

Australia

Total employment in residential care services in Australia (thousands of people) since 1984

Aged care in Australia is designed to make sure that every Australian can contribute as much as possible toward their cost of care, depending on their individual income and assets. This means that residents pay only what they can afford, and the Commonwealth government pays what a resident cannot. An Australian statutory authority, the Productivity Commission, conducted a review of aged care commencing in 2010 and reporting in 2011. That review concluded that approximately 80% of care for older Australians is informal care provided by family, friends and neighbours. Around a million people received government-subsidised aged care services, most of these receiving low-level community care support, with 160 000 people in permanent residential care. Expenditure on aged care by all governments in 2009-10 was approximately $11 billion.

The need for increasing amounts of care, and known weakneses in the care system (such as skilled workforce shortages and rationing of available care places), led several reviews in the 2000s to conclude that Australia's aged care system needs reform. This culminated in the 2011 Productivity Commission report and subsequent reform proposals. In accordance with the Living Longer, Living Better amendments of 2013, assistance is provided in accordance with assessed care needs, with additional supplements available for people experiencing homelessness, dementia and veterans.

Australian Aged Care is often considered complicated due to various state and federal funding. Furthermore, there are many acronyms that customers need to be aware of, including ACAT, ACAR, NRCP, HACC, CACP, EACH, EACH-D and CDC (Consumer Directed Care) to name a few.

In Developing Nations

Nepal

Due to health and economic benefits, the life expectancy in Nepal jumped from 27 years in 1951 to 65 in 2008. Most elderly Nepali citizens, roughly 85%, live in rural areas. Because of this, there is a significant lack of government sponsored programs or homes for the elderly. Traditionally, parents live with their children, and today, it is estimated that 80% of the elderly do. This number is changing as more children leave home for work or school, leading to loneliness or mental problems in Nepali elderly.

The Ninth Five-Year Plan included policies in an attempt to care for the elderly left without children as caretakers. A Senior Health Facilities Fund has been established in each district. The Senior Citizens Health Facilities Program Implementation Guideline, 2061BS provides medical facilities to the elderly, and to those that are poverty stricken, free medicine and health care in all districts. In its yearly budget, the government has planned to fund free health care to all heart and kidney patients older than 75. Unfortunately, many of these plans are overly ambitious, which has been recognised by the Nepali government. Nepal is a developing nation and may not be able to fund all of these programs after the development of Old-Age-Allowance, or OAA. OAA provides a monthly stipend to all citizens over 70 and widows over 60.

Several charitable organisations have since opened in Nepal, with roughly 1500 elderly citizens living in them. Most of these are not government sponsored and are volunteer staffed.

Thailand

Thailand has observed global patterns of an enlarging elderly class: as fertility control is encouraged and medical advances are made, births shrink and lives age. The Thai government is noticing and concerned about this trend, but tends to let families care for their elderly members rather than create extraneous policies for them. As of 2011, there are only 25 state sponsored homes for the elderly, with no more than a few thousand members of each home. Such programs are largely run by volunteers and are questionable on the basis of quality of care, considering there is not always a guarantee care will be available. Private care is very difficult to follow, often based on assumptions. Because children are less likely to care for their parents, private caretakers are in demand. Volunteer NGOs are available but in very limited quantities.

While there are certainly programs available for use by the elderly in Thailand, questions of equity have risen since their introduction. The rich elderly in Thailand are much more likely to have access to care resources, while the poor elderly are more likely to actually use their acquired health care, as observed in a study by Bhumisuk Khananurak. However, over 96% of the nation has health insurance with varying degrees of care available.

India

India's cultural view of elderly care is similar to that of Nepal's. Parents are typically cared for by their children into old age, most commonly by their sons. It should be noted that in these countries, elderly citizens, especially men, are viewed in very high regard. Traditional values demand honour and respect for older, wiser people. India is facing the same problem as many developing nations in that its elderly population is increasing tremendously, with a current estimate of 90 million over the age of 60. Using data on health and living conditions from the India's 60th National Sample Survey, a study found that almost a quarter of the elderly reported poor health. Reports of poor health were clustered among the poor, single, lower-educated and economically inactive groups.

Under its eleventh Five-Year plan, the Indian government has made many strides similar to that of Nepal. Article 41 of the Indian Constitution states that elderly citizens will be guaranteed Social Security support for health care and welfare. A section of the 1973 Criminal Procedure Code, alluding to its traditional background, mandates that children support their parents if they no longer can themselves. NGOs, however, are prevalent in Indian elderly care, providing homes and volunteer care, but governmental policies and organisations are more popular.

Chapter 6

Social Institutions and Ageing

Rethinking Retirement

Ageing population with falling birth rates can't sustain 'early retirement': The age at which people retire is already rising, from what will surely be seen in the years ahead as unreasonably young. The notion of 'early retirement' which was meant to represent economic progress is fundamentally flawed, especially with an ageing population and falling birth rate! The maths don't stack up. In an ageing population, with falling birth rates, it is a recipe for economic decline.

Don't aspire to retire' in your 50s any more: Since the 1980s, an expectation had developed that people should aspire to retire in their 50s. This is simply not sensible or sustainable, especially as life expectancy has risen significantly, general health has improved and the physical demands of most types of work have eased. Even those in physically demanding jobs can retrain to do other work but often need to be supported to do so.

People are still retiring younger than in 1950s: In fact, increasing numbers of people are already choosing to work longer. In the 1950s, the average age of retirement for men was 67. At that time life expectancy was much lower than it is today, yet people are retiring earlier. That means their lifetime income is lower (especially as they often start work much later too) and they have less chance to save for a good later life income. It is clear that change is needed, but we have to manage that change carefully.

Not everyone can keep working but good for those who can: Clearly, if you are not well, or your work requires heavy physical labour, or if you are exceedingly wealthy and choose not to work at all, that is your choice. Nobody should be forced to work longer if they do not wish to, but most people could benefit from rethinking retirement if they are in reasonably good health.

There is no official 'retirement' age any more – individual choice: The traditional idea of stopping work as soon as you reach a 'pension age', whether that be state pension age, or the age at which a private or company pension starts, is now out of date. There is no official 'retirement' age any more, even though many commentators refer to the state pension age as a 'retirement age'. In fact, average retirement age for women is just over 63, which is beyond their state pension age although for men it is still a little under age 65. There can be more individual choice about when to stop working altogether, rather than being forced out by employers or assuming you must stop at pension age.

Redefine 21st Century retirement: The traditional idea of retirement meaning stopping work altogether needs to change – it is already happening, but there is far more that could be done to help it become a reality. The 21st century concept of retirement should be a phase of life with less work, rather than no work. This has the potential to improve millions of people's lives. The longer you work, the higher your lifetime income will be, and the better your pension prospects too. By having a period of part-time work in later life, you can also enjoy a better work-life balance, have time for grandchildren, hobbies or holiday breaks and still be part of the social interaction of work.

Hidden boost to economic growth and individual or family incomes: By keeping the skills of older people in the labour force, national output and national income will be higher, which can boost economic growth. At the same time, individual and family incomes will be higher too, which means more spending both now and in future.

Retirement should be an ongoing process, not a one-off event: This needs changed attitudes among employers and individuals. The old idea of retirement as a one-off event, rather than an ongoing process over a period of years, should be consigned to history. Flexible later life work opportunities, which retain the skills and experience of older people as well as enabling them to earn more if they want to, can boost society as well as the economy.

Work has non-financial benefits too, improve national well-being: There is evidence that stopping work altogether when still healthy can damage health and many surveys also show that people value working for non-financial reasons too. Many enjoy the social interaction and feelings of worth that are associated with work and others find they enjoy self-employment rather than no work. Society's attitude to later life working can change to benefit all of us. That is the real message we need. It's not just about retiring later, or raising retirement ages, it's about a whole new vision for retirement in the 21st century. The sooner we can make this happen, the better all our futures will be.

The Role of Ageing in Adult Learning: Implications for Instructors in Higher Education

Humans begin learning at birth and generally continue this process throughout life, but how much is learned and the value of that knowledge varies greatly from one individual to the next (Sheppard, 2002). Historically, the perception of adult learning and its value has varied greatly among individuals and groups. In the past, many people considered formal education and learning beyond age fifty of little value to society given the limited life span to use such knowledge. Many individuals might have considered such pursuit of knowledge as self-centred at best and viewed work beyond age sixty or sixty-five as unwarranted unless financial considerations dictated otherwise. Other critics of adult learning may have cited various reasons such as illness, genetic longevity, environment, ethnic differences, and individual habits as limiting the career and thus restricting the need for learning. Many of these attitudes were linked to a study by Moody (as cited in Lowy and O'Connor, 1986) suggesting that older adults perceive learning from the vantage point of approximately how much time is left to live. Although never exact, this perspective of time dramatically influences the educational goals of the older adult.

Regardless of these popular attitudes, more recently people have come to view ageing differently and have tended to classify learning in that same context. There appears to be an ongoing shift regarding the issue of adult learning that can be dated back to the post-World War II era and the GI Bill of Rights which resulted in millions of veterans flooding college campuses (Sheppard, 2002). In the United States, this legislation further promoted the growing notion that higher education was available for the common citizen and not just the wealthy aristocrat. Out of that setting came a generation of adults forming different views as to who could learn and when such learning was appropriate. Post WWII generations began taking a lifelong approach to learning resulting in an important cultural change that has increased economic productivity while improving the quality of life as well. Increasingly, older adults are seeking formal educational opportunities echoed in the demographic that reports 33 percent of postsecondary students are age 25 or older (King, Anderson, and Corrigan, 2003).

Changing demographics have had a lot to do with continuous lifelong learning by adults. Increased life expectancy during the last half of the 20th century is believed to be higher than any increases from recorded history until 1900 (Swain, 1995). Legislation regarding retirement age for full social security benefits was initiated in the in the mid 1930's which set that age as sixty-five and this retirement age was actually borrowed from the 19th century when people were estimated as living only a couple of years beyond there working careers. The legislation passed in the 1930's has changed very little since then even though life expectancies have increased dramatically. Consequently, until recently the assumption has been that people who live longer will most likely have more leisure time but not, necessarily, longer working careers. The Baby Boomers, those individuals born between 1946 and 1964, resulted in 80,000,000 new Americans, many of whom entered the workforce. Some writers such as Kaplan-Leiseson (2001) believe that a severe labour shortage will come about as the bulk of this group retires. Although more lenient immigration standards may offset the problem somewhat, the idea that people will continue to work and learn as they grow older seems important from an economic standpoint.

An even more apparent demand for adult education is supported by research that suggests a twenty year old today can expect to make six to seven job changes over the course of a working career (Aslanian and Brickell, 1980). Often, these vocational changes lead to additional adult learning out of necessity.

Clark and Caffarella (1999) explain that adult learning can be defined in numerous ways, but that a widely accepted definition refers to those learners as having completed mandatory public schooling, usually around age eighteen. While that may be a common convention among educational theorists, there are various definitions in use and this manuscript will refer to the adult learner as (at a minimum) having finished mandatory schooling in addition to having gained experience in the work force prior to engaging in additional education. Consequently, the focus here is on the adult that has had life experiences and has often been referred to as a non-traditional student in the higher education setting. The age range for this type of student is extremely wide and, for the most part, includes adults over age 25.

Bok (1990) has noted the importance of the adult learner by asserting that the college or university is a central institution of the current post-industrial society. Therefore, the effect of ageing on the adult learner and implications for educators will be examined in that context.

Physiological Aspects of Ageing on Learning

As one ages chronologically, not only are physical changes taking place such as reduced vision and hearing ability, but other age related factors can impact cognitive function well. Factors such as impaired blood circulation, decreased neurotransmitters, depression, stress, and chronic illness can all have an effect on the ability of the individual to learn (Merriam, 2001).

In 1927 Edward L. Thorndike reported that the ability to learn declined very slowly and very slightly at about 1% per year after age twenty-five. Until then, adult educators had mostly operated under the notion that "you can't teach old dogs new tricks". But later studies by Lorge revealed that the decline was that of speed of learning, not intellectual power, and that even this was minimized by continual use of the intellect (Knowles, 1980). Therefore, to say that one's ability to learn peaks at a young age and then tapers off slowly is generally true for most individuals, but it is also too simplistic and ultimately deficient in describing how ageing affects the complex process of learning.

Most theorist believe that intelligence consists of several factors. These factors can be separated into primary mental abilities and secondary mental abilities (Cavanaugh and Blanchard-Fields, 2002). A common subset of the primary mental abilities is made up of numeric facility, word fluency, verbal meaning, inductive reasoning, and spatial orientation.

Using a longitudinal study over a period of several decades, Schaie (1994) noted that scores on primary mental abilities improved gradually until about age forty at which time the abilities tend to stabilize until approximately age sixty. The decreases are small until the mid seventies at which time scores are usually measurably lower than they were in the mid twenties. Therefore, when a composite measure of mental abilities is used, learning ability does not decrease until the sixth or even seventh decade for most individuals. The significance of this seminal study seems to be that noticeable overall mental decline in the primary abilities does not generally occur until later in life.

Additionally, it should be noted that research pertaining to the secondary mental abilities usually focuses on two: fluid intelligence and crystallized intelligence (Cavanaugh, et. al., 2002). Younger people perform at a higher level where rote memorization that is part of fluid intelligence is measured whereas older, more experienced people make up for this in what is called crystallized intelligence through better developed verbal abilities and judgment (Merriam, 2001).

The good news here is that research supports the notion of lifelong learning in healthy individuals at least well into their seventies. While no one can stop the ageing process, there are some things that have been associated with increased retention of mental processes: education; exercise; absence of chronic diseases and illness and otherwise stimulating activities to the brain have all been shown to help the cognitive process (Merriam, 2001). While older adults are not as quick to learn as are younger people, they can often make up for this through a wealth of experiences that tend to support superior reasoning and judgment abilities if given time to think and reflect on the learning activity.

Experiential Aspects of Ageing on Learning

Adult learners have already been partly educated through life experiences. The concept of the experienced adult engaged in learning is an interesting and popular concept in higher education where it is generally accepted that adults have more experiences, different kinds of experiences, and that these experiences are organised differently (Long, 1983). According to Knowles (1980), adults derive much of their self identity from their past experiences. In that respect, they are much different from children who tend to view themselves largely from external sources. Because of this factor, adult learners place a great deal of value on their experiences and if they cannot use those experiences, or, if those experiences are rejected, it may feel similar to being rejected as an individual. Related to this is the fear of failure that an adult learner may bring to the classroom, particularly if this is a new environment where they might fear further rejection from their peer group (Kennedy, 2003) or their instructor.

While it may be true that adults often have a highly specialised or even expert knowledge base via extensive past learning activity, some researchers speculate that slowing of new information may occur because of a large knowledge base (Sternberg & Berg, eds. 1992). Additionally, adults may or may not bring experiences with them that are related to their current learning. Not all experiences are of equal value to the task at hand. Finally, not only can experiences be unequal in value, in some cases those experiences might actually be detrimental to their learning. Kennedy (2003) notes this phenomenon and indicates, "past experiences can also be a handicap in acquiring new learning." This type of handicap could occur from past habits or old ways of thinking about some important issue. A preconceived way of thinking and doing something is not always easily changed, especially when it has been previously backed up by some perceived expert advice. It could be added then, that adults are more skeptical about accepting new information, especially if it appears to contradict what they already believe.

Determining the trade offs between the size and value of the prior knowledge base and an older adult's ability to access information and add to that knowledge base is a challenging agenda for the teacher of an adult learner (Sternberg & Berg, eds., 1992). Many teachers may enjoy the challenge that adults bring to the table while others might feel threatened because of the expertise that such a student could use to challenge the instructor. These are both important issues that must be addressed by the instructor when developing a learning environment for the experienced adult learner.

Psychological Self-Image of the Adult Learner

Havinghurst (as cited in Knowles, 1980) asserts that people do not simply pass into adulthood and then just coast along to old age. He claims that adulthood has transition points and developmental periods as complete as that of childhood. Other theorists such as Erikson and Levinson also present stage or phase theories sometimes linked to life events and transitions that adults encounter and pass through (Clark and Caffarella, 1999). Kohlberg's (as cited in Merriam and Caffarella, 1991) 1973 theory of moral development promotes three stages that individuals pass through from youth to adulthood in relation to moral and ethical judgments influenced by the relationship of the individual to his or her social setting. All of these theorists tend to break development into various stages and recognise that although adults do not always fit neatly into each of these categories, by and large each phase has its own challenges and adjustments that could be viewed as developmental.

Regardless of which theory is most correct, Knowles (1980) argues for a dramatic change to self-image when one defines him or herself as an adult. The switch is away from being a full-time learner to one that takes on other responsibilities and thus creates more of a self-directed personality. People reaching adulthood do not just inherit a chronological progression of ageing but also often include taking an attitude that is more self-directed along with a need for others to view them as such.

Much of the self-directed image of the adult is mirrored in how they view work. The working role of many people often provides a significant and meaningful factor in self-identification. The old notion of "we are what we do" is an apt description of how a person may view his/her own self-image. While work itself is usually an important factor, another factor appears to be the differences in occupations among individuals. Many times lives outside of work are strongly influenced if not dictated by occupational activities (Long, 1972).

Another aspect of work that appears to influence the adult's perspective to learning has to do with job dissatisfaction. Rapid changes in technology and other socioeconomic factors may influence a great number of individuals to change occupations over the course of their working lives. The need to update or acquire new skills for vocational reasons may be significant for a growing number of adults.

Learning Expectations of the Adult

The notion of the adult learner as being self-directed is generally accepted in the literature on adult learning. Self-directed learning means that the learner tends to be systematic yet independent while not focusing exclusively on the instructor or the classroom (Merriam, 2001). Additionally, it means that as individuals mature, they may choose the precise means by which to learn certain subject matter and may become selective as to which content they learn. Self-regulation is a similar but not exact term used for traditional students in an educational setting where the student monitors the learning progress independently. Likewise, the self-directed learner is able to monitor learning in the classroom but can take that a step further to learning experiences outside of the traditional classroom as well.

Being self-directed has an important influence upon expectations of the adult learner which is one of the major differences between adults and children in the learning environment. Draves (1984) notes that adults are often eager to learn and approach learning from a mentality of readiness, problem orientation, and time perspective. All of these factors contribute to an internal motivation to learn that is sometimes missing in children.

Learner readiness is evident of a true learning mentality and can stem from the awareness that there is a need to learn. Reasons for learning range from specific career objectives to factors such as personal growth and accomplishment. Long (1983) points out that participation by adults in formal education is multifaceted and that realistically it is difficult to classify adult learners into one category without asking them personally about their education. Regardless of the need to learn, it is a very real need to the learner and thus results in readiness to learn.

Aslanian and Brickell (1980) noted that 83% of adult learners describe "some past, present, or future change in their lives as reasons to learn." These learners encounter change that requires learning in order to make the transition successful. Of this group, the vast majority (56%) named career changes as the reason. Additionally, it was noted that some life event separate from those transitions was the actual "trigger" that prompted them to start the process at that time. Sometimes this triggering event was momentous while other times it was of less significance.

Adult learners are more problem-centred and want to make learning apply to their lives. They view learning as most desirable when it is relevant and can be used currently rather than as something to be accessed in the distant future. Thus, they might be more interested in narrow issues than broad philosophical principles. Related to this issue is that adults also view learning from a different time perspective than children. As learners get older, time becomes more limited and, in many ways more precious (Draves, 1984). Placing a higher value on time seems logical when considering the ageing process that adults are experiencing coupled with awareness that they cannot recover lost time. In short, this same concept holds true for adult learners who do not want to waste valuable time in educational pursuits that they view as pointless.

Implications for Educators in Higher Education

Understanding adult learners and the role of ageing on their learning processes is one thing, but what about the implications of this information as it pertains to practicing educators in higher education? Knowing that there is more diversity among adult learners than there is among children who have had fewer experiences means that adult educators may be well advised to take a different approach when applying principles of good teaching to this group. Educators prone to using a cookie cutter approach to teaching may find student dissatisfaction with the instructional efforts that result in few rewards and less professional satisfaction for the instructor and student. Therefore, it seems imperative to develop some inferences appropriate to teaching in the higher education setting given the discussion of the ageing process and its relationship to adult learning.

Most educators may be somewhat disappointed to find that the majority of adults do not learn for the sheer pleasure of learning. Neither the process nor the possession of knowledge is the main reason for their participation (Aslanian and Brickell, 1980). Quite clearly, the main reason that adults are engaged in learning is because they want to be able to apply and use the knowledge. In fact, many adults are learning out of necessity because of some transition that has interrupted their life and they want learning to be relevant and to the point so that they will succeed at this transition. The corresponding message to educators seems apparent; the instruction must meet the needs of the adult students.

Adults are self-directed learners and are generally capable of monitoring their own progress. One implication is that they are usually more capable of interpreting flexibility that is built into a course such as a choice of assignments. As educators, the challenge may be to understand the various student interests and develop methodology and assessment techniques that allow for flexibility yet adheres to the constructs of the course content. This may be as simple as assigning writing requirements where there are choices for developing a topic within a certain conceptual framework.

Motivation is generally not a problem for the mature adult learner because they are ready to learn. They are often motivated to learn due to or in anticipation of a career change and desire to be successful in obtaining that goal. Because of this, problem centred types of assignments appeal to adults and they are usually eager to demonstrate this ability that is so commonly used on the job. Working in groups by role-playing, using case studies, or simulations may be an appropriate method of engaging the student in this type of learning.

The literature supports the idea of lifelong learning as viable for healthy adults and while the speed of learning may slow over time, the older learners make up for speed through their experience and knowledge base and are usually able to mentally process at a higher cognitive level with respect to such things as analysis, conceptualization, creativity, and judgment abilities. Overall, this means that the instructor needs to implement only slight and subtle modifications for an older learner in a course of study. While most adult learners are not as fast at rote memorization and may not be interested in content driven courses that contain a lot of memorization, they appear to be very adept at contextually based relevant coursework that requires critical thinking.

Draves (1984) suggests that group discussion is the most common format used for adult learning but that care must be used so as to prevent the discussion from wandering and becoming irrelevant to the topic at hand. The instructor is advised to introduce a topic of discussion at the beginning of each session and then facilitate from that point on. Giving adult learners the ability to share their stories among a group of learners is highly desirable because it creates a feeling of collegiality among the group and helps reduce fear among some of the quieter students. If the group is large, it may help promote discussion by breaking up into smaller groups first. This type of environment will promote an atmosphere of trust where students feel they can share narratives and dialogues regarding their own experiences. Some authors assert that humans are instinctively storytellers and are able to make meaning from narrative (Merriam, 2001). The sharing of experiences among adults is an important part of developing a learning community within the classroom.

Adult learners often bring a wealth of experience to the classroom that sometimes results in a dominating personality emerging from the group. This can be threatening to other students as well as to an instructor who is unprepared to deal with this kind of situation. To defuse such a dominating personality, it may be advisable for the instructor to understand when and how to intercede so as to bring others in for participation in the learning process. Creating a non-threatening and more informal atmosphere appears to work best when dealing with adult learners. In addition, it makes the class as a whole feel more at ease and willing to participate in discussion.

Like all learners, adults prefer an atmosphere that is favourable to the task at hand. It may seem obvious to note that the physical surroundings should be free of undue noise and that the temperature in the room is appropriate but the instructor should be cognizant of such things as decline in auditory and visual acuity with age. Instructors need to ask students if they can see or hear adequately in order to fully comprehend the material. Long (1983) says that beyond these physical issues there is some indication that architectural and environmental variables might influence interaction and learning but exactly how is not known.

Conclusion

The literature supports the idea that adults are very capable of learning well into their seventies which is a good reason to accept lifelong learning as more than just a pleasant mantra. Likewise, it seems beneficial for faculty in the higher educational setting to be aware of differences between the older learner and the traditional college age student. The differences are somewhat subtle, so it will take effort on the part of the instructor to understand and implement strategies appropriate to the nuances of the adult learner. Even though it takes time and energy to explore for the optimal environment and teaching methodology, the payoff could be well worth the effort if the result is an enjoyable and satisfying learning experience for the student. While it may be true that adults will learn in spite of the professor's shortcomings, faculty that choose to ignore learner differences run the inherent risk of mediocrity in their teaching.

The Ageing of the Population: Opportunities and Challenges for Human Factors Engineering

Dramatic changes are taking place in the demographic structure of the United States and other countries. An estimated 22 percent of the population will be over the age of 65 by 2030, and the fastest growing cohort within this subgroup will be people over 75. Currently about 44.5 million people are over the age of 75; by 2050 they will number almost 50 million (NCHS, 2005). Similar changes are occurring worldwide. By 2030 the percentage of people aged 65+ will be about 24 percent in Europe and about 12 percent in Asia and Latin America.

The ageing of the population presents vast societal challenges to ensuring that our infrastructures can support the needs of older people enabling them to live healthy, independent, and productive lives. To meet these challenges, we must rethink our conceptualizations of ageing and redefine what it means to be "older." The cohort of older adults today is very different from previous cohorts of older people, and the next cohort of the elderly, who will be mostly "baby boomers," is also likely to be different from today's elderly.

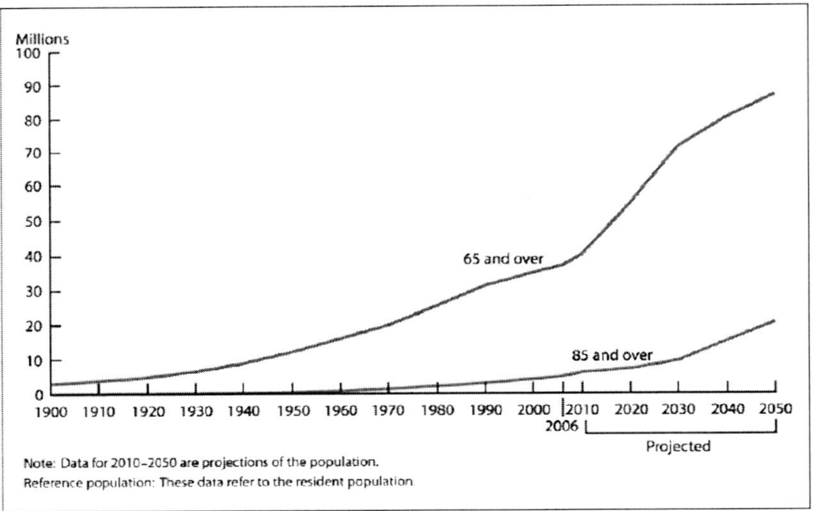

Figure: *Changes in the age distribution of people 65 and older in the U.S. population over the last century and projected through 2050. Source: U.S. Census Bureau, Decennial Census, Population Estimates and projections.*

In general, older people today are healthier, more diverse, and better educated than previous generations, and many are pursuing active lives. For example, many older adults, either out of need or by choice, remain employed in a full- or part-time capacity; some are even pursuing new careers, and many are engaged in volunteer work. The increase in the number of older workers requires changes in government and organisational policies, work procedures, and educational and training systems. Many older people are also engaging in continuing education, recreational activities (e.g., competitive sports), and travel.

Overall, older people are living longer than ever before, and the number of older people reporting very good health and improvements in physical functioning (e.g., the ability to walk a mile or climb stairs) has increased in recent years. Nevertheless, the likelihood of a person developing a disability or chronic illness increases with age. Many older adults are disabled in one or more aspects of self-care and, in general, the elderly require more health care services and incur higher health care costs than younger people. As the elderly population increases and people live longer, more people will require help with aspects of daily living and disease management.

Normative changes in function also occur with ageing. For example, ageing is accompanied by declines in visual and auditory acuity, a slowing of reaction and response times, declines in motor skills and agility, and changes in cognitive processes such as lapses in memory and attention. Thus there is a clear need for strategies to help healthy older people remain productive and independent and to ensure that those who are frail or disabled receive care and support so that they can live in their communities for as long as possible. Age-related changes in function have vast implications for the design of products, environments, and activities.

Diffusion of Technology

Simultaneously with the ageing of the population, we are witnessing unprecedented development and the diffusion of technology into all aspects of everyday life. Currently, all forms of technology, including computers, communications, safety, and health monitoring devices, are being used to perform routine tasks and activities. The use of technology has become an integral component of work, education, communication, and entertainment.

Technology is also being increasingly used in the health care arena for the delivery of services, in-home monitoring, interactive communication (e.g., between patient and physician), the transfer of health information, and peer support. As communication protocols evolve, we can anticipate more sophisticated network applications that can provide faster and more powerful interactive services in the future. Intelligent technologies will also increasingly become embedded in our interactions with the environment, and robots performing daily tasks will be commonplace. People of all ages will interact with some form of technology to function independently and engage effectively in their surroundings.

Technology has great potential for improving the quality of life for older people. For example, telemedicine/e-health will improve the physical and emotional well-being of older people. Technology can also enable older people to remain connected to family and friends, especially with those who are distant. Technology can also help older people remain employed and maintain or upgrade their skills, or it can ease the transition to retirement.

To date, however, evidence shows that the potential benefits of technology for older adults have not been realised. In 2007, about 32 percent of people age 65+ were Internet users, as compared to 65 percent of people age 50 to 64 and 83 percent of people age 30 to 49. Older adults who use computers and the Internet tend to be well educated and white and have more social resources and fewer functional impairments than non-technology users. The number of older people who have adopted home broadband is also lower than in the general population. In 2007, only 15 percent of people aged 65+ had broadband access at home, which limits the scope and potential of their online experience (Pew Internet & American Life Project, 2006, 2007). The widespread use of technology in the larger society suggests that the lack of technology use among older adults will have increasingly negative implications. For example, older people, who are most likely to need medical care, may not have access to health care technologies.

To date, older adults have largely been ignored as a viable user group by designers of technology systems. Although older people will have more technology experience in the future, they may still have problems adopting or negotiating technologies with new features unless system designers perceive older adults as an important user group and take their needs into account. The age-related digital divide could be closed if efforts are focused on that goal.

Human Factors Engineering

Human factors engineering, the study of human beings and their interactions with products, equipment, and environments in the performance of tasks and activities, could have great benefits for improving the independence and quality of life of older people. The overall objective of human factors engineers is to improve the "fit" between people and the designed environment to maximize performance, safety, comfort, and user satisfaction and minimize the likelihood of errors, inefficiencies, injuries, fatigue, and user dissatisfaction. To achieve this objective, human factors engineers espouse a user-centred, systems approach to design in which age-related changes in capabilities, tendencies, and preferences are incorporated into guidelines for design of products, tasks, and environments (Rogers and Fisk, 2000).

User-centred design can address the problems of older adults and help them retain and enjoy independence in their later years. In the following sections, some examples are presented of how older people could benefit tremendously, especially in the areas of information technologies, health care, and employment, from the application of human factors principles and concepts. These examples illustrate opportunities for human factors engineers.

Health Care

The likelihood of developing a disability or chronic illness increases with age, and many older adults are unable to perform one or more self-care tasks. In general, the elderly require more health care services and incur higher health care costs than younger people. The application of human factors and ergonomics principles and methods to the design of assistive and information technologies can improve the lives of elders in the areas of e-health, medication adherence, health care delivery, warnings and instructions, home safety, and the design of assistive devices.

Improving Medication Adherence

Failure to take medications as prescribed is a common problem among older adults and a significant predictor of hospital admissions. Generally, the person fails to take a prescribed medication, takes the incorrect dosage, takes medications at improper times or in the wrong combinations, or fails to comply with special instructions such as dietary restrictions. Noncompliance is particularly problematic for older people who take multiple drugs and are susceptible to side effects and drug interactions.

The problem of medication non-adherence is complex and may be attributed to numerous factors, such as an individual's perceptions or beliefs (e.g., the person does not believe that he or she is ill or that the medication is effective), cognitive problems (difficulty comprehending or remembering medication instructions), or ineffective strategies to encourage compliance. Many of these factors can be addressed by engineering solutions to help offset memory problems associated with comprehending and integrating medication schedules.

Products and devices could be designed to improve the organisation of medications, such as calendars, electronic pill dispensers, and compartmentalized containers that are congruent with a medication schedule. Voice mail or beepers might be used to remind individuals to take medications. Automated telephone messaging is effective not only for medication adherence, but also for reminding people of appointment times and for monitoring chronically ill patients and older adults who live in the community and are not being monitored in health care, assistive, or other facilities. Other engineering solutions include improvements in the packaging and labelling of medications and educating individuals about the nature of their illnesses and the importance of medication in illness management. The appropriate intervention depends on an understanding of the reason for non-adherence (Park and Jones, 1997).

Improving Health Care Delivery

Engineering and technology applications can improve health care delivery for people who are frail or have limited mobility, facilitate access to health care information and services, and make it easier for health care professionals to deliver care. For example, computers and information technologies, such as e-mail and the Internet, can give older people access to information about a particular illness, medication, diet, or exercise program. Technology can be used by health care providers to communicate with older patients; remind them of appointments and home health care regimens, such as dietary schedules; and check on a patient's general health status.

Interactive health communication, or "e-health," generally refers to the interaction between an individual and an electronic device or communication technology (such as the Internet) that provides access to information, transmits health information, or provides health-related guidance and support (Robinson et al., 1998). The scope of e-health applications is fairly broad, but most applications involve searching for health information, participating in support groups, and consulting with health care professionals. Millions of websites currently provide health information, and in 2006 about 113 million Americans searched for health information online on a typical day (Pew Internet and American Life Report, 2006).

The fact that consumers have access to e-health applications has significant implications for both patients and providers. On the positive side, access to health information can empower patients to take an active role in their health care. Patient empowerment can result in more informed decision making, better and more individualized treatment decisions, stronger patient-provider relationships, increased patient compliance, and better medical outcomes. On the negative side, access to such a wide array of health information can overload both patient and physician, disrupt existing relationships, and lead to poor decision making on the part of consumers.

The Internet can help older people communicate with health care providers or other people with similar problems. Several studies have shown that online support groups are beneficial for this population (Fogel et al., 2002). The Internet may be particularly beneficial for hearing impaired or aphasic individuals. However, for these technology-based applications to be successful, the technology must be relatively simple to use, readily available, and affordable, and adequate training must be provided. In addition, designers should take into account the credibility of information, privacy issues, and trust.

The term "telemedicine" refers to a wide range of technologies, from simple telephone connections to live two-way video and audio transmissions (interactive television). With telemedicine, physicians can directly assess patients and measure blood pressure, gait, and cognitive status. Physicians can also measure vital signs and ask hypertensive patients about disease manifestations and drug side effects. The cost of the technology varies with the sophistication of the system.

Finally, personal health records, especially patient-oriented electronic medical records (EMRs), can bring together fragmented information from multiple sources. A study committee of the Institute of Medicine concluded that EMRs are necessary to improve the quality and decrease the costs of medical care and recommended that patients have unfettered access to their own medical information (IOM, 2001). Patient-oriented EMRs are being designed to provide tailored information that can be accessed through on-line patient portals. Patient portals to EMRs also have the potential to personalize health education according to an individual's demographic characteristics and medical conditions. In addition, they can supply decision-support tools that can synthesize a great deal of medical information into linguistically appropriate messages for that individual.

Despite the growing popularity of EMRs, little research has been done on the usability of these tools for patient self-management, especially for at-risk populations such as older adults who are already experiencing a much larger variety of health problems than other segments of the population. Although the number of patient-accessible EMRs is increasing, many of them have not been evaluated to establish their usefulness and usability. Widespread public acceptance of EMRs and other e-health tools will require that designers pay more attention to the needs and circumstances of intended users, including their experience with health information and digital technologies and their capacities for health self-management (DHHS, 2006).

Employment and Work Settings

Current demographic projections indicate that by 2010 there will be about 26 million workers in the United States age 55+, a 46 percent increase since 2000. By 2025, the number will increase to approximately 33 million (GAO, 2003). The number of workers age 65+ will also increase substantially. Parallel trends have been identified in other developed countries throughout the world.

In addition to changes in demographics, we are also witnessing changes in the structure of work organisations. For example, vertically integrated business organisations are becoming less-vertically integrated, specialised firms. Decentralized management, collaborative work arrangements, and team work, and a new paradigm of knowledge-based organisations in which intellectual capital is an important organisational asset are also becoming commonplace. These changes in work structures and processes will have a pronounced effect on the nature of work and on the required capabilities of workers.

Ongoing developments in technology are also reshaping work processes, jobs, workplaces, and the delivery of job education and training. The introduction of automation and computer technologies into the workplace has dramatically changed the nature of many jobs and work situations.

To ensure that older adults can adapt to new workplace technologies, employers must provide them with access to retraining programs and incentives to invest in learning new skills and abilities. In addition, training and instructional materials should be designed for older learners, and technologies themselves should be designed (or modified) to be usable and useful for older adults, especially people with some type of impairment.

The benefits of new work arrangements (e.g., teleworking) should also be explored for older workers. Telework may be particularly appealing to older adults, who are more likely than younger people to be "mobility impaired" or engaged in some form of care giving (Schulz and Martire, in press). Telework also allows for flexible work schedules and autonomy and is amenable to part-time work.

There are also challenges, however, associated with telework for both workers and managers. The challenges for workers include isolation, managing home and work responsibilities, and the lack of technical support and feedback from managers and co-workers. For managers, the challenges relate to supervision and management of workers and decisions about which workers are best suited to telework. A more fundamental concern is that most teleworkers must interact with computers and the Internet or some other form of technology to perform their jobs. Although some data suggest that older workers are receptive to telework opportunities (Sharit et al., 2004), in general limited systematic evaluations of telework, especially with older workers, have been done.

Areas for Future Research

Human factors engineering focuses on improving interactions among people, tasks, environments, and products. The application of human-factors and ergonomics principles can improve the health, safety, and quality of life of older people. The basic premise of human factors and ergonomics is that user-centred design, based on a fundamental understanding of user capabilities, needs, and preferences, will lead to improvements in performance. Thus, according to this principle, improving the health and quality of life of older people requires that the knowledge of ageing be applied to the design of products and environments.

For example, in today's health care and work environments the ability to use technology is a critical skill. Technology can greatly improve the well-being and quality of life of older adults, and studies indicate that older people are receptive to using new technologies. However, they often encounter difficulties because they receive inappropriate training or because designers of the technology have not taken into consideration the needs of older people. User testing and user-centred design are critical to the success of technical systems. Guidelines for human-computer interaction suggest how computers and other forms of technology can be useful to, and usable by older adults (Czaja and Lee, 2002, 2006; Fisk et al., 2004).

We currently know very little about the efficacy of design aids and support tools for older adults. We also need more information on the best way to train older adults to use new technologies, and there are many unanswered questions about the best designs of online training programs and multimedia formats.

Issues of privacy and trust in technology are critical areas for research. There are also many questions about the Internet, such as how access to Internet information impacts health care behaviour and how we can teach seniors to identify and integrate relevant information from the enormous amount of information available on the Internet. In the workplace, research on how technology impacts employment opportunities and the work performance of older people would be extremely helpful. Not much research has been done on telework as it relates to older people or the factors that influence technology adoption, especially for minority elderly people and people who are not highly educated or well off economically.

Finally, many questions related to quality of life and socialization have not been fully explored. Many of the needs of older people could be addressed, or partly addressed through technological solutions. However, we will first need a systematic effort to understand their needs and incorporate them into the design of products for the marketplace.

The Changing Family in Today's World

Most of today's grandparents (Mennonite Brethren) raised their families in villages that resembled churches, whether Gnadental in southern Manitoba or Corn, Oklahoma. Each began as a village of a few families, a church and a school. As agricultural people, they were sustained by the land and the labours of the whole family. Marriage was not designed for personal fulfillment but to bear children and fulfill obligations. Divorce was unthinkable.

Our parents moved with their families to towns. Here it was assumed that fathers worked outside the home in factories, businesses or schools. Mothers cared for the children inside the home. Church was now what one goes to. And divorce was the way "other" families solved their problems.

My generation lives in the city. Our families are often dual career. We talk about the importance of friendship and companionship in marriage. We feel the freedom not to have children and to select a church that meets our personal preference. Over half of our marriages will end in divorce.

It seems hackneyed by now to state *{13}* that there are profound social changes in the past century which have molded and shaped the contemporary family (Skolnick and Skolnick, 1989). Both the difficulties and the resources of the contemporary family are a consequence of these changes. A list illustrative of changes follows.

- The decline of infant mortality means one doesn't have to have six children so four will survive.
- The fact that people live longer means more time together and more adjustment after the children leave.

- The use of birth control allows for more choice in family and career planning.
- The spread of mass education increases employment opportunities for men and women.
- Women have surged into the work place and so increased family income.
- Birth rates have declined, leaving more time for activities other than parenting.
- The women's movement has affected both the way men and women think and act towards one another.
- Social and sexual rules continue to be relaxed so that unmarried couples live together and unmarried mothers raise children.
- Abortion is legal but under attack.
- Remaining single and childless is increasingly acceptable.
- Divorce rates have skyrocketed and then leveled off; now we begin to assess the after-effects.

These are changes that reflect a changing culture. Most of the changes that have shaped the structure of our family life are less a result of Christian conviction than the result of societal shifts. The church will not be able to understand or respond to these families unless it reflects on the social changes that have occurred in this century. The family in times past was embedded in a community, not a private place of refuge from the world of work. Research has demonstrated that between 1957 and 1976 a major psychological revolution had taken place in American society such that in the past, fulfillment meant satisfactory performance of traditional roles of spouse and provider, while 20 years later fulfillment meant finding intimacy, meaning and self-definition. There are fewer functions (education, entertainment, religious socialization, etc.) served by the family than in time past and more of the *{14}* functions are relegated to institutions outside of the family. What is left is a need for companionship without the structures which mediate family closeness.

Furthermore, for Mennonite Brethren the change from the Ukraine to North America has had significant impact on the structure of our families. Our grandparents grew up in a culture which accepted Czar Nicholas II as ruler and their family life reflected that version of the state, a small autocracy. There were clear parallels between socio-political ideals and family structure. The family hierarchy was patterned after social and political hierarchy. But our generation grew up in a Western democracy. Giving unilateral commands, however kindly, is simply not considered appropriate. In a democratic family, greater emphasis is placed on respect for the other member's ability to make decisions.

While the past shapes us, what will be the constellation of the family in the 21st century? What will be the context, the environment of the family then? What will be the strengths of the different family constellations? How will the church relate to the changing family? Will the church respond with confusion, embarrassment, tolerance, acceptance or distance?

This article will reflect on four family constellations. We will not examine the family portrayed in "Little House on the Prairie." It is doubtful that it was ever that idyllic. Nor will we look at the traditional family where father worked in the marketplace and mother worked at home raising the children. That family is rapidly disappearing. Only 13% of North American families fall into this category. Rather, our four constellations are based on rough estimates of these types of households in North American society:

a. the two-earner family, 15-20%
b. the step family of remarriage, 10%
c. the single parent family, 15%
d. the empty nest couple, 20%

Dual Career

This family seems familiar, like the traditional family with two parents and two children. But what is unique about these two parents is they both have careers. In 1985, 54% of all American women over the age of 16 were working. Of these 56% were married (Cox, 1987).

Why the emergence of this family constellation?

1) Inflationary pressure and rising expectations of living standards have combined to bring many women to work.
2) It is less expensive to be working than to be staying home, given the fact that real wages have increased dramatically.
3) Declining birthrates contribute to women working more.
4) A college education has increased the number of jobs available to women.
5) Attitudes have changed.

In 1930 only 18% of surveyed women believed that married women should take a full-time job outside the family, whereas in 1970 it was 73% (Cox, 1987).

The Structure of the Dual Career Family

These parents probably met in college, married after graduation, and then for the next several years traded off working and going to graduate school. Both are now professionals in high-status, high-paying positions. They are homeowners and frequently vacation abroad. This family sees itself as very different from its more traditional parents. Two-career families provide an increased measure of autonomy for each of the individuals.

The practice of combining two careers has radically altered the balance of power. Negotiation, consultation, and friendship are the norm now. No longer is the woman's identity derived from that of the male. The changes in this family may not have come because the wife is an ardent feminist. As a college student she may have become interested in a particular field and wanted to pursue a career. The structure of the family then followed the negotiation of two careers in marriage rather than a particular ideology (Herz, 1989). Sometimes the relationship between the two marriage partners seems closer to a business partnership where a major issue is fairness. This is an active family. Their calendar is full of engagements. As a result, family activities and time schedules are negotiated and that consumes considerable energy.

Resources

This family has incredible resources: college and graduate education, high-paying jobs and broad social networks of friends. They tend to come from families that are already educated and have a middle- to upper-middle-class lifestyle. This kind of family is, however, dependent on a high level of *{16}* income. A labour force which they can hire enables them to save time.

The dual career family may be active in a congregation but scheduling is a problem. If its members are involved, they bring a sense of competence and confidence to the tasks they perform in church. However, the couple may have consciously selected a particular congregation because they felt it would meet their family needs. They would choose another congregation if they felt their needs would be better met. This couple often feels a large gap between their professional lives and the life of the church community and are not sure what to do about it. In all probability this couple will not have regular family devotions the way their parents did, but will occasionally read the devotional literature and share their spiritual concerns.

What are its Stress Points?

This is a family constantly under stress. Whether to have children and how to care for them are among the most difficult issues that these families face. Career women may postpone childbearing until they are promoted to higher ranks. Having children may mean promotions will be denied. At the same time, the biological clock is ticking; when is the best time to have a child? These couples also worry that their children in day care centres are not receiving the kind of nurture they deserve. Sometimes this family has difficulty finding outside labour to perform household and child-care chores. Occupationally, they experience greater difficulty finding careers for both partners in the marriage in the same location. When they find one they must adapt to competing employer demands.

This family prides itself on being more egalitarian. Women continue, however, in dual career marriages to assume responsibility for child-rearing while these fathers seldom talk about the importance of fathering. The research (Cox, 1987) indicates that 89% of the married men and women agree that household cleaning should be shared by both partners when both work. In actuality 40% of the full-time employed wives and only 8% of the husbands reported doing most of the housework. Not surprisingly, these working mothers report not having enough time for themselves.

In spite of all the resources the family possesses, there is fragility:

a. This family has virtually no models to guide them in creating marital relationships.

b. The notions of family self-sufficiency and autonomy are myths with the dual career couples. They must purchase individual and institutional services in order to fulfill traditional family functions. "Dual career couples trade time for money, and, instead of bartering their own labour with friends and relatives as lower-class families do, . . . they buy domestic services from strangers." (Herz, 1989, 296)

c. The lifestyle of this couple has been inflated to the point where both incomes are necessary to maintain their way of life. They can pursue a lifestyle available only to the wealthy. The dual career family is a social and economic elite within a capitalist society.

d. Increased personal fulfillment has meant sometimes that there is not as strong a commitment to home life and traditional marital relationships.

In all probability this type of family will not only survive but increase in the 21st century. It will bring with it its strengths and weaknesses, its needs and gifts.

Stepfamilies

A stepfamily is defined as a remarried family with a child under 18 years of age who is the biological child of one of the parents and was born before the remarriage occurred. The step family, also called the "blended" or "reconstituted" family, is different from the "natural" family. For one thing, it has a larger supporting cast, including former spouses, former inlaws, and absent parents, as well as assorted aunts, uncles and cousins on both sides. Furthermore, it may be "contaminated with anger, guilt, jealousy, value conflicts, misperceptions, and fear" (Einstein, 1986). It is, in short, burdened by much baggage not carried by an "original" family.

Stepfamilies must deal with stress that arises from losses (as a result of death or divorce), which can make both children and adults afraid to trust and to love. A welter of family histories complicates present relationships. For example, previously established bonds or loyalty to an absent adult may complicate new bonding. *{18}*

Statistics: Present and Projected

So, how many families are there in this group? According to a recent issue of *Newsweek Magazine*, which featured the "Family in the 21st Century," about one-third of all children born in the 1980's may live with a step-parent before they are eighteen. According to the latest available census figures, there were close to seven million children living in stepfamilies in 1985. That's an increase of 11.6% in just five years.

In the early 1900s death was the major cause of marital dissolution. Today a typical couple has only a small probability of being separated by death during their first 15 years of marriage, but perhaps 10 times as high a probability of being separated by divorce (Becker & Landes, 1977). Approximately 4/5 of those who divorce will remarry, and half of those who remarry will marry previously divorced persons (Messinger, et al, 1977). Prosen and Farmer (1982) reported that every year one-half million adults become stepparents and that one out of every six American children under 18 is a stepchild. They also predicted that by 1990 the stepfamily could well be the norm. Research conducted by Glick (1989) shows that 17.4% of married-couple families with young children in 1987 were stepfamilies, but he projects that 40% may be expected to become stepfamilies before their youngest child becomes 18 years old.

Questions and Issues Often Faced

Couples planning on remarriage do not spend much time talking together about such things as previous marriages, finances, doubts about the relationship, etc. Many of them live together before remarriage because they think that is the best way to discover whether the marriage will work. In the study by Ganong and Coleman (1987), very few persons contacted professionals before entering remarriage.

Those who did go to a pastor said that the pastor did not bring up specific issues that would be relevant to remarriage or stepfamilies. That is a significant omission. Only about 2% of the men and 8% of the women attended a support group. This particular study indicates that the couples who remarry are either overly optimistic or naive (Ganong and Coleman, 1989). Few potentially important issues were discussed prior to marriage. People often enter the new relationship with a lot *{19}* of optimism. They expect, for example, their new partner to have a good relationship with their children. Only 7 to 9% thought that the stepparent/child relationship might be bad. However, about 30% considered and discussed the possibility of divorce.

For those who did seek help, much of the counselling received was oriented toward solving divorce-related problems rather than focusing on remarriage and stepfamily issues. Stepchildren and finances were the two concerns most often mentioned. There tends to be an assumption that unless there is overt conflict prior to remarriage, then nothing needs to be done.

Problems and Strengths

Disagreements over stepchildren appear to be a frequent problem, as do relationships with former spouse(s). These two items alone may create considerably more conflict than in a nuclear family. The lack of societal guidelines for stepfamily roles is confusing at times, and there may be certain legal problems, for example, the rights of stepparents to sign for medical care for stepchildren and access to children following a subsequent divorce. Economic reintegration can be complicated, and commitment and cohesiveness may decrease. Difficulties in merging two different lifestyles and blurred boundaries can also create problems.

How do children experience living in a stepfamily? In Patricia Lutz's (1983) study of 103 teenagers between the ages of 12-18, eleven categories of stress were identified by the researcher: discipline, divided loyalty, biological parent elsewhere, member of two households, desire for natural parents to reunite, unrealistic expectations, social attitudes, compounded loss, family constellation, sexual issues, and pseudomutuality.

Of all of these categories, the teenagers only noted two of them as stressful: discipline and divided loyalty. Feeling caught in the middle between the two natural parents, and liking a stepparent more than one's natural parent of the same sex were the highest stressors. Interestingly, none of the other items were felt to be stressful. It appears that once the initial adjustment is made (this usually takes about two years), living in a stepfamily may not be that difficult for teens.

There are also some significant strengths of stepfamilies. One of these is the availability of more adults, who may *{20}* provide stability and new experiences for the children. The biological parents may be happier as a result of the remarriage, making life more pleasant for the children. A happy remarriage presents to children a positive model of adult intimacy and marriage. They learn that love is not just automatic; it takes time to grow and develop. The stepfamily may help individuals to have a more realistic view of marriage. There may also be some long-term advantages; some people feel that stepchildren potentially become more adaptable and are able to deal more flexibly with life as adults.

An Opportunity for the Church

The kind of integration that is called for in a remarriage creates many opportunities for the church to step in and help with education, ministry and support. The church needs to broaden its models of family relationships in the church, so that all experience greater openness. A lot of the remarriage concerns are not identified, either by the couple entering it, or by the church, or by those who may be parenting these persons who are remarrying. So it seems this is an opportunity for the church to enter much more fully, both in premarital sessions and in providing individual and group support and counsel.

Single Parent Family

The single parent family is a contrast to the other family constellations. This is the family with a single parent. Most single parents do not live the life of "Kramer vs. Kramer."

In contrast to the descriptions of the previous family structures, we will begin with a profile of Sharon, a 38-year-old single parent with two children: Jeryl (12) and Kirk (14). She divorced her husband Frank, after 15 years of marriage. Jeryl reported that her father had touched her inappropriately over a long period of time and had physically forced himself upon her on numerous occasions. When he continued to deny it publicly and at the same time became physically abusive to Sharon in private, Sharon filed for divorce.

Sharon holds down a full-time job that brings in $14,000 per year, $1,000 per month after taxes. She works as a clerk in a shopping centre. Her monthly rent is $425. Frank does not provide her with child support and is currently earning *{21}* $38,000 per year. While Frank had finished some years of college and begun a career, Sharon had raised the family. She completed a year of college before marriage and now has no marketable skills.

Both children attend school but carry the emotional scars of abuse and their difficult divorce. Jeryl is withdrawn and finds it hard to make friends. Kirk has been a problem in school. He is not doing well academically and has been unruly in class. Shortly after the divorce, Sharon moved from their modest home into a rather cramped apartment since house payments were beyond her means. The children changed school systems, and thus left behind old friends and teachers.

Sharon has sole custody of the children but the father has visiting rights every other weekend. Jeryl refuses to see her father. Since Frank sees Kirk only occasionally, he plans special events. He places no restrictions on Kirk and so Sharon has considerable difficulty setting limits when he returns.

When Sharon first approached her pastor regarding the sexual abuse of Jeryl, she found him sympathetic and understanding. He encouraged her to confront Frank with the truth. He did not feel it was his responsibility to notify the authorities. When she indicated that she was filing divorce papers, her pastor encouraged her to continue in the relationship. Reluctantly, she agreed to return. When Frank became physically abusive, she proceeded with the divorce without her pastor's support. Sharon has felt like a second-class citizen in the congregation. There have been some individuals who have reached out to her in friendship. She has received no financial assistance.

Single Parent Stresses

This home has multiple stressors:

1) The most frequently voiced complaint of the single parent is the enormous emotional and physical drain that single parenthood imposes. The work role seems to absorb most of the single parent's energy and there is little left for homemaking and parenting (Schlesinger, 1979).
2) Single mothers become stricter and fathers more lenient in relationship to the children after the divorce, which creates adjustment problems for the children (Krantz, 1989). The children need additional discipline and support. A single parent

lacks the validation and parental authority which tends to exist in two-adult homes.

3) The single parent may experience feelings of guilt and confusion trying to answer the question, "Who is to blame?" Not knowing how to relate to the ex-spouse is a problem.

4) Women after many years of divorce indicate that loneliness and depression were their major problems. They also indicate that this was not offset by the gains of autonomy and competence.

The Church and the Single Parent

Reed (1986) has suggested concrete ways in which the church can respond to the needs of single parents:

1. Redefine family to include single parents and their children.
2. Provide respite by taking the children for an evening or a weekend.
3. Arrange childcare for church events.
4. Plan support groups for single parents.
5. Give workshops on parenting, discipline, communications and finances.
6. Organise resources for sharing clothing, childcare, etc.
7. Find appropriate role models for the children.
8. Reach out and respond in a friendly manner to single parents.
9. Understand and accept the single parent.

Empty Nest Families

The empty nest is a term for the transitional phase of parenting following the last child's leaving the parents' home. For some it is a time of completion, fruition, and opportunity; for others it may be overwhelming loss, general disintegration, and may even lead to disruption through divorce. Today more marriages are ended by divorce, but couples who manage to stay together can look forward to twenty or more years of married life after the last child has left the home. For some it may be thirty to forty years. Four- and five-generation families may become quite common.

Structure and Demographics

The duration between the last child's leaving home and the death of one spouse has increased since 1910 from a median of less than two to almost twenty years, due to the younger age of the mother when the last child leaves, the small family, greater employment of women, changing role definitions and greater life expectancy.

The 1981 Census Bureau report includes in middle age all those between 45 and 64. In 1979 in the U.S. there were 44 million, or 20% of the population in this group. By the year 2010, the number will almost double to 75 million, or approximately 25% of the population. Nine out of 10 live in families and the vast majority with spouses (U.S. Bureau of Census, 1981).

Financially the empty nest families are the group who are most well-off. In 1986 the 45-54 age group had the highest mean household income, $31,516. In 1984 62.9% of all women aged 45-54, and 41.7% of all women aged 55-64, were in the labour force (U.S. Bureau of Census, 1986). The kinds of work the women are doing is significant.

Problems and Strengths

Launching children and moving on is the newest, the longest stage and in many ways the most problematic of all phases. This phase can lead to parental feelings of emptiness and depression. It has the greatest number of exits and entries of family members: deaths of parents, entry of in-laws and grandchildren. The move up to grandparent position may come at the same time one's own parent becomes dependent. Or this phase may be a liberating time, with more finances and more free time and potential for moving into new and unexplored areas—travel, hobbies, careers. This phase necessitates a restructuring of the marital relationship once parenting responsibilities have ended. Marital adjustment is pivotal; new opportunities and growth for the relationship become possible. If solidification of the marriage has not taken place and reinvestment is not possible, the family often mobilizes itself to hold onto the last child, or the couple may divorce (Solomon, 1973).

When the nest does not empty when expected, or is refilled by fledgling adults returning home to live, there is sometimes tension as parents are forced to accommodate to the presence of their full-grown offspring (Lindsey, 1984). In 1984, 37% of 18- to 29-year olds in the U.S. were in households headed by their parents. About 7% of the men and 10% of the women were in school, and most had not yet married. This situation creates sources of possible psychological conflict. *{24}*

Adult children living with parents may fall into immature, dependent habits, while the parents continue or resume the role of caregivers. Meanwhile the parents may be deprived of long-postponed freedom to renew their own intimacy, to explore personal interests, and to resolve marital issues that were pre-empted by parental responsibilities. Almost half of the still-married parents complained of strains on their marriages.

Eleven percent of divorces and annulments during 1982 were for individuals who had been married 20 years or more. These couples are more likely to see divorce as personal failure. They also experience less peer support. The prospects of new marital roles and relationships are drastically different for men and women, due to the combined effects of sex differences in the death rates and the double standard of ageing. Men have a much larger pool of possible partners to choose from.

Some women who have a heavy investment in mothering experience problems at this time; but they are far outnumbered by those who find it liberating not to have children in the home any more. There is some evidence that this stage may be harder on fathers, who may react to their children's leaving with regrets that they did not spend more time with them when they were younger (Rubin, 1979). The empty nest also appears to be hard on parents whose children do not become independent when the parents expect them to, and on women who have not prepared for the event by reorganising their lives through work or other involvements (Harkins, 1978; Targ, 1979).

Many women may see this time as a release from the dual demands of family and career. But family needs do not cease as the children leave; the growing old-old population (85 and over) is presenting unprecedented dilemmas to the generation in the middle regarding caregiving.

Some of the other problems and needs of this group are: mutual help between the generations, reducing the strain of caregiving, lifelong parenting, and new creative ways to relate which call for mutual giving and receiving. Elder abuse, including neglect, physical and psychological abuse, is a pressing social concern of the 1980s and 1990s. Estimates of victims of such abuse vary from 600,000 to 1 million, which involves about 4% of the older population. *{25}*

There are strengths in the empty nest family as well. The years immediately after the children leave home may bring as much contentment as the honeymoon. The couple has more privacy, the freedom to be spontaneous, fewer money worries, and a new opportunity to get to know each other as individuals. The post-child rearing stage is often a time of consolidation, since the couple has experience, maturity, and financial solvency. The death of a parent may resolve an attachment and help offspring feel more responsible for self, and provide a never known sense of freedom. Sometimes the family rituals around engagements, marriage, birth, and death can give people an opportunity to work out previous unfinished business. People in middle age often learn a lot about themselves while helping elderly parents with their life reviews. Learning to deal with declining physical faculties, ageing, etc., may help persons focus on internal, spiritual growth, and develop inner resources. The heightened awareness of one's own mortality may help set priorities and bring new appreciation for relationships. Change is essential and autonomy, responsibility, and connectedness are key issues. The development of adult relationships with adult children is often positive.

Marital Satisfaction

Current literature on marital satisfaction suggests that it follows a U-shaped curve (Gruber-Baldini and Shaie, 1986). From a high point early in the marriage, it declines until late middle age and then rises again through the first part of late adulthood. The least happy time seems to be the period when most couples are heavily involved in child rearing and careers. Positive aspects of marriage, such as discussion, cooperation, and shared laughter, seem to follow the U-shaped pattern, while negative aspects, such as sarcasm, anger, and disagreement over important issues, decline from young adulthood through age 69.

What makes middle-aged couples split up? Middle-aged couples are separating for many of the same reasons as younger couples: their greater expectations, their growing willingness to end an unsatisfactory relationship, increased acceptance of divorce even for older couples, the less stringent divorce laws. Broderick says, "The chief cause of divorce is disappointment.

If it was a long-term marriage, the disappointments are long-term" (1990, 9). But divorce can be especially *{26}* traumatic for middle-aged and older people. People over 50 suffer more distress. Indeed, divorce has become so prevalent that sociologists are now studying why some marriages do not break up. Reasons frequently given for lasting marriages are a positive attitude toward the spouse as a friend and as a person; belief in the commitment to, and sanctity of marriage; and agreement on aims and goals in life.

Opportunities for the Church

There is a lack of role models for later-life family relations. Present role definitions and labels may not fit. The successful functioning of families in later life requires a flexibility in structure, roles, and responses to new developmental needs and challenges. Patterns that have been functional may no longer fit and new options must be explored. Previous losses and adaptive patterns also affect responses to later life challenges. The church needs to speak forthrightly to invisibility and ageism which are two major problems in society.

The church also needs to be aware that the marriage relationship may be more seasoned, stable, and more satisfactory than any other time. It might also be more conflictual, more tenuous, and more alienated. In the absence of children, the conjugal bond, whatever its nature, will gain prominence. By the same token, more reliance on it will make existing strains more obvious. The couple may adopt either more constricted or more expanded roles. If areas of conflict have been sealed off, there will be significantly less self-disclosure. To stay in emotionally safe areas, there will be avoidance, which means less intimacy, and may lead to emotional distance and physical distance. Both the amount of love expressed, and the number of problems they have declines—thus, there appears to be less happening between them, for good or for ill. Therefore, the empty nest stage seems to be a key time for marriage enrichment and involvement in ministry.

Conclusion

By highlighting dual income, blended, single parent and empty nest families we have tried to show that in the family of God, there is much diversity and that persons in each of these families are of inestimable worth. It behooves us to develop new models and find a new language for caring. An awareness *{27}* among leaders that the family has changed, is changing, and will change is critical. Change is not evil in and of itself. Yet the church often fears change. Why insist on labels and stereotypes that hurt other people? Why be so hesitant to change the language and the conception of the family? We would do well to work harder to affirm families that feel they are second-class citizens. The kinds of families we have described are families that need the church. They challenge the church with a new set of problems and strengths. They can motivate the church to develop new structures and new models of ministry. Let us mobilize ourselves, our gifts, and our congregations to nurture families that reflect the Reign of God.

Creating 'Age-Friendly Cities': Developing a New Urbanism for All Generations

Developing 'age-friendly' cities has become a key issue for improving the quality of life of all generations. Population ageing and urbanization have in their different ways become the dominant trends of the 21st century, raising issues for all types of communities. By 2030, two-thirds of the world's population will be residing in cities. By that time many of the major urban areas of the Global North will have 25 per cent or more of their population aged 60 and over. Cities will remain central to economic development, attracting waves of migrants and supporting new industries. However, the extent to which what has been termed the 'new urban age' will produce 'age-friendly communities' remains uncertain. Cities have many advantages for older people in respect of easy access to medical services, provision of cultural and leisure facilities, shopping and general necessities for daily living. However, urban life can also create threatening environments, producing insecurity, feelings of exclusion, and vulnerability with changes to neighbourhoods. These issues affect all age groups and not just older people. However, with older people spending 80 per cent of their time in the home and home environment, support from the immediate neighbourhood and beyond becomes crucial. What is the scope for developing age-friendly cities to take account of these issues? Some questions to be considered in the debate will include:

Cities are viewed as key drivers for economic success but can they integrate ageing populations as well? Can the resources of the city be used to improve quality of life in old age – just 1 in 20 households may have the money to take account of what cities such as Manchester have to offer? Can cities be designed in the interests of all age groups? What are the options for responding to different housing needs across the life course? How can older people be central to the regeneration of urban neighbourhoods? Can older and younger age groups work together to identify common needs and secure 'rights to the city' which work in the interests of all generations.

Our panellists will give us their perspectives on these issues on Tuesday. A short preview is given below.

Graeme Henderson, Research Fellow, IPPR North

If recovering from the financial crisis is the key fiscal policy challenge of this decade, an ageing population will be the biggest of the next decade, and the one after that. Too often population ageing is seen only as a burden on the economy but this plays down its potential benefits and the opportunities it will bring. Making work better for older people who want to remain in the workforce for longer can help increase our country's economic capacity in the same way that the influx of women into the workforce did in the post-war period. Adapting products and services, homes and even cities, to fit with the requirements and preferences of older citizens is opening up potential growth markets which we should be every bit as on focused on as emerging economies on the other side of the world.

Equally, older workers often have built up a vast amount of experience from working in the same or similar fields for many years.

There is a justified perception that this expertise is not being properly utilised in workplaces and by society. A cultural shift is necessary to ensure that this accumulated knowledge is better understood and fully made use of.

While there is a moral case for developing age-friendly cities, we must not let take understate the economic case either.

Cities in the North of England already aspire to be at the frontier of embracing the silver economy. However, while they are home to several ground-breaking initiatives, these initiatives are largely isolated from wider economic strategies and have yet to deliver a breakthrough in turning around economic challenges. For example, the northern regions have the lowest levels of economic activity among older age men, while for women the three northern regions account for three of the lowest five performers amongst 50-59 year olds, and the three lowest among over 60s.

In most regions and cities, the response to ageing has been on the perceived costs of population change, its impact on service delivery, a focus on attracting a relatively declining cohort of younger workers and new sources of economic growth rather than considering the potential economic contribution of their growing 'silver' cohort. Ageism is sadly rife in our society and is perhaps the main obstacle standing in the way of a flourishing silver economy. There is also a perception that older workers extending their careers prevents young people finding jobs.

IPPR North's new Silver Economies project will seek to address these challenges and look at how to better harness the economic potential of our maturing society.

Stefan White, Manchester School of Architecture

The role of urban research and design in making cities age-friendly: (con)testing the WHO design guidance in a Manchester Neighbourhood

We have just completed a participatory urban research *and* design project for of an age-friendly neighbourhood in 'Old Moat', Manchester, UK for Southway Housing Trust.

Our reflection on the Old Moat project is focussed on how the WHO age-friendly city programme and policies enable us to both understand (Research) *and* produce (Design) more inclusive urban environments. The key issues which have arisen in trying to come to know a particular neighbourhood of the city *and* then attempting to arrive at concrete proposals for making it more 'Age-friendly' are how we decide to define and act in relation to the three broad categories of 'City', 'Neighbourhood' and 'Age-friendly'.

City

We have taken the view that the City should be understood as a complex entity where physical and social issues and causes interact and interlock with one another: A multiplicity of networks at different spatial scales constituted through territorialised relations that stretch beyond its limits (Robinson 2005). Urban research and design for a city of networks involves understanding and changing the relations between places, groups and services as well as the physical environments, organisations and provisions themselves.

Using the example of 'Old Moat' we argue that urban design should not be understood as limited to removing 'unfriendly' objects or surfaces but include stimulating both formal and informal enabling services, socialities and infrastructure networks.

E.g more benches are a common request heard in age-friendly research and a sensible proposition with regard to the average mobility of older people – however concerns over management and anti-social behaviour often prevent them from being installed or are the reason for their removal. How can we *design* a neighbourhood with more benches?

Neighbourhood

We have approached the concept of Neighbourhood as comprising both the community and the space in which it is practiced (DeCertau, Petrescu). This means it is not just a space on a map but made what it is by the people who live there. This approach asks that we address the political engagement or involvement of a community in parallel with any environmental 'improvements'.

In this context we have found that the design of age-friendly cities presents immediate challenges in terms of both negotiating and understanding territorial relationships between specific *neighbourhoods* and the general resources of 'City'.

We argue that age-friendly urban research and design must facilitate community-led negotiation of interventions within both a neighbourhood and the wider city networks to which it relates. E.g making an area especially suited for Older people may have the effect of reducing the provision elsewhere, how can we *design* an 'Age-friendly' neighbourhood in an 'Age-friendly' city?

Age-friendly

Following these relational definitions of city and the neighbours who both 'inhabit' and create it, we contest that while 'Age-friendliness' (as defined in the eight interlocking World Health Organisation 'domains') presents a social model for the understanding (*research*) of the impact of the city on older people – and promotes participation as part of this – it currently limits its definition of the role of *design* to a medical model (Hanson 2007). This either assumes that the relations between 'Citizens' are not what, in fact, makes 'the City' liveable or friendly – or that *design* can have no role in changing these things.

We argue instead that making a city more age-friendly is a participatory process of research and design for the development of urban environmental proposals which should negotiate: *both* physical and social aspects of territory; within each specific neighbourhood; across a range of scales and time frames of the city.

Paul McGarry, Senior Strategy Manager, Valuing Older People Team, Manchester City Council

Ageing in cities, and specifically in disadvantaged urban areas, involves risks that can lead to ill health and poor quality of life. Accordingly, the primary focus of age-friendly programmes has been on older people and ageing.

In the age of austerity the argument for all-age improvement social programmes is persuasive and intuitively 'right'. However there is evidence that without a specific focus on older people, especially in cities, the policy and delivery drivers that can create 'good places to grow old' are often overlooked.

The emerging debates, policy focus and city-based programmes concerned with age-friendly cities reflect a number of key demographic, economic and policy drivers.

The first of these is the compelling demographic driver. As the Dublin Declaration, signed by 42 municipalities in September 2011, argues,

> *"In a world in which life expectancy is increasing at the rate of over two years per decade, and the percentage of the population over 65 years is projected to double over the next forty years, the need to prepare for these changes is both urgent and timely."*

So by 2030 two-thirds of the world's population will live in cities, whilst one-quarter of urban populations in high income countries will be aged sixty and over. And by 2050 one-quarter of urban populations in less developed countries will be aged sixty and over. (Phillipson 2010)

These are well known and well-worn facts that we often tire of hearing, but they signal profound social and economic changes which will create new types of communities, not just in the relatively rich north, but also across the BRIC countries and beyond.

We know that ageing in cities, and specifically in disadvantaged urban areas, involved risks that can lead to ill health and poor quality of life. Health inequalities affecting such areas are well documented and extremely persistent. And as Gierveld and Scharf (2008) argue,

> *"There is emerging evidence that urban environments may place older people as heightened risk of isolation and loneliness."*

The position of older people in cities, at least in a UK context, is described by an Audit Commission (2008) report in these terms:

> *"Some Councils will see an outward migration of affluent people in their 50 and 60s...the remaining older population ...tends to be...poorer, isolated and more vulnerable with a lower life expectancy and a need for acute interventions."*

Unfortunately, for most part the dominant narratives of ageing have concerned pension and health and care service reform. I will leave aside for now the content of these narratives, but insofar as ageing is discussed in political and social discourse it is at this level. There is also an important subplot developing in this story. That of generational competition and the notion of the baby boomer generation having accumulated wealth (and power) for itself at the expense of the generations following it. The impact of these narratives is all too often to prevent public policy moving beyond first base.

In response to these challenges the World Health Organisation age-friendly environments programme was launched in the mid 2000s and resulted 33 cities collaborating on the production of a good practice guide. The WHO guide is based on eight 'domains' which include social and civic participation, the built environment, transport, housing and so on. (WHO 2007)

In 2010 a Global Network of age-friendly cities was declared, bringing together around a dozen partners – including Manchester – signed up to ambitious plans. 138 cities have now signed up to the WHO network.

A criticism of the focus on older people in mainstream age-friendly programmes is that they either represent a missed opportunity to improving cities for all age groups and/or that they exclude young people or potentially create generational fractures. In my experience this is an imagined risk. And at a delivery level it is commonplace in age-friendly programmes that intergenerational approaches such as

Manchester's 'Generations Together' initiative, figure highly. More widely, in a UK context there is little to suggest that the ageing agenda crowds out those aimed at younger generations.

The implications of the age-friendly approach that I've outlined suggest a broad range of national and local actions. Partners should:

- Work within the framework of the WHO Global Network of Age-Friendly cities and promote the Dublin Declaration on age-friendly cities and environments;
- Respond to local needs, desires, inequalities and the specific challenges of growing older in each area with a holistic approach to cover the range of services, opportunities and neighbourhood needs important to residents, including healthy ageing in mid-later life;
- Include cross-generational approaches in age-friendly programmes;
- Adopt inclusive approaches that are flexible to the strengths of local communities, voluntary organisations and frontline staff;
- Shift the focus of support services towards earlier interventions, ill-health prevention, whole populations and multi-faceted initiatives;
- Learn from academic and expert partners and independent scrutiny and evaluation; and
- Maintain a citizenship perspective on engagement to create communities of interest with older people in the lead.

Conclusion

The demographic, economic and policy drivers outlined above demand a linked up, programmatic response at international, national and local levels. So for now at least, the international movement which aims to create age-friendly cities and communities should be encouraged to flourish.

It is being realistic to acknowledge that, in particular, in the western economies, the cold economic climate presents us with significant policy and delivery challenges in respect of disadvantaged urban populations. In this context the specific and growing needs (and assets) of the urban old requires a distinctive voice, of which the age-friendly movement is an inspiring example.

Developing 'Age-Friendly' Communities

The ageing of the human population and the onset of urbanisation are taking place in all types of areas, ranging from isolated regions to those with high population densities. By 2030, two-thirds of the world's population will live in cities.

Developing what has been termed "age-friendly" communities has become a significant issue for social policy, embracing questions ranging across urban as well as rural environments. The reasons for such attention include demographic change, with the emergence of a wide spectrum of housing and community needs among those in the 50-plus age group. Pressures affecting different types of localities, with the impact of accelerated urbanization for some and de-industrialization for others; environmental factors affecting the quality of life of older people and policy debates about what constitutes "good" or "optimal" places to age, as reflected in the work of the World Health Organisation (WHO) around "age-friendly" cities (WHO, *Global Age Friendly Cities*, 2007).

Population ageing and urbanization have in their different ways become the key social trends of the twenty-first century, raising issues for all types of communities – from the most isolated to the most densely populated. By 2030, two-thirds of the world's population will be residing in cities; by that time, the major urban areas of the developed world will have 25 per cent or more of their population aged 60 and over. To review the implications of ageing and urbanisation, this article will consider the following questions: what have been the main factors driving the debate on creating age-friendly cities? How age-friendly is the urban environment? What are the options for improving urban environments for older people? What are the restrictions and barriers likely to be encountered when implementing an age-friendly policy?

The theme of age-friendly communities arose from policy initiatives launched by the World Health Organisation (WHO). A precursor was the notion of "active ageing" developed during the United Nations' Year of Older People in 1999 and elaborated by the European Union and the WHO. The idea of maintaining "active" ageing referred to the notion of older people's 'continuing participation in social, economic, cultural, spiritual and civic affairs, not just the ability to be physically active or to participate in the labour market' (WHO 2002, *Active Ageing: A Policy Framework*, p:12). Achieving this was seen as requiring interventions at a number of levels, including maintaining effective supports within the physical and built environment.

The theme of age-friendly environments was subsequently applied to urban contexts, with work beginning in 2005 around the theme of "Global Age-Friendly Cities." Subsequent work by the WHO, based upon focus groups with older people, caregivers and service providers, produced a guide and checklist of action points focused on producing an "ideal" city relevant to all age groups. This work concluded that: "It should be normal in an age-friendly city for the natural and built environment to anticipate users with different capacities instead of designing for the mythical 'average' (i.e. young) person. An age-friendly city emphasises enablement rather than disablement; it is friendly for all ages and not just 'elder-friendly'." (WHO 2007, *Global Age-Friendly Cities*, p:72)

Such ideas were consistent with new perspectives influencing urban development over the course of the 1990s and early 2000s, notably ideas around "sustainable" and "harmonious cities". The idea of "sustainable" development raised questions about managing urban growth in a manner able to meet the needs of future as well as current generations. The idea of "harmonious" development emphasized values such as "tolerance, fairness, social justice and good governance", with these regarded as essential in order to achieve sustainable development in urban planning. These themes were also influential in the elaboration of ideas associated with "lifetime homes" and "lifetime neighbourhoods", which emerged alongside recognition of the need for more systematic interventions to support population ageing at a community level.

An additional influence was recognition of the development in many localities of what has been termed "naturally occurring retirement communities" (NORCS), i.e. neighbourhoods that, with the migration of younger people, have effectively evolved into communities of older people. The key issue behind the "lifetime" concept was an understanding that effective support for older people within neighbourhoods would require a range of interventions linking different parts of the urban system – from housing and the design of streets to transport and improved accessibility to shops and services. Physical environments have a significant impact upon all age groups, but may be especially important for older people who become increasingly reliant on their immediate community for support and assistance. Older people may in fact be especially sensitive to changes to the physical and built environment, given its significance for the maintenance of identity, and because of the length of time spent at home – 80 percent of the time of those 70 and above.

Scharf and his colleagues interviewed 600 older people living in deprived urban areas of the United Kingdom. Their study found that older people in these areas (inner city communities of Liverpool, Manchester and London) experienced a sense of being 'excluded' from society. Poverty was a major aspect of people's lives, affecting nearly half of those interviewed. A significant minority of older people described themselves as being socially isolated and/or severely lonely. Many of the respondents could be considered as excluded from involvement in formal social relationships and civic activities within their communities.

Neighbourhoods characterized by high levels of economic and social deprivation may present a particular challenge to older people. This may reflect the high rates of personal and property crime that characterize such neighbourhoods. There may even be some parts of neighbourhoods, such as parks and cemeteries, which are effectively out of bounds to older people even during daylight hours.

Older people may be especially susceptible to problems arising from poor-quality housing. Particular types of urban housing have been linked to mental health problems in later life. Research in the USA found that older residents living in high-rise dwellings were more depressed, had higher rates of psychiatric disorder and were more socially isolated than those living in detached homes in the community

On the other hand, the advantages – both existing and potential – of urban areas for supporting ageing populations must also be highlighted: First, the resources associated with urban communities bring opportunities for enriching the experience of growing old. Libraries, museums, parks and communal spaces may all be used to expand the potential of life in old age. Second, even in areas of great economic and social deprivation, older people may still report a strong sense of identification with their community. In the Scharf et al. study of three districts in major cities of the United Kingdom, three out of four respondents identified positive features about their neighbourhood, with most of these commenting on the presence of good neighbours, friends and family. Third, rather than providing limited social support, urban environments may offer assistance from a wider range of networks as *compared with rural areas*. Friendship networks, for example, appear to be especially robust in urban communities and may provide an important support mechanism for those who are single or widowed. Urban settings are of particular importance to migrant groups, especially in respect of access to special forms of cultural, social, religious and economic support.

Radical Initiatives

Creating a better "fit" between urban environments on the one side and ageing populations on the other is assuming some urgency within social policy. The WHO (2007:4) develops the point that "making cities more age-friendly is a necessary and logical response to promote the wellbeing and contributions of older urban residents and keep cities thriving." Equally, measures to support the inclusion of older people within cities must be viewed as a key part of the agenda for creating sustainable and harmonious urban environments. Implementing this agenda will, however, demand radical interventions across urban areas.

A number of themes can be identified in this area. First, developing new forms of "urban citizenship" which recognise and support changing needs across the life course; second, developing an age-friendly approach within the context of lifelong/lifetime communities; and third, ensuring the engagement of older people in the planning and regeneration of neighbourhoods.

The first argument concerns the need to link the discussion about age-friendly cities to ideas about urban citizenship and rights to the benefits which living in a city brings. Older people may find that despite having contributed to an urban world in which they have spent most of their life, it may present major obstacles to achieving a fulfilling existence in old age. On the one hand, cities are increasingly viewed as key drivers of a nation's economic and cultural success. On the other hand, the reconstruction of cities is often to the detriment of those outside the labour market, especially those on low incomes. Achieving recognition of the needs of different generations within cities, and exploiting the potential of the city for groups of whatever age will be central to implementing an age-friendly approach.

Second, some of the issues associated with the above are being developed through the ideas associated with lifetime communities and neighbourhoods. The key issues that need to be considered here include aspects such as: the accessibility of the built environment; the appropriateness of available housing stock; the fostering social capital; the location and accessibility of services; the creation of public spaces that promote a sense of place and social cohesion; the integration and planning of services; the building of intergenerational relationships through shared site usage; the better use of information technology.

Work by the Atlanta Regional Commission (ARC) (*Lifelong Communities,* 2009:7) made the point that although mobility begins inside the individual unit or house, it must carry on throughout the entire built environment: '...from inside the dwelling, down the street and into the restaurant, theatre or store...continuously across the entire urban environment." This argument applies equally to all types of communities – suburban as well as inner and outer city. In relation to suburbs, for example, these have frequently been designed to cater for families and commuters in mind, rather than for the specific needs of older people and/or smaller households. There is scope here to explore the urban design implications of a different population mix together with neighbourhoods that explicitly have a longer lifespan. Strategic guidance on urban design might be developed further to indicate how "lifelong" adaptability for an ageing population can be built into communities from the start.

Third, a critical issue for an "age-friendly" approach concerns ensuring the involvement of older people in urban regeneration policies. Scharf et al. (2002) found that older people were often "invisible" in regeneration policies. The problem here was less the absence of older people in consultations around policies, and more an underlying "ageism" which viewed them only as "victims" of neighbourhood change. Regeneration practice could benefit from the experience of older people, their attachment to their neighbourhoods, and their involvement in community organisations. At the same time, there is also a need to develop urban regeneration strategies targeted at different groups within the older population, with awareness, for example, of contrasting issues faced by different ethnic groups, people with particular physical or mental health needs, and those living in areas with poor housing alongside high population turnover.

Obstacles to an Age-friendly Perspective

Despite the benefits of applying an age-friendly approach, some critical questions also need to be faced to ensure effective implementation of such a policy. At the present time, discussions around age-friendliness have been largely disconnected from the pressures on urban environments in the global north, where private developers remain the dominant influence on urban planning. The tension here is between the social needs of older people, as an increasingly important constituent of urban populations, and the pressures on public space arising from private ownership of land. This may lead to a distortion in provision in terms of meeting the needs of competing groups within the urban system.

Another important issue concerns applying "age-friendliness" in a way that recognises the complexity of the urban environment. The techniques for ensuring an age-friendly approach will vary considerably depending on the characteristics of urban change and development. While the trend towards urban living is world-wide, the pattern of urban growth demonstrates huge variation: shrinking city populations in the developed world (Europe especially); and accelerating urbanization in Africa and Asia, with both continents demonstrating a mix of rapidly expanding cities in some cases, declining ones in others. "Age-friendliness" will also need to reflect the size of a city: The approach might, for example, be different in Europe, where small cities with fewer than 500,000 residents are the norm, as compared with the USA, where large urban agglomerations (with populations of between 2 and 5 million) are much more common. Securing "age-friendliness" in the context of the rise of "mega-cities" and "hyper-cities" (the latter with populations of 20 million or more) provide another variation. At the same time, processes for developing "age-friendliness" will need radical adaptation given the "slum cities" prevalent in Southern Asia and sub-Saharan Africa. The bulk of population growth in these continents has taken place largely through the rise of slums, many of these located on the periphery of capital cities. The problem of reaching older people and migrants who are "ageing in place" and housed in temporary accommodation bereft of basic facilities underlines the need for new models of intervention that can respond to the highly unequal contexts experienced by older people in urban areas across the world.

Finally, we might also note the need to link the debate around environmental change with that concerned with urbanization and population ageing. The vulnerability of older people in periods when urban environments are challenged through extremes of temperature has already been highlighted. But other problems may also be cited. Air pollution is a major hazard, especially in newly industrializing countries in the global south. The WHO estimates that more than 1 billion people in Asia alone are exposed to outdoor air pollutant levels that exceed WHO guidelines, leading to the premature death of half a million people annually. Older people, especially those with chronic health conditions – these exacerbated or caused by environmental degradation – will be among the worst affected in terms of their quality of life.

Looking ahead, rising sea levels associated with climate change may bring particular risks for older people living in cities. Fourteen of the world's 19 largest cities are port cities located along a coastline or within a river delta. In Asia, the dominance of port cities is even greater: 17 of the region's 20 largest cities are coastal, or on a river bank or in a delta. Many of the world's most prominent global cities (e.g. Mumbai, Shanghai, New York City) will be among the most exposed to surge-induced flooding in the event of sea-level rise. The consequences for their substantial populations of old and very old people are immense, and will require detailed planning and assessment.

Older people are especially vulnerable in periods of environmental crisis, with the potential for displacement from their home, from relatives, and from services and support. These aspects were clearly demonstrated in crises such as Hurricane Katrina in the USA and the 2003 heatwave in France. In both cases, older people were disproportionately affected compared with other age groups, but failed to receive the special help and assistance required. In these instances, environmental disaster undermined the ability of urban areas to respond quickly and effectively to the needs of their older inhabitants.

Changes in Research and Planning

Securing age-friendly cities remains an important goal for economic and social policy. The future of communities across the world will in large part be determined by the response made to achieving a higher quality of life for their older citizens. A crucial part of this response must lie in creating supportive environments that provide access to a range of facilities and services. However, the research and policy agenda will need to change in at least three ways if this is to be realised.

First, the issues raised by developing age-friendly communities within complex urban environments will require a more coherent link between research and policy than has thus far been achieved. Research on environmental aspects of ageing has an impressive literature to its name, yet it remains detached from analysing the impact of powerful global and economic forces transforming the physical and social context of cities. To remedy this will require closer integration with developments in disciplines such as urban sociology, urban economics and human geography. Understanding optimal environments for ageing must be seen as an interdisciplinary enterprise requiring understanding of the impact on older people of developments such as the changing dynamics of urban poverty; the impact of urban renewal and regeneration; the influence of transnational networks; and changing relations between different class, gender, ethnic and age-based groups.

Second, in keeping with the approach taken in this article, given the rapid changes affecting many urban areas, new approaches to understanding older people's relationship to urban change – and city development in particular – is urgently required. In particular, there is a strong case for more research in "urban ethnography" to capture the disparate experiences of those living in cities that are now experiencing intense global change and that are strongly influenced by complex patterns of migration on the one side and population ageing on the other. Detailed research will be necessary to understand the impact of urban growth on groups such as migrants ageing in place, single people, and those on low incomes. Urban sociology was founded (through the work of the Chicago School from the 1920s) upon detailed studies of experiences of urban life, particular of disadvantaged and insecure people from different migrant populations. Ethnographies would bring to the surface the attitudes, motivations and experiences of older people who are "ageing in place" and will deepen our understanding about the way in which cities are changing, and about the positive and negative contributions that the changes have on the quality of daily life in old age.

Third, it might be argued that the benefit of thinking about age-friendliness lies more in its challenge to re-assessing the values (and ideals) that might be nurtured within urban communities. From the 1960s onwards, writers such as Jane Jacobs (*The Death and Life of Great American Cities*, 1961) argued the case for celebrating the diversity of city life. Giradet ('Sustainable Cities' in David Satterhwaite, ed, *Sustainable Cities* 1999:424) put forward his vision of the city "as a place of culture and creativity, of conviviality and above all else of sedentary living." In the United Kingdom, Richard Rogers and Anne Power (*Cities for a Small Country*, 2000) developed a new approach to urban planning, one calling for a sharing of spaces for the collective good and for a reversal of the drift towards suburbanization. All of these – and similar ideas – are relevant to developing age-friendly cities and arguably need closer integration to the sociology of ageing. Thus despite the many obstacles to implementing this approach, its potential for reminding us of the values to be nurtured for harmonious city living are important and certainly relevant for building communities fit for populations of older people.

Life Course Approach

The life course approach, also known as the *life course perspective* or *life course theory*, refers to an approach developed in the 1960s for analyzing people's lives within structural, social, and cultural contexts. Origins of this approach can be traced to pioneering studies as Thomas' and Znaniecki's "The Polish Peasant in Europe and America" from the 1920s or Mannheim's essay on the "Problem of generations". The life course approach examines an individual's life history and sees, for example, how early events influence future decisions and events such as marriage and divorce, engagement in crime, or disease incidence. The primary factor promoting standardization of the life course was improvement in mortality rates brought about by the management of contagious and infectious diseases such as smallpox. A life course is defined as "a sequence of socially defined events and roles that the individual enacts over time". In particular, the approach focuses on the connection between individuals and the historical and socioeconomic context in which these individuals lived. The method encompasses observations including history, sociology, demography, developmental psychology, biology, public health and economics. So far, empirical research from a life course perspective has not resulted in the development of a formal theory.

Life course theory, more commonly termed the life course perspective, refers to a multidisciplinary paradigm for the study of people's lives, structural contexts, and social change. This approach encompasses ideas and observations from an array of disciplines, notably history, sociology, demography, developmental psychology, biology, and economics. In particular, it directs attention to the powerful connection between individual lives and the historical and socioeconomic context in which these lives unfold. As a concept, a life course is defined as "a sequence of socially defined events and roles that the individual enacts over time" (Giele and Elder 1998, p. 22). These events and roles do not necessarily proceed in a given sequence, but rather constitute the sum total of the person's actual experience. Thus the concept of life course implies age-differentiated social phenomena distinct from uniform life-cycle stages and the life span. Life span refers to duration of life and characteristics that are closely related to age but that vary little across time and place.

In contrast, the life course perspective elaborates the importance of time, context, process, and meaning on human development and family life (Bengtson and Allen 1993). The family is perceived as a micro social group within a macro social context—a "collection of individuals with shared history who interact within ever-changing social contexts across ever increasing time and space" (Bengston and Allen 1993, p. 470). Ageing and developmental change, therefore, are continuous processes that are experienced throughout life. As such, the life course reflects the intersection of social and historical factors with personal biography and development within which the study of family life and social change can ensue (Elder 1985; Hareven 1996).

Life course theory also has moved in a constructionist direction. Rather than taking time, sequence, and linearity for granted, in their book "Constructing the Life Course," Jaber F. Gubrium and James A. Holstein (2000) take their point of departure from accounts of experience through time. This shifts the figure and ground of experience and its stories, foregrounding how time, sequence, linearity, and related concepts are used in everyday life. It presents a radical turn in understanding experience through time, moving well beyond the notion of a multidisciplinary paradigm, providing an altogether different paradigm from traditional time-centred approaches. Rather than concepts of time being the principle building blocks of propositions, concepts of time are analytically bracketed and become focal topics of research and constructive understanding.

Chapter 7

Social Relation with Ageing

In social science, a social relation or social interaction is any relationship between two or more individuals. Social relations derived from individual agency form the basis of social structure and the basic object for analysis by social scientists. Fundamental inquiries into the nature of social relations feature in the work of sociologists such as Max Weber in his theory of social action. Categorising social interactions enables observational and other social research, such as Gemeinschaft and Gesellschaft (lit. "Community and Society"), collective consciousness, etc. However different schools and theories of sociology and other social sciences dispute the methods used for such investigations.

Forms of Relation and Interaction

Forms of relation and interaction in sociology and anthropology may be described as follows: first and most basic are animal-like behaviours, i.e. various physical movements of the body. Then there are actions - movements with a meaning and purpose. Then there are social behaviours, or social actions, which address (directly or indirectly) other people, which solicit a response from another agent. Next are social contacts, a pair of social actions, which form the beginning of social interactions. Social interactions in turn form the basis of social relations. Symbols define social relationships. Without symbols, our social life would be no more sophisticated than that of animals. For example, without symbols we would have no aunts or uncles, employers or teachers-or even brothers and sisters. In sum, Symbolic integrationists analyze how social life depends on the ways we define ourselves and others. They study face-to-face interaction, examining how people make sense out of life, how they determine their relationships.

This sociological hierarchy is illustrated in the table below:

	Physical movement	*Meaning*	*Directed towards others*	*Await response*	*Unique /rare interaction*	*Interactions*	*Accidental, not planned, but repeated interaction*	*Regular*	*Interactions described by law, custom or tradition*	*A scheme of social interactions*
Behavior	Yes									
Action	Yes	Yes								
Social behavior	Yes	Yes	Yes							
Social action	Yes	Yes	Yes	Yes						
Social contact	Yes	Yes	Yes	Yes	Yes					
Social interaction	Yes	Yes	Yes	Yes	Yes	Yes				
Repeated interaction	Yes	Yes	Yes	Yes	Yes	Yes	Yes			
Regular interaction	Yes	Yes	Yes	Yes	Yes	Yes	Yes	Yes		
Regulated interaction	Yes	Yes	Yes	Yes	Yes	Yes	Yes	Yes	Yes	
Social relation	Yes	Yes	Yes	Yes	Yes	Yes	Yes	Yes	Yes	Yes

What Social Relationships can Do for Health

Social relationships have as much impact on physical health as blood pressure, smoking, physical activity, and obesity, as demonstrated in 1988 by House, Landis, and Umberson. Their meta-analysis of 148 longitudinal studies found a 50 percent increase in survival of people with robust social relationships, regardless of age, gender, country of origin, or how such relationships were defined. Just as obesity has taken centre stage in our cultural self-awareness, social relationships belong on the list of potent risk and protective factors for morbidity and mortality.

Consider the following brief examples of older adults whose relationships show a link to health outcomes:

- Mrs. L lives in an assisted living facility and her son visits frequently, involving himself in the community by getting acquainted with his mother's friends there, and doing projects such as building a raised-bed vegetable garden that all residents tend. The facility cook routinely incorporates the garden's produce into the daily menus, and much of residents' mealtime conversation focuses on "their" vegetables and herbs. Mrs. L experiences obvious bursts of energy and motivation to attend exercise classes after each of her son's visits, increasing her strength and cardiovascular functioning.
- Mr. and Mrs. M have a kind, loving friendship within their marriage; this functions well as an invisible protective shield, buffering their physical health from impacts of day-to-day stresses that wear on other older adults' health.
- Ms. C's bitterness about her arthritis is exceeded only by her bitterness at the many people who have betrayed and disappointed her over her lifespan. She views both her physical and social health as poor, with little insight into how her negative approach to mental health undermines both.
- Mr. K's recovery from a quadruple heart bypass was aided significantly by his wife's deliberate adjustment of their diet and activity patterns to match his health provider's recommendations. Without her involvement, he was unlikely to adhere to recommended lifestyle changes that were key to his recovery.
- Ms. B and Mrs. J maintain a regular schedule at the local elementary school, where they read to children. Afterward, they sit and swap funny stories together over a healthy lunch. The children keep them on the move physically, and the students' improvement in reading ability bolsters the women's sense of personal meaning. The volunteer role helps build psychological and social health.

Many health benefits of relationships are likely to be more subtle than those illustrated in these examples. An uplifting conversation that introduces hope and joy into the morning may influence physical activity, healthy food selection, or the choice to engage further in proactive social relationships later in the day or week. Open communication with a physician may encourage stronger engagement in answering health questions. A social service agency that provides volunteers to maintain landscaping or home maintenance enables many older adults to live in long-term neighbourhood social networks. The range of examples is broad, and the individual variation almost infinite.

Researchers have generated a substantial body of knowledge about the positive benefits of relationships on health. This article explores the question of how the size and composition of a network might influence health, considers how different types of social engagement or support benefit health, demonstrates how physical environments can shape social experiences that might influence health, and explains how healthcare systems could use the power of social relationships to benefit health.

Is More Always Better?

The quantity and quality of social relationships have powerful effects on health across the lifespan. Although older adults experience some shrinkage in the size of their networks as they age, the size of their close network tends to remain relatively stable (Fung, Carstensen, and Lang, 2001). Social losses occur with increasing frequency in advanced old age (Rook, 2000), but most older adults adapt relatively well to those losses. Indeed, satisfaction with relationships increases with age (Carstensen, 1992), including higher levels of positive affect with friends and family, and a better balance of positive-to-negative affect when compared with younger adults (Charles and Piazza, 2007; Newsom et al., 2005). Carstensen's socioemotional selectivity theory claims that older adults respond to their awareness of reduced years ahead by pruning social networks selectively, with the goal of maintaining only those relationships that support emotional well-being (Carstensen, Isaacowitz, and Charles, 1999). Of course, many older adults also experience involuntary network downsizing through death or illness (Rook, 2000).

The benefits of social network size on health are robust (Berkman and Syme, 1979). Older adults with larger networks show higher levels of health and well-being in many areas, including executive function and episodic memory (Seeman et al., 2011), cognitive decline (Barnes et al., 2004), and allostatic load (Seeman et al., 2002).

Health benefits vary across type of relationship because not all relationships are equal. Marriage and intimate partnerships generally offer protective functions to health (Burleson et al., 2013). Marital partners can offer the widest range of support functions because of the high rate of integration in each others' lives, including companionship, emotional support, and instrumental assistance. Adult children are important sources of emotional and instrumeninstrumental support, and sibling relationships increase in value and importance in later life (Blieszner, 2009). Friendships are important sources of well-being, too, including positive effects on physical health as discussed by Blieszner.

Relationships formed within the context of volunteering also have positive effects on health (Konrath and Brown, 2013).

We live within overlapping social networks, with some relationships nested in other networks, such that the effects of relationships on health can be multifaceted and overlapping. Among women diagnosed with breast cancer, midlife and older women with high social support showed a benefit of marriage in reduced mortality from breast cancer compared to those with lower social support (Kroenke et al., 2012). So marriage may not have a simple, nor singular, effect on health. A good marriage, embedded within a socially supportive broader family or community network, may have a different impact on health than a good marriage in a socially isolated world, or a difficult marriage within a non-supportive social network. The broader social context in which particular relationships are embedded can alter the impact of those relationships on health.

By What Mechanisms Do Relationships Impact Health?

The bio-psychosocial model (Engel, 1977) offers a framework for conceptualizing health as being made up of biological, psychological, and social components. Each component represents a domain of health within which the mechanisms of relationship health effects have been investigated.

Biological Mechanisms

Relationships impact physical health through multiple biological mechanisms. Early studies focused on effects of social support on cardiovascular health indicators including blood pressure, heart rate, and cholesterol levels (Ryff, Singer, and Love, 2004). Recent attention has been focused more on the hypothalamic pituitary adrenal axis that produces cortisol in response to stressful events (Friedman et al., 2012).

A recent review (Eisenberger and Cole, 2012) of the physiological mechanisms by which social relationships may impact health suggests a twopronged impact: threats to social connection may prompt activation of a physiological alarm system, and supportive social relationships may buffer that same type of physiological alarm to any type of threat. So there is a reciprocal relationship between social relationships and biological threats. Not surprisingly, lifetime accumulated benefits of social integration and emotional support are evident in comprehensive measures of biological risk for older adults (Seeman et al., 2002).

Psychological Mechanisms

Of the many possible mechanisms, two are described here. A positive conversation may positively influence health through its impact on positive affect and reductions in physiological arousal, as was shown in long-term married couples (Levenson, Carstensen, and Gottman, 1994).

A second psychological mechanism relates to perceptions and appraisals of social relationships. Judgments about whether an interaction or a relationship is positive or negative are referred to as appraisals. The appraisal of one's network as adequate, supportive, positive, and helpful may also influence health separately from the actual number of persons in the network. Those who view friends and families as supportive report a greater sense of meaning in life and a stronger sense of purpose (Krause, 2007), and perceptions of social support are more powerful predictors of well-being than the actual amount of support (Barrera, 1986). Appraisals of positive and negative social exchanges in older adults influence well-being (Newsom et al., 2005) in ways that are similar to findings in young and midlife adults (Croezen et al., 2012). In short, what we tell ourselves about our relationships is as important as the number of people in our networks.

Social Mechanisms

A category system for examining social benefits to health distinguishes between social support (aid or care), companionship, and control or regulation (Rook, August, and Sorkin, 2011). All three types of social benefits impact health and can be provided by a range of social partners.

Social support, which includes practical assistance (often referred to as instrumental support) and emotional support, helps individuals cope with life stressors. Instrumental support is of particular importance to a person's experience of health problems that result in functional disability. Reduced mobility, vision, hearing, or strength can all limit a person's ability to accomplish the instrumental activities of daily living that support independence. Often, instrumental support services are accompanied by emotional support or other types of social engagement that fulfill more than one social need.

Companionship refers to the pleasant benefits of shared activities, camaraderie, and enjoyable interaction. The benefits of companionship are expected to be found in the mood-enhancing effects of good interactions—effects that may alleviate or buffer stress, enhance positive affect, support resilience, and support a person's sense of self-worth (Rook et al., 2011). Friends often are sought out for companionship benefits rather than to gain social support per se. Family relationships may provide companionship, but often bring a mix of role obligations as well as chosen companionship opportunities.

Social control, or regulation, uses some form of constraint on risky behaviour, and this assists with stabilizing health behaviours (Rook et al., 2011). A spouse's encouragement of their partner's choosing healthy foods from a restaurant menu or engaging in exercise are two examples of social control. But social control can lead to feeling nagged, coerced, or bossed around in ways that undermine a strong sense of efficacy or positive well-being. High levels of social skill are required to generate positive benefits from social control interactions. Although we may not seek social control in relationships, we may still benefit from it if our network pushes us toward health-promoting behaviours. On the other hand, the potential for negative effects of social control interactions (e.g., loss of self-efficacy, increased distress, and lack of self-control) are high. Social control is most likely to lead to positive health outcomes when it does not generate negative affects.

As the findings reviewed above illustrate, the bio-psychosocial model of health can organise the search for mechanisms by which social relationships affect health. External factors can also influence health, including physical environments, and the ways in which the healthcare system operates.

Physical Environments Set the Stage

Physical environments such as urban, architectural, or interior design shape social relationships in ways that can impact health. A large lobby in a senior housing complex may invite or impede social interaction, depending upon the layout of the space, lighting, and furniture selection.

The power of encouraging social interaction through thoughtful design is evident when walking through dining spaces in some assisted living facilities. Spaces designed to encourage interaction can help residents feel at home more quickly, leading to lower rates of anxiety, higher life satisfaction, and more engagement in cognitive and physical stimulation. Memory boxes used as a design element outside apartments of people with dementia can also influence social interaction. Although designed primarily to support recognising and identifying a room, the boxes may also serve social functions, such as helping other residents and staff know something about each person's life. Does that support for knowing one another and knowing oneself translate into improved engagement, activity, or relationship development in ways that influence health? Designers of environments for older adults are increasingly paying attention to the direct and indirect impacts of environments on relationships and on health, and the connections between them (Brawley, 2006).

Relationships Within Healthcare Delivery Systems

The power of the link between social relationships and health is hard to overstate, and yet it is almost ignored in healthcare service delivery systems. The patient-centred medical home emphasizes the value and importance of collaboration within that primary care relationship (Rittenhouse and Shortell, 2009). The medical home concept is relational at its core, with an emphasis on stabilizing the relationship between health providers and patients, while engaging patients and providers in addressing patients' health goals in a bilateral planning process. Ironically, primary care still does not systematically view patients within the context of personal relationships at work, home, and in community, even though those relationships almost certainly impact the patient's health. The potency of social relationships for health and well-being warrants understanding and application by those tasked with improving public or personal health.

The intertwining of relationships and health may be more visible outside the healthcare service delivery system. To sustain a new exercise routine, most people recognise they need either a trainer for accountability or an exercise buddy to join them. Smoking cessation program staff know people who live with others who smoke are going to struggle to maintain abstinence. Yet health intervention programs all too often limit their focus on changing the behaviour of the patient, without engaging that person's social network.

The healthcare system should take advantage of the social embeddedness of human lives to influence health behaviour and lifestyle changes that are central to preventing and managing chronic disease. Engaging key family members in healthcare visits could be encouraged and welcomed. Chronic disease treatment plans could include social influences as useful strategies to encourage and empower older persons to achieve their healthcare goals. Patient portals to electronic health record systems could offer the option of including social network members in communications about health.

Conclusion

The social portion of the bio-psychosocial model may be the next frontier for targeted interventions to improve health across the lifespan, with direct impact on the experience of ageing. As a colleague once quipped to me, "We are surrounded by insurmountable opportunity." Where do we begin to engage social relationships in building a healthier ageing population? From personal trainers to public policy makers, the power to influence health through relationships begs to be explored.

Scientists must continue to explore the linkage, from the molecular level effects of social interactions to evaluation of interventions designed to soften the negative effects of toxic relationships in persons with chronic illness. Perhaps we need to create a health-focused "decade of relationships"!

Epidemiology

Epidemiology is the science that studies the patterns, causes, and effects of health and disease conditions in defined populations. It is the cornerstone of public health, and informs policy decisions and evidence-based practice by identifying risk factors for disease and targets for preventive healthcare. Epidemiologists help with study design, collection, and statistical analysis of data, and interpretation and dissemination of results (including peer review and occasional systematic review). Epidemiology has helped develop methodology used in clinical research, public health studies, and, to a lesser extent, basic research in the biological sciences.

Major areas of epidemiological study include disease etiology, transmission, outbreak investigation, disease surveillance and screening, biomonitoring, and comparisons of treatment effects such as in clinical trials. Epidemiologists rely on other scientific disciplines like biology to better understand disease processes, statistics to make efficient use of the data and draw appropriate conclusions, social sciences to better understand proximate and distal causes, and engineering for exposure assessment.

Etymology

Epidemiology, literally meaning "the study of what is upon the people", is derived from Greek *epi*, meaning "upon, among", *demos*, meaning "people, district", and *logos*, meaning "study, word, discourse", suggesting that it applies only to human populations. However, the term is widely used in studies of zoological populations (veterinary epidemiology), although the term "epizoology" is available, and it has also been applied to studies of plant populations (botanical or plant disease epidemiology).

The distinction between "epidemic" and "endemic" was first drawn by Hippocrates, to distinguish between diseases that are "visited upon" a population (epidemic) from those that "reside within" a population (endemic). The term "epidemiology" appears to have first been used to describe the study of epidemics in 1802 by the Spanish physician Villalba in *Epidemiología Española*. Epidemiologists also study the interaction of diseases in a population, a condition known as a syndemic.

The term epidemiology is now widely applied to cover the description and causation of not only epidemic disease, but of disease in general, and even many non-disease health-related conditions, such as high blood pressure and obesity. Therefore, this epidemiology is based upon how the pattern of the disease cause changes in the function of everyone.

History

"History of epidemiology" redirects here.

The Greek physician Hippocrates, known as the father of medicine, sought a logic to sickness; he is the first person known to have examined the relationships between the occurrence of disease and environmental influences. Hippocrates believed sickness of the human body to be caused by an imbalance of the four Humors (air, fire, water and earth "atoms"). The cure to the sickness was to remove or add the humor in question to balance the body. This belief led to the application of bloodletting and dieting in medicine. He coined the terms *endemic* (for diseases usually found in some places but not in others) and *epidemic* (for diseases that are seen at some times but not others).

In ancient India, Ayurveda considered disease to be a manifestation of imbalance in 3 bodily humors, called Doshas. Around this theory, systems of diagnosis were based.

One of the earliest theories on the origin of disease was that it was primarily the fault of human luxury. This was expressed by philosophers such as Plato and Rousseau, and social critics like Jonathan Swift.

In the middle of the 16th century, a doctor from Verona named Girolamo Fracastoro was the first to propose a theory that these very small, unseeable, particles that cause disease were alive. They were considered to be able to spread by air, multiply by themselves and to be destroyable by fire. In this way he refuted Galen's miasma theory (poison gas in sick people). In 1543 he wrote a book *De contagione et contagiosis morbis*, in which he was the first to promote personal and environmental hygiene to prevent disease. The development of a sufficiently powerful microscope by Anton van Leeuwenhoek in 1675 provided visual evidence of living particles consistent with a germ theory of disease.

Another pioneer, Thomas Sydenham (1624–1689), was the first to distinguish the fevers of Londoners in the later 1600s. His theories on cures of fevers met with much resistance from traditional physicians at the time. He was not able to find the initial cause of the smallpox fever he researched and treated.

John Graunt, a haberdasher and amateur statistician, published *Natural and Political Observations ... upon the Bills of Mortality* in 1662. In it, he analysed the mortality rolls in London before the Great Plague, presented one of the first life tables, and report time trends for many diseases, new and old. He provided statistical evidence for many theories on disease, and also refuted some widespread ideas on them.

Modern Era

John Snow is famous for his investigations into the causes of the 19th century cholera epidemics, and is also known as the father of (modern) epidemiology. He began with noticing the significantly higher death rates in two areas supplied by Southwark Company. His identification of the Broad Street pump as the cause of the Soho epidemic is considered the classic example of epidemiology. Snow used chlorine in an attempt to clean the water and removed the handle; this ended the outbreak. This has been perceived as a major event in the history of public health and regarded as the founding event of the science of epidemiology, having helped shape public health policies around the world. However, Snow's research and preventive measures to avoid further outbreaks were not fully accepted or put into practice until after his death.

Other pioneers include Danish physician Peter Anton Schleisner, who in 1849 related his work on the prevention of the epidemic of neonatal tetanus on the Vestmanna Islands in Iceland. Another important pioneer was Hungarian physician Ignaz Semmelweis, who in 1847 brought down infant mortality at a Vienna hospital by instituting a disinfection procedure. His findings were published in 1850, but his work was ill received by his colleagues, who discontinued the procedure. Disinfection did not become widely practiced until British surgeon Joseph Lister 'discovered' antiseptics in 1865 in light of the work of Louis Pasteur.

In the early 20th century, mathematical methods were introduced into epidemiology by Ronald Ross, Janet Lane-Claypon, Anderson Gray McKendrick and others.

Another breakthrough was the 1954 publication of the results of a British Doctors Study, led by Richard Doll and Austin Bradford Hill, which lent very strong statistical support to the suspicion that tobacco smoking was linked to lung cancer.

In the late 20th century, with advancement of biomedical sciences, a number of molecular markers in blood, other biospecimens and environment were identified as predictors of development or risk of a certain disease. Epidemiology research to examine the relationship between these biomarkers analyzed at the molecular level and disease was broadly named "molecular epidemiology". Specifically, "genetic epidemiology" has been used for epidemiology of germline genetic variation and disease. Genetic variation is typically determined using DNA from peripheral blood leukocytes. Since the 2000s, genome-wide association studies (GWAS) have been commonly performed to identify genetic risk factors for many diseases and health conditions.

While most molecular epidemiology studies are still using conventional disease diagnosis and classification system, it is increasingly recognised that disease evolution represents inherently heterogeneous process differing from person to person. Conceptually, each individual has a unique disease process different from any other individual ("the unique disease principle"), considering uniqueness of the exposome (a totality of endogenous and exogenous / environmental exposures) and its unique influence on molecular pathologic process in each individual. Studies to examine the relationship between an exposure and molecular pathologic signature of disease (particularly, cancer) became increasingly common throughout the 2000s. However, the use of molecular pathology in epidemiology posed unique challenges including lack of research guidelines and standardized statistical methodologies, and paucity of interdisciplinary experts and training programs. Furthermore, the concept of disease heterogeneity appears to conflict with the long-standing premise in epidemiology that individuals with the same disease name have similar etiologies and disease processes. To resolve these issues and advance population health science in the era of molecular precision medicine, "molecular pathology" and "epidemiology" was integrated to create a new interdisciplinary field of "molecular pathological epidemiology" (MPE), defined as "epidemiology of molecular pathology and heterogeneity of disease". In MPE, investigators analyze the relationships between; (A) environmental, dietary, lifestyle and genetic factors; (B) alterations in cellular or extracellular molecules; and (C) evolution and progression of disease. A better understanding of heterogeneity of disease pathogenesis will further contribute to elucidate etiologies of disease. The MPE approach can be applied to not only neoplastic diseases but also non-neoplastic diseases. The concept and paradigm of MPE have become widespread in the 2010s.

The Profession

To date, few universities offer epidemiology as a course of study at the undergraduate level. Many epidemiologists are physicians, or hold graduate degrees such as a Master of Public Health (MPH), Master of Science of Epidemiology (MSc.). Doctorates include the Doctor of Public Health (DrPH), Doctor of Pharmacy (PharmD), Doctor of Philosophy

(PhD), Doctor of Science (ScD), Doctor of Social Work (DSW), Doctor of Clinical Practice (DClinP), Doctor of Podiatric Medicine (DPM), Doctor of Veterinary Medicine (DVM), Doctor of Nursing Practice (DNP), Doctor of Physical Therapy (DPT), or for clinically trained physicians, Doctor of Medicine (MD) and Doctor of Osteopathic Medicine (DO). In the United Kingdom, the title of 'doctor' is by long custom used to refer to general medical practitioners, whose professional degrees are usually those of Bachelor of Medicine and Surgery (MBBS or MBChB).

As public health/health protection practitioners, epidemiologists work in a number of different settings. Some epidemiologists work 'in the field'; i.e., in the community, commonly in a public health/health protection service and are often at the forefront of investigating and combating disease outbreaks. Others work for non-profit organisations, universities, hospitals and larger government entities such as the Centres for Disease Control and Prevention (CDC), the Health Protection Agency, the World Health Organisation (WHO), or the Public Health Agency of Canada. Epidemiologists can also work in for-profit organisations such as pharmaceutical and medical device companies in groups such as market research or clinical development.

The Practice

Epidemiologists employ a range of study designs from the observational to experimental and generally categorized as descriptive, analytic (aiming to further examine known associations or hypothesized relationships), and experimental (a term often equated with clinical or community trials of treatments and other interventions). In observational studies, nature is allowed to "take its course", as epidemiologists observe from the sidelines. Conversely, in experimental studies, the epidemiologist is the one in control of all of the factors entering a certain case study. Epidemiological studies are aimed, where possible, at revealing unbiased relationships between exposures such as alcohol or smoking, biological agents, stress, or chemicals to mortality or morbidity. The identification of causal relationships between these exposures and outcomes is an important aspect of epidemiology. Modern epidemiologists use informatics as a tool.

Observational studies have two components: descriptive, or analytical. Descriptive observations pertain to the "who, what, where and when of health-related state occurrence". However, analytical observations deal more with the 'how' of a health-related event.

Experimental epidemiology contains three case types: randomized control trial (often used for new medicine or drug testing), field trial (conducted on those at a high risk of conducting a disease), and community trial (research on social originating diseases).

Unfortunately, many epidemiology studies conducted cause false or misinterpreted information to circulate the public. According to a class taught by professor Madhukar Pai MD, PhD at McGill, "...optimism bias is pervasive, most studies biased or inconclusive or false, most discovered true associations are inflated, fear and panic inducing rather than helpful; media-induced panic, cannot detect small effects; big effects are not to be found anymore".

The term 'epidemiologic triad' is used to describe the intersection of *Host*, *Agent*, and *Environment* in analyzing an outbreak.

As Causal Inference

Although epidemiology is sometimes viewed as a collection of statistical tools used to elucidate the associations of exposures to health outcomes, a deeper understanding of this science is that of discovering *causal* relationships.

"Correlation does not imply causation" is a common theme for much of the epidemiological literature. For epidemiologists, the key is in the term inference. Epidemiologists use gathered data and a broad range of biomedical and psychosocial theories in an iterative way to generate or expand theory, to test hypotheses, and to make educated, informed assertions about which relationships are causal, and about exactly how they are causal.

Epidemiologists Rothman and Greenland emphasize that the "one cause – one effect" understanding is a simplistic mis-belief. Most outcomes, whether disease or death, are caused by a chain or web consisting of many component causes. Causes can be distinguished as necessary, sufficient or probabilistic conditions. If a necessary condition can be identified and controlled (e.g., antibodies to a disease agent), the harmful outcome can be avoided.

Bradford Hill Criteria

In 1965 Austin Bradford Hill proposed a series of considerations to help assess evidence of causation, which have come to be commonly known as the "Bradford Hill criteria". In contrast to the explicit intentions of their author, Hill's considerations are now sometimes taught as a checklist to be implemented for assessing causality. Hill himself said "None of my nine viewpoints can bring indisputable evidence for or against the cause-and-effect hypothesis and none can be required *sine qua non.*"

1. *Strength:* A small association does not mean that there is not a causal effect, though the larger the association, the more likely that it is causal.
2. *Consistency:* Consistent findings observed by different persons in different places with different samples strengthens the likelihood of an effect.
3. *Specificity:* Causation is likely if a very specific population at a specific site and disease with no other likely explanation. The more specific an association between a factor and an effect is, the bigger the probability of a causal relationship.
4. *Temporality:* The effect has to occur after the cause (and if there is an expected delay between the cause and expected effect, then the effect must occur after that delay).
5. *Biological gradient:* Greater exposure should generally lead to greater incidence of the effect. However, in some cases, the mere presence of the factor can trigger the effect. In other cases, an inverse proportion is observed: greater exposure leads to lower incidence.
6. *Plausibility:* A plausible mechanism between cause and effect is helpful (but Hill noted that knowledge of the mechanism is limited by current knowledge).
7. *Coherence:* Coherence between epidemiological and laboratory findings increases the likelihood of an effect. However, Hill noted that "... lack of such [laboratory] evidence cannot nullify the epidemiological effect on associations".
8. *Experiment:* "Occasionally it is possible to appeal to experimental evidence".
9. Analogy: The effect of similar factors may be considered.

Legal Interpretation

Epidemiological studies can only go to prove that an agent could have caused, but not that it did cause, an effect in any particular case:

> *"Epidemiology is concerned with the incidence of disease in populations and does not address the question of the cause of an individual's disease. This question, sometimes referred to as specific causation, is beyond the domain of the science of epidemiology. Epidemiology has its limits at the point where an inference is made that the relationship between an agent and a disease is causal (general causation) and where the magnitude of*

excess risk attributed to the agent has been determined; that is, epidemiology addresses whether an agent can cause a disease, not whether an agent did cause a specific plaintiff's disease."

In United States law, epidemiology alone cannot prove that a causal association does not exist in general. Conversely, it can be (and is in some circumstances) taken by US courts, in an individual case, to justify an inference that a causal association does exist, based upon a balance of probability.

The subdiscipline of forensic epidemiology is directed at the investigation of specific causation of disease or injury in individuals or groups of individuals in instances in which causation is disputed or is unclear, for presentation in legal settings.

Advocacy

As a public health discipline, epidemiologic evidence is often used to advocate both personal measures like diet change and corporate measures like removal of junk food advertising, with study findings disseminated to the general public to help people to make informed decisions about their health. Often the uncertainties about these findings are not communicated well; news articles often prominently report the latest result of one study with little mention of its limitations, caveats, or context. Epidemiological tools have proved effective in establishing major causes of diseases like cholera and lung cancer, but experience difficulty in regards to more subtle health issues where causation is more complex. Notably, conclusions drawn from observational studies may be reconsidered as later data from randomized controlled trials becomes available, as was the case with the association between the use of hormone replacement therapy and cardiac risk.

Population-based Health Management

Epidemiological practice and the results of epidemiological analysis make a significant contribution to emerging population-based health management frameworks.

Population-based health management encompasses the ability to:

- Assess the health states and health needs of a target population;
- Implement and evaluate interventions that are designed to improve the health of that population; and
- Efficiently and effectively provide care for members of that population in a way that is consistent with the community's cultural, policy and health resource values.

Modern population-based health management is complex, requiring a multiple set of skills (medical, political, technological, mathematical etc.) of which epidemiological practice and analysis is a core component, that is unified with management science to provide efficient and effective health care and health guidance to a population. This task requires the forward looking ability of modern risk management approaches that transform health risk factors, incidence, prevalence and mortality statistics (derived from epidemiological analysis) into management metrics that not only guide how a health system responds to current population health issues, but also how a health system can be managed to better respond to future potential population health issues.

Examples of organisations that use population-based health management that leverage the work and results of epidemiological practice include Canadian Strategy for Cancer Control, Health Canada Tobacco Control Programs, Rick Hansen Foundation, Canadian Tobacco Control Research Initiative.

Each of these organisations use a population-based health management framework called Life at Risk that combines epidemiological quantitative analysis with demographics, health agency operational research and economics to perform:

- *Population Life Impacts Simulations*: Measurement of the future potential impact of disease upon the population with respect to new disease cases, prevalence, premature death as well as potential years of life lost from disability and death;
- *Labour Force Life Impacts Simulations*: Measurement of the future potential impact of disease upon the labour force with respect to new disease cases, prevalence, premature death and potential years of life lost from disability and death;
- *Economic Impacts of Disease Simulations*: Measurement of the future potential impact of disease upon private sector disposable income impacts (wages, corporate profits, private health care costs) and public sector disposable income impacts (personal income tax, corporate income tax, consumption taxes, publicly funded health care costs).

Types of Studies

Case Series

Case-series may refer to the qualitative study of the experience of a single patient, or small group of patients with a similar diagnosis, or to a statistical technique comparing periods during which patients are exposed to some factor with the potential to produce illness with periods when they are unexposed.

The former type of study is purely descriptive and cannot be used to make inferences about the general population of patients with that disease. These types of studies, in which an astute clinician identifies an unusual feature of a disease or a patient's history, may lead to formulation of a new hypothesis. Using the data from the series, analytic studies could be done to investigate possible causal factors. These can include case control studies or prospective studies. A case control study would involve matching comparable controls without the disease to the cases in the series. A prospective study would involve following the case series over time to evaluate the disease's natural history.

The latter type, more formally described as self-controlled case-series studies, divide individual patient follow-up time into exposed and unexposed periods and use fixed-effects Poisson regression processes to compare the incidence rate of a given outcome between exposed and unexposed periods. This technique has been extensively used in the study of adverse reactions to vaccination, and has been shown in some circumstances to provide statistical power comparable to that available in cohort studies.

Case Control Studies

Case control studies select subjects based on their disease status. It is a retrospective study. A group of individuals that are disease positive (the "case" group) is compared with a group of disease negative individuals (the "control" group). The control group should ideally come from the same population that gave rise to the cases. The case control study looks back through time at potential exposures that both groups (cases and controls) may have encountered. A 2×2 table is constructed, displaying exposed cases (A), exposed controls (B), unexposed cases (C) and unexposed controls (D). The statistic generated to measure association is the odds ratio (OR), which is the ratio of the odds of exposure in the cases (A/C) to the odds of exposure in the controls (B/D), i.e. OR = (AD/BC).

.....	*Cases*	*Controls*
Exposed	A	B
Unexposed	C	D

If the OR is clearly greater than 1, then the conclusion is "those with the disease are more likely to have been exposed," whereas if it is close to 1 then the exposure and disease are not likely associated. If the OR is far less than one, then this suggests that the exposure is a protective factor in the causation of the disease. Case control studies are usually faster and more cost effective than cohort studies, but are sensitive to bias (such as recall bias and selection bias). The main challenge is to identify the appropriate control group; the distribution of exposure among the control group should be representative of the distribution in the population that gave rise to the cases. This can be achieved by drawing a random sample from the original population at risk. This has as a consequence that the control group can contain people with the disease under study when the disease has a high attack rate in a population.

A major drawback for case control studies is that, in order to be considered to be statistically significant, the minimum number of cases required at the 95% confidence interval is related to the odds ratio by the equation:

total cases = (a+c) =

$$(1.96)^2 \times (1+N) \times (1 \div ln(OR))^2 \times ((OR + 2\sqrt{\ }OR + 1) \div \sqrt{\ }OR) \approx 15.5 \times (1+N) \times (1 \div ln(OR))^2$$

where N = the ratio of cases to controls. As the odds ratio approached 1, approaches 0; rendering case control studies all but useless for low odds ratios. For instance, for an odds ratio of 1.5 and cases = controls, the table shown above would look like this:

.....	***Cases***	***Controls***
Exposed	103	84
Unexposed	84	103

For an odds ratio of 1.1:

.....	***Cases***	***Controls***
Exposed	1732	1652
Unexposed	1652	1732

Cohort Studies

Cohort studies select subjects based on their exposure status. The study subjects should be at risk of the outcome under investigation at the beginning of the cohort study; this usually means that they should be disease free when the cohort study starts. The cohort is followed through time to assess their later outcome status. An example of a cohort study would be the investigation of a cohort of smokers and non-smokers over time to estimate the incidence of lung cancer. The same 2×2 table is constructed as with the case control study. However, the point estimate generated is the relative risk (RR), which is the probability of disease for a person in the exposed group, $P_e = A / (A + B)$ over the probability of disease for a person in the unexposed group, $P_u = C / (C + D)$, i.e. $RR = P_e / P_u$.

.....	***Case***	***Non-case***	***Total***
Exposed	A	B	$(A + B)$
Unexposed	C	D	$(C + D)$

As with the OR, a RR greater than 1 shows association, where the conclusion can be read "those with the exposure were more likely to develop disease."

Prospective studies have many benefits over case control studies. The RR is a more powerful effect measure than the OR, as the OR is just an estimation of the RR, since true incidence cannot be calculated in a case control study where subjects are selected based on disease status. Temporality can be established in a prospective study, and confounders are more easily controlled for. However, they are more costly, and there is a greater chance of losing subjects to follow-up based on the long time period over which the cohort is followed.

Cohort studies also are limited by the same equation for number of cases as for cohort studies, but, if the base incidence rate in the study population is very low, the number of cases required is reduced by ½.

Outbreak Investigation

Validity: Precision and Bias

Different fields in epidemiology have different levels of validity. One way to assess the validity of findings is the ratio of false-positives (claimed effects that are not correct) to false-negatives (studies which fail to support a true effect). To take the field of genetic epidemiology, candidate-gene studies produced over 100 false-positive findings for each false-negative. By contrast genome-wide association appear close to the reverse, with only one false positive for every 100 or more false-negatives. This ratio has improved over time in genetic epidemiology as the field has adopted stringent criteria. By contrast other epidemiological fields have not required such rigorous reporting and are much less reliable as a result.

Random Error

Random error is the result of fluctuations around a true value because of sampling variability. Random error is just that: random. It can occur during data collection, coding, transfer, or analysis. Examples of random error include: poorly worded questions, a misunderstanding in interpreting an individual answer from a particular respondent, or a typographical error during coding. Random error affects measurement in a transient, inconsistent manner and it is impossible to correct for random error.

There is random error in all sampling procedures. This is called sampling error.

Precision in epidemiological variables is a measure of random error. Precision is also inversely related to random error, so that to reduce random error is to increase precision. Confidence intervals are computed to demonstrate the precision of relative risk estimates. The narrower the confidence interval, the more precise the relative risk estimate. There are two basic ways to reduce random error in an epidemiological study. The first is to increase the sample size of the study. In other words, add more subjects to your study. The second is to reduce the variability in measurement in the study. This might be accomplished by using a more precise measuring device or by increasing the number of measurements.

Note, that if sample size or number of measurements are increased, or a more precise measuring tool is purchased, the costs of the study are usually increased. There is usually an uneasy balance between the need for adequate precision and the practical issue of study cost.

Systematic Error

A systematic error or bias occurs when there is a difference between the true value (in the population) and the observed value (in the study) from any cause other than sampling variability. An example of systematic error is if, unknown to you, the pulse oximeter you are using is set incorrectly and adds two points to the true value each time a measurement is taken. The measuring device could be precise but not accurate. Because the error happens in every instance, it is systematic. Conclusions you draw based on that data will still be incorrect. But the error can be reproduced in the future (e.g., by using the same mis-set instrument).

A mistake in coding that affects *all* responses for that particular question is another example of a systematic error.

The validity of a study is dependent on the degree of systematic error. Validity is usually separated into two components:

- Internal validity is dependent on the amount of error in measurements, including exposure, disease, and the associations between these variables. Good internal validity implies a lack of error in measurement and suggests that inferences may be drawn at least as they pertain to the subjects under study.

- External validity pertains to the process of generalizing the findings of the study to the population from which the sample was drawn (or even beyond that population to a more universal statement). This requires an understanding of which conditions are relevant (or irrelevant) to the generalization. Internal validity is clearly a prerequisite for external validity.

Three Types of Bias

Selection Bias

Selection bias is one of three types of bias that can threaten the validity of a study. Selection bias occurs when study subjects are selected or become part of the study as a result of a third, unmeasured variable which is associated with both the exposure and outcome of interest. For instance, it has repeatedly been noted that cigarette smokers and non smokers tend to differ in their study participation rates. (Sackett D cites the example of Seltzer et al., in which 85% of non smokers and 67% of smokers returned mailed questionnaires.) It is important to note that such a difference in response will not lead to bias if it is not also associated with a systematic difference in outcome between the two response groups.

Information Bias

Information bias is bias arising from systematic error in the assessment of a variable. An example of this is recall bias. A typical example is again provided by Sackett in his discussion of a study examining the effect of specific exposures on fetal health: "in questioning mothers whose recent pregnancies had ended in fetal death or malformation (cases) and a matched group of mothers whose pregnancies ended normally (controls) it was found that 28% of the former, but only 20% of the latter, reported exposure to drugs which could not be substantiated either in earlier prospective interviews or in other health records". In this example, recall bias probably occurred as a result of women who had had miscarriages having an apparent tendency to better recall and therefore report previous exposures.

Confounding

Confounding has traditionally been defined as bias arising from the co-occurrence or mixing of effects of extraneous factors, referred to as confounders, with the main effect(s) of interest. A more recent definition of confounding invokes the notion of *counterfactual* effects.

According to this view, when one observes an outcome of interest, say Y=1 (as opposed to Y=0), in a given population A which is entirely exposed (i.e. exposure $X = 1$ for every unit of the population) the risk of this event will be R_{A1}. The counterfactual or unobserved risk R_{A0} corresponds to the risk which would have been observed if these same individuals had been unexposed (i.e. $X = 0$ for every unit of the population). The true effect of exposure therefore is: R_{A1} ” R_{A0} (if one is interested in risk differences) or R_{A1}/R_{A0} (if one is interested in relative risk). Since the counterfactual risk R_{A0} is unobservable we approximate it using a second population B and we actually measure the following relations: R_{A1} ” R_{B0} or R_{A1}/R_{B0}. In this situation, confounding occurs when R_{A0} “‘ R_{B0}. (NB: Example assumes binary outcome and exposure variables.)

Some epidemiologists prefer to think of confounding separately from common categorizations of bias since, unlike selection and information bias, confounding stems from real causal effects.

Ageism

Ageism (also spelled "agism") is stereotyping and discriminating against individuals or groups on the basis of their age. This may be casual or systematic. The term was coined in 1971 by Robert Neil Butler to describe discrimination against seniors, and patterned on sexism and racism. Butler defined "ageism" as a combination of three connected elements. Among them were prejudicial attitudes towards older people, old age, and the ageing process; discriminatory practices against older people; and institutional practices and policies that perpetuate stereotypes about older people.

The term has also been used to describe prejudice and discrimination against adolescents and children, including ignoring their ideas because they are too young, or assuming that they should behave in certain ways because of their age.

Ageism in common parlance and age studies usually refers to negative discriminatory practices against old people, people in their middle years, teenagers and children. There are several forms of age-related bias. Adultism is a predisposition towards adults, which is seen as biased against children, youth, and all young people who are not addressed or viewed as adults. Jeunism is the discrimination against older people in favour of younger ones. This includes political candidacies, jobs, and cultural settings where the supposed greater vitality and/or physical beauty of youth is more appreciated than the supposed greater moral and/or intellectual rigor of adulthood. Adultcentricism is the "exaggerated egocentrism of adults." *Adultocracy* is the social convention which defines "maturity" and "immaturity," placing adults in a dominant position over young people, both theoretically and practically. Gerontocracy is a form of oligarchical rule in which an entity is ruled by leaders who are significantly older than most of the adult population. Chronocentrism is primarily the belief that a certain state of humanity is superior to all previous and/or future times.

Based on a conceptual analysis of ageism, a new definition of ageism was introduced by Iversen, Larsen, & Solem in 2009. This definition constitutes the foundation for higher reliability and validity in future research about ageism and its complexity offers a new way of systemizing theories on ageism: "Ageism is defined as negative or positive stereotypes, prejudice and/or discrimination against (or to the advantage of) elderly people on the basis of their chronological age or on the basis of a perception of them as being 'old' or 'elderly'. Ageism can be implicit or explicit and can be expressed on a micro-, meso- or macro-level" (Iversen, Larsen & Solem, 2009).

Other conditions of fear or aversion associated with age groups have their own names, particularly: paedophobia, the fear of infants and children; ephebiphobia, the fear of youth, sometimes also referred to as an irrational fear of adolescents or a prejudice against teenagers; and gerontophobia, the fear of elderly people.

Implicit Ageism

Implicit ageism is the term used to refer to the implicit or subconscious thoughts, feelings, and behaviours one has about older or younger people. These may be a mixture of positive and negative thoughts and feelings, but gerontologist Becca Levy reports that they "tend to be mostly negative."

Ageist Stereotyping

Ageist stereotyping is a tool of cognition which involves categorizing into groups and attributing characteristics to these groups. Stereotypes are necessary for processing huge volumes of information which would otherwise overload a person, and they are often based on a "grain of truth" (for example, the association between ageing and ill health). However, they cause harm when the content of the stereotype is incorrect with respect to most of the group or where a stereotype is so strongly held that it overrides evidence which shows that an individual does not conform to it. For example, age-based stereotypes prime one to draw very different conclusions when one sees an older and a younger adult with, say, back pain or a limp. One might well assume that the younger person's condition is temporary and treatable, following an accident, while the older person's condition is chronic and less susceptible to intervention. On average, this might be true, but plenty of older people have accidents and recover quickly and very young people (such as infants, toddlers and small children) can become permanently disabled in the same situation. This assumption may have no consequence if one makes it in the blink of an eye as one is passing someone in the street, but if it is held by a health professional offering treatment or managers thinking about occupational health, it could inappropriately influence their actions and lead to age-related discrimination. Managers have been accused, by Erdman Palmore, as stereotyping older workers as being resistant to change, not creative, cautious, slow to make judgments, lower in physical capacity, uninterested in technological change, and difficult to train. Another example is when people are rude to children because of their high pitched voice, even if they are kind and courteous. A review of the research literature related to age stereotypes in the workplace was recently published in the Journal of Management.

Ageist Prejudice

Ageist prejudice is a type of emotion which is often linked to the cognitive process of stereotyping. It can involve the expression of derogatory attitudes, which may then lead to the use of discriminatory behaviour. Where older or younger contestants were rejected in the belief that they were poor performers, this could well be the result of stereotyping. But older people were also voted for at the stage in the game where it made sense to target the best performers. This can only be explained by a subconscious emotional reaction to older people; in this case, the prejudice took the form of distaste and a desire to exclude oneself from the company of older people.

Benevolent Prejudice

Stereotyping and prejudice against different groups in society does not take the same form. Age-based prejudice and stereotyping usually involves older or younger people being pitied, marginalized, or patronized. This is described as "benevolent prejudice" because the tendency to pity is linked to seeing older or younger people as "friendly" but "incompetent." This is similar to the prejudice most often directed against women and disabled people. Age Concern's survey revealed strong evidence of "benevolent prejudice." 48% said that over-70s are viewed as friendly (compared to 27% who said the same about under-30s). Meanwhile, only 26% believe over-70s are viewed as capable (with 41% saying the same about under-30s).

The figure for friendliness of under-30s is, conversely, an example of Hostile Prejudice.

Hostile Prejudice

"Hostile prejudice" based on hatred, fear, aversion, or threat often characterizes attitudes linked to race, religion, disability, and sex. An example of hostile prejudice toward youth is the presumption without any evidence that a given crime was committed by a young person. Rhetoric regarding intergenerational competition can be motivated by politics. Violence against vulnerable older people can be motivated by subconscious hostility or fear; within families, this involves impatience and lack of understanding. Equality campaigners are often wary of drawing comparisons between different forms of inequality. But it is unquestionably true that abuse and neglect experienced by vulnerable older people (which is closely linked to hostile prejudice) kills more people each year than the shocking but relatively isolated cases of public violence motivated by race, religion, or sexual orientation.

The impact of "benevolent" and "hostile" prejudice tends to be different. The warmth felt towards older or younger people and the knowledge that many have no access to paid employment means there is often public acceptance that they are deserving of preferential treatment—for example, less expensive movie and bus fares. But the perception of incompetence means older and younger people can be seen as "not up to the job" or "a menace on the roads," when there is little or exaggerated evidence to support this. Prejudice also leads to assumptions that it is "natural" for older or younger people to have lower expectations, reduced choice and control, and less account taken of their views.

Discrimination

Age discrimination refers to the actions taken to deny or limit opportunities to people on the basis of age. These are usually actions taken as a result of one's ageist beliefs and attitudes. Age discrimination occurs on both a personal and institutional level.

On a personal level, an older person may be told that he or she is too old to engage in certain physical activities, like an informal game of basketball between friends and family. A younger person may be told they are too young to get a job or help move the dining room table. On an institutional level, there are policies and regulations in place that limit opportunities to people of certain ages and deny them to all others. The law, for instance, requires that all young persons must be at least 16 years old in order to obtain a driver's license in the United States. There are also government regulations that determine when a worker may retire. Currently, in the US, a worker must be between 65 and 67 years old (depending upon his or her birth year) before becoming eligible for Social Security retirement benefits, but some company pension plans begin benefits at earlier ages.

A 2006/2007 survey done by the Children's Rights Alliance for England and the National Children's Bureau asked 4,060 children and young people whether they have ever been treated unfairly based on various criteria (race, age, sex, sexual orientation, etc.). A total of 43% of British youth surveyed reported experiencing discrimination based on their age, far eclipsing other categories of discrimination like sex (27%), race (11%), or sexual orientation (6%). Consistently, a study based on the European Social Survey found that whereas 35% of Europeans reported exposure ageism, only 25% reported exposure to sexism and as few as 17% reported exposure to racism.

Ageism has significant effects in two particular sectors: employment and health care.

Employment

The concept of ageism was originally developed to refer to prejudice and discrimination against older people and middle age, but has expanded to include children and teenagers.

Like racial and gender discrimination, age discrimination, at least when it affects younger workers, can result in unequal pay for equal work. Unlike racial and gender discrimination, however, age discrimination in wages is often enshrined in law. For example, in both the United States and the United Kingdom minimum wage laws allow for employers to pay lower wages to young workers. Many state and local minimum wage laws mirror such an age-based, tiered minimum wage. Midlife workers, on average, make more than younger workers do, which reflects educational achievement and experience of various kinds (job-specific, industry-specific, etc.). The age-wage peak in the United States, according to Census data, is between 45 and 54 years of age. Seniority in general accords with respect as people age, lessening ageism.

Statistical discrimination refers to limiting the employment opportunities of an individual based on stereotypes of a group to which the person belongs. Limited employment opportunities could come in the form of lower pay for equal work or jobs with little social mobility. Younger female workers were historically discriminated against, in comparison with younger men, because it was expected that, as young women of childbearing years, they would need to leave the work force permanently or periodically to have children.

Labour regulations also limit the age at which people are allowed to work and how many hours and under what conditions they may work. In the United States, a person must generally be at least 14 years old to seek a job, and workers face additional restrictions on their work activities until they reach age 16. Many companies refuse to hire workers younger than 18.

While older workers benefit more often from higher wages than do younger workers, they face barriers in promotions and hiring. Employers also encourage early retirement or layoffs disproportionately more for older or more experienced workers.

Age discrimination in hiring has been shown to exist in the United States. The Equal Employment Opportunity Commission's first complainants were female flight attendants complaining of (among other things) age discrimination. More recently, Joanna Lahey, professor at The Bush School of Government and Public Service at Texas A&M, found that firms are more than 40% more likely to interview a young adult job applicant than an older job applicant.

In a survey for the University of Kent, England, 29% of respondents stated that they had suffered from age discrimination. This is a higher proportion than for gender or racial discrimination. Dominic Abrams, social psychology professor at the university, concluded that Ageism is the most pervasive form of prejudice experienced in the UK population.

According to Dr. Robert M. McCann, an associate professor of management communication at the University of Southern California's Marshall School of Business, denigrating older workers, even if only subtly, can have an outsized negative impact on employee productivity and corporate profits. For American corporations, age discrimination can lead to significant expenses. In Fiscal Year 2006, the U.S. Equal Employment Opportunity Commission received nearly 17,000 charges of age discrimination, resolving more than 14,000 and recovering $51.5 million in monetary benefits. Costs from lawsuit settlements and judgments can run into the millions, most notably with the $250 million paid by the California Public Employees' Retirement System (CalPERS) under a settlement agreement in 2003.

In the UK, age discrimination against older people has been prohibited in employment since 2006. Since then, the number of age discrimination cases rose dramatically. The laws protect the anyone over the age of 16 who is young as well as old. There were over 6,800 claims submitted to the Employment Tribunal in 2010/11 compared with just 900 in 2006/2007 (immediately after the Regulations came in force). However, the figures for 2011/2012 show a 47% fall in the number of claims, and commentators have suggested that the repeal of the Default Retirement Age may be the reason behind this.

Some political offices have qualifications that discriminate on the basis of age as a proxy for experience, education, or accumulated wisdom. For example, the President of the United States must be at least 35 years old; a United States Senator must be at least 30; and a United States Congressman must be at least 25.

Healthcare

There is considerable evidence of discrimination against the elderly in health care. This is particularly true for aspects of the physician-patient interaction, such as screening procedures, information exchanges, and treatment decisions. In the patient-physician interaction, physicians and other health care providers may hold attitudes, beliefs, and behaviours that are associated with Ageism against older patients. Studies have found that some physicians do not seem to show any care or concern toward treating the medical problems of older people. Then, when actually interacting with these older patients on the job, the doctors sometimes view them with disgust and describe them in negative ways, such as "depressing" or "crazy." For screening procedures, elderly people are less likely than younger people to be screened for cancers and, due to the lack of this preventative measure, less likely to be diagnosed at early stages of their conditions.

After being diagnosed with a disease that may be potentially curable, older people are further discriminated against. Though there may be surgeries or operations with high survival rates that might cure their condition, older patients are less likely than younger patients to receive all the necessary treatments. It has been posited that this is because doctors fear their older patients are not physically strong enough to tolerate the curative treatments and are more likely to have complications during surgery that may end in death. However, other studies have been done with patients with heart disease, and, in these cases, the older patients were still less likely to receive further tests or treatments, independent of the severity of their health problems. Thus, the approach to the treatment of older people is concentrated on managing the disease rather than preventing or curing it. This is based on the stereotype that it is the natural process of ageing for the quality of health to decrease, and, therefore, there is no point in attempting to prevent the inevitable decline of old age. Differential medical treatment of elderly people can have significant effects on their health outcomes, a differential outcome which somehow escapes established protections against Ageism.

Effects of Ageism

Ageism has significant effects on the elderly and young people. The stereotypes and infantilization of older and younger people by patronizing language affects older and younger people's self-esteem and behaviours. After repeatedly hearing a stereotype that older or younger people are useless, older and younger people may begin to feel like dependent, non-contributing members of society. They may start to perceive themselves in terms of the looking-glass self—that is, in the same ways that others in society see them. Studies have also specifically shown that when older and younger people hear these stereotypes about their supposed incompetence and uselessness, they perform worse on measures of competence and memory. These stereotypes then become self-fulfilling prophecies. According to Becca Levy's Stereotype Embodiment Theory, older and younger people might also engage in self-stereotypes, taking their culture's age stereotypes—to which they have been exposed over the life course—and directing them inward toward themselves. Then this behaviour reinforces the present stereotypes and treatment of the elderly.

Many overcome these stereotypes and live the way they want, but it can be difficult to avoid deeply ingrained prejudice, especially if one has been exposed to ageist views in childhood or adolescence.

Australia

Australia has had age discrimination laws for some time. Discrimination on the basis of age is illegal in each of the states and territories of Australia. At the national level, Australia is party to a number of international treaties and conventions that impose obligations to eliminate age discrimination. The Australian Human Rights Commission Act 1986 established the Australian Human Rights Commission and bestows on this Commission functions in relation to a number of international treaties and conventions that cover age discrimination. During 1998-1999, 15% of complaints received by the Commission under the Act were about discrimination on the basis of age.

Age discrimination laws at the national level were strengthened by the Age Discrimination Act 2004, which helps to ensure that people are not subjected to age discrimination in various areas of public life, including employment, the provision of goods and services, education, and the administration of Australian government laws and programs. The Act, however, does provide for exemptions in some areas, as well as providing for positive discrimination, that is, actions which assist people of a particular age who experience a disadvantage because of their age.

In 2011, for the first time a position of Age Discrimination Commissioner was created within the Australian Human Rights Commission. The new Commissioner's responsibilities include raising awareness among employers about the beneficial contributions that senior Australians as well as younger employees can make in the workforce.

Canada

In Canada, Article 718.2, clause (a)(i), of the Criminal Code defines as aggravating circumstances, among other situations, "evidence that the offence was motivated by ... age".

Mandatory retirement was ended in Canada in December 2011, but 74% of Canadians still consider age discrimination to be a problem.

Nigeria

In November 2011, the Nigerian House of Representatives considered a bill which would outlaw age discrimination in employment.

United States

In the US, each state has its own laws regarding age discrimination, and there are also federal laws. In California, the Fair Employment and Housing Act forbids unlawful discrimination against persons age 40 and older. The FEHA is the principal California statute prohibiting employment discrimination, covering employers, labour organisations, employment agencies, apprenticeship programs and/or any person or entity who aids, abets, incites, compels, or coerces the doing of a discriminatory act. In addition to age, it prohibits employment discrimination based on race or colour; religion; national origin or ancestry, physical disability; mental disability or medical condition; marital status; sex or sexual orientation; and pregnancy, childbirth, or related medical conditions. Although there are many protections for age-based discrimination against older workers (as shown above) there are very few similar protections for younger workers.

The District of Columbia and twelve states define age as a specific motivation for hate crimes – California, Florida, Iowa, Hawaii, Kansas, Louisiana, Maine, Minnesota, Nebraska, New Mexico, New York and Vermont.

The federal government governs age discrimination under the Age Discrimination in Employment Act of 1967 (ADEA). The ADEA prohibits employment discrimination based on age with respect to employees 40 years of age or older as well. The ADEA also addresses the difficulty older workers face in obtaining new employment after being displaced from their jobs, arbitrary age limits. The ADEA applies even if some of the minimum 20 employees are overseas and working for a US corporation.

The United States federal government has responded to issues of youth-bias in governance through several measures in the past. They include the creation of the 1970s-era National Commission on Resources for Youth, which was created in the late 1960s as to promote youth participation throughout communities. Recently the federal government implemented the Tom Osborne Federal Youth Coordination Act, aiming to curb redundancy among federal service providers to youth.

The Children's Online Privacy Protection Act has been criticized by some as ageist.

As it approaches its fiftieth anniversary, one author argues that America's leading law against age discrimination, the Age Discrimination in Employment Act of 1967, offers little real protection to older workers. In her 2014 book, Patricia G. Barnes, an attorney and judge, argues the ADEA was riddled with loopholes to begin with and has been eviscerated over time by the U.S. Supreme Court. Moreover, her book, *Betrayed: The Legalization of Age Discrimination in the Workplace*, argues the "legalization" of age discrimination has caused a trickle down affect. Workers who are otherwise considered to be young - workers in their 30s, 40s and 50s - are increasingly experiencing age discrimination.

European Union

The European citizenship provides the right to protection from discrimination on the grounds of age. According to Article 21-1 of the Charter of Fundamental Rights of the European Union s:Charter of Fundamental Rights of the European Unio. EQUALITY, "any discrimination based on any ground such as (...) age, shall be prohibited".

Additional protection against age discrimination comes from the Framework Directive 2000/78/EC. It prohibits discrimination on grounds of age in the field of employment.

Germany

On 18 August 2006, the General Equal Treatment Act (Allgemeines Gleichbehandlungsgesetz, AGG) came into force. The aim of the AGG is to prevent and abolish discrimination on various grounds including age.

A recent study suggested that youths in Germany feel the brunt of age discrimination.

France

In France, Articles 225-1 through 225-4 of the Penal Code detail the penalization of Ageism, when it comes to an age discrimination related to the consumption of a good or service, to the exercise of an economic activity, to the labour market or an internship, except in the cases foreseen in Article 225-3.

Belgium

In Belgium, the Law of 25 Feb 2003 "tending to fight discrimination" punishes Ageism when "a difference of treatment that lacks objective and reasonable justification is directly based on ... age". Discrimination is forbidden when it refers to providing or offering a good or service, to conditions linked to work or employment, to the appointment or promotion of an employee, and yet to the access or participation in "an economic, social, cultural or political activity accessible to the public" (Article 2nd, § 4). Incitement to discrimination, to hatred or to violence against a person or a group on the grounds of (...) age (Article 6) is punished with imprisonment and/or a fine. Nevertheless, employment opportunities are worsening for people in their middle years in many of these same countries, according to Martin Kohli *et al.* in *Time for Retirement* (1991).

United Kingdom

In the UK, laws against Ageism are new. Age discrimination laws were brought into force in October 2006, and can now be found in the Equality Act 2010. This implements the Equal Treatment Framework Directive 2000/78/EC and protects employees against direct discrimination, indirect discrimination, harassment and victimisation. There is also provision in the Equality Act 2010 to prohibit age discrimination in the provision of goods and services, though this has not yet been implemented by the current UK Coalition Government and will not be implemented before October 2012 at the earliest.

Despite the relatively recent prohibition on age discrimination, there have already been many notable cases and official statistics show a 37% increase in claims in 2009/10 and a further 31% increase in 2010/11. Examples include the case involving Rolls Royce, the "Heyday" case brought by Age UK and the recent Miriam O'Reilly case against the BBC.

Recent research suggested that the number of age discrimination claims annually could reach 15,000 by 2015.

The European Social Study survey in 2011 revealed that nearly two out of five people claim to have been shown a lack of respect because of their age. The survey suggested that the UK is riven by intergenerational splits, with half of people admitting they do not have a single friend over 70; this compares with only a third of Portuguese, Swiss and Germans who say that they do not have a friend of that age or older. A Demos study in 2012 showed that three quarters of people in the UK believed there to be not enough opportunities for older and younger people to meet and work together.

The "Grey Pride" campaign has been advocating for a Minister for Older People and its campaign has had some success, with Labour Leader Ed Miliband appointing Liz Kendall as Shadow Minister for Older People. The artist Michael Freedman, an outspoken advocate against age discrimination within the art world says that "mature students, like me, come to art late in life, so why are we penalised and demotivated? Whatever happened to lifelong learning and the notion of a flexible workforce?"

Advocacy Campaigns

Many current and historical intergenerational and youth programs have been created to address the issue of Ageism. Among the advocacy organisations created in the United Kingdom to challenge age discrimination are Age UK and the British Youth Council.

In the United States there have been several historic and current efforts to challenge Ageism. The earliest example may be the Newsboys Strike of 1899, which fought ageist employment practices targeted against youth by large newspaper syndicates in the Northeast. During the Franklin D. Roosevelt Administration, First Lady Eleanor Roosevelt was active in the national youth movement, including the formation of the National Youth Administration and the defence of the American Youth Congress. She made several statements on behalf of youth and against Ageism. In one report entitled, "Facing the Problems of Youth," Roosevelt said of youth,

> *"We cannot simply expect them to say, 'Our older people have had experience and they have proved to themselves certain things, therefore they are right.' That isn't the way the best kind of young people think. They want to experience for themselves. I find they are perfectly willing to talk to older people, but they don't want to talk to older people who are shocked by their ideas, nor do they want to talk to older people who are not realistic."*

Students for a Democratic Society formed in 1960 to promote democratic opportunities for all people regardless of age, and the Gray

Panthers was formed in the early 1970s with a goal of eliminating Ageism in all forms. Three O'Clock Lobby formed in 1976 to promote youth participation throughout traditionally ageist government structures in Michigan, while Youth Liberation of Ann Arbor started in 1970 to promote youth and fight Ageism.

More recent U.S. programs include Americans for a Society Free from Age Restrictions, which formed in 1996 to advance the civil and human rights of young people through eliminating ageist laws targeted against young people, and to help youth counter Ageism in America. The National Youth Rights Association started in 1998 to promote awareness of the legal and human rights of young people in the United States, and the Freechild Project was formed in 2001 to identify, unify and promote diverse opportunities for youth engagement in social change by fighting Ageism.

Related Campaigns

- In 2002 the Writers Guild of America, West has waged a legal battle within the entertainment industry to eliminate age discrimination commonly faced by elder scriptwriters.
- Director Paul Weitz reported he wrote the 2004 film, *In Good Company* to reveal how Ageism affects youth and adults.
- In 2002 The Freechild Project created an information and training initiative to provide resources to youth organisations and schools focused on youth rights.
- In 2006 Lydia Giménez-LLort,PhD an assistant professor of Psychiatry and researcher at the Autonomous University of Barcelona coined the term 'Snow White Syndrome' at the 'Congrés de la Gent Gran de Cerdanyola del Vallès' (Congress of the Elderly of Cerdanyola del Vallès, Barcelona, Spain) as a metaphor to define Ageism in an easier and more friendly way while developing a constructive spirit against it. The metaphor is based on both the auto-Ageism and adultocracy exhibited by the queen of the Snow White fairy tale as well as the social Ageism symbolized by the mirror
- Since 2008 'The Intergenerational Study' by Lydia Giménez-LLort and Paula Ramírez-Boix from the Autonomous University of Barcelona is aimed to find the basis of the link between grandparents and grandsons (positive family relationships) that are able to minimize the Ageism towards the elderly. Students of several Spanish universities have enrolled in this study which soon will be also performed in USA, Nigeria, Barbados,

Argentina and Mexico. The preliminary results reveal that 'The Intergenerational study questionnaire' induces young people to do a reflexive and autocritic analysis of their intergenerational relationships in contrast to those shown towards other unrelated old people which results very positive to challenge Ageism. A cortometrage about 'The International Study' has been directed and produced by Tomás Sunyer from Los Angeles City College.

- Votes at 16 intends to lower the voting age to 16, reducing Ageism and giving 16 year olds equal pay on the National Minimum Wage. The group claims that 16 year olds get less money than older people for the same work, angering many 16 year olds. They additionally postulate that 16 year olds will have their voice listened to by older people more often.

Accusations of Ageism

In a recent interview, actor Pierce Brosnan cited ageism as one of the contributing factors as to why he was not asked to continue his role as James Bond in the Bond film *Casino Royale*, released in 2006.

Also, successful singer and actress, Madonna spoke out in her 50s about ageism and her fight to defy the norms of society. Similarly, Sex and the City star Kim Cattrall has also raised the issue of ageism.

A 2007 Pew Research Centre study found that a majority of American voters would be less likely to vote for a President past a given age, with only 45% saying that age would not matter.

Ageing Movement Control

Normal ageing movement control in humans is about the changes on the muscles, motor neurons, nerves, sensory functions, gait, fatigue, visual and manual responses, in men and women as they get older but who do not have neurological, muscular (atrophy, dystrophy...) or neuromuscular disorder. With ageing, neuromuscular movements are impaired though with training or practice, some aspects may be prevented.

Force Production

For voluntary force production, action potentials occur in the cortex. They propagate in the spinal cord, the motor neurons and the set of muscle fibres they innervate. This results in a twitch which properties are driven by 2 mechanisms: motor unit recruitment and rate coding. Both mechanisms are affected with ageing. For instance, the number of motor units may decrease, the size of the motor units, i.e. the number of muscle fibres they innervate may increase, the frequency at which the action potentials are triggered may be reduced. Consequently, force production is generally impaired in old adults.

Ageing is associated with decreases in muscle mass and strength. These decreases may be partially due to losses of alpha motor neurons. By the age of 70, these losses occur in both proximal and distal muscles. In biceps brachii and brachialis, old adults show decreased strength (by 1/3) correlated with a reduction in the number of motor units (by 1/2). Old adults show evidence that remaining motor units may become larger as motor units innervate collateral muscle fibres.

In first dorsal interosseus, almost all motor units are recruited at moderate rate coding, leading to 30-40% of maximal voluntary contraction (MVC). Motor unit discharge rates measured at 50% MVC are not significantly different in the young subjects from those observed in the old adults. However, for the maximal effort contractions, there is an appreciable difference in discharge rates between the two age groups. Discharge rates obtained at 100% of MVC are 64% smaller in the old adults than in the young subjects: 31.1 ± 11.8 impulses/s in the old subjects, 50.9 ± 19.5 impulses/s in the young subjects.

Isometric strength and physical cross-sectional area of the elbow flexors and elbow extensors are reduced in old compared with young men. The normalized force (maximal voluntary force to the size of the muscle producing the force) of the elbow extensors is the same for old and young people. The normalized force for the elbow flexors is reduced in the old men compared to the young men. The lower normalized force of the elbow flexors may be due to an increase in agonist-antagonist muscles coactivation.

Compared to the young group, the old group has lower dorsiflexors isometric torque at all angles, has lower knee extensors isometric torque at angles >90°. The impairment in force production is muscle specific. During dynamic exercise, the old group requires more time to reach a target velocity and is less able to attain high velocities. The slowing of voluntary contractile speed with age seems to play a role in the loss of dynamic torque.

Sensory Function

The detection of a stimulus by a receptor in the afferent nerve terminals (vs efferent nerve terminals) is useful to protect the body against unexpected disturbances. Studies in post-mortem subjects support that the thickness of muscle spindle capsules increases with age. There is a slight decrease in the number of intrafusal fibres in the oldest subjects. Some spindles show changes consistent with denervation associated with grouped denervation atrophy. Age-related changes are observed in fine structure of spindle nerve innervation in the form of axonal swelling and expanded/abnormal endplates.

When subject to a task of proprioception, the elderly show increased cocontraction of agonist-antagonist muscles, perhaps to increase gamma drive and spindle sensitivity. It is believed to be used for postural control. Despite a cocontraction strategy, old adults have higher reaction time and also make greater errors in estimating the position of their ankle. The elderly subjects with greater errors for the dynamic position sense also perform poorly on the single limb stance eyes closed test.

Old adults sway more than young adults while maintaining upright standing posture, especially with eyes closed with a narrow base of support. Young adults show "resourcefulness" by shifting from one sensory input (vision) to another (somatosensory) whereas old adults do not rely on the variety of sensory inputs but rather respond by stiffening their ankles across tasks (wide base of support vs narrow base of support, eyes open vs eyes closed).

Sensory receptors can initiate rapid responses to perturbations thanks to short-latency connections between afferent innervations and motor units. Yet, ageing results in decreases in motor conduction velocities. This may be due to losses of the fastest conducting motor units. There is also evidence of slowing of both fast and slow conducting axons which can be explained by decreases in axon diameter through demyelination, by reduction of internodal length. Some studies suggest an overall decrease in the number of myelinated fibres.

Ageing results in slowed reaction time in an aiming task for both eye and hand movements. Comparisons between young and old adults who have to follow a target only with their eyes or with a laser in their hand, show that parameters indicative of motor function such as velocity, duration, and amplitude of initial movement are unchanged. However the duration of corrective movement is longer for old adults. It suggests an impairment to sensory system.

Walking Gait

When confronted to an unexpected slip or trip during walking, compared to young adults, old adults have a less effective balance strategy: smaller and slower postural muscle responses, altered temporal and spatial organisation of the postural response, agonist-antagonist muscles coactivation and greater upper trunk instability. Comparing control and slip conditions, after the perturbation, young adults have a longer stride length, a longer stride duration, and the same walk velocity whereas old adults have a shorter stride length, the same stride duration, and a lower walk velocity.

In an experiment, for a single-task walking, 24% of old adults have gait speed <0.8 m/s but for a dual-task of walking and talking, 62% of old adults have gait speed <0.8 m/s. In practical terms, this means that a large proportion of healthy community-dwelling old adults may not walk fast enough to safely cross the street while simultaneously having a conversation. These findings support the assertion that generating spontaneous speech is highly demanding on cognitive resources and suggest that real world dual-task effects on gait may be underestimated by reaction time tasks.

Fatigue Resistance

Compared to young adults, old adults exhibit muscle fatigue (peripheral fatigue) resistance during sustained isometric maximal voluntary contraction, but they show greater supraspinal fatigue at start of sustained task, and during recovery. The first observation reflects changes in fibre type ratio; with ageing the proportion of type I muscle fibres which are adapted to long effort becomes greater. The second observation is likely a result of cumulative effects of exercise on the central nervous system.

For the knee extensors, old adults produce less torque during dynamic or isometric maximal voluntary contractions than young adults. The mechanisms controlling fatigue in the elderly during isometric contractions are not the same as those that influence fatigue during dynamic contractions, while young adults keep the same strategy. The knee extensors of healthy old adults fatigue less during isometric contractions than do those of young adults who had similar levels of habitual physical activity. In contrast, there are no differences between age groups in the fatigue during dynamic contractions.

Speed, Dexterity

For old adults, the decreased saccadic accuracy, prolonged latency, and reduced saccadic velocity may be explained by cerebral cortical degeneration with age. Old adults show reduced amplitude of primary saccades and they generally more saccades to reach fixation. Old adults show significant delay of saccades in all conditions (predictable amplitude and time target steps, unpredictable amplitude target steps, unpredictabe time target steps). Age-related slowing is only evident for predictable targets; however other studies have show otherwise, but noted higher variance in speed of old adults.

Instructed to look either toward (pro-saccade task) or away from (anti-saccade task) an eccentric target under different conditions of fixation, for young children (5±8 years of age) a long time elapses between the apparition of the target and the onset of the eye movement (Saccadic Reaction Time). Young adults (20±30 years of age) typically have the fastest SRTs. Elderly subjects (60±79 years of age) have slower SRTs and longer duration saccades than any other age groups.

Old adults exhibit reductions in manual dexterity which is observed through changes in fingertip force when gripping and/or lifting. Compared to young adults, old adults show an increase in grip force and safety margins (minimum force necessary to prevent a slip). These increases can be explained by skin slipperiness or it may be result of declining cutaneous information. Force increases are not associated with impaired capacity to modulate fingertip forces smoothly. There is no evidence that old adults were less able to program fingertips based on the memory of a preceding lift.

The prismatic grasp (4 fingers in opposition to thumb) which is common in everyday activities, involves the organisation of the digits into specific tasks and the balance of force/moment production by individual digits. Old adults exhibit an impairment in finger and hand force production. They show excessive grip force which could be related to higher moments produced by antagonist fingers. Both can be viewed as energetically suboptimal but more stable performance.

Old adults often show heightened antagonist muscle coactivation during goal directed movement. Contractions at moderate-to-high force often show activation of other ipsilateral and contralateral muscles. When the itensity of contralateral activity is sufficient to produce movement, this is called "mirror movement". When asked to follow a unilateral task, young and old adults show concurrent activity in contralateral muscle but it is greater in old adults. Contralateral activity is greater for isometric than for anisometric contractions. Contralateral force is greater for eccentric than concentric contractions.

Training Consequences

Type I muscle fibre characteristics (area, number of capillary contacts, fibre area/capillary contacts) of the vastus lateralis are unaffected by age. The old men normal fit or trained have smaller type II muscle fibre areas and fewer capillaries surrounding these fibres than do the young men. The capillary supply per unit type II fibre area is not affected by age but is enhanced by training. The old trained men have succinate dehydrogenase activities within their type IIa muscle fibres similar to those in young men and twofold higher than in old normal fit men.

Neural changes like reduced motor unit discharge rates, increased variability of motor unit discharge activity, altered recruitment and derecruitment behaviour mediate modifications in muscle control. On the other hand, physiological deleterious factors including motor unit loss, increased motor unit innervation ratios also affect muscle force. Through strength training, old adults can significantly improve their force control. The rapid adaptation suggests modifications in motor unit activation, increased excitability of motoneuron pool, and decreased antagonist cocontraction.

Heavy resistance and sensorimotor trainings result in increased maximum voluntary contraction and rate force development. But sensorimotor training shows more positive adaptations in postural reflexes, which is likely due to training of sensory reception/processing, central integration of afferent information, transformation of that information into adequate efferent response. The decreased onset latency and increased magnitude of reflex response with sensorimotor training is associated with increased ankle joint stiffness during perturbations.

When asked to reach a given level of force at a certain moment in time without any visual feedback, old adults are less accurate than young adults. With the practice of goal-directed contractions, old adults can improve the accuracy of novel motor tasks (isometric or dynamic) though their strategy differs from the strategy used by young adults. For both age groups, the greatest improvements in accuracy occur at the beginning of practice.

Old adults are able to improve the modulation of grasping forces after motor practice. Unexpectedly, motor practice fails to reduce grasping performance losses under the dual-task conditions but motor practice reduces the decline in cognitive performance under dual-task conditions. Therefore motor practice seems to free up cognitive resources that were previously monitoring motor performance and old adults seemed to use these resources to improve their cognitive performance under dual-task conditions.

Memory and Ageing

One of the key concerns of older adults is the experience of memory loss, especially as it is one of the hallmark symptoms of Alzheimer's disease. However, memory loss is qualitatively different in normal ageing from the kind of memory loss associated with a diagnosis of

Alzheimer's. Occasional lapses in memory are normal in ageing adults and understanding the distinction between normal symptoms and warning signs of Alzheimer's is critical in maintaining cognitive health.

Mild Cognitive Impairment

Mild cognitive impairment (MCI) is a condition in which people face memory problems more often than that of the average person their age. These symptoms, however, do not prevent them from carrying out normal activities and are not as severe as the symptoms for Alzheimer's disease. Symptoms often include misplacing items, forgetting events or appointments, and having trouble finding words.

According to recent research, MCI is seen as the transitional state between cognitive changes of normal ageing and Alzheimer's disease. Several studies have indicated that individuals with MCI are at an increased risk for developing AD, ranging from 1% to 25% per year; in one study 24% of MCI patients progressed to AD in 2 years and 20% more over 3 years, whereas another study indicated that the progression of MCI subjects was 55% in 4.5 years. Some patients with MCI, however, never progress to AD.

Studies have also indicated patterns that are found in both MCI and AD. Much like patients with Alzheimer's disease, those suffering from mild cognitive impairment have difficulty accurately defining words and using them appropriately in sentences when asked. While MCI patients had a lower performance in this task than the control group, AD patients performed worse overall. The abilities of MCI patients stood out, however, due to the ability to provide examples to make up for their difficulties. AD patients failed to use any compensatory strategies and therefore exhibited the difference in use of episodic memory and executive functioning.

Memory Decline in Normal Ageing

Normal ageing is associated with a decline in various memory abilities in many cognitive tasks; the phenomenon is known as age-related memory impairment (AMI) or age-associated memory impairment (AAMI). The ability to encode new memories of events or facts and working memory shows decline in both cross-sectional and longitudinal studies. Studies comparing the effects of ageing on episodic memory, semantic memory, short-term memory and priming find that episodic memory is especially impaired in normal ageing; some types of short-term memory are also impaired. The deficits may be related to impairments seen in the ability to refresh recently processed information.

Source information is one type of episodic memory that suffers with old age; this kind of knowledge includes where and when the person learned the information. Knowing the source and context of information can be extremely important in daily decision-making, so this is one way in which memory decline can affect the lives of the elderly. Therefore, reliance on political stereotypes is one way to use their knowledge about the sources when making judgments, and the use of metacognitive knowledge gains importance. This deficit may be related to declines in the ability to bind information together in memory during encoding and retrieve those associations at a later time.

Episodic memory is supported by networks spanning frontal, temporal, and parietal lobes. The interconnections in the lobes are presumed to enable distinct aspects of memory, whereas the effects of gray matter lesions have been extensively studied, less is known about the interconnecting fibre tracts. In ageing, degradation of white matter structure has emerged as an important general factor, further focusing attention on the critical white matter connections.

In particular, associative learning, which is another type of episodic memory, is vulnerable to the effects of ageing, and this has been demonstrated across various study paradigms. This has been explained by the Associative Deficit Hypothesis (ADH), which states that ageing is associated with a deficiency in creating and retrieving links between single units of information. This can include knowledge about context, events or items. The ability to bind pieces of information together with their episodic context in a coherent whole has been reduced in the elderly population. Furthermore, the older adults' performances in free recall involved temporal contiguity to a lesser extent than for younger people, indicating that associations regarding contiguity become weaker with age.

Several reasons have been speculated as to why older adults use less effective encoding and retrieval strategies as they age. The first is the "disuse" view, which states that memory strategies are used less by older adults as they move further away from the educational system. Second is the "diminished attentional capacity" hypothesis, which means that older people engage less in self-initiated encoding due to reduced attentional capacity. The third reason is the "memory self-efficacy," which indicates that older people do not have confidence in their own memory performances, leading to poor consequences. It is known that patients with Alzheimer's disease and patients with semantic dementia both exhibit difficulty in tasks that involve picture naming and category fluency. This is tied to damage to their semantic network, which stores knowledge of meanings and understandings.

One phenomenon, known as "Senior Moments", is a memory deficit that appears to have a biological cause. When an older adult is interrupted while completing a task, it is likely that the original task at hand can be forgotten. Studies have shown that the brain of an older adult does not have the ability to re-engage after an interruption and continues to focus on the particular interruption unlike that of a younger brain. This inability to multi-task is normal with ageing and is expected to become more apparent with the increase of older generations remaining in the work field.

A biological explanation for memory deficits in ageing includes a postmortem examination of five brains of elderly people with better memory than average. These people are called the "super aged," and it was found that these individuals had fewer fibre-like tangles of tau protein than in typical elderly brains. However, a similar amount of amyloid plaque was found.

More recent research has extended established findings of age related decline in executive functioning, by examining related cognitive processes that underlie healthy older adults' sequential performance. Sequential performance refers to the execution of a series steps needed to complete a routine, such as the steps required to make a cup of coffee or drive a car. An important part of healthy ageing involves older adults' use of memory and inhibitory processes to carry out daily activities in a fixed order without forgetting the sequence of steps that were just completed while remembering the next step in the sequence. A recent study examined how young and older adults differ in the underlying representation of a sequence of tasks and their efficiency at retrieving the information needed to complete their routine. Findings from this study revealed that when older and young adults had to remember a sequence of 8 animal images arranged in a fixed order, both age groups spontaneously used the organisational strategy of chunking to facilitate retrieval of information. However, older adults were slower at accessing each chunk compared to younger adults, and were better able to benefit from the use of memory aids, such as verbal rehearsal to remember the order of the fixed sequence. Results from this study suggest that there are age differences in memory and inhibitory processes that affect people's sequence of actions and the use of memory aids could facilitate the retrieval of information in older age.

Possible Causes of Memory Decline

People commonly associate memory lapses in their mid-30s, 40s, or 50s as a sign of Alzheimer's disease as they approach later adulthood, but typically this is not the case. Memory lapses can be both aggravating and frustrating but they are due to the overwhelming amount of information that is being taken in by the brain. Issues in memory can also be linked to several common physical and psychological causes, such as: anxiety, dehydration, depression, infections, medication side effects, poor nutrition, vitamin B12 deficiency, psychological stress, substance abuse, chronic alcoholism, thyroid imbalances, and blood clots in the brain. Taking care of your body and mind with appropriate medication, doctoral check-ups, and daily mental and physical exercise can prevent some of these memory issues.

Some memory issues are due to stress, anxiety, or depression. A traumatic life event, such as the death of a spouse, can lead to changes in lifestyle and can leave an elderly person feeling unsure of themselves, sad, and lonely. Dealing with such drastic life changes can therefore leave some people confused or forgetful. While in some cases these feelings may fade, it is important to take these emotional problems seriously. By emotionally supporting a struggling relative and seeking help from a doctor or counselor, the forgetfulness can be improved.

Prevention and Treatment

Various actions have been suggested to prevent memory loss or even improve memory. The Mayo Clinic has suggested seven steps: stay mentally active, socialize regularly, get organised, eat a healthy diet, include physical activity in your daily routine, and manage chronic conditions. Because some of the causes of memory loss include medications, stress, depression, heart disease, alcohol abuse, thyroid problems, vitamin B12 deficiency, not drinking enough water, and not eating nutritiously, fixing those problems could be a simple, effective way to slow down dementia. Some say that exercise is the best way to prevent memory problems, because that would increase blood flow to the brain and perhaps help new brain cells grow. A healthy diet is also critical, partly because it has been demonstrated that healthy eaters are much less likely to develop Alzheimer's disease.

The treatment will depend on the cause of memory loss, but various drugs to treat Alzheimer's disease have been suggested in recent years. There are four drugs currently approved by the FDA for the treatment of Alzheimer's, and they all act on the cholinergic system: Donepezil (Aricept), Galantamine (Reminyl), Rivastigmine (Exelon), and Tacrine(Cognex). Although these medications are not the cure for Alzheimer's, symptoms may be reduced for up to eighteen months for mild or moderate dementia. These drugs do not forestall the ultimate decline to full Alzheimer's.

Also, modality is important in determining the strength of the memory. For instance, auditory creates stronger memory abilities than visual. This is shown by the higher recency and primacy effects of an auditory recall test compared to that of a visual test. Research has shown that auditory training, through instrumental musical activity or practice, can help preserve memory abilities as one ages. Specifically, in Hanna-Pladdy and McKay's experiment, they tested and found that the number of years of musical training, all things equal, leads to a better performance in non-verbal memory and increases the life span on cognition abilities in one's advanced years.

The use of memory aids is helpful in fighting cognitive signs of ageing. Keeping a "to do" list will help assure that certain tasks are completed and not forgotten. Establishing day-to-day routines will make everyday tasks, such as taking medication, easier to remember if they occur at the same time every day. Putting everything in its rightful place will help to avoid confusion. Keeping important items in a place where they can always be seen will save you time when they're needed. Using simple associations to remember names, events, or objects can make recalling things much easier. Finally, keeping a calendar to display important dates and times will make remembering much easier.

The easiest way to prevent memory decline in elderhood is to stay active throughout your 40's and 50's. Being mentally active and learning new skills during middle adulthood and as you age is speculated to lower the risk of Alzheimer's disease. By performing new tasks and learning new skills, the brain is forced to focus more than it would on a task in which you have already mastered. In essence, acquiring new skills is a way to exercise your brain. Those who enjoy learning and want to stay mentally active can participate in a new program hosted at Columbia University, as well as 117 other colleges and universities across the country. This program is focused on the elderly and allows them to take classes in academic courses as well as courses involving exercising and skills without the worry of reading, papers, homework, and grades.

New research has identified specific impaired neurons within the human brain that when stimulated, can be recovered. Through studies with fruit flies, it was discovered by Professor Ron Davis that, "...once the appropriate neurons are identified in people, in principle at least, one could potentially develop drugs to hit those neurons and rescue those memories affected by the ageing process." Research such as this, is bringing us one step closer to developing preventative methods and drugs that can reverse and slow the cognitive declines associated with ageing.

Scientists and nutritionists have linked the consumption of certain foods with improved memory and the prevention of Alzheimer's and age-related memory decline.

In her 2010 publication on Alzheimer's, Jean Carper suggests many food practices to prevent the onset of this disease. She encourages individuals to eat antioxidant-rich foods, choline-rich foods, curry, fatty fish, folic acid, nuts, and vinegar; to drink juices, coffee, tea, and red wine (while practicing moderation with alcohol in general); to avoid sugar; and to follow a low-glycemic index diet and/or Mediterranean diet.

A 2011 study suggests that increasing Vitamin C and Vitamin E in diets can increase verbal memory functions. Vitamin C is an antioxidant that can protect brain tissues from inflammation and oxidation damage. Foods rich in Vitamin C include broccoli, Brussels sprouts, cabbage, cantaloupe, cauliflower, grapefruit, green and red peppers, kale, kiwi, mango, oranges, papaya, pineapple, strawberries, and tomato juice. Vitamin E can protect brain cell membranes from free radicals. Foods rich in Vitamin E include almonds, canola oil, grape seed oil, hazelnuts, papaya, safflower oil, sunflower seeds, and wheat germ oil. Vitamin E is also prevalent in leafy greens, including arugula, beet greens, collard greens, kale, mustard greens, rapini, spinach, and Swiss chard. There are conflicting opinions as to whether such vitamins must be consumed in foods or if dietary supplements are also effective.

2011 and 2012 studies suggest that folic acid and Vitamin B12 may also help prevent memory decline. Foods rich in Vitamin B12 include beef liver, clams, dairy products, fish, poultry, and meat.

Diets high in saturated fats and refined sugars have been associated with increased Alzheimer's risk, while low saturated fat and low-glycemic index diets have been associated with decreased Alzheimer's risk. Lean meats, poultry, and low-fat dairy products characterize a low-saturated-fat diet, as well as avoidance of butter in favour of unsaturated fats, such as canola oil, grape seed oil, olive oil, and sunflower oil. Foods with a low-glycemic index include apples, bran cereal, brown rice, citrus fruits, grain breads with seeds, grapes, legumes, milk, nuts, pasta, pears, steel-cut and large-flake oats, sweet potatoes, wild rice, and yogurt. Omega-3 fatty acids found in oily fish, such as herring, mackerel, salmon, sardines, and trout, can also improve memory functions.

Evidence has accumulated that compounds called flavanols naturally occurring in cocoa beans can enhance brain blood flow and improve cognitive health. In 2014, a publication by a group of scientists from seven American institutes reported a controlled randomized trial applying a high-resolution variant of functional magnetic resonance imaging (fMRI) of the brains of 37 healthy, but sedentary, volunteers aged 50-69, who were daily given over a three-month period a specially-prepared cocoa drink. Each subject was randomly chosen to always receive a drink containing either a large dose of flavanols contained in cocoa solids — 900 mg — or a low dose, 10 mg. Of primary interest in the fMRI images was blood volume in the dentate gyrus (DG), a region in the hippocampal formation whose function declines with human ageing and is therefore considered to be a possible crux of age-related memory decline. Previous studies had shown that flavanol consumption can increase dendritic spine and capillary density in the DG of adult mice. The image data of humans revealed a strong correlation between flavanol dose and enhancement of DG blood volume over this three-month study. The subjects were also challenged before and after the period with a novel object recognition task, selection of which was guided by a previous study that had established that this type of task is a cognitive feature of age-related hippocampal dysfunction that localizes to the DG.

The subjects were shown a series of mathematically generated images that could be varied in a quantitative way, and asked to identify previously unseen patterns, either immediately in sequential pairs or after 41 images had been seen. It was found that the high dose of flavanol resulted in significantly better performance in terms of response time to reject previously unseen patterns. The same test applied to 35 young healthy subjects had shown that their performance correlated with higher DG blood volume in their fMRI images. While cautioning that this small study needs to be confirmed with more subjects, one of the authors summarized the overall result by saying "If a participant had the memory of a typical 60-year-old at the beginning of the study, after three months that person on average had the memory of a typical 30- or 40-year-old", and that "flavanols improves the function of humans' dentate gyrus, particularly in ageing humans". It was also emphasized that the dose of flavanols used in this study is far larger than can be obtained from typical commercial cocoa or chocolate, as the processing typically eliminates most of the natural flavanols.

Caregiving and Daily Life

Caring for an adult with memory issues can be a day to day struggle. Every task can become an extreme chore if not approached and handled correctly. By keeping the patient active, focusing on their positive abilities, and avoiding stress, these tasks can easily be accomplished. Routines for bathing and dressing must be organised in a way so that the patient still feels a sense of independence. Simple approaches such as finding clothes with large buttons, elastic waist bands, or velcro straps can ease the struggles of getting dressed in the morning. Further, finances must be managed. Changing passwords to prevent over-use and involving a trusted family member or friend in managing accounts can prevent financial issues. When household chores begin to pile up, find ways to break down large tasks into small, manageable steps that can be rewarded. Finally, talking with and visiting a family member or friend with memory issues is very important. Using a respectful and simple approach, talking one-on-one can ease the pain of social isolation and bring much mental stimulation.

The most important thing to remember when caring for an adult with memory issues is to give them independence in a respectful manner. Finding tasks for them, keeping their mind busy, and rewarding them for a job well done will promote a desire for mentally stimulating activities.

Domains of Memory Mostly Spared

In contrast, implicit, or procedural memory, typically shows no decline with age. Other types of short-term memory show little decline, and semantic knowledge (e.g. vocabulary) actually improves with age. In addition, the enhancement seen in memory for emotional events is also maintained with age.

Recently (2010), experiments that have tested for the significance of under-performance of memory for an older adult group as compared to a young adult group, hypothesized that the deficit in associate memory due to age can be linked with a physical deficit. This deficit can be explained by the inefficient processing in the medial-temporal regions. This region is important in episodic memory, which is one of the two types of long-term human memory, and it contains the hippocampi, which are crucial in creating memorial association between items.

Losing working memory has been cited as being the primary reason for a decline in a variety of cognitive tasks due to ageing. These tasks include long-term memory, problem solving, decision making, and language. Working memory involves the manipulation of information that is being obtained, and then using this information to complete a task. For example, the ability of one to recite numbers they have just been given backwards requires working memory, rather than just simple rehearsal of the numbers which would require only short-term memory. One's ability to tap into one's working memory declines as the ageing process progresses. It has been seen that the more complex a task is, the more difficulty the ageing person has with completing this task. Active reorganisation and manipulation of information becomes increasingly harder as adults age. When an older individual is completing a task, such as having a conversation or doing work, they are using their working memory to help them complete this task. As they age, their ability to multi-task seems to decline; thus after an interruption it is often more difficult for an ageing individual to successfully finish the task at hand.

Additionally, working memory plays a role in the comprehension and production of speech. There is often a decline in sentence comprehension and sentence production as individuals age. Rather than linking this decline directly to deficits in linguistic ability, it is actually deficits in working memory that contribute to these decreasing language skills.

Theories about Memory and Ageing

Tests and data show that as people age, the contiguity effect weakens. This is supported by the associative deficit theory of memory, which asserts old people's poor memory performance is attributed to their difficulty in creating and retaining cohesive episodes. The supporting research in this test, after controlling for sex, education, and other health-related issues, show that greater age was associated with lower hit and greater false alarm rates, and also a more liberal bias response on recognition tests.

Older people have a higher tendency to make outside intrusions during a memory test. This can be attributed to the inhibition effect. Inhibition caused participants to take longer time in recalling or recognising an item, and also subjected the participants to make more frequent errors. For instance, in a study using metaphors as the test subject, older participants rejected correct metaphors more often than literally false statements.

Working memory, which as previously stated is a memory system that stores and manipulates information as we complete cognitive tasks, demonstrates great declines during the ageing process. There have been various theories offered to explain why these changes may occur, which include fewer attentional resources, slower speed of processing, less capacity to hold information, and lack of inhibitory control.

All of these theories offer strong arguments and it is likely that the decline in working memory is due to the problems cited in all of these areas.

Some theorists argue that the capacity of working memory decreases as we age, and we are able to hold less information. In this theory, declines in working memory are described as the result of limiting the amount of information an individual can simultaneously keep active, so that a higher degree of integration and manipulation of information is not possible because the products of earlier memory processing are forgotten before the subsequent products.

Another theory that is being examined to explain age related declines in working memory is that there is a limit in attentional resources seen as we age. This means that older individuals are less capable of dividing their attention between two tasks, and thus tasks with higher attentional demands are more difficult to complete due to a reduction in mental energy. Tasks that are simple and more automatic, however, see fewer declines as we age. Working memory tasks often involve divided attention, thus they are more likely to strain the limited resources of ageing individuals.

Speed of processing is another theory that has been raised to explain working memory deficits. As a result of various studies he has completed examining this topic, Salthouse argues that as we age our speed of processing information decreases significantly. It is this decrease in processing speed that is then responsible for our inability to use working memory efficiently as we age. The younger persons brain is able to obtain and process information at a quicker rate which allows for subsequent integration and manipulation needed to complete the cognitive task at hand. As this processing slows, cognitive tasks that rely on quick processing speed then become more difficult.

Finally, the theory of inhibitory control has been offered to account for decline seen in working memory. This theory examines the idea that older adults are unable to suppress irrelevant information in working memory, and thus the capacity for relevant information is subsequently limited. Less space for new stimuli due may attribute to the declines seen in an individual's working memory as they age.

As we age, deficits are seen in the ability to integrate, manipulate, and reorganise the contents of working memory in order to complete higher level cognitive tasks such as problem solving, decision making, goal setting, and planning. More research must be completed in order to determine what the exact cause of these age-related deficits in working memory are. It is likely that attention, processing speed, capacity reduction, and inhibitory control may all play a role in these age-related deficits. The brain regions that are active during working memory tasks are also being evaluated, and research has shown that different parts of the brain are activated during working memory in younger adults as compared to older adults. This suggests that younger and older adults are performing these tasks differently.

Qualitative Changes

Most research on memory and ageing has focused on how older adults perform worse at a particular memory task. However, researchers have also discovered that simply saying that older adults are doing the same thing, only less of it, is not always accurate. In some cases, older adults seem to be using different strategies than younger adults. For example, brain imaging studies have revealed that older adults are more likely to use both hemispheres when completing memory tasks than younger adults. In addition, older adults sometimes show a positivity effect when remembering information, which seems to be a result of the increased focus on regulating emotion seen with age. For instance, eye tracking reveals that older adults showed preferential looking toward happy faces and away from sad faces.

Bibliography

Alfredo, Morabia: *A history of epidemiologic methods and concepts*, Birkhäuser, New York, 2004.

Andrews, GJ. and Phillips, DR.: *Ageing and Place: Perspectives, Policy, Practice*, Routledge, London, 2005.

Barbara, Logue: *Death Control and the Elderly in America,* Lexington Books/ Macmillan, London, 2005.

Blalock, H.M.: *Conceptualization and measurement in the social sciences*, Sage, Beverly Hills, 1982.

Colleen, Johnson and Barbara, M. Barer: *Life Beyond 85 Years:* Prometheus books, United States, 2003.

Erikson, E.H.: *Childhood and Society*, Norton, New York, 1963.

————: *Identity: Youth and Crisis*, Norton, New York, 1968.

Gavrilov, L.A., Heuveline P.: *Aging of Population*, Macmillan, New York, 2003.

————, Gavrilova NS.: *Reliability Theory of Aging and Longevity*, Academic Press, San Diego, CA, USA, 2006.

Hage, J.: *Techniques and problems of theory construction in sociology*, Wiley Interscience, New York, 1972.

Hayflick, Leonard: *How and why we age*, Ballantine Books, New York, 1994.

James H. Schulz and Robert H. Binstock: *Aging Nation: The Economics and Politics of Growing Older in America,* Johns Hopkins, 2008.

Kaplan, Abraham: *The Conduct of Inquiry: Methodology for Behavioral Science*, Transaction Publishers, US., 1964.

Kennedy, G.J.: *The epidemiology of late-life depression.* John Wiley and Sons, New York, 1996.

Laura, E. Berk: *Development Through the Lifespan*, Allyn & Bacon, 2010.

Laura, Katz Olson: *The Not-so-golden Years: Caregiving, the Frail Elderly, and the Long-term Care Establishment,* Rowman and Littlefield, 2003.

Leonid, A. Gavrilov & Natalia, S. Gavrilova: *The Biology of Life Span: A Quantitative Approach*, Harwood Academic Publisher, New York, 1991.

Masoro E.J. & Austad S.N.: *Handbook of the Biology of Aging*, Academic Press. San Diego, CA, USA, 2006.

Miquel, Porta: *A Dictionary of Epidemiology,* Oxford University Press. New York, 2014.

Moody, Harry R.: *Aging: Concepts and Controversies*, California, Pine Forge Press, New York, 2014.

Muriel R. Gillick M.D.: *Choosing Medical Care in Old Age*: *What Kind, How Much, When to Stop,* Harvard, 1998.

Nortin M. Hadler: *Rethinking Aging: Growing Old and Living Well in an Overtreated Society,* University of North Carolina, 2011.

Nussbaum, J. F., Thompson, T. L., & Robinson, J. D.: *Barriers to conversation*, Harper & Row, New York, 1989.

Ooyman, N.R.; Kiyak, H.A.: *Social gerontology: A multidisciplinary perspective,* Pearson Education, Boston, 2011.

Patricia, M. Burbank: *Vulnerable Older Adults: Health Care Needs and Interventions,* Springer, New York, 2006.

Priscilla, Ebersole: *Gerontological nursing and healthy aging*, Elsevier Health Sciences, Amsterdam, Netherlands, 2005.

Ray, M. Merrill: *Introduction to Epidemiology*, Jones & Bartlett Learning, Burlington, MA., 2010.

Richard, A. Posner: *Aging and Old Age*, University of Chicago, United States, 1995.

Rowles, Graham D. and Bernard, Miriam: *Environmental Gerontology: Making Meaningful Places in Old Age*, Springer Publishing Company, New York, 2013.

Scheidt, Rick J. and Schwarz, Benyamin: *Environmental Gerontology. What Now?,* Routledge, New York, 2013.

Stuart-Hamilton, Ian: *The Psychology of Ageing: An Introduction*, Jessica Kingsley Publishers, London, 2006.

Vern L. Bengtson; Norella Putney: *Handbook of theories of aging*, Springer Publishing Company, 2009.

Andrew, W. Achenbaum, *Crossing frontiers: gerontology emerges as a science*, Cambridge University Press, 1995.

Wahl, H-W.; Scheidt, R.J.; and Windley, P.G.: *Annual Review of Gerontology and Geriatrics*, Springer Publishing Company, New York, 2004.

Weil, David N.: *The Economics of Population Aging*, New York, Elsevier, New York, 2004.

Index

L

M

N

O

P

R

S

T

V

W

❑❑❑